Beyond *The Godfather*

. . . .

ITALIAN AMERICAN WRITERS

ON THE REAL

ITALIAN AMERICAN EXPERIENCE

WITHDRAWN

A. Kenneth Ciongoli and Jay Parini, editors

University Press of New England

Hanover and London

University Press of New England, Hanover, NH 03755
This collection © 1997 by University Press of New England
"Respect" © 1997 by Alane Salierno Mason
"Scents: A Selection from a Memoir of Italian American Life" © 1997 by Maria Laurino
All rights reserved
Printed in the United States of America
5 4 3 2 1
CIP data appear at the end of the book

Acknowledgments for previously published pieces:

"The Edge of Night" by Frank Lentricchia: From *The Edge of Night* by Frank Lentricchia. Copyright © 1994 by Frank Lentricchia. Reprinted by permission of Random House, Inc.

"Origins of a Nonfiction Writer" by Gay Talese originally appeared in *Writing Creative Nonfiction: The Literature of Reality*, ed. Gay Talese and Barbara Lounsberry, published by Watson-Guptill, 1995.

"What Grandma Knew" by John Agresto originally appeared in *Boston College Magazine*, summer 1991.

"On Being White, Female, and Born in Bensonhurst" by Marianna De Marco Torgovnick originally appeared in *Crossing Ocean Parkway*, published by the University of Chicago Press, 1994.

The lines from "Firsts" by John Ciardi quoted by Dana Gioia on p. 169 are reproduced from *The Collected Poems of John Ciardi*, ed. Edward Cifelli, published by the University of Arkansas Press, 1997.

"Breaking and Entering: An Italian American's Literary Odyssey" by Fred L. Gardaphé is an expanded version of the Introduction to *Italian Signs, American Streets: The Evolution of Italian American Narrative*, published by Duke University Press, 1996; it first appeared in the premiere issue of *Forkroads: A Journal of Ethnic-American Literature*, fall 1995.

"A Song from the Ghetto: Tina De Rosa's *Paper Fish* " by Edvige Giunta from the afterword to *Paper Fish* by Tina De Rosa. Afterword Copyright © 1996 by Edvige Giunta. Reprinted by permission of The Feminist Press at The City University of New York.

"Finding My Way," from *Vertigo* by Louise DeSalvo. Copyright © 1996 by Louise DeSalvo. Used by permission of Dutton Signet, a division of Penguin Books USA Inc.

The royalties from the sales of this book are being donated to the National Italian American Foundation to fund an annual literary prize.

· ·

To Ambassador Boris Biancheri

CONTENTS

. . . .

Part One: Memories and Memoirs

. . . .

Part Two: Italian American Literature

· ·

Part Three: Identity Politics

· ·

FOREWORD

· ·

The timely and appropriate essays in this beautiful book by twenty-three well-known writers of Italian descent bring to the wider public the unending quest of a great American reality for its rightful place in the vibrant New World.

Signers of the Declaration of Independence, advisors to the Founding Fathers long before Italy existed as a country, emigrant laborers, exiled intellectuals, scientists, technicians, and businessmen, millions of Italians have come to the shores of America to bring their talents to a society-in-the-making totally different from theirs. All have been sons and daughters of their times, diverse from one another yet keenly aware of their heritage. Many chose to stay and adopt the new country of opportunities without forgetting the old one which, in turn, changed in less than two centuries from Metternich's "geographical expression" to a great European country.

Language, customs, education, the frontier myths, the common law as opposed to Roman codes, the religious environment—all were foreign to them. Most painful of all was the "trickle transplant" as families emigrated separately and later reunited, sometimes only in part, over the years. Still, the journey of the Italians of America can rightfully be written, as our authors do at the close of this century, as a success story in which the interweaving of two worlds, and above all, of two cultures, produced a sense of self-awareness and indeed opened a timely debate on the identity and role of the Italians in the United States and their contribution to the shaping of American society.

That debate suggests to me several considerations. What made us what we are—present-day Italians, the descendants of Latins, Etruscans, and Celts, of Greeks and Longobards, of French and Spaniards, and heirs to so many different histories—was indeed a unique capacity to forge a common identifiable system of values that is proper to us, the identity that in the "Risorgimento" could overcome differences and made possible the achievement of unity and independence. This cultural identity was shaped throughout the centuries to comprise the common traditions of material, social, and spiritual life that are made of economics and art, re-ligious sense and family life, solidarity and the day-to-day way of living, technology, myths, and poetry. The originality of Italian culture is that of a polycentric society, and it originated both from above and from below in a process of cross-enrichment.

The experience of the past concretely enriches a people and enables it to operate better in the present with a sense of historic continuity that gives solid ground to innovation. In this sense, the Italians who came to America brought with them their identity and transmitted the values of Italian culture to the new country, grafting them on an existing foreign tissue.

In the span of more than thirty years during my three tours of duty in the United States, I have been privileged to witness the coming to life of an awareness among the younger generations of Italian Americans. The awareness is of the continuing foundation of their values in the great Italian culture, a culture that always, even under the most difficult circumstances, has looked forward and aimed at progress, beauty, and humanism.

The circle is about to be closed. The Italians of America have forged an elite which, through its own original experience and its success, has come to the fore to reclaim the continuity with our culture and values. They will discover in turn that the continuity was never interrupted and that the quest for excellence unites us.

Ferdinando Salleo
AMBASSADOR OF ITALY TO THE UNITED STATES OF AMERICA

PREFACE

A. Kenneth Ciongoli and Jay Parini

. . . .

Mario Puzo's vastly successful novel *The Godfather* was even more successful as a film, or sequence of films. Too successful, really. *The Godfather*
seems to have held up an image of Italian American life that has obliterated the reality. This anthology of essays on the Italian American experience is meant to offer a glimpse into this important ethnic community, a
look "beyond" *The Godfather,* or behind it.

There has, in fact, been a long tradition of Italian American writers,
going back to the nineteenth century, and this tradition is elaborated in
many of the essays in the collection. Nevertheless, the existence of this
tradition has been relatively unknown, even to prominent Italian Americans such as Gay Talese, who a few years ago asked a piercing question in
The New York Times Book Review: Where are the Italian American writers? He surveyed the American intellectual landscape and found very few
writers of this particular heritage, and he wondered why this was the case.
Was it merely that most Italians who came to America in the late nineteenth and early twentieth centuries had been laborers who could not
read and write? Were Italian American families not encouraging their
children in ways that led, eventually, to an intellectual class?

While nobody can doubt that the Italian immigration to America constitutes a noble part of this country's history, and that Italian Americans
have had a huge impact on our culture (usually in the fields of business,
politics and entertainment—especially the film industry), there has been
a surprising absence of literary writing from a community with a powerful
literary tradition. The Italian intellectual tradition, too, with its roots in
Roman times, was somehow not carried over into the New World—at
least not until recently.

This anthology brings with it the good news that a change has occurred.
A new crop of writers with Italian American roots has recently come of
age, and many of them are represented here, including Frank Lentricchia,
Dana Gioia, Maria Laurino, Regina Barreca, Louise DeSalvo, Claire Gaudiani, Alane Salierno Mason, Marianna De Marco Torgovnick, Sandra

Gilbert, and Mary Cappello. It seems especially interesting that so many of these writers are women, and that they have chosen as their main form of expression the literary memoir. It is as if a new generation has suddenly felt a need to explore their roots, to seek out and affirm a tradition that reaches back to the Old Country but which has found a lively presence here.

Part One of this collection consists mostly of personal reflections—pieces of autobiography. As a whole, these essays provide a strong testament to the impact of an Italian American childhood on each of these writers. Part Two consists of essays on the Italian American literary tradition, beginning with Dana Gioia's robust survey of the field in poetry. Fred L. Gardaphé considers the "literary odyssey" of the Italian American writer, while Anthony J. Tamburri and Edvige Giunta look at particular writers. Part Three contains essays by some leading Italian American intellectuals on aspects of their heritage. Michael Barone, for example, writes about the impact of Italian Americans on politics, while Linda Hutcheon and Richard Gambino take up the hot issue of ethnic identity. Rudolph J. Vecoli offers a unique angle on this question, asking (rather impishly), "Are Italian Americans Just White Folks?" Matilda Cuomo and A. Kenneth Ciongoli find something unique in the Italian American tradition: a particular allegiance to family and home. Joseph V. Scelsa recounts his own story as a pioneer in the field of Italian American studies and his efforts to establish a center for this subject within the academy.

This anthology is by no means exhaustive, nor was it meant to be. A rich crop of Italian Americans exists in the world of literary and intellectual writing. One thinks immediately of Don DeLillo, the novelist; John J. DiIulio, Jr., the social scientist; Larry J. Sabato, the political theorist; Barbara Grizzuti Harrison, the memoirist; Camille Paglia, the cultural critic; and dozens of other leading figures on the scene today. The latest generation of Italian Americans is making itself felt, and the values one associates with this unique heritage—independence of mind, a love of family and food, a commitment to community values, and a vivid sense of personal morality—are reflected in widely different ways, as this anthology suggests.

PART ONE

. . . .

Memories and Memoirs

. . . .

Finding My Way

When my mother meets someone new, she always manages to interject into the conversation what she believes is the amazing fact that I started school when I was only four years old.

"Louise was only four years old when she started first grade in 1947," my mother boasts, as soon as the other mother crows about one of her child's accomplishments.

"Because she knew how to read," my mother continues. "She taught herself how to read. Before I knew what was happening, she could pick up anything at all and read it without any help from me. And if there wasn't a book around the apartment to read, she would read the back of the cereal box. Anything. Anything at all."

My mother explains to her by-now-reluctant audience how she took me over to Sacred Heart Academy the summer before I started school; how the nuns gave me a reading test, a hard one; how they told her that, because I seemed old for my age, I was ready to start school, and they would accept me into the first grade.

The rest of her summer is taken up with making the blue serge uniforms and white cotton blouses that are required wear at Sacred Heart. Though sewing them is hard work (especially the blouses with their darts and puffy, set-in sleeves), my mother says she thinks that wearing uniforms is a very good idea because it makes everyone seem the same so that, during school hours, no one can tell the rich kids from the poor kids, and this means no one will get preferential treatment. This is what's so good about Catholic schools, she maintains, though she is no devout believer in the faith into which both she and my father have been baptized, into which they baptize my sister and me.

Once I enter first grade, my mother's concern for presenting me to the

3

world beautifully dressed subsides and soon vanishes. My sister, Jill, she dresses in my or my cousins' worn hand-me-downs. And through the years she herself stops dressing in the latest, most sophisticated clothes; by the end of her life, it becomes a "chore" for her to enter a store to buy anything. "Too many choices," she tells us. "I get all confused."

After my father comes home from the war and my sister is born, my mother worries about spending money, and she tries to save as much as she can for that house in the suburbs that she and my father dream of one day buying. She will buy what's cheapest on a clothes rack, even if she doesn't much like it, even if it doesn't look all that good on her, and as my sister and I get older, she will force us to do the same. When we argue with her, she always tells us "a penny saved is a penny earned." But the truth is that she has enough money to spend; she just can't treat herself well, and she acts as if she doesn't deserve anything beautiful, anything expensive. By the end of her life, though she always looks nice when she dresses, she wears what she calls "garbage" around the house, and she possesses only one very good and conservative suit (though in an unusual shade of pink), the suit that I choose for her burial.

My mother's story about my starting school at four is something of an exaggeration. Although it is literally true that I start school when I am four, I turn five just a few weeks later, and so it would have been more accurate if my mother had said that I was nearly five years old when I started first grade. And although I *have* learned to read, in my recollection, I do not learn by myself; it is my mother who teaches me. But my mother's story, her pride in describing my precocity, suggests that she has secret aspirations for me that she never openly shared. Perhaps she dreams that I can fulfill her thwarted ambition of one day attending college, of one day becoming a writer, which, many years later, she shares with me as she shows me a medal she won for an essay she wrote in high school.

My mother stands behind me while I sit on top of the telephone book at the kitchen table, "writing." I am about three, and I haven't learned how to write, really. But my mother gives me blank sheets of paper and a pencil, and I fill them with seismic shocks and waves of meaning. I am very serious. I am writing.

Years later she tells me that when she asks me what I am doing, I reply that I am making a story.

"What's the story about?" she asks.

"I don't know," I answer, but I suspect I mean to say "I can't tell."

"When will you know?" she asks.

"When I'm finished," I answer.

"When will you be finished?" she asks.

"Yesterday," I answer.

"You mean 'tomorrow'?" she asks. I often say "yesterday" when I mean "tomorrow" and "tomorrow" when I mean "tomorrow." This confuses my mother. Time is something I haven't yet figured out. "Yesterday" and "tomorrow" are all the same to me.

That I start school when I am four years old becomes an important family story that sticks, that is told through the years, that grows true with its repetition. It means that, despite my difficult infancy (marked by hours of my crying because of the strict feeding schedule my parents adhered to), despite my difficult early childhood after my father comes home from the war (when I give my parents what seems like nothing but trouble because my father believes I am spoiled and I think he's an enemy who's returned from the war to do battle with me), I have turned out all right, and I might turn out all right in the end.

The story about my starting school so young signals that I am special. It differentiates me in my paternal grandparents' eyes from my cousins (and from my sister), none of whom, they believe, can match my intellectual accomplishments no matter how hard they try. And my cousins will be reminded of this at every family gathering.

One Easter my grandmother cooks a lamb's head as a special treat for the family dinner. With great ceremony my grandfather plucks the lamb's eye out from its socket and gives it to me to eat. I shake my head no, refusing. "You have to eat it," my father says, "it's an honor; it's for good luck." But I refuse my grandfather's offering; I can't imagine putting such an offensive thing inside my mouth, much less swallowing it. My grandfather shrugs his shoulders, pops the lamb's eye into his mouth, and pats his stomach as if to say, "Delicious," and we all laugh.

I don't know why I am singled out in this way. Nor do I know whether I would have been singled out in this way, despite my accomplishments, if my father wasn't my grandparents' only son or if I had an elder brother or cousin, for, in Italian American families, males usually get the best treatment. But in many Italian American families, too, one child is often selected by family elders to carry all the hopes for success of the family.

For whatever reasons, in my family, I am that child. What this means for me is that my cousins treat me not as one of a gang of eight tightly knit, rambunctious, mischievous youngsters but as someone around whom they feel uneasy.

There I am in a family picture taken on Easter Sunday, standing off to one side, separated from the rest of them, posing like the models I have seen in magazines, one foot in front of the other, clutching my pocketbook in front of me, looking as I always look, far too old for my years.

"Why can't the rest of you be like Louise?" my grandparents harangue my cousins, in Italian.

"Louise is the smartest; she's going to go far," my grandmother says to the others as she hands me an extra five dollars for making the honor roll.

As the years pass and I grow older, I become my paternal grandfather's favorite companion at the Brooklyn Dodger games he frequents and the Metropolitan Opera's performances he attends regularly. He never takes my grandmother or my father or my sister or my cousins to either.

At the Met he can afford only standing room, but he implores an usher to find me an empty seat; I am too young to stand for so long a time. During intermission he asks me what I think of the performance and reminisces with his cronies about Caruso, for my benefit. At the ball games he buys me hot dogs and loves that I remember the batting averages and the RBIs of my favorite players and that I can predict, more accurately than he can, whether a player will bunt.

When I am fifteen, in a wildly romantic phase, he takes me to the Met to see Samuel Barber's Pulitzer Prize–winning opera *Vanessa*. My grandfather and I disagree vehemently about its merits, to the amusement of the standing room regulars. He doesn't like any opera but Italian opera. Thinks you have to be Italian to compose opera, to conduct opera, to sing opera, even to appreciate opera. But I have found the music of the American opera *Vanessa* deeply haunting. To my grandfather's chagrin, I try to hum the aria "Do Not Utter a Word" on the bus ride back to New Jersey. I think he thinks I am a traitor. *Vanessa* is the last opera I remember seeing with him.

When I start school in September 1947, when I am nearly five years old, emotionally I am not ready for school, though the nuns assume I am. In public, I put on a good show; alone, I am afraid, I am always afraid, but I don't share my fears with my mother, who herself seems even more afraid than I am.

During the first few days at school, at lunch, which is taken at long tables in the school basement, its frosted windows letting in a weak light, I sit underneath the table with my lunch box open between my knees, trying to swallow my food through huge sobs I try to stifle in hopes that no one will hear me. No one does. No one notices I am there.

That my mother packs me off for a full day when I am so little suggests to me now that, raised in the absence of my father and lavished with her attention and that of my grandparents, I have grown to be a very demanding child, and so she wants some time away from me as soon as she can manage it. That and the fact that she is having a hard time raising both my sister (born the previous February) and me, and she wants me out of the cramped apartment for the better part of the day.

Our tiny railroad apartment in the Italian neighborhood of Hoboken, New Jersey, is barely suited for two people, it is true, and certainly not for four. There is absolutely no privacy. No doors separating the kitchen from the bedroom or the bedroom from the parlor.

We all wash up standing in front of the kitchen sink, in full view of everyone else. There is no bathtub, no shower.

Five of us share the toilet that is in a cubicle between two apartments, and unless you remember to lock both doors, someone inevitably opens one when you are inside; and when you do remember, someone knocks on the door, urgently needing their turn. No matter how fastidiously my mother or my grandmother cleans, the room always smells of someone's shit.

I am too short to reach the chain to flush. I am humiliated that I have to fetch a grown-up to pull the cord to dispose of my waste, but I get yelled at if I don't or if I forget. And I won't, I won't balance on the edges of the toilet seat so that I can do it myself. Once, I had managed this. But the fear of falling into the toilet, for there is nothing to grab but the swinging chain, stops me from trying it a second time.

My parents, my sister, and I sleep in the same bedroom. My sister's crib, my parents' double bed, and my cot are shoved so close together that there is no room at all between my cot and my parents' bed and barely enough room between my sister's crib and my parents' bed for them to squeeze by when it is time for them to go to sleep.

When my sister awakens in the night, she wakes us all. When I awaken in the night with a nightmare, which happens frequently, I wake everyone else.

And there is the sound of my parents' lovemaking going on so close to me, too close.

When I am awakened by their stifled moans or by the movement of their bed, I turn my back to them, feigning a profound but restless sleep; and to distract myself, I concentrate on the holy picture of the Sacred Heart of Jesus tucked into the corner of the mirror on my mother's bureau, illuminated by the dim glow of the night light at the foot of my cot.

Jesus is holding his bleeding heart out in front of him on an outstretched gold plate. The sounds and smells and movements of my parents' sex and the sight of the bleeding Sacred Heart of Jesus commingle.

My parents' nearness upsets. In the middle of one night, long after I am toilet-trained, I shit in my cot, which perplexes my mother and my father as they tend to me and my stinking mess.

I delight in the attention I am getting, and in interrupting them. And the need for some kind of release, any kind of release, as if there is too much inside me. Too much that I have seen, too much that I have heard, too much that I have felt, and too too much that has happened.

Though I grow to love school in time, initially, I hate it because I think that my mother is trying to get rid of me. I am jealous that she and my sister will be alone all day, and I wait impatiently for the day to end so that I can see my mother again.

I imagine that, while I am at school, my mother and sister are spending the day going to the playground, playing peek-a-boo, and visiting other kids on the block, as my mother and I did during the war years. But I know now that this wasn't happening. My mother had far too much work to do to play games with my sister, to give her much attention at all.

She rises early to prepare breakfast. She dresses me and my sister and walks me to school. The walk to my school and back home takes her over an hour. Then she starts her day's work. The washing alone takes her hours and hours. She does it all—my sister's diapers and clothes; my father's work clothes, which he changes daily; my blouse, socks, and underclothes—each day, by hand, on a washboard in the kitchen sink. She heats the water on the stove. Leans out the window to hang the clothes to dry. Or in winter, hangs them on a portable rack, inside. Heats the iron on the stove. Starches and presses the clothes. Then there is the cooking and cleaning. Everything she buys for us to eat, she has to cart up four flights of stairs; she has to shop every day, for our tiny kitchen has no pantry. We have no heat in winter, either. Then it is so cold inside that there are ici-cles inside the living room windows.

My mother now works hard. Too hard to enjoy my sister, too hard to be very much of a mother to her. My sister doesn't smile often. She spends much of her day in the crib, trying to amuse herself with the few toys my mother provides so that she can get her day's work done before she picks me up from school.

"When Jill was a baby," my mother will later say, "she never smiled at all." And the proof is there, in the pictures of her in infancy. Eyes down-cast, baby lips pulled into a frown, dull, vacant stare. I had gotten the best, the most my mother could give. My mother didn't have enough left over to give my sister.

What I like about school, though, is being away from my mother and grandmother's battles, the vicious shouting matches between them that now erupt frequently when my father and grandfather are not there. For by now my mother and grandmother are enemies; they are fighting all the time. My grandmother is my grandfather's second wife; his first (my mother's mother) died of influenza soon after my mother was born. My grandmother insists that my mother shows her no respect, that she wants her dead; my mother insists that my grandmother has never loved her, never treated her as kin. When they fight, their eyes lock, their backs arch, like birds that have been trained to peck one another to death. When my mother and grandmother fight, they pay no attention to me, to Jill. We could hurt ourselves, or disappear; they wouldn't notice. Often, my mother breaks things or hurts herself as they argue. She picks up the iron the wrong way and burns her hand. Pours the water for the washing carelessly and scalds herself. When this happens, she bursts into ago-nized cries. When, at last, one of their fights ends, it is impossible to get my mother's attention. A question, a request, provokes either no response or an angry one.

However many problems I might face in school, there are times, like when all the children are bent over their work, that it is blessedly peace-ful and quiet, nothing like the maelstrom I've left behind at home. The maelstrom in which my sister grows to be a toddler.

In time, because it is such a safe, quiet place for me, I grow to love the order, the rhythm, the regularity and predictability of the school day, its hours demarcated into periods of time devoted to penmanship, reading, spelling, arithmetic, catechism, geography. Even now, I like to plan my day in blocks of time devoted to different subjects and tasks, replicating, for comfort, this pattern that I found such a soothing respite from the whirlwind of my mother and grandmother's fights that leave my mother red in the face and in tears and unable to care for me and my sister, my grandmother angry and distant. I am left confused, because my grandmother is always kind to me when my parents are not, and my sister is withdrawn. And during the early, hard times of my marriage, before I am able to snip away the worst things from my past, when my husband and I fight as viciously as my mother and grandmother had, I retreat then, too, to the sanctity and order of my workday.

In the Catholic grammar school that I attended, the first- and second-graders were taught by the same nun and were schooled in the same room. The first-graders were ranged alphabetically in rows to the teacher's right, the second-graders to the teacher's left. While the first-graders were receiving instruction (in spelling, math, geography, reading, or catechism), the second-graders did work in their workbooks. While the second-graders received instruction, the first-graders worked in *their* workbooks. The nun who taught us (whose name I have by now forgotten but whom I will refer to by the name Sister Mary) made it a habit to write on the board directly in front of the first-graders when she instructed them and to move to the other side of the blackboard to write on the board directly in front of the second-graders when she instructed them.

But because my last name began with an S, my assigned desk was all the way in the back of the room and right next to the first row of second-graders. This meant that I couldn't see the first-grade work on the board because I was the shortest child in the class and also because we were required to "sit up straight" (no leaning to the right or left even if it was the only way we could see what was being written on the blackboard). But I *could* see the second-grade work on the board. Because the first-graders were learning how to read and write and I already knew how to read and write, I could complete the assignments in my workbooks quickly, which gave me time to attend to Sister Mary as she taught the second grade, and I learned their lessons as well.

On the first day of school, after Sister Mary settled us into our assigned places, she asked a red-headed girl in the second grade—with the strange name of Miranda Panda—to come to the front of the classroom for a demonstration to which we should all pay careful attention. Miranda Panda was going to show us something that, if we were good pupils, we would be able to do by the end of the first grade.

I hated Miranda immediately. I hated her because I was petrified and because she looked so cocky and sure of herself as she flounced to the front of the class. I hated her because she was in the second grade and I was in the first. I hated her because she wore long red banana curls and a big bow in her hair. I hated her because she was rich and lived on the hill in a big brownstone near Stevens Institute of Technology. I hated her because she had such a stupid name and yet no one dared make fun of her. Miranda Panda was someone special, someone not to be trifled with.

I had already been laughed at for my long, unpronounceable Italian last name (which contained twelve letters in all, seven consonants and five vowels), both in the school yard when kids asked me who I was and in the classroom when Sister Mary called the roll. I had already heard the insults that would become standard fare throughout my years of schooling: "Your name is bigger than you are" from the bigger kids, or the far more common "That's gotta be a Wop name; who else but a Wop would have a name like that?"

I had defended my name to a slovenly boy I instantly despised, with a series of remarks uttered with all the disdain that a nearly five-year-old girl can muster when she wants to be dismissive, contemptuous, and superior.

"I already know how to spell my last name," I told him, my nose pointed high in the air. "My mother says that if I can learn how to spell my last name, there isn't anything I can't learn. I already know how to read and write. And I know all the names of the states in the United States and their capitals. What do you know? You don't look like you know anything."

As the dirty little boy backed off, I knew that I had won. I had used the weapon of words, the only ones in my arsenal, but they were already considerable, and I had already used them in dizzying volleys against my father, who wasn't ever as quick-witted in that regard as I was. I was a girl, too young for school, very small for my age, and working-class, and Italian. In the eyes of the world, I wasn't worth much and wouldn't amount to anything. But my father had already told me that I had a "big mouth" and a penchant for "back talk" and that whenever we argued (which was often) I needed to have the last word. He said it in a way that was critical but also admiring. I *did* have a big mouth; I expressed my opinions whether they were wanted or not; I always talked back if someone said something that I regarded as wrong or stupid, despite the consequences; I never started talking unless I was sure I had something to say, and I never stopped talking until I had proved my point and gotten the other person to agree with me or to give up in despair.

I had refined these skills in the ongoing conversations I had with my mother, her women friends, and my friends' mothers during the war. With no men to talk to, with no one but us children to talk to, these women conversed with us as if we were their equals. They answered our "why" questions without interruption whenever we asked them. And they asked us for our opinions. My mother asked me which dress I preferred to wear, what I wanted for dinner, when I wanted to eat, which book I wanted to hear read, and whether I wanted to go to the park or to the movies (where there were always scary newsreels). My mother and my friends' mothers asked us what we had been doing outside in the courtyard while we were playing, and they listened to us as we told them our very long-winded stories. With the men away at war and no television to entertain or distract them, these women regarded their children as a source of companionship and entertainment, and engaging conversation became a high priority.

By the time Miranda Panda made it to the front of the room to show the class the special thing she had learned the year before on that first day of school, I had declared her the enemy. What I felt as she stood there, waiting for further instructions from Sister Mary, was a moment of envy. Within seconds, though, I felt a keen competition. Miranda Panda had what I wanted: everyone's attention. I decided that it was very important that I beat her.

"Now, boys and girls in the first grade," Sister Mary intoned, "Miranda Panda will demonstrate for you the wonderful kinds of things you will be learning this year. How many of you know your alphabet?"

A flurry of hands from the more eager, more intelligent first-graders. I kept my hands folded on my desk.

"Boys and girls," Sister Mary gushed, with much pride in her voice, "Miranda Panda will now recite the alphabet for you, but she will recite it *backwards.*"

Sister Mary stepped aside. Miranda Panda stepped forward, made a sign of the cross, took a deep breath, and began.

"Z, Y, X, W, V, U, T, S . . ."

When Miranda Panda got to the letter *R*, I stopped listening. My mother had told me that I was going to learn wonderful and important and interesting things in the first grade. Sister Mary had told me that I was going to learn wonderful and important and interesting things in the first grade. And here was a display of the wonderful and important and interesting things I was slated to learn.

After Miranda was finished, Sister Mary beamed at the class. "Now, class," she asked, "what have you learned?" And then, answering her own question, she said, "When you reach second grade, you'll know the alphabet so well, you'll be able to recite it *backwards*, just like Miranda Panda."

Miranda Panda, very pleased with herself, flounced back to her seat. I noticed that she wore ruffled socks in defiance of the academy's strict orders that we wear only socks that were white and plain and without adornment. Yet Sister Mary had singled Miranda out as special though she broke the rules. Whatever else Sister Mary wanted us to learn from Miranda Panda, when she settled herself smugly into her seat on the second-grade side of the classroom, I had already learned that there were insiders and there were outsiders and that the roles apply to some people but not to others.

"Now, class," Sister Mary said, "are there any questions?"

I waited a few moments, sure that every child in the first grade wanted to ask the same question as I, but although some children moved about in their seats, no one raised a hand. I did not yet know that in certain circumstances the question "Are there any questions?" uttered by a nun or a teacher standing in front of a room did not mean "Are there any questions?" but "How can there be any questions?"

I waited a bit longer, but when it seemed that no one was going to ask my question, I shot up my hand.

Sister Mary did not yet know my name, and so she acknowledged me with a little nod of her head.

"Sister Mary, Sister Mary," I began, having been instructed in the niceties of addressing nuns by my mother. ("You must always be very polite to the nuns. You must always use the word 'Sister' before their names.") "But *why* is it important to know the letters of the alphabet backwards as well as forward?"

I had asked the obvious question, one I would have asked my mother and one to which I wanted an honest answer, but here it seemed forbidden.

Sister Mary paused to consider her response. Of course, there was no legitimate answer that she could make to this question, and I knew it.

I wasn't easily fooled. When I asked my question, I had already decided that reciting the alphabet backward wasn't anything important, wasn't anything you could use, wasn't anything you had to know. It was simply a bravura display of useless knowledge. My father, a working-class utilitarian if ever there was one, repeatedly asked me, "But what good will it do you to know that? But what good will it do you to do that?" It was not just enough to know something or do something; you had to do something worthwhile with what you learned, with what you knew. His pragmatic attitude toward learning was something that, without realizing it, I had already come to share.

The truth was, I wanted Sister Mary to admit that knowing the alphabet backward wasn't important at all. In my mind it was the only truly honest answer to my question. And Sister Mary couldn't answer in that way without surrendering her authority, which, of course, she wasn't prepared to do.

I do not now remember the answer that Sister Mary made to my question, if she answered it at all. But I do remember not being allowed to go to the bathroom later the same day when the need to pee was so urgent that I felt sure I would wet my pants. And later in the day, after lunch, Sister Mary took a giant piece of Scotch tape and taped my mouth shut when she caught me asking the boy seated next to me about what had been written on the blackboard because I was too short to see over the head of the tall boy in front of me. Sister Mary told me that the Scotch tape would remind me, if I could not remind myself, that in her classroom there was to be no whispering at any time and no talking unless you were called on to answer a question.

As I sat in my seat, tape over my mouth, eyes stinging with tears, staring at the birthmark on the thumb of my left hand to steady myself, I vowed that whatever else I might learn in the first grade, no matter what the cost, I would never, ever, learn how to say the letters of the alphabet backward. I had decided that if that's what it took to gain recognition by Sister Mary, then I would forgo it. I also decided that I would beat Miranda Panda at the game of knowledge but that I wouldn't do it her flashy, attention-getting way. I would work hard and learn everything I could as well as I could, for sitting down at the kitchen table, my books before me, always earned my parents' praise, always temporarily halted my mother and grandmother's battles. ("Shh," my mother would hiss at my grandmother, "Can't you see Louise is trying to do her homework?") And by the end of my first year at Sacred Heart Academy, I *had* beaten Miranda Panda. I had been selected to crown the Blessed Virgin Mary during the school's May pageant.

The nuns told us that many factors were considered in selecting the person who would crown the Virgin. First, she had to have earned good grades; second, she had to have been a model student. I had been selected, Sister Mary told the class, because I had taken it upon myself to complete the work for the second grade while I was still in the first grade and also because I was the shortest girl in the first grade, and it would look very nice if I led the procession.

Before the crowning, the girls in both classes spent days decorating the classroom with blue and white crepe paper streamers, preparing the shrine of the Blessed Virgin Mary in the small garden in back of the school, decking the statue with flowers, and learning to sing: "O Mary we crown thee with blossoms today / Queen of the Angels, Queen of the May." My mother sewed me a baby blue eyelet gown with puffed sleeves and a bow that tied in front.

On the day of the crowning, the nuns gave all of us girls crowns of flowers to wear in our hair. And I was given a special tiger lily to hold for the procession. My father, very proud of me, took off a day's work and put on his best suit to come see me.

In the picture that my father has taken of us girls standing in front of the statue of the Blessed Virgin, I am in the center, in front of the statue. Miranda Panda stands to my right, wearing a store-bought dress, her hair arranged in perfect ringlets. And though the picture is in black and white, you can see that she is wearing a trace of lipstick. She is richer than I and older and taller, but I am smarter than she is; I know it, and I have proved it, and you can see the satisfaction on my face. And it has taken me less than a year to get what I want—Sister Mary singling me out for special merit, as she had singled out Miranda Panda on my first day at school.

In the years that I attend Catholic grammar school—in Hoboken and later in Ridgefield, New Jersey, after we move there—the lessons that I learn from the nuns are prodigious. They go beyond book learning. They will stay with me for a lifetime, long after I renounce my faith. They will inform my intellectual work.

I learn to see life as a titanic moral struggle between good and evil; I learn that we are all God's children; I learn the importance of neatness, order, discipline, rigor, practice, and routine in learning. The virtue of work. The spiritual, soulful nature of work. That work is another form of prayer. That you must teach others what you have learned. That you teach, too, by example. That there is beauty in the structure of a well-balanced sentence. That language must be used carefully, correctly, and precisely. I learn about the beauty of austerity and renunciation. That you are important not for what you have but for what you are, and for what you make of yourself. That human beings can perfect themselves but that they must constantly fight the allure of evil. That you should treat others as you wish to be treated. That generosity is a greater good than selfishness. I learn the value of intuition as a way of knowing. I learn the importance of pageantry and ceremony; I learn that having flowers nearby enriches the spirit and the soul. And that taking care of your spirit and your soul is as important as taking care of your body.

And as one nun after another after another rewards us by reading to us after a hard day in the first and second grades and throughout the rest of my grammar school years, I learn to listen to stories and to respect them. Although I do not now remember the names of any of the books that were read to me throughout the years, I remember that they were grown-up books, gargantuan books, filled with action, with the pulse of history, or with love and passion (though never with any sex as I recall). I learn to see reading as a privilege and pleasure and to glean the lessons to be learned from those who had taken the time to write beautifully, powerfully, and well.

But at first, school isn't such a welcome part of my life as it becomes in time, and at first, I can't wait for the school day to be over.

I sit anxiously outside school on the stone steps that lead up to the huge wooden front door, waiting for my mother to pick me up, balancing, on my knees, all my books (as usual, I have much homework) and my empty lunch pail (as usual, the milk from my leaky thermos has befouled the yellow cheese sandwich, which I detest and wouldn't have eaten anyway, and I have thrown the sappy mess away). I keep my possessions close to me because I am afraid that the bigger children will snatch at them and take them from me.

I guard my blue loose-leaf binder most carefully; in it is all my homework, neatly separated into subjects by tab inserts. If you do excellent work, you get a gold star. If you do very good work, you get a red star. If you do good work, you get a blue star. If you do average work or poor work or unacceptable work (work that isn't done according to the rules), you get no star at all. Everything you do is judged and ranked and marked. And you never get a star for making an effort. (One boy, transferred from public school, asks this question.) Making an effort is expected, not rewarded.

There is a concrete statue of the Sacred Heart of Jesus (Jesus, his hand on his heart, which is circled with a crown of thorns) in the front of the school. As I await my mother, I count the times that a pigeon lands on

Jesus' head. It's something that amuses me, though I know it shouldn't. When Sister Mary heard some boys laughing at this, she said, "Even pigeons are God's children; Jesus welcomes them to him, just as he welcomes you." Welcome or not, they make a mess, and at the beginning of the year, I watched a younger nun, sleeves rolled above her elbows, scrubbing down the statue of Jesus, making sure that it was clean. I wait to catch a glimpse of my mother coming down Washington Street, pushing my sister in her sand-colored wicker stroller. I wait to see, by the lock on my mother's face, whether it has been a good or a bad day or a really bad day.

If my mother is a few minutes late, I become panicky, sure that she has forgotten me, sure that she has died on the way or been captured and taken somewhere, sure that I will never see her again.

Once, when she is very late, I decide that she isn't coming, that another war has been declared, that something terrible has happened to her, or that my father has been killed, and so, dizzy and disoriented, I run all the way home. Across Washington Street and down and left and right and down and across many, many blocks. I stop several times along the way to pick up the books and belongings that I keep dropping in my haste. Once, my loose-leaf opens, and I have to put all the pages back.

It is a very long distance for a very little girl to travel, even when she has a mother beside her. And I have no mother beside me.

When I arrive at our apartment, and buzz and buzz and buzz and no one answers, I buzz my grandparents to be let in and then run up the stairs and knock and knock on my grandmother's door, only to be told that nothing is wrong, that my mother has left to pick me up, that she was a little late getting started.

And out the door and down the stairs I fly in a panic before my grandmother can stop me, to find my mother, who, I am sure, has come to harm but who, by now, has safely arrived at my school to find me not there. Suspecting that I have tried to walk home by myself, not believing I can find my way home alone but not knowing what else to do, she is returning home, as quickly as she can push my sister along, but by a way different from our usual way home. She is afraid I've been kidnapped, gotten lost, been taken to the hospital. She was late. It's all her fault.

And so we miss each other again.

When my mother finally finds me around the corner from where we live, in front of Our Lady of Grace Church, she is exhausted. She kneels down and gathers me to her, sobbing and shaking in her terror at what might have happened to me.

But I am strangely calm. My earlier fear has dissipated. I have found my way back, and to school, and home again, alone. And I have crossed Washington Street by myself *three times*. A bond between us has snapped, and though I am tired and tearful, I feel good.

"What did you learn today?" my mother asks me after she composes herself, trying to impress upon me a lesson she believes I must understand.

She expects, I think, that I will say that I have learned to wait for her patiently on the school steps even if she is late, that she will always come to get me, and that I should never again leave school until she has come for me.

"I learned that I can find my way home," I reply, which is the right answer for me but the wrong answer for her, and I know this because she frowns at me. Still, I mean it, and I don't take the words back or change them.

She looks at me as if I am a very strange child. For, just as much as she needs me to be gone for the day, so too she needs to come and get me at school, needs me to wait for her there, needs to walk me back home, just as I need to face the fear of losing my mother, need to make my way home without her even if it scares me, even if I have to scare myself to do it.

I have found my own way home. And I have learned that I can find my way again, anytime I need to, anytime I want to.

But my mother? What has she learned?

She has learned that she doesn't like this in me, this new bold and intrepid spirit that I have shown her on this day despite the fearfulness she knows I share with her. It is this that, in time, will separate us. Her fear will keep her where she is. Mine will propel me beyond her, sometimes with no apparent direction but, sometimes, with a homing instinct as sure and true as the pigeons who live in coops on the roof of our tenement display when they spiral their way down from the sky to find home.

Regina Barreca

. . . .

My Aunts Taught Me to Dance

There were dozens of them, fat and small, in floral print dresses, looking like ottomans scattered across the long, dark living room in Brooklyn. They had round faces and completely black or completely white hair, and they were always smiling or yelling, shaking fat fists at the ceiling to punctuate a story. And yet they could dance, gracefully, wildly stamping their improbably tiny feet and flinging one another around the room to jukebox music from the cheap red radio.

They could have taught me other lessons, like how to cook sweet sausage sauce or how to survive an early loveless marriage, but they didn't. Instead they swung me around the room in a two-armed gesture more often used by longshoremen unloading freight than by dance instructors. But with one another they practiced the intricate moves, raising eyebrows and half-smiling when they got it perfectly right, when fingertips touched just as the music stopped. It didn't have a name, but it was the only dance they knew and the only one I've learned in thirty-nine years.

They taught me to dance, and from them I learned what life had in store. One aunt was married to an uncle everybody called "the saint" because they apparently had lived together for forty years without having sex. "Your uncle Johnny is a saint," a random aunt would whisper in a voice as easy to hear as a stage villain's. For my first few years I knew only that he was called a "saint" by these women but did not know why. When I was about seven, they felt I was mature enough to handle the reason behind the title. I still had no idea what they meant, but I learned to raise my eyebrows slightly and nod.

So they kept speaking—believing for some lunatic reason that I knew what on earth they were talking about—and I kept quiet, silently and secretly remembering what they said. I knew I would need to figure it out later. The way kids from some other families on the block stole and hoarded food under their beds for the middle of the night, I craved and stole these stories, illegal in my ignorance, so that I too could get up after midnight and gnaw on them, filling myself up with stuff I could barely grasp or digest but couldn't get enough of.

"Your Uncle Johnny is a saint," as it turned out, meant that he didn't bother my Aunt Grace for sex. Now I wonder whether he dressed up in her slips when she wasn't home or caressed her shoes or found other like-minded saints in small basement clubs for a slow waltz. But maybe he just liked her company and wanted somebody to make cinnamon toast for him when he came home from driving a truck to and from New Jersey every day. Maybe they did everything except have sex, and there are certainly relationships less intimate than that. They slept in tiny separate twin beds, like children at a boarding school, but that still doesn't make it a tragedy. Sleeping in the same bed next to somebody every night doesn't mean you know what they're dreaming, after all.

The story about Aunt Grace ranked right up there with stories about "the change of life." "The change of life" sounded like what you got back after you bought something with "the bill of life," but after a while I realized that it wasn't currency they were talking about, at least not the way the word was usually understood. It's true, however, that hearing "Your Aunt Clara went through the change early" sounded as though she had emptied her pockets prematurely; and "Teresa never admitted having the change" sounded as though Teresa was cheap. Maybe they weren't too far off the mark; maybe blood was the going currency, with soft tissue as the floating bond of matrimony.

I overheard warnings about how people who came into the family through marriage could not be trusted. You might have to trust them a little maybe, but the family was still the only place you could count on the truth. The kind of truth you could count on, for example, was made clear by the way one uncle could bring his mistress to his sister's house for a drink every week before they went out for the evening, and my aunt would never think to tell her sister-in-law, his wife, what was going on because she, the wife, just wouldn't understand. The truth was that this uncle really loved his wife and was a good, good husband; that was the real truth. The little, incidental, small truth of an affair that lasted eighteen years was a truth his wife could not be trusted with. That made his wife untrustworthy. That was the logic of matrimony.

I also learned about matrimony and romance from looking at the cousins around me. At sunset the heat and the energy made it seem as if everything in the neighborhood might explode; these firecracker night-times filled my early summers. Humidity in the hot air rose like city in-cense out of garbage and Evening in Paris. "If you're not married by twenty, then kiss it good-bye," I heard my cousin laugh to his sister, who was seventeen and whom I adored. From the next door over we all heard my great-uncle yell, "There ain't no socks that stink like a woman's nag-ging." The steamy streets were thick with an undergrowth of children tan-gled in gritty games until way after dark. In this warm darkness my cousin Marie and her friends were future mothers out looking for future fathers.

It was clear to me even then that there weren't decisions to be made, only choices. Choosing by eye color, height, or a single noble gesture, my female cousins picked boys the way boys picked jobs: taking what offered the most in the long run. Time set boundaries around them like fences. "Nobody has forever," said Marie to me as she ran down the steps in a hurry, "least of all us. You'll see. Wait." I was maybe ten years old, but I tucked the warning away for later. The beautiful shark-eyed teenage boy who waited in a car beside the curb seemed Marie's best bet, I thought. His white smile broke through the heat like a wave on a beach.

I was thirteen at Marie's wedding. I wore a homemade dress in forest green: I looked like an avocado, and worse, I knew it. I pleaded homework and cramps, but there I was, on the way to a hotel on Long Island, back-seat window rolled up against the breeze from the river, curls of hair, like snails, already damp against the back of my neck. It wasn't pretty. But something was different in the slick, false ballroom. The cake was a car-toon, vaulted high as a cathedral. The bride and groom walked in, black and white with her red bouquet like a blush in her arms. We all knew what they were thinking. Yet the priest had blessed them, and what five minutes before was a slap-in-the-face sin was now a sacrament, sanc-tioned by God, between the marital sheets. Anything could happen.

Old ladies in purple and black looked like eggplants, moving together around the perimeters of the room until the music started.

The music was magic. It was like Lourdes. Women who had hardly walked in years got up to dance. They laughed and smiled, doing dances as old as their whisperings, dancing done for harvests and fertility.

Something in me thumped recognition, but when Aunt Grace pulled me in I pulled myself out. I wasn't ready. But I was ready to dance with the friends of my cousin, rough boys with black hair, boys from vocational schools, boys otherwise out of bounds. My skirts flung out, my legs showed, and for a minute fear raked nails across my arched back; but everybody was smiling. It was a wedding. I danced harder, as if something depended on it, until my father's hand, reaching through the music, pressed against my shoulder to say we had to go. Looking at my partner, he said, "The long drive back . . ." The boy nodded, and I smiled like a chorus girl, thinking the green dress brought out my eyes, looked like a river running over me. My cousin's husband, like a tycoon in his striped tie, kissed his wife as we were leaving. The wedding guests rapped spoons against their glasses in a fine silver shower of sound. My new shoes were like little boats of pain, but I didn't mind; I could hear every note in the music, the way you hear your own name in a crowd. Who cared that the band wasn't good; who cares who calls your name as long as somebody shouts it?

My Sicilian great-grandmother, well into her nineties, wished Marie luck and said a prayer for her. My grandmother would stay up late but sleep in intervals, waking to pray, or curse, or make a prediction. Then she'd fall asleep, fall back into her dreams like a shriveled dark pear that had fallen from one of the fruit trees that grew, unceremonious and undaunted, behind the house.

This great-grandmother could not imagine a world immune to magic, so she applied magic to her wish that all the women in the family would marry, considering every girl a woman. She lit votive candles that glowed red on every table. She prayed out loud. When the backyard bushes were hung with fireflies shining like rhinestones, she would tell stories about eating figs right off the tree and talk about how she met her husband when she was only fifteen. He died when he was forty-seven and she was forty-one, and this was more than fifty years ago, but she spoke about him as though he had just gone to the store for a few minutes.

(When this old woman fell, not like a piece of fruit but like a kitten flung from a rooftop, down two flights of stairs, it was my twenty-two-year-old mother, not one of her own children, who dared to go with her in the ambulance to the hospital. My aunts wouldn't, being more terrified of doctors and places where no one understood your screamed questions than they were of their mother's solitary death. You agreed to see a doctor in my family only if you were ready to die, and since no doctor ever came to the house before a priest was already set up to perform the last rites, it turned out to be true. My relatives saw doctors and then died; that there was a flaw in the causality of the relationship didn't occur to me until much later on.

My mother said the old woman looked into her eyes with a full understanding of all that was happening, apologetic for all the others who were too cowardly to be with them. They placed my great-grandmother on a stretcher and wheeled her away—but not before she smiled good-bye to another immigrant imported wife with no way to make herself understood. My mother herself would die only a few years later. Did she have a premonition of this, escorting the old woman to the hospital where she would soon spend so much time? (I didn't want to ask the question.)

Tough questions at home were answered with the line "Life is great, not easy." Questions at school were easier. My brother looked through my seventh-grade marbled science notebook, crossed out "electron, neutron and proton" and wrote instead "fire, air and water," exercising his prerogative of years to reconstruct my education. It was the beginning of something for me, his knowledge of crossing out, this permission to scribble across block letters and print outside the lines. Few things were easy, what with mistaking words for truth and me with my pudding heart. I discovered a nasty satisfaction in survival. Tips for survival were thrown around freely. My father believed that you had better keep your back against the wall because They will be there to pick you off, one by one, like cherries from a tree, birds on a fence, suckers at a card table, unarmed wops at a restaurant.

(When did I consciously think of myself as Italian? I was trying to break a statue of the Virgin Mary while listening to my parents fight with my brother when they found dope under his bed and my mother came upstairs, cigarette dangling from her lips like Bette Davis in *Now Voyager*, saw me smashing the statue, and casually remarked, "That's very Italian." It was hardly the slogan for Prince Spaghetti Day or anything, but it took, like a dye or an inoculation, and marked me.)

High school was madman boyfriends writing across my curriculum and my wondering whether Einstein had a daughter. Bigger girls blamed it on the bossa nova, and their guys wore jeans so tight you could see where all the blame could lie. They walked the halls like rope dancers, balanced on high shiny heels, upright. If only I were called Cheryl, Sharon, or Cindy, I thought, and had a name like a whistle. My weapons were a high wail of right answers, a tattoo of information. I was incandescent in my correctness. I wanted to get the right answer, not to be right but to be heard.

There were no long answers in my family, only short ones. Asked why, at seventy-five, one great-uncle moved himself into the attic, moving a staircase away from his wife of forty-eight years, the only answer was "That's where he wanted to live." Asked why Aunt Louise never married, the answer was "She never found the right man," which always sounded as if she had carelessly misplaced him or at least misplaced the map that would lead her to him. There was never a hint that she might not be looking.

The aunts who danced on Saturday evening went to church on Sundays and some went during the weekday, too, to cover their heads with lace and cry. Churches locally seemed filled with women in mantillas weeping and making excuses. The pews also held a few frowning men, making their own excuses, looking more defiant than unhappy when confronting their Maker with their own sinfulness. My talent, clearly, was for breathlessly overhearing things, not minding my own business, and storing away what I did not understand, in order, it seems, to invent interpretations that only coincidentally coincided with the truth.

While I did not know specifically for what sins my aunts cried in the brick churches, I figured that these sins must have happened in the past. Surely, they were incapable of sinning at their advanced ages. Sinning was a youngster's game, something to look forward to for me and something to look back on for them. My aunts led complex lives in a simple setting, and I, wrongly, thought I had their story straight before I was even starting my own. I thought their marriages, their loves, their passions, their furies were diluted by their years and buried by their shapeless flowered dresses. I separated myself from their circles and found other rhythms strumming beneath my feet.

That I went to college was a surprise to my family. "College" was a concept I patched together from an illicit reading of *The Group* as well as from seeing Sandra Dee in a movie called, I think, *Tammy and the Professor*. I didn't fully realize that "college" was as foreign to my family as a camping trip or a welcome call from a government official. Living as I was in a house decorated in Sicilian Gothic, full of small rooms with people telling contradictory stories in every one of them, I was surprised to find that the aunts were, in this matter, uniform in their response.

The aunts were suspicious. No girl had ever left the neighborhood for a good reason. So when I said, "I'm going to New Hampshire," pleased with myself for getting a scholarship, they paused. They eyed me, were uneasy, wary, frowning. "You're pregnant, right?" they said. I denied it. They told me it was okay, that it had happened to a cousin, that I could come back home when it was all over. They clucked in sympathy, and I could not convince them that I didn't need their sympathy but instead needed their enthusiasm. They shook their heads. I left, heading north with no idea of what to expect.

"My aunts taught me to dance," I said to somebody when I was eighteen and starting at this college where I was, I believe, the only person on campus whose last name ended in a vowel.

We'd just finished dancing, this beautiful boy and I, and I was sorry to lose the feel of his hip against my own. He was tall, just golden enough to be interesting, and he had blond hair falling over a high forehead. He was as different from everyone I'd ever met as I was from everyone he'd probably ever met. It occurred to me even as he brushed his hand against the back of my neck that my grandparents would have been working in factories his grandparents owned, that my uncles would have been fixing his father's shoes, that my aunts would have been sewing his mother's dresses, and that, in only a slightly different world, I would have been the nameless waitress at a place he went for coffee. But the world had shifted, however slightly, on its axis, and we were locked together in a moving embrace, presumably as equals.

When I looked up at him I felt what I could only identify as my stomach contracting, like someone sketching a detailed picture on my belly like ice skates on a frozen pond. But what was happening that evening was the beginning of a thaw, of a new season having nothing to do with winter.

Let me tell you about that dance. That was the night I found out that dancing lets you take a stranger and hold him in your arms and that such holding is one of the best things about it. You move together, briefly and silently. I was so conscious of my body while I danced with the beautiful boy that my fingers still remember the feeling of the skin on the back of his hands, of the slight pressure of his leg brushing against mine, and the way I felt my mouth forming words for the sheer pleasure of making my lips move so near to his he must have felt my warm breath on his throat.

I was glad I wore perfume in my hair, I was glad that my hair was long, and for the first time I was really glad that it was black and curly because everyone else had straight fair hair. He could ask, "What happened to the girl with the curly hair?" and it would only be me he was asking about. If he asked at all, that is. Who knew what he was thinking? Maybe he was thinking about the girl he came with, a small-faced woman who wore pearls and clean shoes, and who kept an eye out for him while I kept my eye on her.

I was thinking about this boy taking my hand and then pulling me toward him, his hands in my hair, his mouth against mine. I was thinking of nights when I was sixteen, in the long backseats of cars with one-night-stand boys, never going below the waist as dictated by morality, and a need not to have to bother: who needed to be that busy on those July evenings? I was remembering hands on my breasts and kisses that went on for hours and the deep hunger for tongues and sweat and breaths that were as shallow and as far-reaching as a stone skipped across a pond.

In my head I told him, "Dancing with you is a dressed rehearsal, an upright version of a deed with a downside. Threading my fingers with yours as if we are playing a child's game of church and steeple is, for me at least, only a prelude to the grown-up game. Your leg against mine even in a dance is no game; my hand spread open against your back and feeling the movements of your shoulder with my fingertips is no mechanical motion. Slipping muscle against bone as you maneuver me across a polished wooden floor to music is serious, serious business." I tried to signal this message to him like a lighthouse or a secret agent, tapping it out in the unspoken but, I thought, universally understood code of desire.

I tried to make him understand the message through the hieroglyphs of the heart, but he didn't hear.

He heard how I sounded, my voice—not my arms—capturing his attention. "Say that again," he said, dimpling his perfectly smooth cheek, keeping me inside the gravitational pull of his charm. I smiled because I didn't dare not smile in front of a handsome man at that point in my life, but I was puzzled; and whatever else he was blind to, he wasn't blind to my slightly blank look.

"Say what again?" I ventured, no doubt fluttering a few eyelashes for good measure; if I was going to look like a fool, then at least I could also look like a flirt and pretend it was intentional. He smiled. "Say 'My aunts taught me to dance.' You have a real New York accent."

I didn't think of myself as having an accent. I didn't think of myself as bearing the stamp of difference in my language, with words having always been my allies, the one thing I could count on. But that evening I suddenly heard myself the way he must have heard me, with a voice like Brooklyn traffic, saying "aunts" as if I were talking about insects instead of relatives. I didn't even try pronouncing the word differently. In part I knew too well that by mimicking his way of saying "Aahnts" not only would I make myself ridiculous but I would at that moment be swapping a strong and real inner voice for something that was merely correct.

I knew in that moment that I couldn't have been his girlfriend, even if he'd wanted it, couldn't have been softly sweet or constantly agreeable any more than I could have spoken like a debutante or hit a brilliant backhand; I could not do these things. My past was too dense with choice to let myself be thinned, like paint, in order to be applied more easily to him. I'd been taught too well in those basement kitchens by women who tried to make sure my life would be better than theirs. He wouldn't have given up altering me, showing me what he thought was right, despite the fact that he genuinely liked what he saw in me that night. I would always have seemed like something out of a "Dondi" cartoon to him or the front of the Contadina tomato paste can, the ripe Italian who offered a little spice but who had to be measured out carefully in order not to be overwhelming.

The boy and I danced together only that one evening. He probably went on to dance slowly but not too closely with the girl with the pearls and the New England accent.

As for me, I learned to rely, increasingly, on my aunts' advice: life's too short to hold onto a guy who thinks there's only one way to say words or one way to move to the music.

I moved across other dance floors in my day, small, flat, wooden countries full of miraculous mobility, slipping and regaining my footing, sometimes with a man's arm around me as a prop or a guide, sometimes just part of a circle of strangers or friends, sometimes with my aunts as they made their ways, more and more slowly, to the place where their lessons were learned without being questioned and their lead was followed without hesitation.

They taught me better than I realized. I follow gratefully in the surprising, smiling grace of their footsteps.

Frank Lentricchia

. . . .

The Edge of Night

Even you don't know what you meant by you.
—Raging Bull

Christmas season 1987, give or take a year. I can't remember exactly. Hillsborough, North Carolina. A kitchen. Three real people, who must not be called characters, though that's what they, along with all the other real people, must become. A woman, about seventy; her son, her son-the-author, late forties; his wife, late thirties. The older woman (the mother, the visiting mother-in-law) speaks, directing most of it to the non–Italian American daughter-in-law, but all the time keeping the son in view, occasionally shooting him a challenging glance or remark. Her mood is better than you think; her mood is better than she thinks. She speaks as if the conversation has been rolling for some time. In fact, her words inaugurate it:

"But what I want to know is why are we so involved, because they'll never change. Change? With us? Change my ass. I have to ask you something. What kind of a look do you call that on my son's face? He's just like his father. And his father is just like *his* father, that's where it all comes from, but my husband's father was the worst. He's the one who scared me. With their friends they're different, then they change in a hurry. My father-in-law was so cold you don't even know what I mean by 'cold.' I was ashamed to smoke, he never said a word and I was ashamed. You think I don't notice your husband when you smoke? I notice everything. And what are you looking at? What is he looking at? Naturally your husband is not as bad as my husband, but after all what do you expect me to say? With his friends I bet he's different, then all of a sudden they're warm, because their friends, the men especially, make them happy, let's face it, not us, and not their kids. Don't look at me like that, you don't scare me. I changed your diapers. He looks at his mother and his wife with that face. *Che faccia brutta!* The Lentricchia men, they're all the same, believe me, except for one of my brother-in-laws who went to the other extreme. At least our husbands didn't do that, but maybe they should have, maybe they did that, too. Because let's face it, sex is another joke. What do you want me to say? *Why* are they like that around us? You went to college, you tell me. To be honest, I don't think even they know, and I don't care anymore because in their own homes they don't want involvement, they go inside themselves. What are they doing in there? If they didn't want involvement, who told them to get married in the first place, if they didn't want involvement. What I want to know is how long are you going to kid yourself? If you have the answer, don't think I want to hear it, because I don't want to hear it, but if you have to, you can tell me."

I can't remember the words, I can't remember the context, maybe there wasn't one, because she doesn't need a context, but that's how I remember it now, five or six years later, my father in another room watching TV, my mother right in front of us, and I don't have to remind you who "us" is. She probably had a context; I just couldn't see it.

It should be mentioned that my mother is prone to opera. She talks in arias. Any and all disturbances presage apocalypse. Her enemies ought to croak, the bastards. All wounds are fatal, and anything can cause a wound, even nothing can cause a wound. It should also be mentioned that I've heard it said that I'm nothing like my father, who I'm not saying is what my mother says he is. According to him, I'm very like my mother. We're the same. "What do you expect? He exaggerates. He exaggerates everything. He gets it from his mother. He gets excited, don't you, Frank?" Arias without discernible context; emotions for which I can find no matching circumstances. Apocalypse twice a week. Wounds that cannot be healed, not even by affection. Affection, in fact, makes them much worse, opens them right up again.

About a year ago, in New York, an editor at a major publishing house said to me that I ought, up front, tell my readers who I am. Otherwise readers would have to crawl inside my head. She said "crawl inside." She felt that in order to understand the chunk she had just read, she would need to crawl inside my head, in order to find out who I am. When she told me that, I felt a strong urge to find out who she was. I wanted to open up her head. I should have said, "If I knew who the fuck I was, do you think I'd be writing this?" Or I should have said, "If I knew what the fuck I was doing, do you think I'd be writing this?" I was about to revise out "fuck," but if I did you might think that I was talking metaphorically when I said I wanted to open up her head. In order to see what was under the skull, what was actually in there.

I was talking to the New York editor in my favorite Italian pastry shop, way over on the East Side, near the East Village, a place I liked to frequent because any time I went in there I saw an elegantly dressed elderly man, utterly manicured, a shave every four hours, a haircut every five days, who would occasionally walk outside to talk to youngish guys built like bulls in flowered shirts, with envelopes in their hands who kissed him on the cheek when they left. It was a movie, post-*Godfather.* They knew they were in a movie; they were enjoying themselves in the movie.

The elegantly dressed elderly man scared me. I had to look at him out of the corner of my eye, which I became very good at, because I didn't want to be in his movie in the wrong role. I've never seen a face that brutal when he thought no one was looking at the face. It was the best brutal face I'd ever seen. I liked to look at it. Maybe a plastic surgeon could give me a duplicate. They say anything can be arranged in New York.

It would have been nice to call him over, to introduce him to the New York editor at a major house. Then I could have said, "Now say the words 'crawl inside your head' to this man." If only she could have coffee with this man every day, if only she could, she would become more sensitive in her relations with writers, she would become a good woman. Because if she didn't, with his demitasse spoon, and his little pinky sticking way out, he'd eat what was under her skull. I don't like questions about who I am or what I'm doing. If you wish to know who I am, ask my parents; they know. Or my friends, with whom it is said I'm different.

I'll tell you what I like about writing. When I'm doing it, there's only the doing, the movement of my pen across the paper, the shaping of rhythms as I go, myself the rhythm, the surprises that jump up out of the words, from heaven, and I am doing this, and I *am* this doing, there is no other "I am" except for this doing across the paper, and I never existed except in this doing.

I'll tell you what I hate about writing. Finishing it. It comes to an end. You can't come forever. When I'm finished, I can't remember what it was like inside the doing. I can't remember. When I'm not writing, I want to become the man with the brutal face.

A sentence, a sentence, my family for a sentence.

This time it's only a few months back that I'm trying to remember, so I'm fairly confident about the words. A telephone call to my parents, for the purpose of conducting research on a word famous in second-generation Italian American households, who get it from the first generation, and then pass it on to the third, where I am, dead end of tradition. Forget the fourth, where my kids are. I was writing about this word. Once I heard this word spoken by Robert De Niro in Martin Scorsese's *Mean Streets* (I like to write out those names) and felt secretly addressed, even thrilled, a member of a community. Its pronunciation varied startlingly in my family, according to affective context: *c*'s become *g*'s; final vowels could disappear. It all depended. The word was deeply rooted, yet flexible. It gave what was needed. A genial word, from the unprinted lexicon of Italian American. I pose the question of its meaning to my mother, who says immediately, "Pecker, your pecker." She's totally confident, so I don't mention that the interesting word takes the feminine definite article, because some part of me, maybe most of me, wants her to be right, with the feminine definite article, yes. My father only says, "Ann." That's all, you can hear him. My mother is not intimidated. She comes back: "I know that word." My father: "It's the woman's, he knows it's the woman's." He's totally confident. He tells her that I'm kidding around. He knows that, if asked, which I wasn't (because they don't do that), I'd side with him. After such phone calls, what knowledge?

I am an Italian American, one of whose favorite words bears his grandparents, his parents, his neighborhood, his favorite movie director, but not his children, not his colleagues, not where he lives now, and not most of his friends. I'm not telling you that I'm alienated from my ethnic background. I'm not unalienated from it. It's an issue that doesn't much preoccupy me anymore.

This word dancing in my head cannot tell the difference between the man's and woman's. The New York editor, who is an Italian American, thinks it important to tell you that I'm an Italian American. Are you glad to know that? Am I becoming clearer to you by the sentence? I know a word that means the man's and woman's. Do you want to know my secret word? Shall we play with it together? You starting to crawl in?

.   .   .

I have a friend who lives in a good place, in South Carolina. His name is Leonard Cunningham. Leonard once said to me, in full knowledge that I am a married man: "You still a grumpy old bachelor?" One time I called the place where Leonard lives. The person at the other end, who was not Leonard, said something that I must have misheard, because I replied, "Am I Father Aelred?" I must have misheard. The person best in a position to know reminds me of a nightmare that I can't remember, king of the roof-rattlers, a full-throated screamer. It seems that I looked into my wallet for my driver's license, found it, it was mine all right, definitely mine, but it bore someone else's name and picture. It was definitely mine all right. Feel free, don't worry about it. Crawl in.

I said nothing when the New York editor said that I ought to tell my reader that I'm a literary scholar, a literary theorist, a professor of English, a critic, and I was rendered speechless when she whipped out a copy of the paperback edition of one of my books—bent and underlined—and quoted some sentences about my favorite philosopher, William James, which I didn't remember writing, then offered a commentary on those sentences (critic of a critic of a philosopher), which I couldn't understand, sipping my decaf cappuccino, then declared that *that* very passage, and others like it in my critical books, would help my readers to understand who I am. Tell them you're a literary critic.

At which point, in a tone as dead flat as I could manage, I should have said, "I've concluded, after much consultation with experts in the field, and much reflection, that, in spite of all the obvious resemblances, I'm nothing at all like T. S. Eliot." That's what I should have told the New York editor when we were sitting there in that pastry shop way down on First Avenue. "For example," I should have said, "what are the chances that Eliot ever ate" *(academic, very dry, hands about the coffee cup)* "three cannoli in one sitting, even as I do now?" I can tell she needs to think I'm funny, rather than something else. She'd prefer not to think of me and something else. I'd prefer that she think of me and something else. I say, "You think I'm funny? What's so funny? You want to be edited?" She is trying to smile, but she cannot do it. I'm winning. At which point I call over the wonderful brutal face and say *(leaning in, with concern)*, "Which one of us would you prefer to ride home with on the deserted subway at 1:00 A.M., to the end of the line in Brooklyn, just one of us and you in the car? Which one? Be careful, don't answer too fast, and don't say both because we're not kinky. Don't even suggest kinky. You got a gun? Which one? Choose, I'll count to five, then I'll tell him" *(broad winning grin)* "to do that thing with his demitasse spoon, which I imagined eight minutes ago, which I haven't told you about, because I want you to be surprised and tickled pink. You want to taste my cannoli? I'm Al Pacino in *Godfather II*. Who are you? All work and no play makes Frank a dull boy. Name that movie with Jack Nicholson!"

I teach English in a distinguished university. In my distinguished department, which is like all English departments I have known or heard about, we have virtually nothing in common, not even literature.

For the last two years I've been writing about T. S. Eliot; I'd better say trying to write about him. All work and no play. He is a fascination and a crisis. Honey, I'm home. The job of the literary critic is to explain, whatever else he may do, but Eliot's poetry is beyond explanation, though it has been explained *ad nauseam*. I get nauseous. His poetry, and I say this with total admiration, is unreasonable. Not unreasonably difficult, just unreasonable, which is why I find it fascinating. I'm also drawn to his explanations of the writing process. He means the process of writing a poem. I mean the process of writing anything, including a letter, or this, maybe especially this. What is this? I hate that question. Make me happy and hate it too, hate it too.

Eliot is responding to a German writer, Gottfried Benn, Eliot is always responding to some other writer, building, ripping off, making something new. Theft and the individual talent. Eliot says that writing begins with an "obscure impulse" (in other words, you don't know what you're doing). Or, he says, you're haunted by a demon "with no face, no name, nothing" (in other words, you don't know who you are, you don't have a face). Benn says, says Eliot, that we start with an "inert embryo," a "creative germ." Plus the language. "He has something germinating in him for which he must find words, but he cannot know what words he wants until he has found the words." When you have found the right words (which you can't know are right in advance) then the thing for which the words have to be found disappears. You have a poem. Writing is a journey in and through language; writing is discovery. That's Benn. Here's Eliot's twist: the writer "is oppressed by a burden which he must bring to birth in order to obtain relief." Eventually, the writer gains "relief from acute discomfort" (sounds like an ad for something) and experiences "a moment of exhaustion, of appeasement, of absolution, and of something very near annihilation, which is in itself indescribable." Benn never mentioned acute discomfort; Benn maybe likes the process. Eliot feels labor pains, or maybe a sharp gas pain in the lower intestinal tract. The pain gives no pleasure. What gives pleasure is the end, when relief is obtained, and the poem is fully born. The last *t* has been crossed, *then* Eliot is satisfied.

Coleridge is better than either Benn or Eliot on the writing process. He says readers "should be carried forward, not merely or chiefly by the mechanical impulse of curiosity, or by a restless desire to arrive at the final solution" (we know who you are, you're under arrest), "but by the pleasurable activity of mind excited by the attractions of the journey itself." He's talking about readers who almost don't exist, who don't ask questions that make me unhappy, who do not seek the final solution. No reader could possibly experience what Coleridge wants readers to experience unless (Coleridge is not talking now, it's me) there were writers who wanted to feel the same thing, "the pleasurable activity of the mind excited by the attractions of the journey itself." The meandering adventure through language (writing as drafting as revising as improvising), not the thing at the end but the unfolding process itself, the journey, the ride, every step of the way, never sure what's unfolding, never caring that much, happy to go off the track, screw the track. Outside the process, the demon has no name. The process names the demon and you are the demon, the demon *in* and *of* and *as* the process, and you like the demon. For once, you like yourself. The annihilation you experience is indescribably good, because it is the death of everything you were outside the process. The opaque burdens of your self-consciousness are lifted. When the process ends, you go back—the opacity, the weight, the stasis, and other things best not to mention, that's what you are. There you are, on the track.

When I'm doing this, whatever "this" is, and that's not my problem, that's your problem, if you want that problem, which you don't have to have because nobody is holding a gun to your head and demanding that you tell us what this is, when I'm doing this, I like taking walks, driving, riding in airplanes (I have an extra ticket, you want it free?), sitting in the waiting lounge, doing it there in public, when will my flight board? I can't wait. Motion like the motion of my pen. I can write in airplanes now. I become a dangerous driver, things come into my head when I drive and walk, writing as motion sickness, I better walk more. I *am* writing; *l'écriture, c'est moi.*

In a letter—on this one he didn't go public—Eliot had something to say about bad writing. Bad writing is writing that repeats what you've already written. To avoid it, you must "defecate" the self that produced it, if it is possible (which it isn't) to say a "self" produces the kind of writing that Eliot has in mind. Defecate the self *of* that writing, that's better, my graduate students might like that, or run the risk of writing feces. To avoid it, void it. Birth and defecation, labor pains and gas pains, life and crap. Does Eliot know the difference? Does anybody? Flesh of my flesh, shit of my shit. Shit of my death. I'm a literary critic.

It was in the place where Leonard lives that I first read these lines from Psalm 144:

> No ruined wall, no exile,
> No sound of weeping in our streets.

"Flesh of my flesh": Eliot's poem, his metaphorical child. I have two children, not metaphorical. We, I risk speaking for the three of us (I mean the two kids and me, Eliot has no part in this), we feel unrelieved, unappeased, not absolved, annihilated in quite specific ways, the details of which I'm never going to tell you. We are certainly exhausted. "Annihilated" is heavy, but I'm using it anyway. Eliot used it, why can't I? I'm not giving you the details because this isn't *People* magazine. The domestic details are banal, anyway. They don't explain. The opium of the middle class. You already know the details. You know the soap opera, so don't ask.

One weekend, a long time ago, about fifteen years back, when they were about five and six and a half, they were visiting us. You know who "us" is and you know why they were "visiting." While she was cooking dinner (no, I won't tell you her name, you don't need to know that, either), we played a game involving the stairs to the second floor. Daddy, you stand at the bottom. Daughter Number 1 climbs to the third stair. Daddy says, Amy Amy Amy. She jumps into his arms. Daughter Number 2. Rachel Rachel Rachel. Jumps into his arms. Daddy, let's do it again. Lots of giggling. We do it for the fourth stair. We do the fifth. Giggling becoming intense, hysteria creeping in, the little bodies flying, love-missiles right on target. Daddy Daddy Daddy. Amy Amy Amy. Rachel Rachel Rachel. Crash. The sixth is painful, gravity is beginning to talk tough. Daddy was not ready. The kids want the seventh. Daddy braces, the seventh is accomplished. Higher! Let's go higher! We do the eighth, my God. We do the ninety-eighth; we do the four hundred and fifty-eighth stair. Flesh of my flesh. We open up each other's heads. "I'll get you through our kids, you son of a bitch." *I'll get the kids through you, you son of a bitch, I'll put*

the kids through you, you son of a bitch, I'll put the son of a bitch through the
kids, you son of a bitch, I'll put the son of a bitch through the son of a bitch,
with the full cooperation of the son of a bitch, you son of a bitch. What do
you expect? I'm middle-class. I like soap opera too.

We didn't have a name for the game we played. I think I was saving
them. It was the game of I Saved the Kids. "He exaggerates. He exaggerates everything." Like my mother, I'm prone to it, prone to the real thing,
where they go all the way, all the time the four hundred and fifty-eighth
stair. The real thing is Italian opera. Can this shit live? Can this shit sing?

"You need to tell us where you're from."

"I'm one hundred percent from literature."

"No, seriously."

"Okay. I'm one hundred percent from the movies."

A conversation that never took place, with the New York editor or with
anyone else. No real conversation about my first place. Good thing, it
would have been too hard to explain in conversation, to say just what I
mean. The first place, my so-called origins, the Hydrogen Bomb of explanation. Then everything becomes clear. Then everything becomes dead.
In conversation with strangers I tend to be sloppy and anxious, sometimes
with intimates, too, what an experience that is. Conversation is too hard.
Better to write. Forget the telephone, forget talking altogether. Except
after long, enforced absences, talking is overrated.

Yeats said that he was always discovering places where he wanted to
spend his whole life. One of the places where I want to spend my whole
life is in Yeats. Like Yeats, I don't know exactly where I'm supposed to be.
Long after I left, long after it seemed to have drifted out of my mind for
good, Yeats helped me to recover my first place, my grandfather's house on
1303 Mary Street, Utica, New York, where we lived on the second floor
until I was a senior in college. But "recover" is misleading, suggesting I got
something back that I used to possess. I used to sleep and eat there, but I
never possessed it, it never possessed me (that's better), I never actually
lived there until I imagined myself all the way back through the medium
of some of Yeats's poems about the great country houses of Ireland,
specifically Lady Gregory's, Augusta Gregory's (she had just the right first
name), in the west of Ireland, Coole Park, where Yeats was taken in every
summer, nurtured and sustained and respected from who he was, a writer.
Coole Park was the place where he wrote well and about which, much
later, he would write better than well, he would write magnificently, out of

his memory of loving sustenance and respect, poems about the place it-self, writing when he had a bitter hunch, and he was right, that the place would be leveled, imagining its and his own not being there, and the vines and the saplings winning, forcing themselves up through the broken stone, the rubble. He wrote magnificently because he was haunted.

Absurd to think of my grandfather's house—my mother's father's house—and Coole Park in tandem, neck and neck in my imagination, ab-surd to say that I possessed it as if for the first time, not as if but actually, reading poems about an aristocratic mansion, where my grandfather would have been employed to "shovel shit," which is what he would say whenever I asked him to tell me what he did in the old country, when he was young. He shoveled it for *il padrone,* the landlord, which he said in his dialect: *u padron.* He was speaking literally, and he said *u padron* with a tone perfectly mixed with resentment, awe, and desire.

He, my mother's father, Tomaso was his name, could have been one of Lady Gregory's writers, because he was the best storyteller I ever heard. He had an endless supply featuring surprising savage ironies, beautiful twists of revenge, twists of revenge are always beautiful, those stories were wonderful because people got what they had coming to them, the bastards. And the supply must have been endless because he told them every night and he never repeated himself except by special request. I never heard of any of them before or since. I believe he made them up, I hope he did, as we are there around the kitchen table, spurring him on just by showing him how happy we were because he was telling us stories. He could see we hung on his words and gestures. We were helping him to make them up, that's what we were doing, though nobody could have known that, much less said it. We were imagining together, that's what I believe. Of course, we could never have done what he did, and he was not born to listen to stories.

After supper, after the espresso, the anisette, and the Stella d'Oro cookies, and several of us there waiting for him to start, he would turn it on without warning. We would sometimes ask for repetitions, a story he told last month, and he would oblige, but on occasion he would balk (briefly) and display a flare of irritation (briefly), when my father or I (the main requesters) would ask for a certain story too soon, like four days later (at which point we became the main aggravations). He would look at us, say oh my Jesus Christ, then deliver it as if for the first time, as if for a vir-gin audience, as if he himself had heard it for the first time six minutes ago, he himself laughing hard in the funny moments. Later, my father and I would say some of the key lines and words to each other, going back upstairs, as if we never heard them before, doing some of his gestures, going to bed with his voice jumping in our heads. If I could tell you how good he was, I mean so that you knew the way we knew, you'd miss him even though you never experienced him in the flesh.

One night, we got out of hand, my father and I. We asked for the one we liked best too soon, we asked the night after he told it, and then we became worse than an aggravation. Tomaso said nothing. He just got up, walked over to the refrigerator, looked in for about twelve seconds (which in a situation like that you can imagine what it felt like), took nothing out, even though he must have needed something bad, shut the door, came back to the table, then told it ferociously. His fury made it new. When he was finished, he got up and went to bed. It was barely dusk. I wish that I could remember that one, I'd tell it to you right now. But maybe that's what you get for abusing the storyteller, you lose your memory of the story. He withdrew that night, and now the story is withdrawn forever.

His sons and sons-in-law referred to him openly as the King of Mary Street, without irony, with pride. His depressions were rare but deep, and if he happened to be suffering one when they addressed him as the King of Mary Street, he'd come back with, I am the King of Pig Street. Or he'd say the King of the Pricks, I am the Prick of Mary Street, I am the King of the Pigs. I wonder if Lady Gregory ever thought of herself as the Cunt of Coole Park? You can't tell about those aristocrats. Like artists and peasants like Tomaso, they're capable of anything. They tend not to give a damn what people think.

One of my father's brothers came up with the one he liked best. The King of the Mushrooms (always with the definite articles), not because of the quantities he could put away, but because of the huge Santa Claus sacks full he would bring home every weekend, every autumn—he knew where they were in the damp and shady secret places in the hills around Utica, to which he'd walk, then, twelve miles round-trip every weekend (one time I heard twenty-two miles), usually on a Sunday morning when Natalina, his wife, was at church. Even into his late sixties. At today's prices who knows the value. Maybe 300 pounds per autumn. Which my grandmother would put up, and her daughters and daughters-in-law would put up, a year's worth for the family, free.

On Thanksgiving he took everybody, about forty people, to an "American" restaurant, because if I want Italian food I'll stay home. But on most major holidays, we all ate at his table, two or three shifts, too many courses, the men falling asleep right there during coffee. I never saw one of the woman fall asleep.

I never saw him reading. The only thing he ever wrote were the bills, with curses against the Blessed Virgin Mary. Lady Gregory listened to Irish peasants, then wrote it all down (who knows what she changed) and made books out of illiterate genius. If he had had a Lady Gregory, then you'd know. He was a Lady Gregory and he needed a Lady Gregory, but he couldn't be his own Lady Gregory.

I liked the wide black belt he wore with the huge buckle, I have one just like it, and I like to remember the way his belly, emphasized by the belt, spilled over it. My belly's starting to do the same thing, but he never did what I do. He never held it in; he just let it spill over; he let it cascade. If you could have asked him why he didn't hold it in (the question was culturally inconceivable), he'd reply in one of his favorite idioms. The crude English equivalent is: "Because I don't give a fuck." The crude Italian says: "Because it doesn't fuck me."

Without fail, every third summer, the sons and the sons-in-law painted his house. And every other summer, it bore fruit, that audacious thing he cultivated, that cherry tree—he and the sons and the sons-in-law mounting the longest extension ladder he could buy. He made that thing go beyond itself, "in nature's spite" (Yeats's phrase for a work of art, what we rear "in nature's spite"). He definitely reared that tree. It was thirty-five feet high when it was supposed to be only eighteen, and however wide a thirty-five-foot cherry tree would have to be, that's how wide it was. That cherry tree got too big and too old, so he reared it more, he got up under its ass with two-by-fours, bracing the big limbs that couldn't take it anymore. Then he made those long black belts, gargantuan versions of the one he wore around his waist, he must have bred those tree belts, he must have pulled those tree belts right out of his own belt, and he stopped that tree from doing what it wanted to do, but it started to do it anyway, and the sap ran out of the gashes, so he poured stuff into the gashes that looked like actual concrete, which I think it was, and he stopped the gashes from getting worse, but later they got worse anyway.

And every other summer they climbed it, I was too young to be trusted on the extension ladder, with a great basket and a little hook attached to the great basket's handle, for the rungs, so you wouldn't have to hold the basket once you got up into it, and with a long stick, hooked at the end, it looked like a cane for a giant—I think he made it from an old cane of his, which he grafted an extension onto, which grew one-sixteenth of an inch every other summer—that cane was so the men could reach way out where no ladder could go, where only the goddamn robins could (and did) go, and where (naturally, damn the Virgin Mary) the best cherries were, but that cane at the end of a grown man's arm got out there all right and they pulled in those cherries in robins' spite, fuck those robins, because that's what Yeats was trying to put across, and they pulled in enough cherries for an army. And so they had to put them up, of course, Natalina, and the daughters, and the daughters-in-law.

It was family socialism, the men risking their necks, you could hardly see them up in there, up against that tree that sprawled way over into Louie Spina's yard, who was welcome to pick everything on his side, but he always asked before he did it, even though he knew the answer, and the women getting scalded in the kitchen, you think it didn't happen?, it happened, more than once, and risking their sanity doing that tedious repetitive shit they have to do on an assembly line, without the adventure of the tree, being up in there when the tree belts might go at any minute, the wisecracks going back and forth between the guys on the ground and the guy in the tree. I heard some odd talk in the kitchen, those women let go because I was too young to be harmful, and I saw sullenness in that kitchen, like a pure thing. Those women were anxious to tear into somebody. I think they had a critique of socialism.

He commanded loyalty and energy, I don't know how. Nobody was afraid of him because there wasn't any big inheritance awaiting the best ass-kisser. Some ass-kissing, naturally, went on, because one or two thought there was a pile stashed away, but those one or two kissed his ass in vain. His personality was on the sweet side, and he was known to cry. Maybe it was the fig tree. If you can believe a fig tree at that latitude, which you have to because I'm telling you it was there, but I can't go into all that he did to rear it, it would take too long, and I haven't even gotten to the other grandfather yet, you know, the one who was so cold you don't even know what I mean by cold. The grandfather who produced the son who produced me. The genealogy of ice, according to the leading soprano. ("He gets excited. He thinks he's the leading tenor, don't you, Frank?") Maybe it was the combination of the storytelling, the mushroom mountains he brought home, and the fig tree. Thomas the August. All I'll tell you is that if that cherry tree wanted to put out cherries the size of golf balls, then he gave that fig tree major hubris. There were maybe only seven figs per summer, but they pumped themselves up to the pear level, it's true. Maybe if your grandfather or your father or your father-in-law could do what he did for cherries and figs, you'd want to work for Tomaso, you might not be able to keep yourself from throwing in with him, no matter how irritated you might get sometimes, which you would definitely get because he couldn't or wouldn't drive, and you'd have to pull driving duty once a month, and drag your wife with you against her will, and your kids losing it in the backseat, once a month, on a Sunday, when maybe you were fed up with the extended family routine, who could blame you if you were fed up once a month?, but just on that day when you were completely fed up you'd have to pull driving duty, take him up to his camp on Oneida Lake, "to the beach," *u beach.*

He had two camps at Sylvan Beach, next to each other, and the big one, the size of a small hotel, burned to the ground and almost got the other one, too. They said "some bum" did it in the winter, but the crime was never solved, and he went into a depression almost as long as the one he went into after the near-lethal heart attack, a depression, according to my father, that lasted a year, he was mourning for his own death, but it turned out he outlived death by twenty-four years, no talking except for yes and no and an occasional because it doesn't fuck me. What I'm saying is that if this man is in your family, and I didn't screw up the tense just then, if this man is in your family, you want to be on his side, don't tell me you wouldn't. You wouldn't burn the camp. You wouldn't do something to the cherry tree in the middle of the night. No Italian would do a thing like that. Americans do that.

I know what you're thinking. You're thinking, he's making a story out of that grandfather of his and that cherry tree. (I cannot tell a lie.) You just don't know my concept of truth, my conception (that's better), and I don't think you ought to worry about it either, which I'm not saying you're doing. Those kinds of worries are not worth it. The distinction between truth and fiction, that one gets tougher and tougher for me to get. I'm going to stop trying to get it, because it doesn't fuck me.

The first place, 1303 Mary Street, technically doesn't qualify because the first four or five years of my life were spent a few doors east, up the block. East was always "up"; west was always "down," because it led to downtown Utica. I begin with the basic fact, that the first place wasn't the first place (Yeats wasn't born in Coole Park either); I add to that another fact, that the so-called first place dropped out until I reread Yeats two years ago, just before traveling to Ireland, as I was starting this book, which I didn't know I was starting; then I add an assertion, which I want you to believe, though you might not: that I wouldn't go back, even if I could (and I can) because I don't feel any return-pain (no nostalgia, *that* you don't believe), because what I want from the first place I draw on freely. No, better to say it draws on me, like sucking, even now, sitting here writing. Yeats taught me that the first place was about writing. (No, not "about," "about" should be revised out.) Small second-floor spaces, first on Mary Street in the late forties and through the fifties, now here in Hillsborough, North Carolina, and a relationship to something made possible by those spaces. I am here in the first place.

"A relationship to something": I'm not sure of the name. Not a relationship *to*, no, as if the "something" were a person or geographical point. The relationship *is* the something, and the place is itself the relationship. The place is me-in-the-place, so if I'm not there, then the place is no longer the place, and I am no longer me. If you lose the first place, which almost everybody does, it's not a tragedy. The story still might turn out well.

So I am going to be drawn by these lines in Yeats, drained almost dry:

> O may she live like some green laurel
> Rooted in one dear perpetual place.

Yeats, praying for his newborn daughter, and creating unnecessary pain for himself, and for me, by writing "perpetual." He should have forgotten "perpetual," he should have revised it out, because she's going to be rooted in a dear perpetual place that she'll lose, then, with luck (I have no idea how), she'll find a new perpetual place.

The "something" comes closer when I read this, concerning the pleasures of an ancestral house:

> The pacing to and fro on polished floors
> Amid great chambers and long galleries, lined
> With famous portraits of our ancestors; . . .

Tomaso had one in his dining room, a picture of his mother and father, which now hangs in mine, a portrait famous only in my family, and now among some few of my friends. Yeats was describing the house of a rich man. But it's not the things of the house, it's never the things, no matter how lovely the things, because there are always lovelier. It's the looking and the pacing to and fro. My floors are polished, and I pace the house between sentences, on my polished floors, looking for sentences, they're mine now, these polished floors. Yeats's poetic place, Tomaso's, where I am now, houses that look like they've been meditated upon, they have that kind of look, the look is there in the floors, and in the narrow stairs to the second floor, this is a house, this is, this is what truly is, and it looks like it has been looked at, this house of mine, with a yearning (Yeats gives me these words, they are his gift) with a yearning so great that the yearning drowns in its own excess:

> Beloved books that famous hands have bound;
> Old marble heads, old pictures everywhere;
> Great rooms where travelled men and children found
> Content or joy; . . .

He was there, at Coole Park, to write, that was his role, and to stroll magnificent grounds, and to approach the small lake at Coole, when the sun flares cruelly off the waters, and to gaze as if with lidless eyes into the glare as they climb the air, the swans mounting invisible through the sunflare, just for him, honored guest of gazng. My role—I was the fussed-over grandson (a redundancy)—mine was to study, not to work like the men and the women, and to be sustained at 1303 Mary Street, for the leisure of my intellect, for my long apprenticeship in pure gazing. I, too, was an honored guest ("He gets good marks, he's smart in school").

When I was there, Tomaso was my Lady Gregory, the house on Mary Street my Coole Park. I was Tomaso's apprentice writer. He was the masher, the writer who couldn't write, the talking writer. These lines from "Coole Park, 1929" suck me, too, deep into their vision:

> They came like swallows and like swallows went,
> And yet a woman's powerful character
> Could keep a swallow to its first intent;
> And half a dozen in formation there,
> That seemed to whirl upon a compass-point, . . .

Hard not to notice, it's a small poem, Yeats's saying "there" five times, a strategic incantation, bringing "there" here, making it thingy, and you stand in it, on it, take your stand there.

And because he, Tomaso, was "there," his powerful character holding us all in formation, I could stand there on the small second-floor back porch, a space five by five, the cherry tree at my right, at the twenty-foot level, at the level of the tips where only the robins and the giant cane could go, and the fig tree tucked in against the garage, at the back of the yard, the tomato plants next door on my left, looked at from above, and my grandfather's garden totally shaded by the cherry tree (he made it grow in sun's spite), and Louie Spina in his yard on my right, Louie invisible through the cherry tree, moving heavily about, who laid brick with arms like your thighs, thighs like your boy's waist, and me standing in the dusk after supper, I'd walk out there, drawn, belly full, no one moving now down there in the yards, legs becoming stone, it will take serious effort to leave (turn body, pick up feet), and the yard is quiet, leaning into the railing, automatic hands picking off the flaking paint (it's *next* summer the men must do that), the yard is calm, and the looker looks into quiet and calm more juicy than those huge cherries just hanging there, becomes part of another life, not his, he just drops into it, he goes in, sucked all the way into the juicy quiet and calm, full in his belly, twelve years old, just gazing there.

Okay, the other grandfather, my father's father. If I write down his first name, I'll secure a cheap irony, not to mention the melodrama of shocking coincidence. In melodrama, as in Italian opera, the writer makes deplorably excessive appeals to the emotions of the audience, he'll do anything, like tell you that the name of his father's father, the Patriarch of Ice, the Origin of Ice, is Augusto. Cheap.

It was said he baby-sat me in the early forties. Then, still in the early forties, he and my grandmother, Paolina, moved to Miami because the rich people, for whom he had strong left-wing contempt, like to go there in the winter, and they know the good places, and because he thought it would ease his arthritis, which it didn't. After they moved, I saw him a few times in the summer, when they came to visit, he always sending Paolina ahead, then coming himself two weeks later, and I saw him on two visits that I made to Florida. When he died in 1980, the last of the grandparents to go (I was forty then), his oldest daughter sent me a surprise, several volumes of poetry and notebooks, he had been writing all those years, teaching himself Dante, the poems all written in a consistently elegant hand, in large five-by-eight diary books, the volumes numbered, his picture the frontispiece of volume one, the entire set entitled *Le Memorie di Augusto Lentricchia*. Family pieces (picnics, birthdays, births, deaths, the day Paolina was breaking a box in the kitchen for firewood and the splinter by intention flew into her eye, destroying her sight in that eye); public events (strikes, Sacco and Vanzetti, Hoover, the death of Lenin, especially strikes, laborers in hell); poems to Paolina. From denunciatory satire, to domestic commemorations, to the romantic lyric, 1,200 pages of work, spanning the years between 1920 and his death.

His sons and daughters knew he was writing all those years, but they never thought it important to mention this to me, the professor of English, of whom they were very proud, don't get me wrong. Every year he'd mail a serious book: Michelangelo, Einstein, Thomas Paine, Walt Whitman. He was following my educational progress with pleasure, he said so in his letters. He wrote a poem about his grandson in graduate school at Duke University, but he never showed it to me. They said he was a champion baby-sitter, that's the phrase they used, they always said that. After his death, I quizzed his oldest daughter about it: "Because you would go to bed early, and you were a quiet kid, anyway. The grown-ups would go out and he'd take care of you so he wouldn't have to go out, so he could stay home and write, which he loved." I don't know why he took those thirty-hour train rides from Miami to Utica by himself. I'm guessing he wanted the private time for his writing. Not to mention the two weeks before, all by himself, which must have been wonderful.

He was a neat and a disciplined man. He ironed his own clothes, which always looked as if they'd been laundered and pressed only an hour ago. Calisthenics every morning. Mostly silent at the dinner table. His crew-cut silver hair looked like it was trimmed every five days, and no matter how hot and humid the day, he looked cool and contemplative. Perfect flat belly. When he spoke it was always like he was forcing the voice to come out; soft and cracked, broken up; the voice didn't want to speak; it wasn't used to it; the voice didn't want to go public. He was polite, even courtly in manner, especially with Paolina, but he wasn't interested in conversation. He was interested in reading and writing, and his kids weren't, and when he baby-sat me in the early forties we were a good team. The Patriarch of Ice and Baby Ice. Learning the ropes.

Of course, I've heard some stories, but I'll never tell them. First of all, I consider the sources: nonwriters. Second, I don't care. So what that he did a few things? Of course, my mother wasn't talking about a few things he did, she was talking about the tone of his presence, the quality of being, his and hers, when she had to be in the same room with the man. Am I supposed to believe that Pacino learned how to do *Godfather II* from him? Revenge is a meal best taken cold. Applies inside the family, too. She comes back to see the kids after the separation, you remember, Diane Keaton, who when she told him she was leaving him, when she was leaving him, remember?, he says "I'll change," with that dead look on his face. How come Al didn't say, Diane, you change, because I'm not changing. And so she's standing there, just outside the threshold of the house in Vegas, saying good-bye to the kids, when he comes into view from another room, tanned and terrific looking, Al never looked better, and with the best pitiless look I've ever seen on that face of his that you can't take your eyes off of, and the look is delightful. (I must contact a very good plastic surgeon.) And he says nothing. Diane says, Hello, Michael. Al says nothing. He just closes the door in her face like death. Al didn't change. Later, in *Godfather III,* we see what happens. Diane changed. You changed, Diane, do you feel better now? Let them change, because we're not.

I don't want to contradict my mother, not because she's my mother, and there's nobody I'd rather sit and listen to, but because I believe that her feelings had grounds. All I'm saying is that I don't care. And I'm saying that I consider the source: a nonwriter, by which I don't mean bad. I mean nonwriter. My theory, which I haven't told my mother yet, is that her smoking wasn't the thing. He was aggravated because he couldn't get back to the writing, or because he was blocked, or because he was writing well and wanted to get back to it, or because he worked on the kitchen table, he had no choice, and how was he supposed to write with that loud mob (the family) in the house? The louder the mob and the more he concentrated on that phrase in his head that he was going to write down tomorrow. That's just a theory of mine. Did he find intimacy on a daily basis too much work? The phrase he honed in his head, that was the thing, he liked that phrase.

Pacino and Paolina used to take walks every evening after supper, and they never invited anyone to go with them. What does that mean? I can believe that his family didn't have access, that they felt shut out, because he floated inside his own mind too much, because he wasn't one of those who constantly exude sympathy. You're there and he isn't, and you take it personally. They would think him cold. What else could they do? Assume that he was trying to be himself?

Every afternoon, Monday through Friday, she'd call him (I saw this in Florida) at 4:00 P.M., from the screened-in front porch where he sat with a book. So that they could watch a soap opera together. *The Edge of Night.* "Augu, *Edge'a Night.*" I'm not telling you they were lovers until the day she went into her final coma. He ignored something in her will, according to one of his sons. I have no idea about the nature of their relationship. Did he show her the poems, the ones about herself that she couldn't read? Did he read them to her? What if he didn't? What would that prove? The fact that a man who likes to write writes a tender poem to a woman doesn't necessarily mean what it is supposed to mean. Maybe it means that he enjoyed writing the poem, period.

Paolina was the shyest person I've ever known, but when she said, "Augu, *Edge'a Night,*" and he didn't hear because he was lost in that book of his on the screened-in-porch, she said it again in a surprising tone. He came with a very small grin. He sat down; no talking; they watched the television intensely; no discussion during the commercials. After the episode was concluded, there was talk about plot details, getting it straight, preparing for tomorrow's intensity.

It's possible that marriage and kids were a mistake. It's possible he knew that. It's possible he was, at times, seething underneath because he knew that he shouldn't have gotten married, et cetera, because he did some things that could have been a lot worse, and he knew they could have, but he held back and had waking visions of himself doing the unspeakable, going way over the edge, getting himself onto the front page of the newspaper. It's possible. I have no knowledge of his nightmares; I'm only imagining.

Now I shall write out my desire for a dead man. This is what I want. That he, Augusto, could have been his, Tomaso's, Yeats. That in the warm months a little writing table would be placed for him out there on the second-floor back porch. That he would sleep out there when he wished. That in cold weather he be permitted into the finished part of the cellar, where he'd find a full kitchen and be given a key to the special cellar within the cellar, under lock and key except to Tomaso, Natalina, and now Augusto, a key to the inner cellar, lined with what to my eyes and his look like bookcases, where he shall find space to place his few books and his manuscripts, in between the canned goods, the cherries and peaches and pears, the mushrooms and sausage and *caponata,* and the tomatoes and peppers and beets, and on the floor against the coolest wall, Tomaso's cool homemade wine, as cool as himself. And when he wanted something to sweeten the day, he would only have to speak his desire, and she would bring him one of her homemade cannoli, stuffed only upon the voicing of desire. A pallet would be fit into the inner cellar and he would sleep in there, but only in the cold months. Then one fine day at midmorning in midsummer he would look up from his writing table on the porch (this is what I most want for him) and know the quiet like the pen in his hand and legal pad beneath, part of the lines he writes when he likes the lines, part of what he most wants to be and, in that moment, is, sensing himself inside a relationship more primordial than what it holds in relation. Then he knows, and is, what Yeats said about Homer:

> . . . Homer had not sung
> Had he not found it certain beyond dreams
> That out of life's own self-delight had sprung
> The abounding glittering jet; . . .

Life's, not Augusto's, self-delight, I want him to be lost in that, life's self, which was the world of Tomaso, and then from Augusto would spring, as it had sprung from Homer, the abounding glittering jet, expression pouring forth, piling high upon itself, the lines he would most like, lines that were part of the quiet and the self-delight of which he himself was only part.

And let it be his death room, the second-floor back porch, let it be detached and boarded up, and let him be buried in it between the fig tree and the cherry tree, and upon the grave let there be placed a sprig of cherry, one fig, and, each day, one mushroom, one for every time he could press back, almost without knowing he was pressing back, almost without pain, his urges for marriage and fatherhood. Let it all be.

Augu, *Edge'a Night.*

Sandra M. Gilbert

. . . .

Mysteries of the Hyphen

Poetry, Pasta, and Identity Politics

> I think the notion of a hyphenated American is un-American. I
> believe there are only *Americans*. Polish-Americans, Italian-
> Americans or African-Americans are an emphasis that is not
> fertile.
> —Daniel Boorstin

> Our lives are Swiss—
> So still—so Cool—
> Till some odd afternoon
> The Alps neglect their Curtains
> And we look further on!
>
> Italy stands the other side!
> While like a guard between—
> The solemn Alps—
> The siren Alps
> Forever intervene!
> —Emily Dickinson

Last summer a friend and I spent a week cruising the waters of the
Mediterranean off southern Turkey—sailing in Byzantium, as a matter of
fact—with an Italian couple, a Turkish couple, and a Turkish crew of
three. We were (obviously) a lucky and elite little band: our boat, a traditional wooden *gulet* of the sort that has plied these seas for centuries, was

fitted out with spacious cabins, a cozy galley, and a shaded deck where we spent long, sybaritic mealtimes engaged in absorbing cross-cultural discussions of books, ideas, music, food, computers—the substance of contemporary lives. Our "seminars," we began to call them.

The other passengers were mostly mathematical economists (my traveling companion is a retired mathematics professor, and the Turkish economist who chartered our boat had been a student of his some years ago), fortified by a businessman (one of the Italians was CEO of a computer company based in Milan), but our conversations were so wide-ranging that I usually felt quite at ease, even though I was the only humanist on board.

I was at ease, that is, until strange tensions began to develop between me and the rather elegant Italian couple. I'd told them, of course, that I'm an "Italian-American." More precisely, I'd said, "My mother is Sicilian; she was born in Sicily and went to the States when she was seven. And my father's father was French—Niçois—but his parents were probably from Liguria, originally. From a town called La Mortola, near Ventimiglia, on the French border." My maiden name, I'd added, was Mortola.

I meant these disclosures as a gesture of warmth, one that might inspire bonding of some sort or at least trust. I had intended, indeed, a hands-across-the sea overture ("My people are your people") of a kind that one can only rarely make.

But the Italians responded with curious coolness. The handsome, forty-something Milanese CEO, who liked to regale us with information about the opera CDs he often played while we sipped our aperitifs, went blank when I not only waxed enthusiastic about some of the performances but ventured knowledgeable comments on them. His companion—a Roman woman who taught economics in Brussels and was also handsome, also forty-something—seemed equally oblivious to my remarks, although she talked with considerable animation about her own efforts to educate herself in music, especially opera.

I finally realized that there was something peculiar happening when we had an odd exchange about, of all things, *pasta*. Although the Turkish crew unfailingly produced extraordinary meals, Pietro and Lucia (not their real names) had shopped assiduously for Italian delicacies in the port from which we'd embarked, and I thought there was something winsome in their determination to instruct our cook in the ways of an Italian kitchen. One night, after much discussion, they oversaw the assembly of a splendid pasta—a sort of spaghetti primavera with lots of garlic and zucchini—that we had for a starter at dinner.

Of course I complimented all concerned profusely, congratulated the cook, praised the recipe, and so forth. But why was there a puzzling silence when I added that my mother makes a very similar pasta primavera, as did, I am told, my grandmother before her? Mooning over garlic, zucchini, basil, and freshly grated parmesan cheese as the *gulet* rocked in a glassy inlet known as Cleopatra Bay, I confessed I was nostalgic for the lively Italian odors and flavors of home—of, that is, my mother's shoebox of a kitchen in Jackson Heights, Queens, and my grandfather's not much bigger culinary kingdom not far away in Kew Gardens, along with the big, practically floor-through dining room–kitchen over which my Aunt Francesca used to preside many years ago in Brooklyn. Sipping wine and twirling spaghetti, I celebrated the flavorful familiarity of this dish on which Pietro, Lucia, and the Turkish cook had, I thought, so delightfully collaborated. But although Pietro and Lucia nodded and smiled politely, their smiles seemed forced, and they contrived to nod a bit censoriously, as if I had been, somehow, impertinent.

Impertinent familiarity! That, I realized later, had been the social solecism I had committed. I had professed familiarity with the ways of a culture that, from the perspective of "real" Italians, is not my own. My Italian is dreadful, practically nonexistent (my French-born father and my Sicilian-born mother could speak only English to each other, so that's the language we spoke at home when I was growing up), but I could grasp a few of the words I overheard Pietro and Lucia exchanging as we all lay on deck sunbathing the next morning. They spoke rapid, intimate Italian sentences that they assumed I'd never understand. No. I can't reproduce their words accurately, but I caught their meaning: She's just an American, what does *she* know about Italian cooking, about opera, about *being* Italian?

And truly, after all, the answer is *almost nothing*. The hard cosmopolitanism of Pietro and Lucia was clearly grounded in an unproblematic ethnic sureness to which they had been born. The culture of which and for which they spoke was fully, seamlessly, *theirs* in a way in which it can never be mine—a way in which, as a matter of fact, it had probably ceased even to be my mother's within a year of her landing, the youngest of nine in a family of Sicilian *socialisti*, on Ellis Island. Thus, whether they saw my eagerness to show familiarity with things Italian as a competitive striving toward sophistication or as a sentimental gesture of recuperation, the (really) Roman woman and the (really) Milanese man must have at best ascribed a kind of pathos to me. Rather than supplying me with an engaging internationalism, my insistence that I was an *Italian*-American meant not that I was more than an American but that I was less than an Italian.

"Less" than an Italian: perhaps the sense of lessening or dilution I associate with Italy—and more precisely the *lack* the Italian language signifies in my personal history—gives special poignancy to my experience of a cultural selfhood that is (yet is also somehow not) my own.

I am an Italian-American who doesn't speak Italian, just the way I'm a French-American whose French ranges from tremulous to nonexistent, as well as a Russian-American who barely recognizes the sound of Russian and has never seen a street in Russia. Because of all these complex combinations, moreover, I am an American-American who spent years denying *being* American, years inhabiting a country (or perhaps countries) of hyphenation—maybe even a hyphen-nation. In a confused and tentative fashion that Pietro and Lucia might never be able to understand, I eat hyphenated food, sleep and dream among hyphens, and in a sense am a walking, talking hyphen. But the Italian part of my hyphen-nation looms most grandly, tragically, glamorously, and persistently over the politics of my identity; and therefore it is to Italy as a country and a concept, as a lost land and a sometimes lost, sometimes found history, that I have turned again and again in poetry and more generally in that struggle toward self-discovery of which poetry is a crucial element for me.

Fifty percent of me, through my maternal lineage, is 100 percent Sicilian; and behind my French-born paternal grandfather, who represents another 25 percent of me, there is a heritage that is also, somewhere in the not so distant past, 100 percent Ligurian. So for many years my poetry has dwelt at various times on the mysteries of Italy as they appear to an outsider who is also, in a vexed and vexing sense, an insider.

Indeed, my poetry hasn't just dwelt on these mysteries; it's been both literally and figuratively fed by them. As a number of commentators have observed, we hyphenated Americans often "know" our ethnicity best by knowing our ancestral fare, and for me the stuff and staff of Italian life— for example, pasta—has long been a kind of poetry or anyway a staple of poetry—a sometimes delicious, sometimes poisonous food I cook obsessively on page after written page, now and then, like so many other women writers, even scribbling about its symbolic significance while the real thing bubbles in the oven. The moony roots of spaghetti writhing in a pot, baby zucchini sliced into green-gold coins on a butcher block, mystical minglings of basil and rosemary and garlic—all these are culinary talismans for me.

No wonder, then, that the skepticism of Pietro and Lucia—*How can*

she *be an Italian? What does* she *know about our culture (i.e., our* food?)—
sent me into spasms of alienation.

To be sure, culinary idealizations are not the only ways in which my hyphenated Italian-nation manifests itself to me, though before I went sailing in Byzantium with Pietro and Lucia, they were certainly the least
problematic. As I meditate on the ways in which my heritage has colored
both my poems and my thoughts, I begin to see that Italy has had at least
four, maybe five different kinds of meaning for me as a person and an
artist.

First, and most obviously, the distant provinces that shaped my parents' and grandparents' lives represent an ancestral geography infused (as
such places must be for everyone) with those family secrets in which the
mysteries of origin are perhaps hopelessly embedded. My mother's parents, the Sicilian grandparents who died before I was born, most dramatically incarnate such originatory mysteries for me; but even my father's
Niçois-Ligurian father, to whom I was close until he died when I was in
my thirties, sometimes seemed to me to radiate enigma, as if his own past
and his parents' past and his parents' parents' past seethed with riddle.

In an early poem of mine, titled "The Grandmother Dream," my
mother's mother manifested herself in a cryptic vision:

> My Sicilian grandmother, whom I've never met,
> My Sicilian grandmother, the midwife, who died
> forty years ago, appears in my bedroom.
> She's sitting on the edge of my bed,
> at her feet a shabby black bag,
> and she speaks a tangled river of Italian:
> her Sicilian words flow out like dark fish, slippery and cold.
> her words stare at me with blank eyes.
>
> I see that she's young, younger than I am.
> I see her black hair gleam like tar as
> she draws from her small black midwife's bag
> her midwife tools: heavy silver instruments
> polished like doorknobs, polished—misshapen, peculiar—
> like the knobs of an invisible door.

That this grandmother really was a midwife endowed her, not surprisingly, with a mystical mastery of origins, as if she herself were the keeper
of those invisible doors out of which the present and future emerge from
the past. But it interests me, looking now at this poem from some thirty

years ago in my own life, that back then I felt as alienated from her somehow "slippery" and coldly incomprehensible Sicilian words as, just last
summer, I felt from the chilly Italian with which I felt Pietro and Lucia
were barring me from their country and their culture.

As for my father's father, I knew him too well to meet him in dreams.
For many years, in fact, the kitchen of the big dark apartment in Kew Gardens, Queens, where he lived with his wife (my Russian grandmother)
and unmarried daughter (my favorite aunt) was part of my quotidian architecture. Yet although in reality this room, one of my favorite spots in
the world, was haunted by a curiously seductive aroma of garlic and cigars, it was also shadowed by my own speculations about a long and intricate history I knew I could never understand.

What *had* brought Grandpa to Queens? I was told that sometime in the
mid-nineteenth century his family had left the little town of La Mortola,
near Ventimiglia on the French-Italian border, to settle in Nice. There
they farmed a few acres of land in the hills high above the city, land on
which a canny cousin was to build an inordinately expensive condo-
minium a century later. I was also told that when Grandpa was a teenager,
he worked for a while as a bellboy at the Hotel Negresco: I have pictures
of him looking starched and vaguely embarrassed in a spiffy uniform.
After a while, though, he evidently moved to Paris, whence he embarked
for New York, rather inexplicably planning to study art.

My grandfather's decision to leave Paris in the early 1900s so that he
could study art in New York seems, I've always felt, a bit like Rick's decision to go to Casablanca, in the movie of that name, so that he could "take
the waters." In the succinctly sardonic phrase that Bogart delivers so well,
Grandpa "was misinformed."

Or anyway, even if he wasn't misinformed, he was entangled in a historical narrative sketched out by others, a narrative about which I myself could
never be truly informed. In a sort of elegy I wrote for him some ten years
ago, I had to admit that I didn't know, would never know, what the story
was. Yes, I could start by meditating on specifics—culinary details I myself
remembered, a few biographical facts I'd been able to grasp—but halfway
through the poem I sorrowfully admitted that I could only speculate.

> Garlic and cigars recall you, stuffed mushrooms,
> spinach ravioli, Genoa haunting your kitchen,
>
> and you with your dragging foot—
> bad circulation, maybe a stroke—

5'3", bald, gray forehead, gray mustache, failed
restaurateur, failed painter, thinning as you cooked,

thinning to the one you were in the bottle-green
Hotel Negresco uniform in Nice,

only now in Queens, pining for the old farm,
the hills above the sea. . . .

When they paced the cobbled wharf at Genoa
planning their moves five centuries ago,

what did they imagine? The men
must have been seamen: leaning landward like old walls,

they must have dreamed you as a wave
breaking on some far island. You must

have been their intention for the future. When the great
ship set sail, heeling and running free,

you lay in the hold, naked of uniforms,
painter of frescoes, master of promised spices,

rosy, perfect. What accident
of the mid-Atlantic

turned you into a scrap of cargo
lost by the civilization of the wind—

the calm sea, the prosperous voyage—
that left you and your dragging foot behind?

But if my grandparents on both sides were clothed in enigma, characters enacting dramas I could only dimly comprehend, all of them—along
with all my other Italian relatives—also seemed at times to stand for a history that was itself cloaked in shame, maybe even a site of some cryptic
original sin as ineradicable as its (and my own) Italian origins were mysterious. As Annette Wheeler Cafirelli may be the most recent commentator
to observe, many Italian-Americans were so deeply traumatized by the
very thought of Mussolini that our cultural pride went underground for
quite a while, and I must confess that I was no exception.

Growing up during World War II, I fantasized changing my name from Mortola to something more innocuous (Martell? Morton?), and when at twenty I married into a family whose Jewish surname (Gelbart) had been anglicized on Ellis Island to the WASP-ish Gilbert, I'm sorry to say I was curiously relieved. At that point (in the late fifties) I was no feminist, and as I was to write years later in a poem ("The Leeks") partly on this subject, I wanted "to be an American, / [wanted] a name that ends in a Protestant consonant / instead of a Catholic vowel."

Of course I must have intuited whole volumes of anti-Italian cultural snobbery, the kind that prompted one late-nineteenth-century writer to publish an article titled "What Shall We Do with the Dago?" in *Popular Science Monthly*. I wanted a name that *didn't* reek of garlic and cigars, didn't ooze olive oil, had never drunk red wine! I wanted a name that wouldn't shake hands with Mussolini! I wanted—to be perfectly frank—a name that never met a mafioso!

To this day, I haven't been able to sit through a single one of the *Godfather* movies, despite assurances from friends and (even Italian) relatives that most of these films are cinematic classics. Every time I'm forced to gaze at some Hollywood prince whose hair has been slicked back with shoe polish or obliged to hear an on-screen accordion wheezing a gangland tarantella, I spill diet soda, fling popcorn on the rug, and storm out of the room. "Mafioso," one of the earliest "real" poems I wrote—"real" because it represented a breakthrough into honesty and out of poesy—still speaks my mind on this matter.

> Frank Costello eating spaghetti in a cell at San Quentin,
> Lucky Luciano mixing up a mess of bullets and
> calling for parmesan cheese,
> Al Capone baking a sawed-off shotgun into a
> huge lasagna—
>   are you my uncles, my
> only uncles?
>
>   O Mafiosi,
> bad uncles of the barren
> cliffs of Sicily—was it only you
> that they transported in barrels
> like pure olive oil
> across the Atlantic?
>
>   Was it only you

who got out at Ellis Island with
black scarves on your heads and cheap cigars
and no English and a dozen children?

No carts were waiting, gallant with paint,
no little donkeys plumed like the dreams of peacocks.
Only the evil eyes of a thousand buildings
stared across at the echoing debarkation center,
making it seem so much smaller than a piazza,

only a half dozen Puritan millionaires stood on the wharf,
in the wind colder than the impossible snows of the Abruzzi,
ready with country clubs and dynamos

to grind the organs out of you.

But of course I hope it's clear that in this poem I really blame *American*-Americans, especially those who rule Hollywood, for the pernicious myth that we Italian-Americans are all somehow either mafiosi or nieces, nephews, and "godchildren" of mafiosi. I hope my visions of little donkeys plumed like the dreams of peacocks and of the impossible snows of the Abruzzi make that point. For even while the Italy of my imagination is a province of mystery and a site of shame, it is also a sort of lost Eden, the very opposite of a place of sin, as well as a foreign realm that is a center of otherness—a kind of anti-nation or place of alienation where I might find what Yeats would have called an "anti-self" and perhaps finally, therefore, a symbol of what is eternally desired by me but yet (or thus) perpetually incomprehensible, remote, deferred, inaccessible.

Of the nine children in my mother's Sicilian family, all were much older than she; none ever spoke very good English though all were brilliant, learned, and passionately political (or so I've always been assured); and seven were brothers, as in some monitory medieval tale, which is no doubt why my poems (for instance, "Mafiosi") are heavily populated by mysterious uncles. Understandably enough, however, it was to her one sister—my Aunt Francesca, who was ten years older—that my mother was long closest. With Francesca and Francesca's three children and Francesca's husband, Frank, a self-professedly "communist" architect, my mother and her mother lived for some years, mostly during the Depression, in a big old brownstone in Williamsburg, Brooklyn.

This house had the giant, almost floor-through kitchen–dining room I mentioned earlier, and it also had, in some secret part of the basement (whose layout I never understood), another, more magical and enigmatic "summer kitchen," to which all gastronomic operations were transferred in hot weather. And outside this (to my mind) practically mythic room, it had a concrete terrace roofed over by what I now realize must have been a grape arbor—or maybe it was wisteria—and a little garden where my passionately political uncle grew mysterious herbs and flowers whose names I didn't know, flowers so vividly colored that I wondered if he sneaked out at night and painted them, the way the gardeners paint the roses in *Alice in Wonderland*.

My uncle, who usually scowled and chain-smoked and pounded on the big dining table when the family argued about world affairs, neither scowled nor chain-smoked in the garden, nor did he pound on anything there.

At the center of that garden a tiny birdbath, looking rather like a parodic baptismal font, proffered lukewarm water to any and all citizens of the Brooklyn sky. And on the little concrete terrace I lounged in a sort of small-town-American porch swing, sometimes alone and sometimes with one or another of my cousins, all of whom were significantly older than I, so they seemed almost weary with their understanding of what it meant to be, to be—well—like *us*.

And on that swing I mused, I suppose, about Italian-American mysteries: the clots of wedding guests jostling each other's finery outside the Arion Ballroom across the street, the rush and tumult of Sicilian words I hardly understood ("Che beddu," some gnarled relative would exclaim, pinching my cheek with terrifying ferocity), the pounding, hooting, grinding passage of the noisily American Bushwick Avenue El just a block away.

It seems as though it must have been half a lifetime later, though perhaps it was only a quarter of a century later, that one of my three Williamsburg cousins dismantled the Brooklyn house following her father's death and transported both my aunt and the birdbath (but not the swing) to a suburb outside Boston, where—yet another half a lifetime later, it seems—we taped Aunt Francesca telling us the story of the golden *sala*.

When the nine children of the (according to family legend) quite devout midwife and her slightly more aristocratic but nevertheless socialist husband needed a roof over their heads, my aunt said, they moved into a ruined palazzo in the center of Sambuca, their town of (to me, mysterious) origin.

My mother has always told me that the town is outside Palermo, but when my husband and I went to look for it a little more than a decade ago, we couldn't seem to find it on our otherwise perfectly accurate map of Sicily.

Bearing witness to the real history of Sambuca, however, my aunt said that the midwife and her nine children, along with their rather Laputan father, more or less camped in an erstwhile ballroom of regal proportions, with flakingly gilded walls and no longer gleamingly polished floors.

But the ballroom, indeed the palazzo itself, had become, in anthropological terms, a kind of liminal zone, a place where nature and culture collide in willful clashes over destiny. Chickens high-stepped across the glowing balconies, donkeys brayed through the imperial foyers, and in my visions of the late baroque facade an assertively Sicilian sky pours a scorch of amnesiac blue over angels and gargoyles alike.

My aunt was fated to live to be ninety-nine, just missing that climactic age of one hundred when our American president would have sent her a congratulatory telegram, but she was a mere ninety-three when we recorded her quavering memories of the heat and light of Sicily and of the gold of the golden *sala,* about which I tried to write, with English words that felt oafishly inadequate, an Italian-American poem called "In the Golden *Sala.*"

Sun of Sicilian hillsides,
heat of poppies opening like fierce
boutonnieres of Apollo,
light of Agrigento, fretting the sea and the seaside cliffs—
light of the golden *sala,*
the great *sala* of the ruined *palazzo*
where my Sicilian grandmother and her nine children
camped outside Palermo.

Gold leaf, gold moldings,
shredding tapestries with gold threads.
"Once it belonged to a prince.
Mama kept chickens on the terrace
but they came in sometimes, and the donkey too."
Gold chairs, gilt around the windows,
angels with shining hair and empty eyes
staring from the ceiling.

"Mama made our beds in the corners:
the big room scared us, we thought
the prince's ghost was there."
Gold railings where her laundry hung,

gold curtains, new eggs under them.
Her cooking fire in a corner,
the center of the *sala* a cave of gold
for spankings and scoldings.

"Mama was a midwife, knew
everything about herbs and births.
The peasant women came from farms around Palermo
so she could help them."
On floors still streaked with gold
she made them spaces
in the dazzling spaces where the prince once walked.
Gold of forgotten dances, tattered rugs.

When a new baby slid out in a splash of water
he must have looked up, dazed,
toward the prince's Apollonian light,
and the black eyes of the midwife
and the black eyes of the midwife's nine blackhaired children
would have looked quizzically down
as if from a high cliff by the sea
hot and yellow with new poppies.

After I came back from the Italian vacation on which my husband and
I failed to find Sambuca, incidentally, and shamefacedly confessed to my
Aunt Francesca, still living then, that we hadn't even found the place on
the map, much less visited it, she told me that it was really much closer to
Agrigento than to Palermo. Which is to say, I never really understood
where it was at all, not to mention *what* it was.

And speaking of Sambuca, the town is really (now) called Sambuca
di Sicilia, but it was once known as Sambuca Zalat. Just the other day,
my friend Edvige Giunta—an increasingly influential critic of Italian-
American literary traditions who understands the pained curiosity with
which I try to investigate mysterious origins—forwarded to me a copy of
an article her Sicilian parents had sent her about the place after she told
them that she knew someone who was trying to learn about it.

Even the Xerox she mailed to me looks as though it came from faraway
and long ago. It's blackened at the edges the way "old-fashioned" Xeroxes
tend to be, and the paper feels thick and parchmenty, like paper that
ought to be guarded under glass, at a controlled temperature, in a rare
book collection. But I think it actually comes from a recent issue of a contemporary travel magazine, and it tells me that the name Sambuca Zabut

(or in some formulations Zabut Sambuca) means that the town is very old, that it was primordially inhabited by Greek settlers and Carthaginian traders but that "according to the folk tradition the modern place was later founded by the emir Al-Zabut—a follower of the ascetic Maghreb conqueror Ibn Mankud, who led the troops of Affriyquia as far as the Byzantine capital of the island, Syracuse," in the ninth century B.C.

I sent a copy of this Xerox to one of the Brooklyn cousins, a retired research biologist with whom I have in recent years shared a yearning e-mail correspondence about our mutual history, and he replied with surprising details.

> I did know it was called Sambuca Zabut. Whenever we spoke of the 400-year Arab occupation of Sicily, Mother used to stand up and proclaim in Stentorian tones "SAMBUCA ZABUT! That's Saracen!" And then she would roll her tiny dark brown Arabian-style eyes until the whites showed, in what I think was supposed to be her imitation of the Savage Turk (*turchi, saracenni*, they were all the same to her).
>
> She also spoke many times of the statue of the Santissima Maria del'Udienza in the Chiesa Carmine mentioned in the brochure, in a way which suggested the church might have been located close by to where they lived, leading me to believe that they might have resided near the famed Arab quarter, in a made-up apartment, one of several, on the second floor of an old and partially broken down version of one of those princely or baronial palazzi that are mentioned in the text you sent me. According to her description, there was a masonry coat of arms on the facade which also had a marvelous *fenestrone* on the second floor like the one that is pictured in the brochure, set over a regal arched and vaulted entry-way from the street into the central atrium big enough for a man on a horse or a horse and carriage to enter. It also had a very characteristic third floor ballroom, into which the roof had caved, however, and was unoccupied, thus leaving it open to the elements and the birds. At night, strange sounds would emanate from above and frighten her little brothers and sister, whom she had to comfort by gathering them around her, under her shawl, with a lantern.

What was it that Fitzgerald said? *So we beat on, boats against the current, borne back ceaselessly into the past?* Or perhaps not borne back, some of us, except in little fidgets and glitches of the tide, as in this further sentence from the material Edi Giunta sent me, which may (or may not) have been, as my cousin assumed, drawn from a travel brochure: "*About the meaning of the name Zabut there are many interpretations. Leonardo Sciascia ('Pirandello and Sicily') [associates] the name Sambuca in As-Sambugah with the meaning of 'remote place.'*"

Alane Salierno Mason

. . . .

Respect

It is a love and a rage.

The love you already know about, lurking in all the clichés of ethnicity: pungent, generic. Like garlic, it stays with you.

You already know: the smell of garlic frying. On a Sunday morning, Grandmother with fleshy arms in a housedress, swaying as the kitchen cabinets open and shut, the refrigerator opens and shuts: basil, big cans of tomatoes, the golden blocky pillar of a tin of olive oil, meat for the *braciole* to spread with Crisco and bread crumbs and spices, green-bean salad made on Saturday and chilled. A hard block of pale tart cheese to grate for the table. Grandfather wearing his best vest and ruby ring and cologne for the midday meal, having washed up for company after coming in from the garden with zucchini flowers to be basted in egg and bread crumbs and fried in olive oil. As each aunt and uncle, cousin and second cousin arrives, a kiss for everyone in the room. The great-uncle with the cigar, the favorite great-aunt with freckled arms hardy as a hazelnut. Relatives from the Bronx, New City, Patterson, Saddle River, Suffern, Croton-on-Hudson, all strung like beads from the landings on Ellis Island. Wine, mixed half-and-half with sweet soda for the children. The long table with the lace tablecloth, hours later strewn with orange and apple peels and the hulls of walnuts and roasted chestnuts, to be cleared away and thrown in the fireplace before black coffee and anisette are poured.

In the summer the fruit peels and the nut hulls might be thrown in the garden. "What comes of out the ground goes back into the ground" my grandfather always says as he throws the peelings from the kitchen between the tall stakes of the tomato plants. "Nothing wasted. You get out of the ground what you put into the ground" (referring to the seedlings that sometimes sprouted from discarded peach pits), "and what comes out of the ground goes back in. Dear granddaughter, I'm telling you something very important: you get out of life what you put into it."

When he came to America, he had delivered eggs and milk, worked in a laundry and candy factory, become an apprentice plasterer and ultimately a building contractor, constructing and renovating churches and schools. "You got to have a good foundation," he always told me, pointing out cracked pavement a year after new road work was done, peeling paint in places where no one had bothered to scrape the old coat. "You have to take pride in your work. The problem with this country, nobody anymore takes pride in his work."

And also, "It's very important to have respect for the old people. They know something about life you don't know. Dear granddaughter, listen to what I say: you have to have respect."

II

In this brownstone neighborhood in Brooklyn, there are many old ladies, as hardy to the eye as olive trees. One of these, Mrs. Gianquito, lived on the ground floor of the building I lived in when I moved here ten years ago. She used to cry when I saw her: "Sono sola, sola sola!" (I'm alone, alone, alone!) Sometimes I sat beside her in the building's tiny courtyard, separated from the street by a short iron fence, keeping her company while she talked to me in an Italian I couldn't understand. Perhaps it was mostly dialect; or perhaps because I spoke a few words, she granted me perfect comprehension and spoke very rapidly. In any case, of her torrent of words I understood only *sola* and this single saying: "Se si rispetta, si sera rispettata." "If you respect others, others will respect you." Or did it mean, more literally, "If you respect yourself, you will be respected"?

My grandfather was born in Naples in 1908, and Brooklyn was the first place he lived when he came to America in 1920. He met my grandmother when his eldest sister married a widower, also Italian, with four daughters born in America, one exactly his age. Later they lived in the Bronx, then in Italian East Harlem, and finally in upstate New York, where I was born. I moved to Brooklyn in 1987, a year after I graduated from college. My grandfather said, "I spent my life trying to get the family out of Brooklyn, and now you're going backwards, back where I started!" Now he says, "I'm going to shoot that Brooklyn Bridge!" because he imagines it transporting me away from the family.

In this neighborhood of four- and five-story buildings with gardens in the front and back, there are grapevines growing on the telephone wires. My neighbor yells to her kids, "Get in hee-yah!" On Saturdays in the supermarket, the old ladies' carts jam up against each other; they trade Italian gossip about their friends and advice about different brands. The men stand outside the bakery or in the doorways of their social clubs: The Society of Citizens of Pozzallo. The building with the ground-floor wineshop was owned by the proprietor's grandparents; his grandfather used to make wine in barrels in the backyard, he says, and when he hosed out the barrels the yard was stained purple. The grandson, in his thirties, has lived here all his life; when he decided to open the store, everyone he knew told him he could not succeed, but there has been an influx of Manhattanites into the neighborhood and the store thrives. He flirts with all the young women who go into Manhattan to work. Yet his store hasn't launched him into their world; he is still a fixture of the neighborhood. If he took the subway into Manhattan, he says, he would have to carry a gun, because of the *melanzane:* eggplants, or black people. (And perhaps the *finucchi:* fennel, or gays.)

At the neighborhood church my old landlady, Mrs. Amaroso, used to call the *cathedrale*, there is a Rosary Society, a Cabrini Club, and the Our Lady of Loreto Council Columbiettes; they sponsor card games and trips to Atlantic City and, a few times a year, accompany a statue of the Virgin Mary in promenade around the streets. On Good Friday the women wear black and carry candles in a funeral procession around a wax figure of the dead Christ in a glass casket. The casket is born aloft by burly dark-haired men wearing medals on long red ribbons around their necks.

It was the smell in the bakeries that drew me here, the strong smell of childhood, sharing my grandfather's expectation of an occasion, a holiday or Sunday company. The fresh-baked anisette biscuits and *regine* (sesame) and pignoli (pine nut) cookies, the cannoli and *sfogliatell'* and *pasticiott'*, the boxes tied with red-and-white string. These Brooklyn bakeries even carry Manhattan Coffee Soda, the sweet, carbonated espresso in a small glass bottle with an old-fashioned yellow label. There are also half a dozen places in the neighborhood where they make homemade mozzarella, the firm strings of cheese dripping moisture. My second cousin Roseangela, in the Bronx, has been making it in her father's deli since she was eleven. When I was a child and my grandfather brought this kind of mozzarella home, I would eat it right from the milky wet waxed paper it was wrapped in while my grandmother made us *mozzarell' in carozz'*, in a carriage, that is, between two pieces of bread, dipped in egg and bread crumbs, then baked in the oven.

My grandfather usually buys his pastries in New Jersey, but since I've lived here I like to bring him the real thing from Brooklyn, where they're better and cheaper. Each holiday now, I can expect a call with his "order" (*roccoco* and *mustacioli* for Christmas, *sfingi* and *zeppole* for St. Joseph's Day), which I bring to him in the big white boxes tied with red-and-white string. Sometimes I will remember to ask the bakery for additional small boxes, for my grandfather always buys enough to give away. This is very important, that no visitor should leave the house empty-handed. Between my grandparents' house and my mother's, I am always carrying cheese, vegetables, fruit, half a vat of soup, half a loaf of bread, half a cake, left-overs. An Italian American writer once told me that his mother made him take home half an onion. "Take it, you might need it, I'm not gonna use it," she'd said.

For four of my first five years in Brooklyn, I dated an Italian American lawyer living across the street, who made *biscotti* from his grandmother's recipe and on Sundays liked to make a marinara sauce and espresso with a shot of anisette. His landlady, sitting in a chair on the building stoop, would stop me as I went in to tell me how he did his own laundry and cooking and housecleaning, that he was *un ragazzo buono, oggi e difficile a trovare, un ragazzo buono,* a good boy, the kind difficult to find these days. I wanted my children to have Italian traditions, to know themselves as something other than just plain American. (There is no greater occasion—none so garlanded—as an Italian wedding.) But in the months I tried to bring myself to decide whether to marry him or not, I often lay awake at night, alone, violently trembling with an unnamed emotion.

When my old building was sold, I stayed in the neighborhood. On the old block there was a man in a wheelchair, whose friends always gathered on his stoop. When I told him I was moving a few blocks away, he said, "Eh, you're moving up. You'll find a different class of people over there."

Up in the country, when my grandfather moved house for the first time in forty years, he took with him a couple of wheelbarrows full of topsoil and several of his favorite rocks.

I too collect stones from many of the places I've been.

III

On Sundays, the stairwell of my building smells of garlic frying in oil, of marinara sauce or zucchini in bread crumbs. The landlady and landlord I have had, now, for the past five years are not, as far as I can tell, a different class of people from those a few blocks away. Angelo immigrated in the fifties and still does not speak English well; Angela was born in this building, where her ancient mother lived with her in the same three rooms on the ground floor till her death.

Like my grandfather, I have a sociable streak, and every few months I host an out-of-town guest or have friends over to my home to eat and talk. This is one of my great joys—or was, before Angelo started standing on the doorstep at the beginning of a dinner party, shouting "This is not a club!" and interrogating guests, male or female, about what they were doing here and how soon they were leaving.

Unlike my grandparents, who have been married for sixty-five years, I have been serially monogamous and remain unmarried. Shortly after I moved here, the Italian lawyer moved to California. When I started seeing someone else, Angela began standing at her front window, peeking through the curtains, whenever she heard more than one set of footsteps on the stairs. Now that I have had a man in my life more seriously (truly, the most seriously) for over a year, Angelo and Angela have become increasingly agitated. First, when Angelo saw him on the stairs, he raised the rent fifty dollars. Then Angela started calling on the telephone. "I wanna know what's goin' on up there—that guy, he's been there for a week!" That time he'd been visiting a day or two from the distant city where he is a university professor. "It's none of your business!" I said indignantly, thinking for a moment that I was in America. Angela shouted back, "None of my business! Every week I see a different guy. What'ya do, take every guy in the neighborhood into your bed?" That month I had had two other male visitors, both gay, who stayed in my living room one night each, and earlier that week I'd had a work-related dinner party and had asked my guests to tiptoe down the stairs when they left so as not to disturb the landlords. "The other night you had six people over," Angela added, "and I didn't hear any of them leave. Whaddya have them all sleepin' over?"

I went downstairs to sit at her kitchen table. "Angela, there must be some kind of misunderstanding; I'm not the person you say I am," I tried to tell her, but she insisted. "I have to worry about your reputation," she said. "Angela," I said, "let me worry about my own reputation. I have a very good reputation."

"People around here, they talk," she said. "They ask me, what'sa matter with that girl, she's got so many boyfriends? And I says to them, I donno, they're friends of hers. But I gotta look out for your reputation and the reputation of the house!"

I explained that I had friends in Washington, in California, in North Carolina. "When they come to visit, I shouldn't offer them a place to stay? I'm a hospitable person. I'm Italian!" I tried to tell her. She said, "You wanna have foreigners? Let them find a hotel. Listen to me, you do what I say, you'll be happier. They'll respect you for it. And don't worry, you'll get married eventually, because you're good-lookin'. I'm tellin' ya, listen to me, because I'm tellin' ya for your own good: don't go with a guy just because he likes you. Make sure he has a job!" I rolled my eyes. She said, "Don't you look at me that way. I'm tellin' ya the truth!" As I left, she said, "I'm tellin' ya for your own good! My father would've killed me if I so much as looked at a boy, and I tell ya I'm glad I was brought up that way, to respect myself."

Over the years I've tried giving my landlords plants, homemade panettone and gingerbread, a bottle of anisette, a pleading letter written in Italian. I stopped having parties. I've tried to tell them I want to be left alone to live in peace, in my own way, in my own home. I've tried to rationalize: maybe there's too much noise on the stairs? Maybe they come from the mountains of Sicily and are so suspicious of strangers that they can't stand to see anyone around they don't know? Perhaps because they see me in church, because they know I have Italian blood, they think I should live exactly as they do? "A relative, once in a blue moon, it's all right," Angela once said to me. "I don't have people over; why do you have to have people over?"

My friends say, get a lawyer to write your landlords a letter. They have no right to harass you. You're a good tenant, you're hardly ever there, you're always working; even when you're home, you're working; you're quiet; you pay your rent on time. But the law doesn't matter here, I know; it is the kitchen table that matters.

The next time my boyfriend was in town, the next time the phone rang from my landlords downstairs, I tried to be respectful. I took him to meet Angela. We both paid our respects at the kitchen table. She asked him what his intentions were. Satisfied, she delivered her verdict: "He looks like a nice guy, an intelligent guy. If you're goin' steady, and he's the only one, it's all right. But if I see any other guys around here, I'm gonna snitch on ya! I told her she'd find someone eventually, because she's good-lookin'." I rolled my eyes again. "She doesn't believe me, but I'm tellin' her the truth!"

Then he was away for a month, then here for three days in one week; Angela called up and said, "What's he livin' with you?"

I want to point out that I am a different class of people. I want her to understand that I am respectable, a professional, that I take pride in my work. Yet each time she calls, I shake with anger, then burst into tears. If I were a true American, wouldn't I be living someplace where no one cares what I do?

When my boyfriend and I went to pick up the dry cleaning, the lady who runs the laundromat asked me, "Who's he?" When I shyly said, "mio amico," she gave him a complete report: I was *una buona ragazza, educata, rispettosa, fa i fatti suoi, non riguarda nessuno* (a good girl, well-mannered, respectful, does her own thing, doesn't look at other guys). The next time I saw her, she advised me to find another man, younger, and see both of them for a while, then decide. She asked what my family thought, and I said only that my mother did not approve. I did not say that my grandparents did not know he existed, let alone that he sometimes stayed in my apartment. He is not Italian, not Catholic, divorced, sixteen years older, and has a beard. My mother says my grandfather will have a heart attack if I take him to meet them. Without my saying any of this, the laundromat woman said, "Non odi tua mama" (don't hate your mother); it's natural for a mother to be concerned about such things.

Then there is the man in the family-owned fruit market who flirts with me in front of his mother and brother, but when he asks me why I'm not married yet, such a *bella ragazza,* I know how to behave: flattered, embarrassed, not scornful but reserved, proper. Sometimes he tells me it's better not to get married; that's when I know he has had a fight with his wife. I don't know if he has yet spotted me with my boyfriend, or what he will say, but this is not the neighborhood to live in if you want a life protected from the eyes of strangers.

It strikes me that *rispettare,* to respect, has the same root as *aspettare,* to wait, to expect. To expect something must be to look *toward* its arrival; to respect, then, must be to look again, maybe to see the same thing from another point of view, through someone else's spectacles. When my grandfather says that this generation of today, these kids of today, have no respect, I think he is telling the truth. They are full of disregard— *riguardare* also means to look again—they look away, while the evil eye must see in one direction only. Looking at Angela, I think I begin to understand why, in tribal cultures and small villages, people needed protection against the evil eye.

The other day, Angela tried to raise the rent a second time in six months, and I refused. While she called me "you sonuvabitch, you *tramp,*" I slammed the door in her face. I had had enough. I too was raised to respect myself.

A week before Christmas in this neighborhood, they begin selling fish for the Christmas Eve feast—the *stocca,* the *baccala,* or salt cod, the eels, the *vongole,* or clams—from the back of a truck parked near the fruit market, in front of the bank. They also do this in the south of Italy. Some mornings in summertime, when I look out my window in slanting morning light over the low buildings and see Angelo watering his fig tree in his white sleeveless undershirt and long black shorts with black knee socks and hear someone shouting in Italian in the street, I don't know what country I'm in.

IV

You might say I have a bad case of third generation-itis. I did go to Italy to see the town my grandfather was born in. I saw the dry goods shop my great-grandmother used to run in the corner of their house, the church bell my grandfather used to ring in the dusty town with onions drying on the rooftops and horse-drawn carts returning from the fields. Somewhere near Naples my great-grandfather might be buried. The first of my ancestors to come to America, he was also the only one to set foot again on Italian soil. He did not sponsor his wife and children to follow him to this country. Eventually, they came anyway, sponsored by other, more distant relatives. "That's a mystery," my grandfather says. He tells of how, when he got off the boat in America, his father came to meet them, but he did not recognize him, did not know which man was his father. Shortly after that, his father got sick and went back to Italy to die. Or so he was told. He had been working in a leather factory in Newark, my grandfather told me.

In Naples, I stayed with the daughter of my grandfather's cousin, a grade-school English teacher. When I arrived, she had already read my mail. My Italian cousins could not understand why I was quiet; they thought I was melancholy, depressed. They did not understand the meaning of privacy or solitude. And when they shouted, I couldn't understand that they were just enjoying a conversation; I thought I had made them angry. They would not let me go anywhere alone. They wanted to introduce me: "This is our cousin from America. Her mother was divorced. Do you know that in America the fathers don't come home for lunch with their families? That's why there's so much divorce."

My cousin said she could understand why I wasn't married yet: I didn't have to live with my parents, I lived alone, I had my freedom. Her husband shouted: "Are you sorry you met me? Are you sorry you have those children? What's the most important thing, love or freedom? You want freedom over love? What is freedom compared to love! Love!"

We took a picture of a distant relative to take back to my grandfather; a stout old woman in black, she tried to pull a small boy to her, but he pulled away: he was afraid of having his picture go to America. The old woman cried, and my cousin said to me, "Is your grandfather also very emotional? Yes? You see, they are related."

My grandfather, I understand now, is an idealist of a sort. He has strong ideas about how things *should* be. He was not easy on his children and disapproved of each of their marriages (one too young, another from the wrong side of the tracks, another an artist whom he threatened to shoot), and even now, thirty and forty years later, they have not forgotten. It is a close family full of distances. Lately, when something happens that my grandfather does not understand—when the family does not all come together on a holiday, for instance, or we show up at his house at different times—he has taken to saying, "I must have been born in the wrong country" or simply, "I was born in the wrong place."

He is susceptible to rhetoric: family values, God and country, productivity, not tax and spend. He loves politics and ran for local office three times on his own "Productivity" ticket before finally winning over those whose partisans called him "uneducated" and "a foreigner." Since Hoover was president when he became an American, he became a Republican, to express his loyalty to his new country; but his Italian best friend, a former head gardener for a big estate, is a Democrat; he is a tall, bony man with a freckled forehead, always neatly dressed in jacket and checked shirt and wide, florid tie. They are both nearly ninety, and they like to argue about things on which they don't really disagree: "If we only made a dollar, we were glad to have that dollar, as long as we had a job!" "These kids don't have respect, and nobody tells them any different, not the parents, not the Church!" My grandmother, who doesn't talk much, doesn't participate in the debate; she says her Rosary and votes as my grandfather votes. Once he complained that my grandmother never wants to have a discussion. For sixty-five years of marriage he told her how to vote; now he wants to have a discussion?

Recently, my grandfather told me about his friend who was a friend of Caruso and how Caruso was given a title by Mussolini. I said I didn't think a title from Mussolini was anything to be proud of. My grandfather said, I know, he made that mistake, making friends with Hitler. I said, even without Hitler he was a fascist, he was a bad egg. My grandfather looked confused. Hadn't he told me from childhood that Mussolini made the trains run on time, just as Marconi invented the telegraph?

I always argue. Well, not always; sometimes I boil in silence or gently demur, depending on the subject. My grandmother told me once she loves to hear me talk, I talk so nice: grammatically and with a big vocabulary. Neither does my grandfather seem to mind that I disagree with him. With me, he doesn't consider it a sign of disrespect. He always told me he wanted me to grow up to be president, though when Ferraro ran for vice president, he thought it a bad risk—what if we ended up, God forbid, with a lady president? I reminded him of his plans for me, and he laughed. "That's different," he said, and when I asked why, he answered, "Because you're my granddaughter." When he complains about this generation of today, and I try to defend us, he says, "I don't mean you. I mean the others."

My grandfather points out that it is impractical for unmarried people to live apart from their families: "two phone bills, two electrical, two water bills, heat, groceries." I say, "Grandpa, we don't pay for water in the city." He says, "The landlord pays, but you pay in the rent. You're working for the landlord."

He says, "The problem with this country is no one has time for family. It used to be, everyone came together for Sunday dinner, and they spent the day eating and talking—hours went by, the whole day! Now they eat and run, an hour and then they're off to play golf; if they give you two hours, it's a miracle!" He says, "The problem with this country is career before family. You live to work, instead of work to live!"

He says, "I want to see the mothers home with the children, the way it should be, not the child comes home and the house is empty. A man should bring home the bacon, the wife, put it in the pan"—and laughs.

He says, "I want you to know, dear granddaughter, that family is the most important thing."

V

As for the rage close to grief, you may know that too: like parsley, curly or flat, bitter, individual.

My grandmother suffers from what she calls "nervous tension." Each Christmas, before preparing the Christmas Eve feast of eels and macaroni with fish sauce and lobster, she disintegrates into days of hiccuping burps and sobs, her eyes rubbed red under her glasses, sometimes not even wearing her wig to cover the baldness caused by menopause. Her sons argue and cajole, offer to have the dinner elsewhere, at a restaurant; my grandfather refuses, says they will stay home. "Right away he steams up, gets so excited," my grandmother says; at the last minute she recovers, and the dinner is cooked. Her children say that next year they will do it differently; each year it is the same, even when they bring over the main dishes ready cooked: still the bald head with wisps of white, the red-rimmed eyes, the burping, the wishing to die; my grandfather decorates the house with blue lights and flashing multicolored rosettes still in the box; I roast the nuts, set the table, make the salad, mix the parsley, garlic, and oil into the bread crumbs to stuff the mushrooms; the dinner goes on; at the end, the table is strewn with orange and tangerine peels, the hulls of walnuts and chestnuts.

I wonder, with all the modern tools at hand, is it something in my grandmother's childhood, something about Christmas in the convent school where she and her sisters were raised by nuns? Was it that she learned to cook from her mother-in-law and not from her mother, who died so young; is it the pressure of living up to the ways of an Old Country she herself never knew? Anger at the rigidity of expectations, the tyranny of ritual, the respect for authority, the insistence that certain truths not be uttered and certain feelings not be had? Either my grandmother herself does not know or if she knows, has never told anyone. Or if she told my grandfather, for instance, he then has never told. Or if her doctor, he has only prescribed antidepressants, which she calls her "depression pills."

The past is inscrutable, but not my grandmother's radiance when, inexplicably happy again, the holidays past, she giggles and her eyes shine. In such good spirits she will sometimes sing the songs she sang with the other girls as they worked in the garment district making wedding dresses, sewing thousands of tiny beads. She loves to sew and would have liked to keep working, she once told me, but my grandfather wouldn't let her once they could get by on his earnings alone. "It wouldn't look right," she said; he wanted to appear a man of means. He once told me he wanted to make Salierno a respected name in this country, as it had been in Italy. For the same reason he came home one day, to their apartment in a building full of relatives in Italian East Harlem, to tell my grandmother he had bought a house in the country. They were moving up and out, taking his mother with them.

In the country, within twenty minutes drive (but she won't drive now, which leaves her housebound) of each of her brothers and her parents, my mother suffers, terribly, from the depression that struck each of her parents, as well as a premature decline from Parkinson's disease. Though her husband comes home at night, she is alone, alone, alone, alone! Each time I see her, she cries, "I wish you could come more often. When are you coming again? I wish you didn't have to leave!" She says, "I don't want you to have to quit your job," which means, of course, that in some part of herself she has already imagined, already wished that I will. And is it not the proper role for the only daughter of an only daughter in an Italian family to care for her parents, for the old and the sick? What about my pride in my work? Isn't family the most important thing? What's more important, love or freedom?

If I don't visit for more than three weeks, my grandfather greets me, "Hello, stranger." My grandmother counts the weeks. My friends think I visit my family often; they don't understand that my living alone, visiting only thirty-six or forty-eight hours every two or three weeks, is one version of poverty, just as it is an American form of wealth. The demands of my family are not those of a modernity so fluid it carries effortlessly along even nostalgia for the smell of the marinara sauce bubbling on the stove, the "Kiss Me, I'm Italian," the San Gennaro Festival in Little Italy.

In my neighborhood church in Brooklyn, its walls lined with lurid statues of bleeding saints, two teenage girls gossip in the pew, playing with a beeper, whispering loudly over the pages of a young adult novel. Three times I tell them to be quiet. Each time they ignore me. I tell them, "You may not want to be here, but that doesn't mean you have to be disruptive for people who do." They roll their eyes. These kids of today, they have no respect! My blood boils. I get steamed up right away. I have, I know, my grandfather's cardiovascular system, the same relation between blood and heart.

And some mornings, I wake up with my stomach in knots, burping like my grandmother. I have my grandmother's gut, which twists up with the knowledge that I am not, somehow, what I am wanted to be.

VI

First the garlic, then the parsley, then the bread crumbs and oregano; the landlord's fig tree, the backyard stained with wine; grandfather without a father, grandmother without a mother; holiday dinner with red-rimmed eyes, best vest coffee soda mozzarella black coffee anisette zucchini flowers orange peels hulls of walnuts roasted chestnuts kids today without respect love rage love.

Gay Talese

. . . .

Origins of a Nonfiction Writer

Part I

I come from an island and a family that reinforced my identity as a marginal American, an outsider, an alien in my native nation. But while this may have impeded my assimilation into the mainstream, it did guide me through the wayward yet interesting path of life that is familiar to many searching people who become writers.

My origins are Italian. I am the son of a dour but debonair custom tailor from Calabria and an amiably enterprising Italian American mother who successfully operated our family dress business. I was educated by Irish Catholic nuns and priests in a poor parish school on the Protestant-controlled island of Ocean City, off the southern coastline of New Jersey, where I was born in 1932.

This breezy, sand-swept community had first been established as a religious retreat in 1879 by Methodist ministers wishing to secure the presence of God on the beach, to shade the summer from the corrupting exposure of the flesh, and to eliminate the temptations of alcohol and other evil spirits they saw swirling around them as freely as the mosquitoes from the nearby marshlands. While these sober ministers did not achieve all of their virtuous ambitions, they did instill on the island a sense of Victorian restraint and hypocrisy that exists to this day.

The sale of liquor remains forbidden. Most businesses are closed on the sabbath. The steeples of churches rise prominently in an unpolluted sky. In the center of town are white gingerbread houses with large porches, turrets, and finials that retain the look of late nineteenth-century America. In my youth a voluptuous young woman who strolled on the beach wearing a slim bikini would often prompt mild frowns from the town's proper matrons, if not from the middle-aged men concealing their interest behind dark sunglasses.

In this setting where sensuality and sin are always in delicate balance, I cultivated a rampant curiosity that coexisted with my nun-numbed sexuality. Often I went clam digging after supper with my boyhood friends, but at times I strayed alone toward the beachfront bulkheads behind which the island's most amorous teenaged couples necked every night; later, however, I conformed to the bedtime rules of my parochial school: I slept on my back, with my arms across my chest, and my hands resting on opposite shoulders—a presumably pious posture that made masturbation impossible. At dawn I served Mass as the acolyte to a whiskey-scented priest, and after school I worked as an errand boy in my family's dress shop that catered to decorous women of ample figures and means. These were the ministers' wives, the bankers' wives, the bridge players, the tale bearer. They were the white-gloved ladies who in summer avoided the beach and the boardwalk to spend considerable amounts of time and money along the main avenue in places like my parents' shop, where, amid the low humming of the fans and the attentive care of my mother in the dressing rooms, they would try on clothes while discussing their private lives and the happenings and misadventures of their friends and neighbors.

The shop was a kind of talk-show that flowed around the engaging manner and well-timed questions of my mother; and as a boy not much taller than the counters behind which I used to pause and eavesdrop, I learned much that would be useful to me years later when I began interviewing people for articles and books.

I learned to listen with patience and care, and never to interrupt even when people were having great difficulty in explaining themselves, for during such halting and imprecise moments (as the listening skills of my patient mother taught me) people often are very revealing—what they hesitate to talk about can tell much about them. Their pauses, their evasions, their sudden shifts in subject matter are likely indicators of what embarrasses them, or irritates them, or what they regard as too private or imprudent to be disclosed to another person at that particular time. However, I have also overheard many people discussing candidly with my mother what they had earlier avoided—a reaction that I think had less to do with her inquiring nature or sensitively posed questions than with their gradual acceptance of her as a trustworthy individual in whom they could confide. My mother's best customers were women less in need of new dresses than the need to communicate.

Most of them were born of privileged Philadelphia families of Anglo-Saxon or Germanic stock, and they were generally tall and large-sized in a way typified by Eleanor Roosevelt. Their suntanned, leathery, handsome faces were browned primarily as a result of their devotion to gardening, which they described to my mother as their favorite summertime hobby. They acknowledged not having gone to the beach in years, wearing during those years what I assume were bathing suits too modestly designed to prompt a lifeguard's second look.

My mother had been reared in a Brooklyn neighborhood populated primarily by Italian and Jewish immigrant families, and while she had acquired a certain worldliness and fashion-consciousness during the four premarital years she had worked as a buyer for the borough's largest department store, she had known very little about Protestant America until she married my father. He had left Italy to live briefly in Paris and Philadelphia before residing on the white-bread island of Ocean City, where he started a tailoring and dry cleaning business, and later, in partnership with my mother, the dress boutique. Although my father's reserved and exacting manner, and the daily care he attached to his appearance, gave him a semblance of compatibility with the town's most scrupulous leading men, it was my convivial mother who established our family's social ties to the island's establishment, doing so through the women she cultivated first as customers and eventually as friends and confidantes. She welcomed these women into her shop as if into her home, guiding them to the red leather chairs outside the dressing rooms while offering to send me out to the corner drugstore for sodas and iced tea. She did not permit telephone callers to interrupt her discussions, relying on my father or one of the employees to take messages; and while there were one or two women who abused her forbearance as a listener, droning on for hours and ultimately inducing her to hide in the stock room when she next saw them coming, most of what I heard and witnessed in the shop was much more interesting and educational than what I learned from the black-robed censors who taught me in parochial school.

Indeed, in the decades since I have left home, during which time I have retained a clear memory of my eavesdropping youth and the women's voices that gave it expression, it seems to me that many of the social and political questions that have been debated in America in the second half of the twentieth century—the role of religion in the bedroom, racial equality, women's rights, the advisability of films and publications featuring sex and violence—all were discussed in my mother's boutique as I grew up during the war and postwar years of the 1940s.

While I remember my father listening late at night to the war news on his shortwave radio in our apartment above the store (his two younger brothers were then in Mussolini's army opposing the Allied invasion of Italy), a more intimate sense of the conflict came to me from a weeping woman who visited our shop one afternoon with word of her son's death on an Italian battlefield, an announcement that drew my mother's deepest sympathy and compassion—while my troubled father remained behind the closed door of his tailoring room in the rear of the building. I recall other women complaining during these years of their daughters leaving school to "run off" with servicemen, or to do volunteer work in hospitals from which they frequently did not return home at night, and of middle-aged husbands who were seen bar-hopping in Atlantic City after attributing their absences from home to their supervisory jobs in Philadelphia defense plants.

The exigencies of the war, and the excuses it provided, were of course evident and available everywhere; but I think that large events influence small communities in ways that are uniquely illuminating with regard to the people involved, for the people *are* more involved in places where almost everybody knows everybody else (or think they do), where there are fewer walls behind which to hide, where sounds carry further, and where a less-hurried pace allows a longer look, a deeper perception, and, as personified by my mother, the leisure and luxury of listening.

From her I not only learned this first lesson that would be essential to my later work as a nonfiction writer pursuing the literature of reality, but I also gained from my store-centered upbringing an understanding of another generation, one that represented a variety in style, attitude, and background beyond what I could have encountered in my normal experiences in school or at home. In addition to my mother's customers and their husbands who occasionally accompanied them, the place was frequented by the female employees who helped my mother with the selling and bookkeeping during the busy summer months; the elderly semiretired tailors who worked with my father in the back room altering suits and dresses (and, not infrequently, trying to remove whisky stains from the clothes of the town's many furtive drinkers); the high school senior boys who drove the plant's delivery trucks; and the itinerant black men who operated the pressing machines. All the pressers were flat-footed and had been rejected for military service during World War II. One of these was a militant

Moslem who first made me aware of black anger in this period when even the United States Army was racially segregated. "Draft or no draft," I heard him say often, "they never gonna get *me* to fight in this white man's war!"

Another presser who then worked in the shop, a massive man with a shaved head and knife-scarred forearms, had a small, feisty wife who regularly entered the steaming back room to berate him loudly because of his all-night gambling habits and other indiscretions. I was reminded of her aggressiveness many years later, in 1962, while I was researching an article for *Esquire* on the ex-heavyweight champion Joe Louis, a man with whom I had cavorted through several New York nightclubs on the evening before our flight back to his home in Los Angeles. At the baggage claim area in Los Angeles, we were met by the fighter's wife (his third), and she promptly provoked a domestic quarrel that provided me with the opening scene of the magazine article.

After my colleague Tom Wolfe had read it, he publicly credited it with introducing him to a new form of nonfiction, one that brought the reader into close proximity to real people and places through the use of accurately reported dialogue, scene-setting, intimate personal details, including the use of interior monologue (my mother would inquire of her friends: *What were you* thinking *when you did such-and-such?* and I asked the same question of those I later wrote about) in addition to other techniques that had long been associated with fiction writers and playwrights. While Mr. Wolfe heralded my Joe Louis piece as emblematic of what he called "The New Journalism," I think his complimenting me was undeserved, for I had not written then, or since then, anything I consider to be stylistically "new," since my approach to research and storytelling had evolved out of my family's store, drawing its focus and inspiration primarily from the sights and sounds of the elderly people I saw interacting there every day like characters in a Victorian play—the white-gloved ladies sitting in the red leather chairs, indulging in midafternoon chats while gazing beyond the storefront awning out into the hot, sun-burnished business district in a time that seemed to be passing them by.

I think of them now as America's last generation of virgin brides. I see them as representing nonactive statistics in the Kinsey Report—women who did *not* partake in premarital sex, or extramarital sex, or even masturbation. I imagine that most of them have now departed from the planet, taking with them their old-fashioned values laced tight by bindings of restraint. At other times I feel something of their reincarnated vitality (together with the vigilance of my parochial school's nuns) in the spirit of

1990s neo-Victorianism—their hands in the writing of the Antioch College dating code, their voices in harmony with antiporn feminism, their presence hovering over our government like a governess.

But my memory of the white-gloved ladies remains benign, for they and the other people who patronized or worked in my parents' store (plus the curiosity transferred by my mother) sparked my early interest in small-town society, in the common concerns of ordinary people. Each of my books, in fact, draws inspiration in some way from the elements of my island and its inhabitants who are typical of the millions who interact familiarly each day in stores and coffee shops and along the promenades of small towns, suburban villages, and urban neighborhoods everywhere. And yet, unless such individuals become involved in crimes and horrible accidents, their existence is generally ignored by the media as well as by historians and biographers, who tend to concentrate on people who reveal themselves in some blatant or obvious way, or stand out from the crowd as leaders, or achievers, or are otherwise famous or infamous.

One result is that "normal" everyday life in America is portrayed primarily in "fiction"—in the works of novelists, playwrights, and short story writers such as John Cheever, Raymond Carver, Russell Banks, Tennessee Williams, Joyce Carol Oates, and others possessing the creative talent to elevate ordinary life to art, and to make memorable the commonplace experiences and concerns of men and women worthy of Arthur Miller's plea in behalf of his suffering salesman: "Attention must be paid."

And yet I have always believed, and have hoped to prove with my efforts, that attention might also be paid to "ordinary" people in *non*fiction, and that *without changing the names or falsifying the facts,* writers might produce what is called the "Literature of Reality." Different writers, of course, reflect differing definitions of reality. In my case, it reflects the perspective and sensibilities of a small-town American outsider whose exploratory view of the world is accompanied by the essence of the people and place I have left behind, the overlooked nonnewsworthy population that is everywhere, but rarely taken into account by journalists and other chroniclers of reality.

My first book, *New York—a Serendipiter's Journey,* published in 1961, presents the small-town character of New York neighborhoods and reveals the interesting lives of certain obscure individuals dwelling within the shadows of the towering city. My next book, *The Bridge,* published in 1963, focuses on the private lives and loves of steelworkers as they link a bridge to an island, altering the character of the land and its inhabitants.

My first best-seller, in 1969, entitled *The Kingdom and the Power,* describes the family backgrounds and interpersonal relationships of my former colleagues on the *New York Times,* where I worked from 1955 through 1965. This was my only full-time job, and I spent all my years there in the main newsroom on Forty-third Street off Broadway. This newsroom was my "store."

My next best-seller, *Honor Thy Father,* was written in reaction to my defensive father's embarrassment over the prevalence of Italian names in organized crime. I grew up hearing him claim that the American press exaggerated the power of the Mafia and the role of Italian gangsters within it. While my research would prove him wrong, the book that I completed in 1971 (having gained access to the Mafia through an Italian American member whose friendship and trust I cultivated) was less about gun battles than about the island-like insularity that characterizes the private lives of gangsters and their families.

In response to the sexual repression and hypocrisy that was evident in my formative years, I wrote, almost in dedication to the patrons of my mother's boutique, *Thy Neighbor's Wife.* Published in 1980, it traces the definition and redefinition of morality from my adolescence in the 1930s through the sexually liberating pre-AIDS era that continued into the 1980s—a half-century of social change that I described in the context of the ordinary lives led by typical men and women around the country.

The final chapter in that book refers to the research I did among nude sunbathers at a private beach located twenty mile downstream from my native island—a beach I visited without clothing and on which I would soon discover myself being observed by voyeurs standing with binoculars aboard the several anchored vessels they had sailed over from the Ocean City Yacht Club. In my earlier book about the *Times, The Kingdom and the Power,* I had referred to my onetime profession as voyeuristic. But here on this nudist beach, without press credentials or a stitch of clothing, my role was suddenly reversed. Now *I* was being observed, rather than doing the observing. And there is no doubt that my next and most personal book, *Unto the Sons,* published in 1991, progressed from that final scene in *Thy Neighbor's Wife.* It is the result of my willingness to expose in a book of nonfiction myself and my past influences, without changing the names of the people or the place that shaped my character. It is also a modest example of what is possible for nonfiction writers in these times of increased candor, or more liberal laws with regard to libel and the invasion of privacy, and of expanding opportunities to explore a wide variety of subjects even, as in my case, from the narrow confines of an island.

Part II

I left the island in the autumn of 1949 to attend the University of Alabama. I was then seventeen, acne-scarred, and socially insecure in ways I had not been when younger. The comfort I had found among my elders during my errand-boy days in my parents' shop, and the polite and highly personalized "store manners" that I had inherited from my mother and that had ingratiated me with the elite women who patronized her boutique in summertime, had provided me with no headstart advantages during the previous damp and deserted months of the off-season when I had attended high school. To most of the teenagers with whom I spent four scholastic years in a chilly brick building two blocks from the ocean, I was a classmate in name only.

I was variously looked upon as "aloof," "complicated," "vague," "smug," "quirky," "in another world"—or so I was described by a few former students years later at a class reunion I attended. They also recalled that during our school days I had somehow seemed to be "older" than the rest of them, an impression I attribute partly to my being the only student who came to class daily wearing a jacket and tie. But even if I appeared to be older, I did not feel senior to anyone and certainly never a leader in any of those areas by which we judged one another—athletically, socially, or academically.

In sports, I was too slightly built and insufficiently fast to make the football team; in basketball I was a bench-warming substitute guard; and in baseball I was a fair contact hitter and a shortstop with "good hands" but an erratic throwing arm, and I was inserted into the starting lineup by the coach hesitantly and irregularly. My main athletic contributions usually came *after* the games, when I returned home and used the store's typewriter to write about the contests for the town's weekly newspaper, and sometimes for the daily paper published in nearby Atlantic City. This was not an assignment I had initially sought. It had long been the obligation of one of the assistant coaches to phone in to the press the scores and accounts of those games that the editors deemed too unimportant to be covered by any of their own personnel. But one afternoon during my junior year, the assistant coach of our baseball team protested that he was too busy to perform this chore; and for some reason the head coach asked me to do it, possibly because at the time he saw me standing nearby in the locker room doing nothing, and because he also knew that I subscribed to sports magazines (which he frequently borrowed and never returned). On the mistaken assumption that relieving the athletic department of its press duties would gain me the gratitude of the coach and get me more playing time, I took the job and even embellished it by using my typing skills to compose my own accounts of the games rather than merely relaying the information to the newspapers by telephone. Sometimes this resulted in my receiving bylines on articles in which I was obliged to acknowledge my inadequacies as an athlete: "the game got out of hand in the eighth inning when, with the bases loaded, Talese' wild throw from shortstop bounced beyond the first-baseman's reach and rolled under the stands."

Although there were many young women in high school to whom I was attracted, I was too self-conscious, especially after my bout with acne, to ask any of them out on dates. And while I devoted hours every evening to my school books, what most engaged my interest in those books were ideas and observations that my teachers invariably considered inconsequential and never included in the questions they formed for quizzes and examinations. Except for my excellent marks in typing class, taught by a buxom, flaxen-braided opera buff who was a friend of my mother's— and who sent my spirits soaring one day when she compared my nimble-fingered hands to those of a young classic pianist that she admired—my grades were below average in almost every subject; and in the late spring of 1949, I graduated from high school in the lower third of my class.

Adding to my dismay later that summer was being rejected by each of the dozen colleges to which I had applied in and around my home state of New Jersey. After I had contacted our principal's secretary, seeking the names and addresses of additional colleges to which I might apply, the principal himself paid a rare and unexpected visit to my parents' shop. At the time I was up in my father's balcony office that overlooked the main room of the shop, seated at his desk reviewing the list of late-afternoon delivery stops I was about to make in connection with my summertime job as a driver of one of the dry cleaning trucks. I was not aware of the principal's presence until I heard his familiar stentorian voice greeting my mother, who was standing at a dress rack putting price tags on some of the new fall merchandise I had earlier unpacked.

While I watched anxiously, crouching behind one of the potted palms placed along the ledge of the balcony, I saw my father coming out from the tailoring room to shake hands with the principal before joining my mother in front of the counter while the principal cleared his throat loudly, as he always did in our assembly hall prior to making announcements. A lean and bespectacled man with curly gray hair, he was dressed as usual in a white round-collared shirt adorned with a polka dot bowtie, and hung from a gold watchchain strung across the vest of his three-piece beige suit was his diamond-studded Phi Beta Kappa key that I could see sparkling from a distance of thirty feet. My custom-tailored father, being his own best customer, was also nattily attired, but there was a lofty bearing about the principal that somehow diminished my father, or so it seemed to me, and it made me uncomfortable even though it had no apparent effect upon my father. He stood there calmly next to my mother with his arms crossed, leaning ever so lightly back against the counter waiting for the principal to speak.

"I'm really sorry to burden you both with this," he began, not sounding sorry at all, "for I know your son is a fine young man. But I'm afraid he is not college material. He persists in sending out applications, which I've always advised him against, and now I'm appealing to you to try to discourage him." He paused, as if expecting some objection. When my parents remained silent, he continued in a softer tone, even sympathetically: "Oh, I know you both want the best for your son. But you both work very hard for your money. And I would hate to see you waste it on his tuition. I really think it would be better for you, and for your son as well, if you would keep him here in your business, and perhaps prepare him to take it over one day, rather than to entertain any thoughts of his going on to college, and . . ."

As my parents continued to listen quietly, I stared down at the three of them, humiliated but not surprised by what I was hearing, and yet I was disappointed that my parents had said nothing on my behalf. It was not that I resented the idea of taking over their business. As their only son and the older of their two children, I sometimes thought of it as inevitable and perhaps my best prospect. But I was also eager to escape the familiarity of this island that in wintertime especially was so forlorn; and I had looked upon college as a way out, a destination toward which I had always saved my store earnings and to which my parents had also promised to provide whatever I lacked financially. Still, I was not sure how a college education would serve my career, since I was uncertain I would ever have a career— except, as the principal was cogently suggesting, within the boundaries of the shop.

In recent weeks, perhaps in reaction to my mounting rejection mail, my father had often repeated an offer he had first made months earlier about sending me to Paris to study tailoring on the classical level it was practiced by his Italian cousins on the Rue de la Paix. I might ultimately develop into a high-fashion designer of suits and dresses for women, my father explained, zestfully adding: "Ah, *there's* where the money is!" The renowned dress designer, Emanuel Ungaro, had once worked as a tailoring apprentice in the firm of my father's cousin, and I myself had not dismissed the idea of seeking such an apprenticeship during this uncertain summer after high school.

Another possible option for me existed in journalism. In addition to the sports reporting I did for the town weekly, I had volunteered during my junior year to do a nonathletic feature called "High School Highlights," a column devoted to student programs and activities in drama, art, music, community work, and such social events as the class dances and proms I had always avoided. The editor liked my idea and accepted it on the condition that I expect no higher payment than our already established sports rate, which was ten cents for every inch of my writing as measured within the newspaper's published pages. From the "Highlights" column and sportswriting combined, I soon was receiving weekly checks in the range of two to four dollars—a sum far below what was paid even to the lowest apprentice tailor in Paris, my father reminded me; but I was being rewarded in extra ways that were privately satisfying.

Although I continued to forgo asking young women to dances, I sometimes did go alone in my new role as a social columnist. For individuals who were as shy and curious as myself, journalism was an ideal preoccupation, a vehicle that transcended the limitations of reticence. It also provided excuses for inquiring into other people's lives, asking them leading questions and expecting reasonable answers; and it could as well be diverted into serving any number of hidden personal agendas.

For instance, when my pet mongrel ran away one day while I was at school during my senior year (despite my mother's insistent denials, I've always believed that she gave my dog away or had him "put away," because of my repeated failures at keeping him out of the store), I persuaded the editor to let me write a feature article about the local animal shelter, an idea inspired entirely out of my wishful thinking that I would find my dog there or at least confirm there my worst suspicions about my mother, whose graciousness toward customers did not extend to animals. After three prolonged visits to the shelter, however, where I discovered no evidence of my dog's life or death, I did learn for the first time about the "power of the press"—or rather about the many privileges and courtesies that could be accrued by self-interested people like myself while masquerading as an objective journalist. The town's leading animal rights advocates, including the philanthropists who helped to support the shelter financially, welcomed me cordially every time I arrived there to examine each howling and vibrating steel cage bearing newly arrived animals; and I was also given access (unattended) to the office filing cabinets that contained not only public documents and statistics about lost-and-found pets but also several unpaid parking tickets tagged to the dogcatcher's private car, along with a few fading mistakenly filed love letters received long ago by one of the shelter's deceased volunteer secretaries. In the files I found mortuary records pertaining to a pet cemetery that I never knew existed in the outskirts of Atlantic City; and when I mentioned this to the shelter's director, he insisted on driving me there—filling me with renewed hope and fear that I might at last discover the final destiny of my missing mongrel.

But after being introduced to the head groundskeeper of the sprawling, tree-shaded burial grounds jutted with stone statuary, crosses, and other monuments honoring the memory of some eight hundred pets—dogs, horse, cats, monkeys, guinea pigs, canaries, parrots, goats, mice—I was assured that no mongrel matching my description had recently been brought there. Yet my interest in the pet cemetery continued unabated, and with the groundskeeper's permission I subsequently returned several times alone, driving my dry cleaning truck after work to the site that was ten miles inland beyond the island's bridge. Remaining until twilight to stroll past the gravestones that often displayed the pets' pictures along with their names and their owner's words of affection, I was no longer searching for signs of my own dog but was responding instead to the vast sadness and sense of loss that now allied me to this place.

Here were mourners lamenting the death of their animals in human terms, decorating the gravesites with flowers, and, as the groundskeeper told me, often interring their pets in white lambskin caskets within concrete vaults, and placing silk handkerchiefs over their animal's faces while services were said, services accompanied at times by funeral processions, pallbearers, and requiem music. Many affluent and famous people whose pets had died while the owners were visiting or working in Atlantic City had chosen this place for the burial, and among those who did this were the financier J. P. Morgan, the songwriter Irving Berlin, and the film actress Paulette Goddard. Some of the buried animals had achieved distinction on their own: here were the remains of "Amaz the Wild," a celebrated show dog reputed to be the last of the great Russian wolfhounds raised by the Romanoff family; "Cootie," the revered mascot of Infantry Company 314 of World War I history; and "Rex," a dog which performed for years onstage in Atlantic City and throughout the nation.

The cemetery had been founded in the early 1900s by an animal-loving

couple who resided in the Atlantic City area and whose practice of providing their dead pets with funeral rites and gravestones in their backyard
had gained the approval of their pet-owning neighbors and then the desire
of these neighbors to share the space and the cost of its upkeep. After the
original couple's death, the cemetery was bought and enlarged upon by a
woman who was in her mid-seventies when the groundskeeper introduced me to her; and from her—after minimum of coaxing—I obtained
all the cooperation I needed to write what I hoped would be a lengthy and
poignant article about the cemetery. This story had the elements that appealed to me. I was connected to it personally. It had enduring human appeal. And it was centered in an obscure place that until now had eluded
the attention or interest of other writers and journalists. Since I had already satisfied my obligation to my editor regarding the island's animal
shelter—I had written a brief unsigned piece announcing the director's
latest fund-raising campaign—I was free to submit this more interesting
story in a place where I might attract more readers, namely the *Atlantic
City Press.* From a *Press* copyreader that I knew from my sports assignments, I obtained the name of the suburban editor to whom I should submit the article; and two weeks after I had mailed it to him, I received a
note of acceptance together with a check in a sum sufficiently awesome
to impress my father temporarily—twenty-five dollars.

The 2,000-word piece was run with my byline at the top of the suburban section under a double-decked four-column headline accompanied
by a large picture of the burial grounds taken by a staff photographer.
While I was then years away from the understated literary style I would
aspire to during my *Esquire* magazine-writing period, the cemetery piece
showed early signs of my continuing interest in providing readers with
precise details ("Mr. Hillelson gave his dog, Arno, a funeral with six pallbearers and a three-car procession through the streets") although it also
came with a bit of bathos that the cemetery owner had recounted to me
and that I could not resist ("as the old blind man's dog was lowered into
the ground, he rose and cried, "Oh God! first you take away my eyes, and
then my dog").

The response to the article was immediate. I received many compli-
mentary telephone calls and letters from readers as far away as Trenton
and Philadelphia, along with comments both from the suburban editor
and my island editor indicating that I might have a future in some aspect
of reporting or writing. Neither of these men had attended college,
which were facts I had elicited from them when it began to seem that
this would also be my fate. But it had not been "fate" in their cases, they

had emphasized; they had eschewed college by choice, as had many journalists of their generation, believing that it induced an effeteness in a tough profession then smitten by the flamboyant spirit of the "Front Page," of reporters who talked like big-city detectives, and who typed, if at all, with two fingers.

I do not know if I was finding consolation in this imagery as I sat eavesdropping in the balcony while my principal was characterizing me as ill-prepared for university life. All I recall, as I mentioned earlier, was a certain recurring shame about my lowly academic status and disappointment that my parents had not challenged the principal's assessment of me, leading me to wonder if perhaps they might even be secretly relieved; insofar as the store was concerned, the question of succession was now resolved.

After the principal had departed, and while my parents now began communicating quietly at the counter, I sank softly into my father's chair and listlessly glanced at my delivery route spread out on the desk. I remained there for several minutes, not knowing what to do next, not even knowing if my parents were aware that I was up there—until I suddenly heard my father's voice calling from the bottom of the staircase.

"Your principal is not very smart," he announced, removing an envelope from his breast pocket, and summoning me down to read it. And with a slight smile he added: "You're going to college."

The envelope contained a letter of admission from the University of Alabama. Unknown to me until it was later explained, my father had discussed my difficulties a month earlier with a fellow Rotarian for whom he made suits—an Alabama-born physician who had practiced medicine on the island since the mid-1920s. He was also our family doctor and, and lucky for me, an influential graduate of the University of Alabama. In addition to this, his sister-in-law was my typing teacher, whose limited but laudatory view of my talents represented the most impressive vote of confidence I could ever hope to get from the local faculty; and she, together with the doctor, apparently had written so positively and persuasively about me to the Alabama dean, contending that I had a growth potential beyond what was indicated by my school grades, that I was admitted into the university's freshman class.

Also in my favor perhaps was the desire of many southern colleges in those days to bring to their then lily-white and heavily home-bred campuses some out-of-state diversity that might include students with backgrounds that were Slovak, Greek, Italian, Jewish, Moslem, or anything but black. Long before the terms "affirmative action" and minority "quotas" came into use, such sentiments existed unofficially in places like Alabama with regard to the offspring of people that the Klan might define as marginally white; and I think I was a beneficiary of this slow-moving trend toward tolerance. When I read my father's letter, however, I realized that I did not know where Alabama *was;* and after locating it on a map, I felt some anxiety about attending a college so far away from home. But during the Labor Day weekend, as many of my fellow graduates from high school were preparing to leave the island for campuses within the state, or within neighboring New York and Pennsylvania, I was happy that I'd be far away from them. Where I was going no one would know me. No one would know who I was, who I had been. My high school records were as good as burned. I would have a fresh start, a second chance. As my parents and young sister escorted me on a balmy fall afternoon in early September of 1949 past the stone columns of the Philadelphia train station, where I would soon board one of the silver-paneled rail cars across which was painted a dark streamline-lettered sign reading *The Southerner,* I imagined that I was feeling what my father had been feeling twenty-five years before when he left Europe at seventeen for America. I was an immigrant starting a new life in a new land.

The train moved slowly and jerkily through the night down past the Shenandoah Valley of Virginia into the Carolinas and Tennessee and the northwestern tip of Georgia. The car was filled with attractive, friendly, and neatly dressed young men and women who chatted amiably and laughed often, and who traveled with their tweed jackets and camel's-hair coats folded carelessly up in the overhead racks next to suitcases plastered with stickers announcing: "Duke," "Sweet Briar," "Georgia Tech," "LSU," "Tulane"—and none, I was happy to note, "Alabama." I was still pursuing a singular route.

I did not linger in the club car, where a crap game was being conducted on the floor by several shouting men in their mid-twenties who were students on the GI Bill. I learned this from overhearing two black porters complaining to one another about the ruckus; since neither made any attempt to stop it, it continued through the eighteen hours I remained on board. I spent most of that time staring out the window at a blurred nocturnal landscape, trying to memorize some of the strange and faintly lit station names of the small towns we raced through; and, since I could not sleep, I read a few chapters from *The Young Lions* by one of my favorite authors, Irwin Shaw (I think my being seen on two occasions carrying novels by Irwin Shaw and John O'Hara into senior English had not endeared me to the Virginia Woolf–loving woman who taught the class), and on the train I also perused the Alabama registration catalogue that had arrived on the eve of my departure. I planned to major in journalism. Although I still was not convinced that this would become my career, I believed that taking journalism would challenge me the least in an academic sense. I wanted every chance to remain in school and protect my student-deferment status from the clutches of my draft board.

After the train had arrived at a town in central western Alabama called Tuscaloosa, where I was the single departing passenger, I handed the two cracked leather suitcases I had borrowed from my father down to a top-hatted black jitney driver who soon transported me into what could have been a movie set for *Gone with the Wind*. Stately antebellum buildings loomed wherever I looked from the jitney's windows, structures that were part of the older section of the University of Alabama. Some had been re-stored after the campus had been attacked and torched by Union soldiers during the Civil War. Now all of them were being put to use for classroom study or as social or residential centers for students, faculty, and alumni.

My dormitory was a half-mile beyond, built on lowlands near a swamp that had become an expanding locale of postwar building resulting from the student increase magnified by the GI Bill. My quarters were small, dank, and, as I would discover soon enough, penetrated regularly by wind-blown musky odors emanating from a papermill located outside the school grounds off the main highway. The dormitory was also invaded by the nightly return of ex-GI students from the beer halls that flourished be-yond the "dry" county that encompassed the campus—serenading revel-ers eager to begin playing cards and shooting dice with the vigor I had seen exhibited by those other veterans on the club car.

But far from being disturbed by the nightly commotion—though I con-tributed very little to it even as I began making friends during the suc-ceeding weeks—I became drawn to these older men more than to my contemporaries. In my comfortable role as an observer and listener, I liked watching the veterans playing blackjack and gin rummy, and hearing their war stories, their barracks language, their dirty jokes. Up half the night and rarely cracking a book, they rose daily to attend classes, or cut classes, with no apparent fear of ever failing a course—an attitude that left some of them open for surprises. Not all the survivors of the war sur-vived their first college year.

I of course did not follow their example, lacking the confidence at this point to be casual about anything; but being around these men loosened me up a bit, spared me from having to compare myself exclusively and perhaps unfavorably with my age group, and it seemed to have a favorable effect on my health and schoolwork. My acne had all but vanished within six months of my arrival, a cure I could attribute to the festive atmosphere of the dorm and maybe even the salubrious, if foul-smelling, fragrance that floated in from the papermill. I made passing grades in all of my freshman courses, and near the end of the term I had my first coffee date, then movie date, then first French kiss with a blonde sophomore from Birmingham. She was studying journalism, but would have a career in advertising.

As a journalism student I was usually ranked in the middle of the class, even during my junior and senior years when I was active on the college weekly and worked as the campus correspondent for the Scripps-Howard daily, the *Birmingham Post-Herald*. The tended to favor the reportorial style of the conservative though very reliable *Kansas City Star;* where some of them had previously worked as editors and staff writers. They had definite views of what constituted "news" and how news stories should be presented. The "five W's"—who, what, when, where, why—were questions they thought should be answered succinctly and impersonally in the opening paragraphs of an article. Since I sometimes resisted the formula and might try instead to communicate the news through the personal experience of the single person most affected by it—being doubtless influenced more by the fiction writers I preferred reading to the practitioners of "objective" nonfiction—I was never a faculty favorite.

It should not be inferred, however, that there was any unpleasantness between us or that I was a rebellious student. They were reflecting an era that predated the rise of television as the dominant force in spot-news reporting. I was reflecting my own peculiar background in my ambivalence about who and what was important. In reading through old newspapers and other antiquated periodicals in the school library and elsewhere, as I sometimes did in my leisure time, it seemed that most of the news printed on the front pages was historically and socially less revealing of the time than what was published in the classified and the display advertising spread through the middle and back pages. The advertising offered detailed sketches and photographs showing the then current fashion in clothing, the body styles of cars, where rental apartments were obtainable and at what cost, what jobs were available to the white-collar and the laboring classes; while the front pages were largely concerned with the words and deeds of many seemingly important people who were no longer important.

Throughout my college days that ended in 1953, and in the years following at the *Times,* I sought assignments that were unlikely candidates for page one. Even when I specialized in writing sports, whether it was at

Alabama or at the *Times,* the final results interested me less than who played the game; and if given the choice of writing about people who personified the Right Stuff or the Wrong Stuff, I'd invariably choose the latter. When I became the sports editor of my college newspaper in my junior year, I took full advantage of my position to describe the despair of the infielder whose errant throw lost the game; of the basketball benchwarmer who saw action only during scrimmages; and of many other ill-starred characters on the fringes of the playing field. One of the sports features I wrote for the college paper concerned a big, seven-foot student from the backwoods hill country who did not know how, and did not want to learn how, to play any games. I also wrote about an elderly black man, the grandson of slaves, who was the athletic department's chief locker room attendant; and how in this time and place where there was no interracial contact in sports, the all-white 'Bama football team began each game by stroking the black man's head for good luck. If I wrote more compassionately about losers than winners during my sportswriting days, it was because the losers' stories were to me more interesting, a view I retained long after leaving the Alabama campus. As a *Times* sportswriter I became enamored of a heavyweight fighter, Floyd Patterson, who was constantly being knocked down but who kept getting up. I wrote more than thirty different pieces about him in the daily paper and the *Times Sunday Magazine,* and finally did a long piece about him in *Esquire* entitled "The Loser."

This was done when I was engaged in what Tom Wolfe called the "New Journalism," but, as I hope is obvious, it is founded in old-fashioned legwork, hanging out with the story's subject day after day (just as I'd hung out in my parents' shop as a juvenile observer and listener)—the "Art of Hanging Out," I've sometimes called it—and it is an indispensable part of what motivates my work, together with that other element that I have maybe mentioned too much already, that gift from my mother: curiosity. My mother knew that there is a difference between curiosity and nosiness, and this distinction has always guided me with regard to the people I interviewed and how I presented them in print. I never wrote about anyone for whom I did not have at least a considerable measure of respect, and this respect is evident in the effort I take with my writing and the length I will go in trying to understand and express their viewpoints and the social and historical forces that contributed to their character—or lack of character.

Writing for me has always been difficult, and I would not invest the necessary time and effort on people merely to ridicule them; and I say this having written about gangsters, pornographers, and others who have earned society's disapproval and contempt. But there was in these people also a redeeming quality that I found interesting, a prevailing misconception that I wanted to correct, or a dark streak upon which I hoped to cast some light because I believed it would also illuminate a larger area in which a part of us all live. Norman Mailer and Truman Capote have achieved this in writing about murderers, and other writers—Thomas Keneally and John Hersey—show it to us out of the gas chambers of Nazi Germany and the fatal fumes over Hiroshima.

Nosiness represents mainly the interests of the mean-spirited, the one-night-stand temperament of tabloid journalists and even mainstream writers and biographers seizing every opportunity to belittle big names, to publicize a public figure's slip of the tongue, to scandalize every sexual dalliance even when it bears no relevance to that person's political or public service.

I have avoided writing about political figures, for so much about them is of temporary interest; they are dated people, victims of the recycling process of politics, doomed if they openly say what they truly think. My curiosity lures me, as I've said, toward private figures, unknown individuals to whom I usually represent their first experience in being interviewed. I could write about them today, or tomorrow, or next year and it will make no difference in the sense of their topicality. These people are dateless. They can live as long as the language used to describe them lives, *if* the language is blessed with lasting qualities.

My very first writing in the *Times,* in the winter of 1953 following my June graduation from Alabama, dealt with an obscure man who worked in the center of "the Crossroads of the World," Times Square. I was then a copyboy, a job I'd gotten after walking into the paper's personnel department one afternoon and impressing the director with my fast and accurate typing and my herringbone tailored suit (she later told me). Some months after I'd gotten the job, I was on my lunch hour, wandering awkwardly around the theater district when I began to concentrate on the five-foot-high electric light sign that rotated in glittering motion the world's latest headlines around the tall, three-sided building overlooking Forty-second Street. I was not really reading the headlines; I was wondering instead: *how does that sign work? how do the words get formed by those lights? who's behind all this?*

I entered the building and found a staircase. Walking up to the top, I discovered a large, high-ceilinged room, like an artist's loft, and there on a ladder was a man putting chunks of wooden blocks into what looked like a small church organ. Each of these blocks formed letters. With one hand he held a clipboard on which the latest headline bulletins were attached—the headlines changed constantly—and in the other hand he held blocks that he inserted into the organ that created lettering along the exterior wall's three-sided sign containing 15,000 twenty-watt bulbs.

I watched him for a while, and when he stopped I called to him, saying I was a copyboy from the *Times*, which was located a half-block away but which also owned this small building with the sign. The man greeted me, and, taking a coffee break, he came down the ladder and talked to me. He said his name was James Torpey, adding that he had been standing on that ladder setting headlines for the *Times* since 1928. His first headline was on the night of the presidential election, and it read: HOOVER DEFEATS SMITH! For twenty-five years this man Torpey had been on that ladder, and even with my limited experience in New York journalism I knew that *that* was some kind of a story. After writing some notes about Mr. Torpey on the folded paper I always kept in my pocket, I returned to the main office and typed a short memo about him and put it in the mail box of the city editor. I wasn't being paid to write, only to run errands and perform other menial tasks; but within a few days, I received word from the editor that he would welcome a few paragraphs from me on the high life of the light-bulb man—and this was published (without my byline) on the second day of November in 1953.

That article—and also my bylined piece in the *Times*'s Sunday travel section three months later about the popularity of the three-wheeled rolling chairs that people rode on the Atlantic City boardwalk—brought me to the attention of the editors. Other pieces followed, including a Sunday magazine article that the *Times* published in 1955 while I was on leave with the army. The piece was about a woman old enough to be one of my mother's most venerable customers—a silent screen actress named Nita Naldi, who had once been Valentino's leading lady in Hollywood. But in 1954, decades after Nita Naldi's exit from the film business, it was announced that a new musical called *The Vamp*, inspired by the actress's life and starring Carol Channing, would soon be coming to Broadway.

I had read this item in a tabloid's theater column one morning while riding the subway to work, months before leaving for the army. The column mentioned that Nita Naldi was then living as a recluse in a small Broadway hotel, but the hotel was not named. New York then had close to 300 small hotels in the Broadway area. I spent hours looking in the yellow pages in the *Times* newsroom when I was not otherwise occupied; then I jotted down the hotel numbers and later began placing calls from one of the rear phones that copyboys could use without being in visual range of the city editor's desk clerks, who liked to assert their authority over copyboys.

I phoned about eighty hotels over a four-day period, asking each time to be connected to Miss Naldi's suite, speaking always in a confident tone that I hoped might convey the impression that I *knew* she was staying there. But none of the hotel people had ever heard of her. Then I called the Wentworth Hotel, and, to my amazement, I heard the gruff voice of a man say, "Yeah, she's here—who wants her?" I hung up. I hurried over to the Wentworth Hotel in person.

The telephone, to me, is second only to the tape recorder in undermining the art of interviewing. In my older years, especially while doing publicity tours for one of my books, I myself have been interviewed by young reporters carrying tape recorders; and as I sit answering their questions I see them half listening, relaxing in the knowledge that the little plastic wheels are rolling. But what they are getting from me (and I assume from other people they talk to) is not the insight that comes from deep probing and perceptive analysis and much legwork; it is rather the first-draft drift of my mind, a once-over-lightly dialogue that too frequently reduces the exchanges to the level of talk radio on paper. Instead of decrying this trend, most editors tacitly approve of it, because a taped interview that is faithfully transcribed can protect the periodical from those interviewees who might later claim that they had been damagingly misquoted—accusations that, in these times of impulsive litigation and soaring legal fees, cause much anxiety and sometimes timidity, among even the most independent and courageous of editors. Another reason editors are accepting of the tape recorder is that it enables them to obtain publishable articles from the influx of facile free-lancers at pay rates below what would be expected and deserved by writers of more deliberation and commitment. With one or two interviews and a few hours of tape, a relatively inexperienced journalist today can produce a 3,000-word article that relies heavily on direct quotation and (depending largely on the promotional value of the subject at the newsstand) will gain a writer's fee of anywhere from approximately $500 to slightly more than $2,000—which is fair payment, considering the time and skill involved, but it is less than what was being paid for articles of similar length and topicality when I began writing for some of these same national magazines, such as the *Times Sunday Magazine* and *Esquire,* back in the 1950s and 1960s.

The telephone is another inadequate instrument for interviewing, because, among other things, it denies you from learning a great deal from observing a person's face and manner, to say nothing of the surrounding ambiance. I also believe people will reveal more of themselves to you if you are physically present; and the more sincere you are in your interest, the better will be your chances of obtaining that person's cooperation.

The house phone of the Hotel Wentworth, which I knew I had to use in announcing myself to Nati Naldi, did not present the same obstacle that a regular phone might have: I would, after all, be calling within her own building, *I was already there,* an undeniable presence!

"Hello, Miss Naldi," I began, having asked the operator to be directly connected without my having first announced myself to one of the hotel's desk clerks, a courtesy that—suspecting their mercenary nature—might have boomeranged to my disadvantage. "I'm a young man from the *Times,* and I'm downstairs in your hotel lobby, and I'd like to meet you for a few minutes, and talk about doing an article for the *Sunday Magazine.*"

"You're *downstairs?*" she asked, in a dramatic voice of mild alarm. "How did you know where I lived?"

"I just called all the Broadway hotels I could."

"You must have spent a lot of money, young man," she said, in a calmer voice. "Anyway, I don't have much time."

"May I just come up to introduce myself, Miss Naldi?"

After a pause, she said: "Well, give me five minutes, then come up. Room 513. Oh, the place is a perfect mess!"

I went up to the fifth floor, and will never forget the place. She occupied a small suite with four parrots, and the suite was decorated like a turn-of-the-century movie set. And she was dressed in a style that would have no doubt appealed to Rudolph Valentino himself and perhaps *only* to him. She had dark arched eyebrows and long earrings and a black gown, and jet black hair which I'm sure she dyed daily. Her gestures were very exaggerated, as in the silent screen era they had to be; and she was very amusing. I took notes, went back to my apartment after finishing work that day, and I wrote the story, which probably took three or four days or even longer to complete. I turned it in to the Sunday editor who handled show business subjects and asked if he would be kind enough to read it.

A week later, he called to say he would like to use the article. His response marked one of the happiest days of my young life. The magazine would definitely publish it, he repeated, adding he did not know exactly when. It lay in type for a few months. But finally it did appear, on October 16, 1955, while I was serving in the tank corps in Fort Knox, Kentucky. My parents sent me a telegram. I called them back from a telephone booth, collect, and my mother read the published article to me over the phone. It began:

In order that Carol Channing be flawlessly vampish, beguiling and pleasingly unwholesome as the star of the musical on the silent movie era which comes to Broadway Nov. 10 and is called, not unexpectedly, "The Vamp," she has had as a kind of adviser, aide de camp, critic and coach, that exotic former siren named Nita Naldi. When it comes to vamping roles, no one is a more qualified instructor than Miss Naldi. In her heyday, in the Twenties, Nita Naldi was the symbol of everything passionate and evil on the silent screen. . . .

And it ended:

. . . still very dark and buxom, Miss Naldi is recognized surprisingly often as she travels about. "Women don't seem to hate me anymore," she says with satisfaction. She is often stopped in the street and asked, "What was it really like kissing Valentino?" Young people will remark, "Oh, Miss Naldi, my father has told me so-o-o much about you!" to which the actress manages to respond graciously. Not too long ago a man approached her on the corner of Forty-sixth Street and Broadway and exclaimed in wonder, "You're Nita Naldi, the Vampire!" It was as if he had turned the clock back, restoring Miss Naldi to the world she had inhabited thirty years ago. Eager to live in the present, the actress replied in a tone that mixed resentment and resignation, "Yes, do you mind?"

My mother ordered several dozen copies of the magazine and mailed them out to all the customers who had known me as a boy in the store, and she included in her package my address at the base. In the fan mail I later received from them was also a letter from the city editor of the *Times* informing me that, after I was discharged and had returned to the paper, I would no longer be employed as a copyboy. I was being promoted to the writing staff and assigned to the Sports Department.

In a postscript, he added: "You're on your way."

Maria Laurino

. . . .

Scents

A Selection from a Memoir of Italian American Life

Junior High School. After all these years, those three simple words can still make me wince. The low brick building I occasionally glimpse today from the tinted panes of a commuter train signifies that particular place and time in which sameness is the prize, and a seed of adolescent difference could sprout into a field of skunk cabbage. My most vivid memories of junior high were the physical humiliations that turned even the sturdiest girls into sorry mush: how a slip of the tongue unhooked a tiny elastic band attached to a silver retainer and sent it flying across the room, or how acne cream slathered on bad skin sat in the middle of one's forehead like a platter of hummus left in the sun. For someone like me, whose confidence was sketched in pencil and easily erased, the worst moments took place standing in line before gym class. There our bodies were on display, corporeal objects that symbolized who we were, light or dark, hairy or bare-skinned. Our uniforms were baby blue, the color of surgeons' gowns and prison uniforms, and I felt both sick and trapped during those forced fifty minutes of exercise.

Occasionally I tried to make conversation, but generally I learned the advantages of silence. Once an attractive blonde girl who, unlike most of us, had developed curves that captured the attention of a league of boys, mentioned how she needed to shave her legs. Her passing comment, said with a bored nonchalance, caused me to panic. While the hair on my legs looked like a bed of wilted grass dipped in black ink, the blonde girl's legs were as smooth and silky as a newly varnished oak floor. I couldn't imagine why she'd put a razor to her skin.

97

"Yeah, I need to shave too," I naively replied. To share the truth—that my mother thought I was too young to have a woman's legs—would have been mortifying, but I also lacked the instinct to distract her with a line like "You know, Cybill Shephard couldn't hold a candle to your thighs" and quickly change the topic. The look of horror on that girl's face when she peered down at my calves is as clear to me today as it was back then in 1973. I'm sure she had never encountered the hirsute beauty of the Italian American body.

Soon I began to intuit an important fact: In gym class, as in life, one's innermost fears are exposed inch by inch, no matter how hard the attempt is made to hide or avoid them. In fact, those fears will suck your confidence like an aphid on a dewy green leaf if not addressed head-on. During another class, the girl standing behind me in our alphabetical line began a conversation as we strutted in sync, bare legs and bodies covered in powder blue, to the gymnasium.

"You were shopping at Saks the other day?" she asked, knowing the answer.

"Uh-huh," I said. (She had never spoken to me before; in retrospect I think the visit to Saks provided a necessary credential.)

"Yeah, I told my mother, 'That's the smelly Italian girl who stands in front of me in gym class.'"

I was stunned. I never thought of myself as smelly, nor did I move quickly enough in class even to perspire. But instead of challenging her rude remark, I just stood there. Silently. She continued to chatter while I, in my acquiescence, experienced a deep shame of my body. It seemed impossible to escape the sweat of my ancestors, peasants from southern Italy. Even the name of region, the *mezzogiorno*, or midday, summons the oppressive afternoon heat that parches the skin and then showers it with drops of sweat, the sun's perverse joke on the body's prayer for water.

Yet despite my deep embarrassment, part of me—the part that understood the significance of a junior high social hierarchy—was flattered: this pretty, popular girl was talking to me. Sloe-eyed, with chocolate brown hair, she was Jewish; and unlike the WASPy girls whom I could never be like, I saw myself as a darker, rawer version of her. We were both average height, but she was thin, shaved her legs, plucked her eyebrows, and dyed unwanted lip hairs blonde with a jar of Jolene. I, on the other hand, was chubby, had the leg hairs of a grizzly, a light mustache, and a bristly black feather of an eyebrow that rested proudly at the bottom of my forehead.

Comparing our basic similarities, I saw the potential for my own reform.

So I decided that if she continued to befriend me, I would ignore the nasty comment. In the following weeks, during the strange course of junior high relationships, I tried to ingratiate myself into her world, and she began to accept me. But always, she'd tell classmates about the incident that sparked our first conversation. "I saw her shopping in Saks," she would say with a high-pitched giggle, "and I told my mother, 'that's the smelly Italian girl who stands in front of me in gym class.'"

Soon sympathetic friends pulled me aside to say that I never smelled and she must have confused me with someone else. I burned with embarrassment but politely nodded as they defended me. Looking back on those days, I probably believed them. I did not begin to shower three times a day to assiduously escape my odors. Instead, I continued the same bath regimen (although I can't say precisely if it was every day or every other) and sprayed myself with a fragrance called Love's Fresh Lemon, marketed for teens with a popular Donovan song about wearing your love like heaven. Did I smell like hell and rotten lemons? Probably not. I accepted the definition of being smelly rather than believing that I smelled. That is, if someone thought I had a body odor, there must be something unpleasant about me that needed to be changed.

I remained silent in response to her accusation, lacking the self-confidence to speak. Perhaps, most of all, her exact words made me mute. She never talked about that smelly girl, or that smelly girl who is Italian, but rather that "smelly Italian girl." The structure of that phrase, compared to its other possibilities, implied that being Italian was essential to her particular definition of what it meant to be "smelly"; in other words, I was smelly *because* I was Italian.

Gym class wasn't the only time I heard the words *Italian* and *smelly* placed together, like a pungent clove of garlic sweating in a pan of warm olive oil. Sometime later, I was sitting in the cafeteria with my new gym pal and a friend of hers, sharing gossip and news between bites of our sandwiches. The other girl mentioned that her father was planning a trip to Italy, and my friend and I swayed in delight at the idea of traveling to Europe.

"Are you going with him?" we asked in an enthusiastic chorus.

"Are you kidding?" she replied with a silly, girlish laugh. "And be around all those smelly Italians?"

Suellen Hoy, the author of a recent book on cleanliness, tells this anecdote: In 1957, when she was a teenager and had just shaved for the first time, she was lounging at a pool with several other bare-legged friends. There they saw an older woman in a beautiful bathing suit reveal her hairy legs and armpits. The girls were stunned and repulsed to see this woman's unsightly hair in public, and they decided that she must be "foreign" because someone had told them that European women didn't shave. The incident, Hoy explains, first taught her about America's deep obsession with being clean. She adds that she wasn't alone in her perceptions, citing a "Dear Abby" column from three decades later in which a reader submits this thought: "If 'Rapunzel' legs is too dirty to shave, she should move to Europe."

It may be a peculiarly American trait that leg hair is associated with dirt, and I wonder if I earned the label of being smelly because I seemed more foreign than the rest of the girls in my class, who all acted as if they had received a maternal benediction to rid themselves of unwanted hair. By describing my "foreignness," I don't mean to suggest that we were recent Italian immigrants. Actually, I am a third-generation Italian American; my grandparents came to the United States at the turn of the century, and I am the youngest of their youngest-born. Yet sometimes I must have seemed more Italian than American, especially when a junior high teacher read my name off an attendance list and asked, "Do you speak English?" painstakingly pronouncing each syllable of her question.

Ultimately, however, looking dark and unkempt because of unwanted body hair is very different from being called smelly. The label "smelly Italian" was acceptable to many teenagers in my school for another reason: Body odor suggests that you are ill-bred, a member of the lower class.

For centuries the sweet scents of the upper class and the earthy smells of the lower class differentiated both groups in body and spirit. More than the clothes one wears or the language one speaks, the stink that fills the air of an unwashed person, the dirt and sweat that turn underarms and loins into a triangular estuary of odor, a repository of the unwanted emissions of our bodies, separates the classes. The "basement odor of the masses," as Flaubert once wrote, serves as one of the clearest demarcations between rich and poor.

The issue of smell and class plagued George Orwell for many years. In *The Road to Wigan Pier,* his treatise for a socialist state, Orwell wrote with characteristic bluntness that there are "four frightful words which people nowadays are chary of uttering," that is, "the lower classes smell." Orwell reasoned that class equality could never occur if the bourgeoisie continued to consider the lower classes "inherently dirty," their olfactory pronouncement of *us versus them.* The judgment can be impenetrable, he reasoned, because a physical feeling of dislike is far more difficult to transcend than an intellectual one.

Orwell may have paid particular attention to odors because he had his own fears as a child that he smelled bad. Describing his experiences as a scholarship student in an elite public school, Orwell wrote: "A child's belief in his own shortcomings is not much influenced by the facts. I believed, for example, that I 'smelt,' but this was based on general probability. It was notorious that disagreeable people smelt, and therefore presumably I did too."

Orwell thought that he was "disagreeable" because his family was poorer than those of the other boys at his school, who came from the highest quarters of English society. The writer once described his family's economic status as "lower upper middle class," but because class distinction is relative and children want more than anything to be like their peers, Orwell must have imagined that a lower-class boy smelled—and he took on this trait.

Perhaps I made some similar assumptions because my family's economic position could be described as deep in the basement of upper-middle-class life, or more accurately middle-middle-class life. The notion that I was called smelly because I was Italian seemed as likely as the fact that I was chubby because I ate brownies at lunch. Growing up in Short Hills, New Jersey, a suburb that manufactured debutantes like Detroit produced steel, I learned as a child that the shrill whistle sounding every hour at the station signaled more than an approaching train: the town's dividing line was drawn at the railroad, and we were on the wrong side of the tracks. While many of my friends lived in sprawling ranch houses with stone patios and outdoor pools, our little split-level house in a new development had a modest lawn that blended into the same-size property of our neighbors, who were mostly small businessmen, middle managers, and teachers.

Perhaps any child who is poor among the rich learns to kowtow to the needs of the wealthy and in doing so carries a deep sense of shame of her own inadequacies. The child intuits the sense of privilege that the rich share and knows she'll be rewarded by indulging them, commenting on how lovely their house is, oohing and ahing at the wall of mirrors in the bathroom, enthusiastically accepting the gracious invitation to swim at their pool. Her role is to be a constant reminder, like a grandfather clock that chimes reassuringly, of just how much they have. As my neighborhood pal would remind me, we lived in "the ghetto of Short Hills."

But since people pride themselves on degrees of wealth, it was never lost on me that the real "ghetto" was in a section of Millburn, the neigh-boring town where my father had grown up, that housed an enclave of Italian Americans. Because Short Hills was part of Millburn township, the poor kids and young gents went to school together (the public school was so good that there was not the usual channeling of the elite to private schools). In both junior high and high school, there was a mix of middle-, upper-middle, and upper-class teens, with a smattering of the lower-middle class. Latinos and African Americans were still excluded back then, so the only people of color in my high school were the children of the housekeeper at the local Catholic church. That left Italians as the largest dark ethnic group, and the only kids labeled by an ethnic slur.

In high school the Italian American boys were known as the "Ginzo gang"; they were greasers with beat-up cars that first chugged then soared, thanks to their work in the local gas station (Palumbo's), owned by the father of one of them. Olive-skinned and muscular, they were sexy in their crudeness, and their faint gasoline scent and oiled-down hair de-fined the image of Italian Americans in our school. The young women who hung out with them had little separate identity other than the Girl-friends of the Ginzos.

The Ginzos were my rearview mirror, a reflection of the near past that I wished to move beyond. They were an acknowledgment of my heritage, a recognition that the small sum of money my mother had inherited from her father's construction company, used as the down payment for our house in a neighborhood a mile away, allowed me to escape from their world. But who was I fooling? My grandfather earned his money by dig-ging up dirt with methodical fervor; the loamy earth formed a filmy layer on his body, a talisman linking him to the land that he labored. That sweat and dirt were part of me, an oath of fealty to my peasant past. Yet I pre-ferred to bury the memories of his work, which provided us with some material comforts but not enough to rid me of the label of the Smelly Italian Girl.

The flimsy cover of a gym uniform had unmasked my efforts to look and act the same as everyone else; now I needed to find a new route to ac-ceptance. In the interstice between the accusation of being smelly and an unspoken acknowledgment of my guilt, a denial of my ethnic self emerged. Unprepared to confront my fears, I responded like a criminal who'd do anything to get the charges dropped. If the cause of being called smelly was my Italian roots, then I would pretend not to be Italian.

At first, I rejected the smells of my southern European heritage, re-placing them with the odors of the eastern bloc. Gone were the tastes of my youth: the sweet scent of tomato sauce simmering on the stove, sooth- ing as a cup of tea on a rainy night; the paper-thin slices of prosciutto, salty and smooth on the tongue; and my own madeleine, oil-laden frying peppers, light green in color, with long, curvaceous bodies that effortlessly glide down the throat and conjure up memories of summer day trips to Asbury Park, where we ate ham-Swiss-and-fried-pepper sandwiches pre- pared by my mother.

Instead, I began to savor the sour and smoky odors of pickled herring and cured fish and taught myself to like the blander tastes of brisket, food that I was served when I ate holiday meals with my new friend from gym class. These old flavors of eastern Europe, new to my tongue, provided comfort and relief: I could escape class boundaries by accepting morsels from another culture.

Soon, I not only stripped away familiar smells but wanted to eliminate the extra baggage of vowels from my name, those instant markers of eth- nicity. My hatred of my first name was not abated by my mother's expla- nations of why she chose it: the fact that both my grandmothers were named Maria had little relevance to me because I was five years old when my only living grandmother died; and I was surprised by my mother's in- sistence that she was moved by the beauty of the actress Maria Montez. I decided that the grade B movie actress explanation was more glamorous, but still I repeatedly asked why Laurino couldn't have been changed to Laurin. In my efforts to sanitize myself, washing off an *o* seemed like a clean, decisive stroke.

The physical repulsion attached to the label of being "smelly" makes a person want to escape from body and self, and I was determined to change who I was, stripping away layers of my ethnicity in order to dissociate my- self from the Smelly Italians. It was only years later, having grown a little more confident, that I began the precarious work of trying to replace those layers. The alien surroundings of college created a nostalgia for familiar tastes and allowed me to appreciate the foods that I grew up with, al- though not everyone shared my enthusiasm. One time my freshman room- mate, who was studying to be a nurse, approached me, her face a picture of compassion and concern, as I entered our tiny dorm room. How was my weak stomach, she asked? Momentarily befuddled, I soon realized that she had confused the odoriferous aroma of the provolone I had recently eaten with vomit and believed that I had thrown up in our room.

Traveling to Italy and falling in love with its sinuous hills and burnt or- ange hues made me realize how foolish I had been to believe the comment of the girl at the cafeteria table about the Smelly Italians. By then, my early twenties, I also had learned from the local grapevine that the girl's father had made seasonal trips to Italy to visit his secret mistress and their two children. Now I realize that she probably never was invited on her father's frequent sojourns, and the thoughtless remark was the defense of an insecure child, rejected by a man too busy sniffing the earthy scents of Italians to spend much time with her.

Today I have a new fear about smell; I fear that I lack a defining odor. I feel removed from my own sense of smell and the images it could conjure. I feel a languor in my appreciation of everyday scents, like my pots of dried lavender, whose wildflower fragrance faded to a docile sachet as its deep purple buds grew pale and streaked with beige, a graceful bow to domesticity and old age. I refuse to linger by the coffeepot and sniff my carefully chosen beans or inhale their smoky end, first ground then muddied and scorched by a hot rain; instead, I quickly dump the grounds and wash the pot in soapy water, just as I will rush to lather the summer heat off my body. No smell, no mess. Life is measured, careful, clean, far removed from the chaos of dirt and its primitive pleasures—and the smelly label of my youth. Perhaps after years of trying to rid myself of the perceived stench of my ethnic group and its musty basement-class status, I sanitized my own voice, cleaned it right away.

Certain incidents in life—like being told during gym class that you smell—become emotional markers, and around these events a series of reactions is set into motion. Giving up pizza for pickled herring can take years to undo, if you even discover the fine psychological threads that formed this intricate defense web. Recently, I've come to notice how much time I've been spending scenting my body, covering it with colognes, milks, and creams, giving it a pleasant but artificial character, or voice, you could say. At first I was unaware that in the past year I had become perfume-obsessed, as people can be unaware of their obsessions. But now I think I can link its beginnings to a time and a place.

Initially, I didn't realize the connection between a fragrance fixation and a free-lance writing career, but neither did I fully understand that a spray of cologne can provide a narrative for your body in case your own story currently lacks luster. My aromatic addiction began once I decided not to return (after a brief stint in government) to the newspaper that I had worked at for nearly a decade, which was as familial as family. I was nervous about the decision to free-lance, because it not only took away an important piece of identity but would force me to choose my subjects, instead of writing about what others expected of me. And perhaps even worse, telling people that you are a full-time free-lancer sounds more like a euphemism for unemployment than an adult career choice. So I acted a bit like the child who leaves home for the first time—one part wants to go while the other kicks and drags down the stairs, clutching the newel post. The final decision to step out the door and not return to my old work home coincided with a surprise birthday gift from my husband, a five-day trip to Paris. A perfect distraction, except that I found myself spending a good part of the time thinking about a particular French cologne.

I'd like to chalk it up to coincidence rather than to Freud that I occasionally had been wearing a French cologne with a light lemon scent and a Roman emperor's name, Eau d'Hadrien, which seemed like an elegant version of the Love's Fresh Lemon of my youth. But maybe I needed to consummate the marriage of my new affection for Rome and my old need to hide Italian smells with lemons and had had one of those weird sense memory experiences when I first purchased this cologne. One of my tasks in Paris was to buy a bottle, because I knew it was cheaper there than back home.

I went to a small Left Bank perfumery filled with fluted-glass bottles capped in gold and purchased my scent. The saleswoman handed me the bag and then made an irresistible gesture: she sprayed my body, from my neck to my thighs, with cologne. Her hands flowed gently yet confidently around me, and the idea of being covered in fragrance, not frugally dabbed behind the ears, was so enticing that I went back to the store every day for a purchase and another spray. I had discovered a scented balm to soothe a shaky ego.

"Is this a gift for someone?" she asked upon my return.

"No, it's for me," I happily responded, waiting for the soft mist to drape me like a gossamer veil.

In the two years since that trip, spending long days with my computer and that fragile identity I've befriended since junior high school, I've grown even more attached to the fragrance, or perhaps the idea of this fragrance. Every time I'm in a department store, I allow myself one indulgent purchase. I've bought hand cream, body lotion, perfumed body cream (my favorite; it's as if I'm covered in lemons and cream), soaps, other colognes to mix with my fragrance to create a new, layered smell—the possibilities are endless. I no longer just spray behind the ears but cover myself completely in the scent, letting the perfume conquer the blandness of a scrubbed self. My fragrant protectress sits proudly on the bathroom shelf, an elixir to enliven a diffident voice.

I used to think that my guilt-free desire for an expensive French cologne meant that I was at least coming to terms with the embarrassing bourgeois side of myself, which capitalizes on the chic of a European heritage rather than my real-life peasant roots. But now I realize that like the young girl who wanted to deny her heritage, again I'm ducking for cover. I never quite learned the lesson from gym class long ago, when the voices of my family and my past were silenced as I altered the scents surrounding me. It's easier to shower away a smell, to censor yourself with a scent, than to accept your body's signature, the rawness of odor and sweat.

The Smelly Italian Girl no longer exists, if she ever did. In addition to my fragrance, my body is practically hairless, waxed from lip to toe by a Gallic woman who says "Voile" after finishing each leg and who reminisces about her country, sharing with me the fact that she knows the colorist who knows the colorist who mixes the blonde hair dye for Catherine Deneuve (her six strands of separation from true glamour). During the months between waxings, I let my leg hair grow long, and I run my fingers through it, still mystified by the abundance of those dark strands that I wish to find beautiful but ultimately decide to remove once again.

I have tried to escape the class boundaries of my youth, but sometimes, in that lonely space between me and the bathwater, I wonder what has become of my own smell, what it would be like to drip in sweat and to uncover a voice that could tell the stories of my past.

Jay Parini

. . . .

Amalfi Days

Ten years ago, my wife and I spent the better part of a year in Amalfi, a coastal town in the Naples region of southern Italy. It was during this time that I began, for the first time, to reflect on my Italian American heritage. Suddenly immersed in village life, I realized that my emotional connections to Italy were strong. A peculiarly tribal feeling stirred inside me. Was it blood? Or just a piece of trumped-up sentimentality, a feeling created in the imagination? Was I, in fact, a member of some category called "Italian American," and did this have any bearing on my work as a writer?

My paternal grandmother was, indeed, a peasant woman much like those I encountered everywhere in Amalfi. She lived in a tiny house in a rural part of Pennsylvania, and her daily rituals for decades were not dissimilar to those I saw in place around me in Amalfi. Gardening was central to her life, and she raised most of her own vegetables. She kept chickens, and the eggs played a large role in her diet. She cut her own pasta, letting the long strips of fettucine dry for hours on waxed paper on her kitchen table. I still remember the smell of garlic and olive oil that seemed to permeate her house. I found it again as I wandered into my neighbors' houses in Amalfi.

My grandmother was from Savona, in Liguria, but serendipity led us to the Amalfi Coast, to an old stone villa on a steep cliffside overlooking the sea. The house belonged to the friend of a friend and it came fully furnished with a family of caretakers who lived nearby. This family, it turned out, was willing to clean the house, look after our small boys, replace light bulbs or rolls of toilet paper, or do almost anything else that needed doing. From the first day, we knew we had landed on our feet.

It was impossible not to love this house. Its crisp white walls and vaulted ceilings reminded one of a medieval monastery; one could almost hear the monks chanting as one sat in the living room with the shutters open and looked out to sea. The house was tiled throughout with the colorful, hand-painted tiles typical of the region; they proved irresistible to our children, who could run and slide on them when their feet were wet. My wife and I slept in one big room in a bed that could easily have fit in our two boys as well; a huge wooden crucifix hung above our bed, adding to the religious aura of this house. The boys, fortunately, had a room to themselves. Both bedrooms had balconies with gasp-making views of the sea.

Better than the little balcony off our bedroom, however, was the rooftop terrace. The view of the sea from up there was nothing short of damaging to one's eyes: a dazzle of light reflecting off the sea, with a distant view of the Calabrian hills across the water. For shade, there was a grape arbor, a cozy little niche on the south side of the terrace where one could eat at a garden table or sink into a canvas chair to read. Because the house was built into a cliff, the terrace backed onto a steep hillside that was crammed with lemon trees, their brilliant yellow globes like tiny suns. The hill turned into a limestone cliff about halfway up, with the Villa Cimbrone—a landmark piece of Italian domestic architecture—enthroned high above our heads in Ravello. We could also see the alabaster walls of La Rondinaia, a five-story villa clinging to the cliffside like a swallow's nest and owned, for the past three decades, by Gore Vidal, the American novelist, who soon became our friend.

Looking from the northern wall of the terrace, one got a fine view of Amalfi itself—one of the most entrancing places on earth. The russet roofs and amber stone walls of Amalfi make a haunting vision of medieval town planning, with so many narrow, winding streets converging on a sequence of elegant public squares. Legend has it that Amalfi was founded in ancient times by Hercules, who was in love with a beautiful woman called, of course, Amalfi. She died a tragic death; heartsick, Hercules buried her on this magnificent site, naming the place after her. Myths and legends aside, we have positive proof that Amalfi was a going concern in the early Middle Ages. From the ninth to the eleventh centuries it was an independent republic with influence over a large territory along the coast. It adjoined the powerful dukedom of Naples. Having a wonderful natural harbor, Amalfi became a center for ships and trading, and its fleet sailed to such destinations as Tripoli, Alexandria, Tunis, and Constantinople. Amalfi soon became one of the most powerful maritime republics of Italy, rivaling Genoa and Venice.

Standing on the steps of its magnificent cathedral—begun in the ninth century and finished two centuries later—one can almost imagine the sense of worldly power that must have fueled such grand projects as this one. And one begins to understand the Latin proverb *sic transit gloria mundi*—so pass the things of this world. Which is to say that Amalfi has long since passed its prime: the ships are gone, and so is the access to wealth and power. It has become a small village with a glorious past; apart from tourism, which makes the place bustle in the summer, there is not much going on here in the way of commerce or industry (the only "factory" in town makes handmade paper).

It takes a long time to get the feel of a new place from the inside. I'm by nature a village person, which is to say I adore the feeling of community that can be had only on a neighborhood scale. This, I like to think, is part of my Italian heritage: a world in which family and community were everything. I still like it when I go into a drugstore and the pharmacist knows my name and wonders how I'm doing with my allergies. I am delighted when the bank teller doesn't have to look up my name on the computer to see if he should cash my check or not. The waiters in the local restaurants should be acquaintances if not friends, ready to bring me a cup of coffee the way I like it without asking whether or not I take sugar. In the modern world, of course, these little luxuries are almost unobtainable, but in Amalfi all-of-the-above pertained. My wife and I, with the boys, were taken into the life of the village with open arms. (The fact that my name was Parini did not hurt; countless times I was asked, "Are you related to Giuseppe Parini, the great Italian poet?" I would shrug and say, "Who knows? It's a small world.")

Nevertheless, Amalfi remains a medieval place in many ways, and this has its downside, too. For instance, our youngest son woke up one morning with a very high fever. We became quite panicky and rushed him to the emergency room of the local medical clinic. The place was hardly more than a dark hole-in-the-wall with a cramped waiting room with a drowsy nurse at a bare desk. She did most of the routine work, which consisted of dispensing Band-Aids and cough syrup. The doctor, I was told, was not available (he was at the local bar, I later discovered—his usual hangout). But the doctor's mother was on duty, and she would be glad to see us. The nurse said this without blinking.

A little apprehensive, I said, "Is she a qualified doctor?"

The nurse looked at me queerly. "A doctor's mother," she said, "is as good as a doctor. Maybe better."

There was no choice but to see the doctor's mother, a large woman in her mid-seventies with a big bun of gray hair at the back of her massive head. And we were, after all, satisfied with her help. She took the sick boy into her arms, put her palm on the forehead, then kissed him on the lips. "A virus," she said, as if she had smelled it on his breath. She gave us a packet of suppositories and sent us on our way, reassured. The boy, I should add, recovered beautifully.

One aspect of community—or communal—life in Amalfi that struck us quickly was the way that children were deemed the common possession of the town. In America, children are often treated like property. One hesitates, for instance, to scold a stranger's children in a public place, no matter how badly they are behaving. It's the old obsession with private property. In southern Italy, which remains a peasant society for the most part, everyone feels responsible for the care of children. They are part of the social fabric, and any tear in that fabric affects everyone. I was, at first, horrified when a local restaurateur in Amalfi wagged a finger at my elder boy for slurping his pasta. The boy *was*, however, behaving rudely, and it was my fault for not jumping on him earlier. My wife and I found ourselves quite relieved that the responsibility for tending our children was not so squarely on our shoulders. We were the primary caretakers, of course, but one had a feeling of general public support. Children were, above all, welcome; they were acknowledged as real people; they were cheered on, scolded, listened to, and taught—by everyone.

Wherever one lives, one gradually etches a particular groove in the earth's surface, a familiar network of paths that one plies daily and only rarely alters. It wasn't long before our daily ritual in Amalfi was set. My wife and I are both writers, and we prefer to work in the morning, when our minds have been swept clean by a night of sleep and our energy levels are at their peak. So we arranged for the family attached to our villa to babysit the youngest boy during the morning hours—from 9 till 1. The older boy attended a little grade school run by the Sisters of Mercy. (He didn't know a word of Italian when he started; in a couple of months, he understood nearly everything and could babble in something vaguely resembling Italian.) I would drop the eldest off at the school, then proceed to a small café beside the sea. My wife would make her way to another café. All morning we would sit and write, undisturbed, drinking *caffe latte*. It was lovely. I wrote poems in a spiral notebook. My wife was working on a novel, and because she likes to write on a typewriter, she carried with her a portable, battery-operated electric model that fit neatly into her beachbag. Eventually the *padrone* of what we thought of as *her* café suggested that she simply leave the typewriter behind his cash register; that way she wouldn't have to lug it down the steep path into the village every morning.

When the clock struck one, we expected to sit together with the boys at the big oak table in our dining room. Frequently Elvira, the house-keeper, would have made a spectacular pasta or meat dish; sometimes we just ate cheese and fresh fruit with a loaf of bread from the nearby bakery. We never ceased to marvel at the variety of vegetables available in the local market. Once, having had many salads of arugula in local restau-rants, we tried without success to buy some of that wonderfully tangy green-leafed plant. We asked Elvira where we could buy it, and she looked at us with astonishment. "Nobody in Amalfi *buys* arugula," she told us with mild disdain in her voice. She took us outside, where the hillside was literally overgrown with the stuff. "You want arugula," she said, "and you got it."

When in Amalfi, do as the Amalfitani do. So we took greedily to our beds after lunch. Even the boys seemed quite happy to sleep for an hour or two after eating. In the States, I almost never take naps because I al-ways seem to wake up feeling worse than when I fell asleep. But in Amalfi I could sleep blissfully for two hours after lunch and wake up as fresh as the surf itself. After our siesta, we'd all stroll into town for what-ever the season offered by way of amusement. In the dead of winter, there wasn't much to do apart from sitting in cafés or taking chilly hikes into the countryside. We'd occasionally take a bus to Salerno or, more rarely, Naples, where we'd go shopping or simply walk about. On a day when we felt especially adventurous, we'd take the ferry to Capri—only a couple of hours away. In late spring or summer we'd go to the beach, where you could rent small paddle boats or just swim. The swimming is heavenly, though one worries about tales of pollution. Rumor has it that the Mediterranean is not what it used to be, and I'm sure that a lot of work will have to be done to restore this bit of paradise to its legendary pristine self. Still, the water along the Amalfi coast from Amalfi to Positano—the only stretch I know intimately—puts on a good show; it seems pellucid, full of fish, and dazzling.

Southern Italy is still full of little restaurants that don't overcharge for a plate of pasta and a bowl of fruit, so we tended to eat out in the evenings. Our favorite restaurant was called Zaccharia. It hung out precariously over the sea, and it served a marvelous pasta full of dime-sized clams. There was no menu. Zaccharia himself, a taciturn man in his fifties with black eyes and hair, decided what everyone should eat. The meal usually began with a plate of garlic bread and fresh anchovies, all "on the house." The pasta with clams came next. You could stop there or continue on to something weightier: lobster perhaps, or swordfish. The wine was always the same unbelievably dry and crisp white wine typical of region. According to local legend, Zaccharia's mother made all the wine for her son's restaurant by treading on the grapes in her bathtub. Even if this were true, it didn't matter. I'd walk many miles in a cold sea fog for a glass of that wine.

After dinner the entire town of Amalfi gets dressed up for the nightly parade. About nine o'clock the fun begins. Lovers, arm in arm, compete for space on the sidewalks with ancient widows, with priests and nuns, with local worthies, ne'er-do-wells, teenage gangs, and a genial mix of European tourists. Everyone's out for a stroll, for gossip and story telling, for idle chit-chat. We tended to gather at the Bar Sirena, which has a grand view of the harbor and the chief promenade. The boys would play with the children of the *padrone,* and my wife and I would discuss world as well as local events with any one of a dozen people we had come to know. Quite often, Gore Vidal himself—known to everyone as *Lo Scrittore* ("The Writer")—would join the assembled company and hold forth in his inimitable style.

We left Amalfi on a hot summer morning, with tears in our eyes and our suitcases full of gifts from local friends. Our time there had, quite simply, run out. Much as we liked to pretend otherwise, we were not Amalfitani; we were Americans, and our lives—our "real" lives—lay elsewhere. Our friends in Amalfi, of course, couldn't understand this. "You should move here for good," one of them said, explaining excitedly how I could get a job at the university in Salerno. There were many days when, in my fantasy, I imagined pulling up stakes in the United States and becoming an Italian—a *real* Italian, not just an Italian American. But this was impossible, as I knew only too well. You can't become something you're not. Even in the midst of this little town's extremely warm welcome, my family and I remained foreigners, full of crazy ideas and misconceptions about how to cook pasta and how to dress our children.

The questions relating to my Italian Americanness were never entirely resolved, although I came away firmly believing I must come to terms, on some deep level, with my roots in Italy and my connection to this strange hybrid of Italian America. I began, in fact, to write poem after poem about Italy and about my Italian grandparents in America, trying to connect, in language and image, to some important part of my past.

Heritage is something mysterious and should perhaps remain so. That Italians are family-centered and that—especially in small towns—possess strong communal feelings goes without saying. It is possible that I was connecting more with the European "peasant" tradition in Amalfi than with anything so grand as a national consciousness. The truth is that Italy is not a coherent nation-state; it is a thousand little communities, most of which command the reflexive allegiance of their fellow members. Sicilians and Amalfitani and Genovese seem blithely ignorant, or contemptuous, of each other, although a common tradition is nevertheless discovered in their heritage of fine art, great music, and wonderful architecture. What all Italians have most in common, I suspect, is a devotion to certain daily rituals, which include a plate of pasta at lunchtime or late at night, with a glass of shimmering red or white wine to wash it down.

As one does in such cases, my wife and I swore we'd return to Amalfi again and again. But we knew the truth: that one can have new adventures in familiar places, but that the past is always past. History repeats itself only in the textbooks. Unless we were willing to bite the bullet and become permanent expatriates—and we weren't about to do any such thing—we would have to content ourselves with occasional return visits, with postcards and letters, with photographs and souvenirs. Our one comfort was the knowledge that we had known firsthand this bright and cheerful place that was full of human depth and medieval strangeness and that we had somewhere to go to when, as the poet Wordsworth said, "the world is too much with us."

Claire Gaudiani

. . . .

Of Cheese and Choices

No matter how quietly I tried to replace the spoon and glass top of the container of freshly grated Parmesan cheese on Nonna's dining table, one or the other always clinked. If I was lucky, the animated conversations in the living room masked the clink and no adult voice called out to inquire who might be in the dining room tasting the cheese. My earliest memories of irresistible temptation involved the pursuit of Parmesan, soft and nutty, sitting like a sacrament in its sacred vessel on the linen cloth. The challenge was never walking by silently enough; it was getting the cheese out of the container quietly enough. The sin was not mainly in sneaking the cheese (my family never begrudged its children food, even purloined food); the real sin was in eating it from the cheese spoon, covering the spoon with my germs and putting the germ-ridden spoon back into the cheese server that everyone would use. I knew better. Both of my grandfathers were doctors, but I couldn't help it. I really loved the taste. I knew all about germs and the potential danger I posed to my family. Luckily, even by age six, American pragmatism was shaping me as fast as my Italian taste buds. Bringing a spoon from the kitchen was, I reasoned, out of the question. Nonna's kitchen drawers were very heavy and too noisy for me to open and close alone. Taking a pinch of cheese from the container manually would leave telltale droppings on the tablecloth and finger germs in the server anyway. No, using the little serving spoon was unfortunately the only way to satisfy my temptation.

But as I grew a little older, I continued to worry about the germs and learned to work out moral dilemmas by using the laws and traditions from our Italian culture and the rational pragmatism of our American culture. The combination has served me well. I used what I know now was the grammar schooler's version of Thomistic theology, *lex dubia, non lex est,* roughly translated "where there is doubt (or lack of clarity) there is no law." I reasoned, primitively, that if I was not told specifically on the day we visited Grandma not to spoil my appetite, I was under no direct obligation not to sneak spoonfuls of her Parmesan cheese from the table as often as I could. There was, however, no avoiding the moral responsibility my germs posed. So by age eight, I had developed a germ-free technique. I learned to load the little spoon, throw my head back, and drop the cheese directly into my mouth the way a bulldozer discharges its contents into a dump truck. No contact, just direct delivery of the goods.

A lot of life since then has been about satisfying personal drives and goals while mindful of the well-being of others. And a lot of success has come from the synergy I have experienced between our Italian culture and American values. The stories I heard as a child illustrated this synergy that shaped me before I knew myself and resonated powerfully through my conscious life experience.

My family—maternal, from little towns on the Amalfi Drive; paternal, from Laurino and Rome—created this synergy. My grandfather, Augusto Rossano, arrived in the United States as a boy of nine in 1889, passionate to become a doctor. As children of his youngest, most beautiful, and most spiritual daughter, my five siblings and I heard the stories of how hard he worked in school, how Augusto came home every day to aunts and uncles because he had bravely left his parents to live in New York with relatives who had an import-export business. His parents in Italy expected him to study hard. He wanted to make them proud. He went to Columbia College of Physicians and Surgeons and in 1906 was the first Italian American to graduate first in his class. His personal goal fulfilled in triumph, he choose to practice medicine in East Harlem where he could do the most good among the poor and immigrant people he had grown up with, and whose language he spoke.

His commitment to the poor and to social justice constituted an important weight-bearing structure in the building of my sense of self. I remember hearing how he had returned to his parents' home several years after his graduation from medical school and helped an old workman struggling to unload a horse-drawn wagon full of luggage. The young doctor worked with the old man until the wagon was empty. The town buzzed for weeks. In Italy, educated people, doctors especially, did not do manual labor, did not work with peasants. My mother's interpretation of this text was that in America he had learned that class does not matter, that people help each other when the need arises.

This was not an easy lesson for Italians, as my mother noted when she recounted how her father had explained life in America to his young bride, courted and wed in the summer sojourn he spent in his village. Rosa Cosenza, a young woman from a cultured family in the next town, became the doctor's wife. Once in the United States, he explained, she would have to feel comfortable shaking hands and speaking English with all kinds of people, doctors and lawyers, fishmongers and fruit sellers, gypsies, Jews, blacks and Anglo Saxons. Everyone lived in close proximity in New York, and, unlike in Italy, in the United States everyone she met, regardless of their economic or educational level, would expect to shake her hand.

And so Rosa did shake hands and spoke accented English once she was outside their five-story brownstone on 116th Street between First and Second Avenues, but inside that home she and the family spoke and ate and prayed Italian. The six children she and Augusto raised spoke perfect English and either became professionals or married them. Their son attended MIT in 1935.

Family values were Italian; civic values were American. The connection to both value sets made us Italian Americans. We came to understand without verbal explanation that it was not simply geography, a family from Italy living in the United States, that made us Italian Americans. Rather, it was two carefully integrated value sets that made us Italian Americans starting first thing in the morning. My mother had always told us that her parents began their day by having espresso in bed together, saying the Rosary together, and reading the *New York Times*—physical, spiritual, and intellectual comforts coming from both cultures. When Augusto served in the U.S. Army in World War I, Rosa proudly had a coat that matched his captain's uniform made for her own tiny frame, and she wore it selling war bonds all over East Harlem. She also wrote for the local Italian-language newspaper. Papa helped young Italian immigrants get into the university and medical school. Both of them worked with Mother Cabrini and the Missionary Sisters of the Sacred Heart to start schools in New York for immigrant children and to help found Cabrini Hospital. Papa and Mama were sustaining Italian culture but were active, patriotic, volunteering Americans to the core.

Other stories we were told suggested how both cultures created synergies between our Italian Catholic spirituality and American pragmatism. When Nonna Rosa caught pneumonia one winter and lay dying at home, well beyond the reach of pre-penicillin medicine in 1919, she kissed her four children good-bye. Then she and Augusto prayed to the Blessed Mother, promising that if, by some miracle, her life was spared, they

would both return to Italy, to her village, and give her most prized possessions, her diamond solitaire earrings, to the dressed statue of the Virgin
Santa Maria delle Grazie. Their connection made fast to their Italian culture and spirituality, they called in Augusto's best friend, a brilliant young
Italian American surgeon, who had received his medical degree from the
University of Rome and had studied in Germany with the doctors who invented the catheter, before immigrating to America in 1911 to practice
surgery and continue doing research. Dr. Vincent Gaudiani affirmed that
Rosa's condition was terminal but offered the slender chance of a most
risky experimental operation, opening her chest cavity to relieve the massive pulmonary infection. Faith and pragmatism induced them to go forward. Too sick to live through transport to the local hospital, Rosa's bedroom was draped for surgery. With makeshift lamps but with all his
surgical tools at his command, Dr. Gaudiani opened the chest of his best
friend's wife and saved her life.

Rosa and Augusto fulfilled their promise to the Virgin several years
later. The summer they returned to Italy with the earrings for the statue,
they conceived their last child, Vera, who grew up to marry Dr. Gaudiani's
only son, Vincent, and to bear him six children, continuing his name and
line, including another Dr. Vincent Gaudiani, also a surgeon like his
grandfather. As the oldest of this family of six, I remember these stories
reinforcing the synergy between prayer and professional expertise.

My father's father, Dr. Gaudiani, dominated as a model of a perfection-
ist. He was widely recognized as so demanding in the operating room that
others feared working with him. Patients from all over sought him for his
skills but also found him difficult. Even though he died in 1938, when his
son was only seventeen, the stories of Dr. Gaudiani's skill and pursuit of
excellence were constant models to his grandchildren of the most hard-
hitting, no-nonsense achievement. I always remember his being called
Dr. Gaudiani by everyone in the family except my father. Respect for his
achievements somehow excused his legendary difficult personality.
Through stories about him, my father shaped high expectations of his six
children. I remember, when I was very young, coming home with a 98 on
a test and my father asking me if anyone had gotten a higher grade and
how many others had gotten a 98. I quickly learned that it was not the
grades themselves but their distinctive character that would bring him
satisfaction. He expected me to achieve at the highest level, to succeed
beyond others. A West Point graduate, with a Columbia University master's degree in engineering, he had great impact on my sense of order,
striving, focus, and intensity. Of course, sixth-grade history and geography

detailing the glorious achievements of ancient Rome simply reinforced the notion that my parents proposed. We were descendants of people who had always achieved at the highest level, and we were responsible for carrying on that tradition.

The stories about Augusto and Rosa Rossano made them our models of social justice and optimism. Nonna Rossano's pastoral approach to his patients in his general practice and stories of Nonna Rossano's optimism and celebrated generosity told me how to be with people. Papa Rossano never refused a patient all through the Great Depression and his fifty years of practice of medicine in East Harlem. He accepted whatever payment his patients could bring. My mother told us it was sometimes fruit or fish. One time a Gypsy mother did magic tricks for him with his handkerchief and his quarter after he saw her baby. He was a listener and a healer, a gentler William Carlos Williams. At Christmas, when fruit, vegetables, chocolate, and pastries came from grateful patients, Rosa would make up baskets and take them around to poor families in the neighborhood as quickly as the goodies came in. "God can never be outdone in generosity." "What you do for the least of my brothers you do unto me." The recounting of these stories always closed with what sounded like a perfectly rational explanation for the kindness of both Rosa and Augusto.

For Rosa, life was a celebration, and life in the United States simply meant twice as many holidays to celebrate. She made pumpkin pies for Halloween and stuffed turkey for Thanksgiving, and she decorated the house in green for St. Patrick's Day. She maintained every Italian holiday, religious and otherwise, including March 19, St. Joseph's Day, a celebration of fathers and husbands, a day I have continued to celebrate for my husband in our own family for our own children. Italian and American holidays offered perfect excuses to draw the family together, make memorable meals, and tell stories from old times and new times.

Just as my father always underlined the idea of achievement in the world and competition, my mother would gently remind us that the faith we were given had been likewise handed down, generation after generation, for two thousand years, and we were responsible to draw on its strength and to hand it down in vigorous condition to our own children.

As a child, I felt responsible for a weighty heritage, but the family stories convinced me that I had good models in my family and could expect a lot of help from prayer. The power of prayer and spirituality infused everything we did as children. Prayer connected us to a world of heavenly expertise that we could draw on like senior partners or consultants. Saints and angels were there to help with all our needs, from lost mittens to lost causes: Saint Christopher when we traveled, Saint Francis when the cat was sick, and Saint Anthony and Saint Clare when material desires outpaced our allowance, because they had rejected materialism and chosen simplicity. My dramatic patron saints, Clare and Theresa, gave virtue and learning the kind of dazzle the Material Girl gives vice and vogue. With such helpers, from my guardian angel to our saintly relatives deceased but still watching over us, I never remember feeling the devastating loneliness and powerlessness that can afflict children. My mother helped us understand how to pray. Her devotion to Mary drew us to her to say the family Rosary each day. Fifty-four-day rosary novenas read from a little blue book brought us to her king-size bed to snuggle together in prayer. Hail Mary after Hail Mary, we mediated on the life of Christ and of course daydreamed and babbled too, when we got distracted. Our mother never got distracted. Her focus taught us all the meaning of self-discipline, single-minded devotion, and loyalty.

The meditations we read on each event in Christ's life gave me my wildly vivid imagination, strong powers of concentration, and a deep sense that other people's stories could convey meaning for my own life. At the end of each decade the closing prayer asked for a specific virtue appropriate to the mediation. After the Annunciation we prayed for humility. After the Visitation we prayed for charity. After the Agony in the Garden we prayed for resignation to the will of God. After the carrying of the Cross we prayed for patience in adversity. For years, I had no idea what adversity was, but I knew I needed patience and of course I still do—in adversity and otherwise. But the larger message that I now see from this carefully categorized referencing of events and virtues is that good and bad things are going to happen but that specific personal virtues can be prayed for and developed and will create the power to cope and even triumph. No one ever said this exactly, but prayer like this created a network of connections between God and self to manage life.

Although our mother never worked outside our home, my brothers and sisters and I always felt she had great power through the simplicity and persistence of prayer, to which she drew us gently with her just as she drew us with her to Mass and to making spiritual bouquets as gifts. I felt that whatever she asked God to help me with was going to work out perfectly for me. Our mother's prayer life, anchored in her parents' faith, created an awesome example of a powerful woman as I looked back on my childhood. Actually, my Nonna and my mother were often the most visible signs of the invisible helpers we had been taught to pray to when in a catastrophe. Like the saints and angels they came to the rescue. I must have been four or five, visiting my grandparents, when I was scolded for some now forgotten failing or disaster I had caused. Nonna arrived, taking my hand, and she led me across the marble terrazzo dining room floor, searching for a key in her pocket as we walked. It emerged, shiny and important, and we approached a little door in her massive sideboard next to the dining room table. The key opened the chocolate cupboard—I knew that. Soon I held a Nestle's crunch bar big enough to savor, small enough to eat alone and not to have to share as the oldest child usually must. All problems were over. The world was right, no questions asked, no lessons reviewed, just happiness.

Nonna took control of all disasters with optimistic resolutions. If any one of us spilled anything at her table, even red wine, she exclaimed with joy that this was a sign of special blessings we could all expect. She transformed a child's embarrassment and fright into a strange stillness, the soul's equivalent to a deer caught in the sudden flood of headlights. No one could get angry at a child who had just brought sudden blessings down on the whole family, right? Like the chocolate bar, Nonna's blessing pronouncement stopped the oncoming problem dead in its tracks and well away from her grandchild.

My mother worked that way as well. On Valentine's Day eve in my first-grade year a snowstorm prevented my parents from driving to buy Valentines for our card exchange. I went to bed very worried but prayed to my guardian angel. I awoke to find my mother had hand-made a whole set of little cards and fashioned a little mail bag from a lunch sack and ribbons. When the bus came for me, my problem was over; the day would be a success. As I grew up, the striving and achievement were clearly as important as spirituality, social justice, and optimism. In fact, they were connected. For us, the focus on faith, food, and family, especially tenderness to children and the poor, were as strong as the focus on premier achievement in American society—Italian Catholic spirituality in the context of American striving.

As I grew into adolescence, more stories from this dual heritage prepared me for a good marriage. I had always known how well my maternal grandparents and my own parents had taken care of each other, loved each other, and even remained romantic, for goodness sake. In our culture the men and boys were always special, but I had also always seen the women of the family as very strong, combining power of prayer and expertise in the kitchen and at homemaking in a balance with their beauty. Makeup and manicures, hair setting and eyebrow tweezing were all part of being a woman in our culture. I loved it all and saw no contradiction.

None of this prepared me to connect comfortably with the wave of the women's liberation movement of the early '70s. It took me years to discover why the stories from my Italian ancestry and my life experience in my Italian American household made me a feminine misfit in my own generation.

One afternoon in 1990, after a three-day conference in Washington, D.C., a set of my male and female colleagues and I were decanting in a hotel suite. Conversation turned to weight, nutrition, cooking, and family traditions around food. I began to explain to my colleagues that in my family women cooked so well that food became "the at home sacraments," that we were adored by our husbands and children for our culinary achievements, and that all girls learned the art. Our cooking combined excellent taste and good nutrition. The evening meal each night was a major event no one missed. The table had a cloth, the places were set, and each course was a treat. As I spoke about my family and food, my normal defenses relaxed, and I went on to explain that in my culture not only was cooking an art but ironing was also done to perfection and taught. Initially the housekeepers but eventually my practical grandmother and her five daughters all learned to use the Ironrite mangle, high-tech ironing machines at which the ironer would sit and control the rolling padded cylinder's contact with the hot curved metal platform it fit into by moving levers with quick motions of the right or left knee: right to make contact and to roll or stop rolling, left to hold the contact in place for an extra second or two of pressing on the item placed between the pad and the platen.

In our home, my mother taught me how to use the Ironrite deftly as an early adolescent, and by full puberty I could iron a man's shirt, light starch. I felt proud and competent, I explained, to be developing skill with the Ironrite as I did in the kitchen. I told my colleagues that the Ironrite also created a quiet setting for important mother-daughter talks and that I even remembered coming home from college vacations and discussing Saint Augustine, Saint Thomas, and more contemporary boys as my mother rolled most everything the family wore through the Ironrite. Even my father's boxers were pressed in thirds twice and turned into tiny packages for the second drawer of his dresser. Careful ironing and talking together was as natural as careful cooking and talking together, and both seemed like normal activities I would always do.

When I married, I explained, my husband and I were both graduate students in the same Ph.D. program and were living in a tiny basement apartment. In the first month after we moved in, I put an ad in the local paper and found a used Ironrite in mint condition for only $25! My enthusiastic recall of my achievement must have sounded increasingly alarming to my professional colleagues—all of us then in our mid-forties with several advanced degrees. Stories of my mother and grandmother and the Ironrite were quaint and funny, "but not you, Claire," their eyes seemed to say. They were looking at me like people who had just discovered that the stockbroker they had trusted for years wore a hair shirt and self-flagellated twice a day. Suddenly aware of their eyes, I felt forced to invert my perfectly earnest story about how I intended to carry on the traditions of an Italian American housewife into a self-deprecating joke. As I snapped to my senses, realizing the alarm my story was causing my colleagues, I said, "I was just a bride. I guess I was afraid a marriage could not be officially consummated in a home without an Ironrite." Great laughter. "Whew, she was only kidding," they seemed to say with their eyes and laughter. She actually was not completely kidding of course.

At least I did not tell them that for years of our marriage I used to set a little alarm clock and wake at 4:00 A.M. to freshen my hair, apply light mascara and blusher, and then go back to bed so that when my husband woke up he would find me looking closer to what I wanted him to see rather than to what the night would have left behind. Lack of self-confidence and vanity? Of course. But it always actually felt like not taking David for granted, like keeping the gift of romantic love alive, just as my grandmother and mother had done.

I was much too embarrassed to explain to my colleagues that my grandmother had always told me to take precious care of my husband, to try to please him in what she mysteriously called "personal ways," and never to do or say anything to break his heart. If I had told them that, I would have had to explain the rest of the story—the story of how a woman must be careful and sure that she has met the right man to marry and shower with gifts like these. My mother recounted it to me. When Nonna Rosa was of age to marry, her parents permitted appropriate young men to call at the house, for tea first, and if they seemed interesting, then for dinner. At dinner all the courses were made by the cook, but my grandmother made the dessert herself. When the complicated pastry was served, her own mother announced to the suitor that Rosa had prepared the dessert personally to please her guest. Little did the young man know that his next few words would seal his fate. Only the effusively responsive were permitted to call again, regardless of their education, wealth, or physical appeal. My great-grandmother explained that Italian women bring extraordinary gifts to their husbands throughout a lifetime. Appreciation, really outright enthusiastic gratitude from husbands makes the gifts a continuing source of pride and joy for giver and receiver. Needless to say, any suitor who could not produce more than a "non ch'é male" for a gift a woman offered during courtship would not be worth further consideration. What a lesson about a woman's self-worth and the value of her love and attention! A lesson as well about the importance of a woman's wise discernment and the power she wields in her home.

Yes, my background made me a bit of a misfit in consciousness-raising meetings in graduate school in '71 and after professional meetings in the '90s. The women in my family had not seemed oppressed and did not seem alienated from their fathers or husbands. My own marriage and family life reflected my cultural traditions more than my contemporaries' experiences. I was naive about the problems for which the solutions discussed in those meetings seemed like only a loss: imagine emancipation from service to family!

I was always driven to achieve and knew I would have a profession, but it never occurred to me that I would not also cook, bake, iron, and sew. I remember feeling just as driven academically as I was to continue traditions, to keep a well-managed home, and, maybe in those early transition years, to iron table linens and, for a few years at least, my husband's boxer shorts. In my immense naïveté, I did not know what so many women had struggled with at home, at work, and in getting work. Nor did I have the least idea how many expectations for home life were going to work with my professional life. All that, my husband and I made up as we went along year after year inventing a stable dual-career marriage.

Through the most precarious decades of social change, my own marriage has been the gift of a lifetime, in no small measure because of my husband's generosity and wisdom but also because the stories of my family had as powerful an influence on me as those of my sisters in the movement. With the latter, I shared a drive to knock down barriers to women's achievement and ensure that the women of my daughter's generation would be able to bring their personal gifts and interests to society and not experience discrimination because of their gender. With the former, I shared a continuing commitment to our faith and parish work, to making full dinners each night and baking bread and homemade pizzas. With my husband, the couple we became has been struggling to make sense of both directions. We have helped each other succeed at work, and each of us has moved twice to follow the other to better positions. We shared making school lunches, and David learned to be a great cook. I learned to tile bathrooms and make screened-in porches.

As a part of the women's movement, I was the first woman with a husband and a tiny new baby to complete a Ph.D. in the French and Italian department at Indiana University, the first one for whom the department had to meet and to vote and give special permission to nurse during lunchtime of Ph.D. exam days. The women's movement was part of public life and the expectations for achievement. Changes in American society and my father's expectations made me ready to struggle with high expectations for achievement in public life, but my family stories shaped the structure of my private life, my home life. The generosity of my husband helped us both to create a balance between our public and private lives. To this day our lives begin each morning, like my grandparents', with espresso in bed together, although I have not yet succeeded in inducing David to say an Our Father, never mind an entire Rosary with me. As in the marriages that shaped my own, David and I are soul mates. When we moved our careers for each other, we were both putting the family and each other (and pleasing each other in "personal ways") first. We advise each other on professional challenges and share equally in the great adventure of raising our two children, attempting to offer them the stories, our own and our ancestors', that will be witnesses for them in the complicated world they will engage as they leave our home.

Years later I realize that my own drives in life are to increase social justice and tolerance, to strive for highest achievement myself, and to celebrate life. I get to do that as a mother, wife, and daughter and as a professor, college president, writer, corporate director, community volunteer, and Eucharistic minister. Those early experiences of trying to satisfy personal drives—say for spoonfuls of Parmesan cheese—with responsibility for the well-being of others probably helped me sort through the conflicts between wanting a career and concern for my family life. I still feel power in prayer and find help from my heavenly coaches. I still pray for specific personal virtues and work for justice in civil society. I see that power comes from striving and expertise built through competition and cooperation, that it comes from achievements at home and at the office, from serving others and from leading them, from prayer and from work and from having access to friends in high places—worldly and spiritual. I see that I had a whole set of role models. Our role models do not need to have the same profession or education we aspire to. They need to have the same human impact as we seek to have. My family and patron saints were powerful role models for me, though none of the women ever finished college or received a salary.

Now, more than a hundred years after Augusto Rossano arrived in the United States, more than eighty years after his marriage to Rosa Cosenza, and more than fifty years after their daughter Vera married Augusto's best friend, Dr. Gaudiani's only son, Vincent, our children speak Italian, cook, and pray and celebrate in their Italian culture. All the while they achieve at the highest levels by American standards in some of this country's most prestigious schools, Andover and Princeton. They study art and science. One does architecture; the other, history of science. They are committed to the needy and to excellence, passionate about family, food, children, and their work. The synergy between our Italian family values and our American civic values continues. Their great-grandparents would be proud, I think. My husband and I are grateful.

Mary Cappello

· ·

Shadows in the Garden

Poetics of Loss, Italian/American Style

> Today I have convinced the men in the shop to open the
> shades providing that I close them before dark. What is there
> better than light?
> —From the journal of my maternal grandfather,
> John Petracca

I. Beads

I remember how my Sicilian grandfather, Giacomo Cappello, mourned
the death of his wife, Ninfa, my grandmother. He wore black for one year
and numerous days thereafter; TV was strictly prohibited, as though it
would throw too much light into the room or distract one from the work of
grieving. So when we visited—I was a child—we played cards, made hats
out of newspaper, sat in silence while my grandfather wept. At this point,
my grandfather took up a new habit: each week when my father and I
brought him to our house for dinner, he would take his mute, darkly
clothed place in the front passenger's seat and almost audibly, breathily,
pray. He was reciting the Rosary. Last week, my mother's sister, my aunt
Josephine, died. My aunt made thousands of rosary beads in her lifetime.
After her daughter died at aged two and a half of spinal meningitis, my
aunt took to crafting the beads and to religion, Catholicism became increasingly her life's devotion. My aunt's death was followed by news of a
close friend's serious, possibly fatal illness. Trying to doze this evening
before the television set—*Atomic Cafe* is on—I find myself imagining a

particularly vivid, efflorescent set of blue beads passing between my fingers. And suddenly I—vociferously anti-Catholic—am reciting to myself with crystal clarity the calming repetition of the Hail Mary—ten such songs followed by an Our Father. How could I know those prayers, having not recited them or turned in the direction of their predictable intonations for solace in twenty years? The memory is, to say the least, strange, sometimes charming, in what it will lose and find. Now I find a bead between my fingers, now I lose the space between it. And is the space of who I am in the feltness of bead to finger or in the space between?

I like to think my ancestors can help me in times of need, so now I am calling on Aunt Josephine, her spirit still close to the earth, my mother said. In my imaginary dialogue with Aunt Jo, she tells me she cannot help me unless I pray. Unless I pray— Fill in the blank with all unimaginable disaster, loss. I tell her I can't pray because I don't believe. This is the short version of a longer dissertation on the oppressiveness of organized religion, the damage wreaked upon my psyche by Catholic training, the biases reproduced in the otherwise seemingly contentless utterances of church dogma. "Besides," I remind someone—is it just myself now? myself and my dead aunt? myself *as* my aunt?—"even my aunt who is a nun says she does not pray much: her *day is a prayer,* she says."

Still I wish for the beads. Blasphemous idolater that I am, I want their talismanic lure. Or maybe, really, I want to feel what linked my aunt, my grandfather, to earth, how the string of beads linked them to each other, how this form of meditation in repetition thematized their loss.

I believe that we all carry with us devalued resources attached to unpopular or ghettoized states of mind, and my goal is to find the words, face, song, story—the unintelligible core of those resources—for the new poetic forms they can suggest. Rosary beads, musical notes, the sprocket holes and frames of home movies are some of the handicraft that is my familial legacy. They are marks of something sighted, something sung when voicelessness threatened, instances of remaking in light of traumatic unmakings of their authors' worlds. To read them from the distance of several generations entails the translation of the conviction that they can offer me something I need to know—an inherited artistry, a labor of love, an embodiment—or maybe just something I need to tell.

Every year on January 6, the Feast of the Epiphany, my grandmother Rose and my aunt Josephine would meet at Wanamakers, a popular department store in Philadelphia. They would rendezvous at the store's trademark, an enormous bronze eagle, and, browsing or shopping, they would in this way celebrate what is considered by some Italian Americans the day of the little Christmas, specifically the day on which the three wise men visited the child Christ. January 6, 1954, would be remembered as a profound exception to the rule. On that day, my aunt called my grandmother to say that she would not be able to meet her, that when she was putting Janice's, her daughter's, snowsuit on, something strange and sudden occurred. Janice's head jerked backward and she was unable to stand up. She developed a high fever. My aunt called the doctor. Janice became increasingly ill. My aunt called a rescue squad. It took only eight hours for spinal meningitis to take Janice from their midst. She died on the way to the hospital. Because Janice died on a city street rather than at home or in a hospital, her body had to be taken to the morgue, where my uncle then had to reclaim her as his own.

Family members tried to make sense of the incomprehensible loss in various ways. My grandmother blamed the industrial area where my aunt lived. Whenever she visited, she said, she found the child in her playpen covered with soot. My aunt, the more directly injured by the loss, momentarily exacted a less environmental, more metaphorical, aggressive and superstitious rationale. She said that Janice died because my grandfather, a worrisomely unreligious man, did not go to Communion at my aunt's wedding two and a half years earlier. The pain of this accusation sent my otherwise reasonable grandfather back to church. My uncle, my aunt's brother, on hearing the news of Janice's death punched his fist through a wall. My great-grandmother at unexpected moments shared out loud the thought that burdened her, much to the dismay of my aunt. "Poor Janees," she would say, "it's snowing on her." My mother and her sister Frances were given the job, ordered by the Board of Health, to burn anything that Janice might have touched that day or, if the item was not burnable, to wash it in disinfectant. They found themselves destroying the gifts they themselves had given her as a baby on this, the feast of welcome—a refusal of a second, a little, Christmas. At the viewing it was stipulated that Janice's body be separated from mourners by glass. For the first time ever, my mother's boss told her she could stay away from work for as long as she liked and thus keep at a presumed distance the terror of infectious disease.

It is no doubt true that my aunt lived with a loss from which she never fully recovered, and yet I wonder what that means: "recovered." Aunt Josephine lived. Aunt Josephine made. When she looked at me, her sister's daughter, she knew I knew she saw *her* daughter, but never grudgingly, lovingly. So what would it mean to say she never recovered?

Aunt Josephine recovered enough to care for other children. She adopted a boy whose biological mother had dropped him from a second story window when he was an infant, and she gave birth to another son, referred to by doctors as the miracle baby because she conceived him after a partial hysterectomy. In an interview on trauma, Robert Jay Lifton suggests that for the survivor "insight begins with the shattering of prior forms" (Caruth 134). A new form must be created to attach to the prior shocking event for which one had no experiential referent and therefore no imagery to make sense of the trauma.[1] In the space of unfillable absence, Aunt Josephine made rosary beads and other artifacts that one might not hesitate to call kitsch. Mostly she worked with yarn and rope, crocheting brightly colored afghans, needlepointing keychains in the shape of geometrics, improvising her own imitation Mondrian tissue box covers, and my favorite pieces—the dresses made to fit nothing other than a roll of toilet paper. Any standard-size doll could fit into the roll, to don the sequined miniature cap my aunt also made, and voilà: an aristocratic lady, wearing usually a lime green or neon orange dress, could be found gracing the back of one's toilet, and only you would know what she was stuffed with, what gave her skirt its hoop.

Though my description may sound parodic of the thing itself, what I really mean to imply is the mocking, if not irony, implicit in these particular creations of my aunt. Many of my aunt's craftings had an unutilitarian utilitarian quality. The toilet paper dress had a "use," but one would be hard-pressed to say its use was necessary, immediate, or urgent, even though the presence of the doll meant there would always be an extra roll. Suspended somewhere between pure kitsch and art, the dresses transformed the roll of paper from something useful to something decorative. Like "good art," they got one thinking about the abundance of taken-for-granted useless items produced in the name of capitalist need. In a sense, they were one instance of my aunt's deciphering her loss as a joke, the joke that was played on her, and responding not by mocking others but by mocking the emptiness at the center of objects that would pretend to fill a desire.

Within the realm of aesthetic theory, critics have affiliated kitsch with escapism and political quietism, with the duping of the working class by totalitarian forces, with cheap and superficial sentiment, with an inability to feel complex emotions, and with "killing time" (Calinescu 248). I imagine each tug of yarn drawn through its hole, each tying of a knot to hang an ornament by, each pulling taut of a pipe cleaner like the furred edge of a cat's ear fondling one's fingers, as forms of *facing* time, as ways that my aunt continued to be in time. If kitsch attempts to "assuage a fear of emptiness" (Calinescu 251), I wonder if the emptiness usually at issue is merely an imagined emptiness, even if an originary emptiness, or if certain forms of kitsch can suggest that an emptiness that one had only encountered or been engulfed by has now been confronted.

Teasing a set of beads out from within its blue velvet pouch like a snake charmer, I try to imagine the shape the world may have taken for my aunt after the loss of her daughter. I imagine doorways narrowing and perception funneling to a point. And a great labor required in first moving from that point, into which what used to be distinguishable as tree, cloud, house, sun, self had collapsed, to another point, and much later letting the point open to recalibrate difference, watching a new world issue from the point as though from a spring—not the same tree, cloud, house, sun, self as before but a renewed sense of being in time. I don't want to call it recovery but change for change: the loss as unexpected call, the beads as symbolized response.

There are a great number of sides to a rosary bead, a great many ways to understand how, through their crafting, my aunt may have devised a poetics of loss, a way of confronting emptiness. In the face of the ungraspable, a bead is grasped, pause, and grasped again. Like learning to walk again, what has to be mastered is the movement from bead to bead. A well-wrought rosary bead is as sensual as a nipple hardening between thumb and forefinger, a reattachment to sense. Though the believer is told that reciting the prayers attached to the beads will sanctify her, I think more interesting than cleansing is the idea of the rosary as something held. Rather than induce the disappearance of the self, it seems to encourage a dialogue or double-voicedness, a bass line with improvisatory accompaniment? The Hail Mary that one repeats for ten counts, or a decade, is, for example, supposed to be accompanied by meditation on a so-called Joyful, Sorrowful, or Glorious mystery decided on from the start. Lest one get lost in the mystery, the Hail Mary returns one to ground; lest one be tempted to wallow in dirt, the mystery beckons one to stand, to fly. This is of course my homespun theory made from my aunt's homespun rosaries and not, I hope, an interpretation the Catholic Church would agree with. I'm hoping for a conversion not to faith but from raw materials to making, from fingered to formed.

I know that my aunt did not merely "serve" the church in her rosary making and did not capitulate to the church's attitudes toward women. She addressed letters to me with "Ms."; in those same letters, she let me know she accepted my lover as a member of our family—"Hope all is well with you and Jeannie," "Give my love to Jeannie." As she was going into coma on her deathbed, among the few last words she thought to write on paper my mother read to me over the phone: "Thank you Mary and Jeannie for the flowers." Having spent more than her share of time on so many solitary islands of illness as a child, my aunt, I believe, maintained an independent preserve of fortitude that could not be overcome by consolatory dogma.

I cannot know what, through her rosary making, my Aunt Josephine was trying to "say," nor can I surmise what she envisioned in the solitude of her daily recitations or with groups of people in prayer. I do know that, in the chapel of her own funeral mass, I failed to be consoled by the ritualized prayer that perhaps anesthetized so many there. I realized then that the Catholic church service was entirely "performative" in the sense that linguist J. L. Austin elaborates that term in *How to Do Things with Words*. It did not matter *what* the priest was saying (cf. the automatic trance that the mass cast over the mourners) but *that* he was saying them. His utterances performed an act (vis-à-vis loss) without having much discernible content, especially with regard to the lived life of Josephine Petracca Falter. The mass was a perfect ritual of dissociation, the highest form of superficial feeling, the most magnifying form of kitsch. The way the candles were flickering, like the stuttering of an artificial log fire, I couldn't tell whether the flames were real or electronic flares in red plastic casing. The sound did remind me of the staccato coughs akin to sobs that were my pained uncle's attempts not to cry. If the person traumatized or in mourning is already uncomfortably dissociated, then artificial respiration in the form of more recognizable dissociating mechanisms may only return her to the world deluded once more.

I see in the manufacture of the rosaries something better and more, for in my aunt's decision to *make*, not merely "say," rosaries, she in a sense chose to handle the co-constitutive matter of absence and presence on a daily basis. Making something requiring some meticulous care and imagined beauty, often prepared as a gift for friend or family, resecured my aunt's interest in living; and yet to fashion rosaries is to circumscribe a circle, a hollow, a loop made of luminous orbs. I want to say again that to make rosaries and to say the Rosary are different kinds of acts. What would the poet make if the book and the pen weren't ready-made? If one chose to manufacture one's materials, would one's poetry look different? Would one choose not to make poetry at all? Rather than deposit her prayers, her worries in a journal, my aunt decided on different materials— color of beads, icons, forms of linkage—for making a journal each day. Each set of rosaries that my aunt made was an instrument for someone else to play on. I'm only sorry that the intended, the prefabricated song could not be sung to her but to the anonymous force whose love she perhaps felt she had to earn.

If I cannot know what visions attended my aunt in her cramped living room workshop, I can reenvision rosaries I have known. The rosary of pink beveled beads I wore on my school uniform always felt like a pretend fringe imitating the fringes of the cool late-sixties–early-seventies plastic vest I slunk into after school. The mother-of-pearl rosary *bracelet* that my godmother gave me felt like a chameleon changing colors with my moods—around my wrist now camouflaging, now flashing varying states of mind. A powder blue pair lay nestled like an unexpected toy in the box for storing picks inside my mandolin case. Another pair hung or hovered, a dove on my bedstead, like an amulet. And the sound of beads collapsing into their pouch or into my palm comforted me like the returning retreat of water over pebbles that would not yield to it. I have to admit that saying the Rosary had about the same uninteresting effect as alcohol does on me today—sleep or stupor. If saying the Rosary could, like other meditative practice, encourage openness, alertness, or discipline of mind, I wouldn't know, for my childhood rosaries were more like differently purposed fetishes for me—one for each corner of the room—and less like exercises that properly aligned my soul for the Lord.

If I were a collagist, I could imagine hanging my old rosaries in glass boxes and labeling them with a name for the separate fetishistic purpose they served. On the backdrop that supported them, I would record a script describing the unutterable realities that they tried to keep at bay. Behind the bracelet, for example, I'd record a terrorizing rhyme that members of the Sicilian side of my family would play with me: "Round ball, round ball, pull-ee little hair. One slice, two slice. Tickle under there." While directing this uncanny verse eye-to-eye, the teller would first circle a forefinger into your palm, then tug at a piece of your hair, then slice at *wrist*, at upper arm, and finally tickle under your arm. The verse seemed guaranteed to conjure something, at first to implicate one in a magical ritual, only to later suggest that each part of the rhyme was a red herring, a distraction that gave the teller access to a vulnerable spot. Behind the rosary that doubled as a fringe, I'd write the story of the stomach shred by family violence.

In a related exhibit, I'd display rosaries in which the icons that directed the meditator to funnel her thoughts through Jesus-impaled to Mary-ascended, from martyred son to quintessentially humbled mother, were replaced with common objects that may or may not resonate for the viewer: miniature teabags, telephones, toothbrushes, objects of desire, of bondage, of freedom, of conception and misconception, of moment and of insignificance, with the prayer to be determined by the route the psyche took through the object. (Students could be encouraged to write such rosary poems in creative writing classes.) Vision would be hoped for, and worlds of change.

All is context. In the working-class town where I grew up, wooden rosaries against a nun's habit signify differently than plastic beads on a schoolgirl's uniform. Plastic in itself isn't cool, nor wood warm. Though the rosary was intended for the faithful but unlettered masses, my aunt's decision to spend some important part of her days stringing and positioning beads on wire may not be so far from arranging, as the poet does, words on a line.

There is a shadow in the garden whose source is out of reach. The rosary says you will walk there nevertheless. At the end of a path you will come to a wide circle. Follow it. It may return you to the original path. It may not. Leave the garden gate open as you exit. A poetry that mimicked this would be easy for the part that by some formal arrangement took a reader around and out. Harder though, to make the words cast shadows all the while.

Aunt Josephine did not survive a surgery she was expected to survive. The doctors convinced her to go through with it: they could repair the damage left from a childhood battle with rheumatic fever. Her life would be different. She wouldn't be so tired, so out of breath. Aunt Josephine came out of surgery OK, surprised she had survived, she said, because she "had seen Janice." Several days later, Aunt Josephine died.

II. Notes

It must be understood that the great-grandmother who couldn't stand the thought of the child's body buried under snow associated snow with the foreignness of the country she had migrated to from southern Italy. She disembarked from the boat into Boston harbor snow, the first snow she had ever seen, ever felt. This woman, Josephine Conte, and her only son, John Petracca, my grandfather, came to join the husband and father who was already here. Mother and son fled together but never wholly left behind a great deal of loss: my grandfather was the only one of my great-grandmother's six children to have survived childhood. One wonders if my great-grandmother mourned for herself to see her namesake, my aunt, endure the loss of a child as well.

John Petracca bore the burden of the surviving son and shouldered into adulthood the material losses exacted by the Depression. On a shoemaker's wages he attempted to feed six children of his own. At age thirty-four, in 1934, he started to keep a journal, mostly in English, that began this way:

> From this day February the first of the year of our most Beloved lord, Jesus Christ, 1934, in the middle of my life, I, John Petracca, an obscure cobbler of Llanerch, Pennsylvania, while practicing in order to exist, my trade, taught to me by my loved Uncle, Antonio Conte in Teano have begun to write chronically some of my thoughts.

My grandfather was able to make shoes as well as repair them, and I have very strong memories of the textures, rhythms, and smells that permeated the shop that was attached to his home. He practiced "in order to exist" a number of other arts as well, especially music and writing, a trade he plied daily even though he felt to the end of his life that he failed to serve language well:

> Very hot has been the day but somewhat colder toward evening. Worked all day and earned very little comparing it with the wage that most people receive nowadays. I have bought writing paper to see if I can complete a few of my long ago begun short stories. 'Why do you want to waste time?' You have said. I do not know. I cannot keep away from writing even after realizing I am not able. I cannot spell. I cannot compose. I cannot create. And still I fool myself. I write, write and write. Just for what? That I do not even know! It is perhaps one of those things that cannot be explained neither to oneself. The only consolation that I derive from such undertaking is that I harm none and I am indeed glad!

The musical notes my grandfather scored like beads strung on a wire are what I want to turn to for now though, remembering the passage from his journal: "My mandolin and guitar break my terrible monotony. It is with them that I live, forgetting for the moment my poor social state and live in a world of grandeur all my own!"

When I was ten years old, a series of circumstances, including my grandfather's poor social state, converged to bring me into that world of grandeur. Partly as a scheme to treat my grandfather's material and psychological depression, my mother proposed that he begin to give lessons to me and one of my brothers on mandolin and guitar, respectively. My grandfather wouldn't accept money from his children, even though he was in dire need, unless he rendered them a service such as this. I can't recall how exactly I became the designated mandolinist—my mother asked me if I'd like to try and I said yes?—but I wore the designation from that point on as a kind of privilege and blessing in the familial abode. None of my grandfather's children had learned to play his beloved instrument, so there was a sense that I, a member of the third generation and a female at that, was helping to preserve something from extinction. If the forces of assimilation had wiped any desire for the Italian language from familial consciousness, learning the mandolin stood for a more oblique, symbolic expression of postponing loss. A potential hazard of this might be that it shuttled "things Italian" to a nebulous, untranslatable place— the realm of music—at the same time that it translated the complex of that culture, the culture that was being forgotten, into "feelings" dissevered from intellection. Like my grandfather but differently so, I began to turn to the mandolin for feelings for which there was no outlet nor language in mainstream American culture. The polarizing illusion this fostered was that I was beginning to think in English and feel in Italian. What I could feel in those weekly lessons was a secret to be kept between me, the mandolin, and my grandfather.

Getting to the weekly lessons wasn't easy. My father, who suffered from colitis all of his life, drove like someone desperate for a bathroom, and my mother, who suffered at that time from agoraphobia, made the trip with apparent difficulty. This terrible tension, which I couldn't help perceive even if I couldn't fathom it, would dissipate once we arrived at my grandparents' house. The music really did seem to make people feel better. In the summertime my brother and I had the freedom to take the bus on Wednesday mornings to our lesson, and yet the ride there was still unpleasant. The bus, whose air conditioner was terminally broken, smelled predictably but no less rankly of vomit and body odor. Unlike the adult anxieties that plagued my parents, I "suffered" from a congenital cuteness that, combined with the bright red corduroy mandolin case my grandmother had sewn out of scrap material for me, made it hard to deflect the smiles from strangers who would never see me as the tough tomboy I wanted to be.

The time spent with my grandparents settled upon us like a happy oasis, a glorious routine. After my lesson and while my brother had his, I would pick the herbs and vegetables in the garden that my grandmother would use to make lunch for us. My grandmother's meals were neat as mathematical equations—her sandwiches were perfectly square as though she'd trimmed the edges, even though she hadn't; her fried eggs were perfectly round—and I enjoyed this as an antidote to the fuzzy grasp I had on the numeric aspect of reading music. Occasionally during my lesson my grandmother would emerge from the kitchen to sing or dance. As we prepared to catch the bus, my grandfather would carefully choose now a rose, now a fig, for us to take home from the garden.

Roiling beneath the resplendent color and the quiet forms of those early afternoons was the frustration I experienced in attempting to master the special skills required by the mandolin. As soon as I got home from the lesson, I'd retire to a corner of the basement of our tiny row home, where, sitting on the toy chest with my mandolin, I'd try again to meet the challenge that made the mandolin distinct—its doubled strings and the tremolo that only a limp and nimble wrist could produce. I felt angry with my grandfather, as though he was leaving me with the impossible feat of not only growing wings on my back but making them flutter. Try as I might to make the two strings sound as one, I'd always end up hitting the strings above and below the one I was concentrating on. This, I could tell, would be like learning to keep one's coloring within the lines, and remembering how my colors always spilled over or strayed, I'd abandon the mandolin to the basement and run weeping to my mother: "I can't do it," I'd tell her. "I will never learn the tremolo," I cried. My mother, who at that time was reading Margot Fonteyn's biography and writing poems about Rudolf Nureyev leaping from TV screen into living room "to uplift her to earth," pointed me to the motto inscribed on the front and back cover of the Fonteyn bio: "What a difficult step," she used to say to herself, "I shall never be able to do it."

I did not become the Margot Fonteyn of mandolinists, but I did learn to make nearly beautiful music in the form of solo mandolin, in duet with second mandolin or guitar, and in a quartet consisting of me, my grandfather, my brother, and my grandmother, whom my grandfather had taught to play the guitar in the early days of their marriage even though she never learned to read music. By the end of two years, I could sustain the vast repertoire my grandfather had introduced to me. Tangos, polkas, waltzes, and numerous Italian folk tunes were at the center of our program, but my grandfather had also scored songs like "The Last Rose of Summer," "The Blue Bells of Scotland," and "When Irish Eyes Are Smiling" for the enjoyment of the Scotch-Irish men whom my aunts had married, as well as more intricate, difficult pieces by Haydn and Verdi. Perhaps realizing that I might not carry the mandolin into adolescence unless I could learn to play some music I already recognized, my grandfather made an arrangement of the Beatles' "Yesterday" for me and "Go to the Mirror Boy" from the rock opera *Tommy* for my brother. I had tried, with two of my neighborhood friends, to start a band consisting of mandolin, tambourine, and vocals—we called ourselves "The Bottomless Pits"—but it was clear that no one would be asking us to play our flat melodies at local graduations anytime soon. Another of my friends took to calling my mandolin my "ukelele" (it was the era of Tiny Tim), and I really did feel like an unobliging vaudevillian when a neighborhood mother insisted that my brother and I perform our Italian songs for her Girl Scout troop. At the end of the performance, I received a pin that made me an honorary member. A weirder performance experience I can't recall.

The mandolin is, of course, a staple of American folk music, bluegrass in particular, but perhaps due to the class and ethnic makeup of where we lived, bluegrass never made it to Darby, PA. The mandolin had become for me a very private corner of experience, reserved for dialogue with my immigrant grandfather. In those weekly sessions, I played my heart out, I grew calluses on my fingers, and I felt my jugular vein expand. My grandfather's two major directives to me in his slow, soft voice were "softer, softly," and "slow, slower." Listening to an old recording of myself and my grandmother recently was almost frightening for the seriousness in my child voice. I'm introducing a tune called "Perche Ridere" ("Why Not Laugh?") as though we're about to perform a Wagnerian dirge. The playing is lively and clearly joyous in many parts, but there is an intentness on my part indicative perhaps of a refusal to let the mandolin play me, or of something in excess that the mandolin couldn't meet, or maybe of the sheer difficulty for a child of achieving the modulation necessary to express the qualities of feeling implicit in songs with titles like "Sospiri" and "Valse Pensieroso."

After my third year of lessons with my grandfather and just as I was beginning to learn how to move into second and third positions on the instrument, just as I was entering the public junior high school as a happy egress from Catholic grade school, my grandfather died of the lung cancer that he had lived with in the previous two years. I remember distinctly the day we took my grandfather to the hospital for the last time, for two reasons: he told my uncle what suit he wanted to be laid out in, and my cousin accidentally closed my finger in the car door. It felt as though something had been yanked from me, as though my very body had gotten away from me, it hurt terribly, and I screamed at the top of my lungs.

My grandmother and I continued to play together on occasion, and my brother and I were sometimes coerced into long and frustrating practice sessions together, but for the most part I stopped playing the mandolin after my grandfather died. With my confidante and teacher gone missing, the whole point of the music seemed lost. Many years later, in my tenure year as an academic, I felt drawn to the mandolin again. I had seen a short and wonderful Canadian film entitled "When Shirley Met Florence," in which the special lifelong friendship between two Jewish women, one of whom was a lesbian, was documented. Among other things the women shared, they played gorgeous duets together on mandolin and guitar. It made me see again what was possible with this instrument, and I momentarily considered starting to take lessons again. I do believe that there is more to be found, some resource for a marginalized poetics lurking in my grandfather's musical scores and in this instrument that continues to seem incongruous on the American scene (to this day, my partner wrongly or wryly refers to my mandolin as my "banjo"). There's something more there than a temporarily nostalgic kitschy salve to midlife crisis.

Once per year my grandfather gave me a book of ready-made mandolin music, but most of the time he wrote out each week's self-devised lessons and their accompanying songs. The music he marked wasn't of the fast and furious, dots-and-dashes, fountain pen variety. His notes, formed with a ballpoint, appeared as though he first sculpted them, then inlaid them onto the page or positioned them, collage-like, as in the manner of a Cornell box. G-clefs tilt toward unexpected concatenations of spheres; some steady o's suspended outside gravity, some flecked like meteors, others held upright like pods on their stems; one or two vibrating rattles and every now and then a word advancing or receding: "first lesson to," "June 18, 1970," "staccato," "legato," "half," "quarter," "whole," "to my granddaughter, Mimi." Like Cornell, too, my grandfather hoped a child would be willing to handle the box, to shake it and draw it to her ear, to tilt and balance it on head, shoulder, crook of arm, knee.

How might the practice of scoring music in the form of lessons like this help to navigate loss? You lay something down like so many railroad ties, the staff; you fill something in, like birds or silence moving between the tracks; you wait patiently for yourself or your student to catch up to the movement, to learn its always unexpected time. My grandfather gave me hand-hewn orbs—opened, closed, half-moons, full, eclipsed—so that my fingers pressed to fret could feel something solid, touch something outside me; they could sound, and I could hear the sound, feel it echoed in my belly. But the distinction of the mandolin again is its doubled strings, added to which my grandfather ever encouraged the power and beauty of the duet, as if to say keep your ears open to your friend and, whenever possible, don't scream above her need for you. Like the rosary's play between ground and mystery, solidity and flight, the mandolin called for a two-tiered mobility; but maybe the real trick of bringing out the instrument's sweetness was to play in such a way as not to foster the illusion that the two strings were one.

On the tape of my grandmother and me playing together, there is much less of my grandparents' voices than I would like. They wanted to make a professional-sounding recording, as though nothing but music, not even ourselves, filled the room. Early on the tape there is a snippet of dialogue that I cling to, in which they seem to be saying the same thing but need each other both to say it and to mean it differently:

Grandmother: "Well, that was pretty good."
Grandfather: "It *is* pretty good, isn't it, Rose?
Grandmother: "I think it sounds pretty good, don't you, John?"
Grandfather: "Oh yes."

III. Sprockets and Frames

> It is the 8mm movie that will save us.
> —Jonas Mekas

My great-uncle, Antonio Polidori, husband to grandmother Rose's sister Anne, filled the house that he designed and constructed, aided by his only child, Richard, with novel forms of kitsch. If Aunt Josephine improvised on ready-made kits, Uncle Tony improvised on nature. Such craftings started in his lushly surreal garden, which, though typically appointed with rosebushes and wine-bearing grape arbor Italian American style, also featured trees that bore two kinds of fruit (the result of my uncle's experimental graftings) and unusual plants whose otherworldly bounty my uncle plucked, painted, carved, and decorated to fill a collection of unearthly delights. One plant yielded nothing but seed pods, which, in my uncle's hands, came to resemble birds whose beaks, now clearly tilted to sing, curled around almost to meet their heads. Two dashes of pipe cleaner simulated feet, sequins, eyes. Other plants gave way to gourds ranging in size and shape but mostly pearlike, which my uncle hollowed out to fill with Xmas tableaux or which he reshaped and painted to serve as makeshift musical instruments—mostly crookedly wandering tubular horns intended for parties or parades.

In the basement of his spectacular house, suffused with the light of wide windows reminiscent of Frank Lloyd Wright designs and reflecting the tiles from the outside walkways that he'd painted in harlequin costume colors, my uncle, I'm told, *made* fantastic parties, hung photo collages, and invited friends to screen his latest home movies. By the time I got to know my uncle, in my childhood of the sixties and early seventies, he no longer threw parties, but he did occasionally rescreen his home movies. The parties came to an abrupt end (even though his filmmaking continued) after his son, Richard, aged twenty-one, was killed in a car accident. On Father's Day 1953, my uncle received a telegram from Louisiana, where the accident occurred, informing him of the death of his son.

Uncle Tony had purchased his 16mm wind-up camera at that cultural moment that made such surplus equipment available to amateurs after World War II. In 1950, following a calling from his mother to visit her in Italy, he purchased the camera and made the trip and his first films. (When he returned to the States from his trip, his mother died.) One such film consists entirely of a series of mostly 1950s family weddings, spliced together to form a nearly unbroken chain of ladyfinger yellow, apricot, dusty lavender, or pink flamingo–colored gowns. In ritualistic fashion my uncle brought each wedding troupe to his house and filmed them parading past house and garden in different seasons.

The films instigate feelings that I can only tentatively approach. I feel strange and excited on a cold, dark January evening on a visit with my lover to see if we can convince my ninety-year-old aunt to bring out the films. She is unable to run the projector, but my lover is willing to perform the intricate threading, and we both agree to take responsibility should the film break from brittleness. I need to see those films, knowing full well that my uncle would not document my life, the life of his lesbian niece, even though he treated me dearly if not exactly "tenderly" as a child. (When we visited, he'd squeeze me practically breathless, until once I told him, "Don't squeeze me. I'm not a lemon." Tickled by a four-year-old's metaphor, he greeted me with this refrain whenever I saw him thereafter.)

Much of the wedding-day footage my uncle shot suffuses me with a sense of its subjects' vulnerability. Viewing my relatives on this day of particular consequence and compulsory witness,[2] in a youthful moment, prim and blissfully regaled, I am reminded of the forms of loss and harm outside the purview of the frame that they could never have anticipated. In one frame my aunt Frances, her new husband, and their winter wedding party parade before Uncle Tony's house, but the line is broken by a blonde child who walks beside them rather than behind them. At another wedding, one where the camera seems wandering, at loose ends, with the crowd merely humoring the filmmaker, a wide-smiling and waving Aunt Frances in a bright pink jacket erupts within the frame, consolingly. Now I read the child in the first frame as a knowing angel, an accompanist out of order, for my aunt Frances suffered from undiagnosed mental disorders all of her life and died in her early forties from a combination of kidney failure and depression. My mother wanted me as company to visit her in intensive care, but I was ever after plagued by images of my aunt's help-lessness as she coughed up blood into a respirator tube. Especially diffi-cult to view is the wedding of the cousin whose future will yield a son gruesomely murdered by a stranger who plucked the child from a hotel hallway where the family was vacationing, then slit the child's throat atop a Bible as though the child were a sacrificial lamb.

At moments like these, when the film seems rife with the threat of something as simple as its figures' missed steps or something much less comprehensible and dark, I concentrate on the sound of the projector's motor. Worn from disuse, the motor revs like an electric mixer at different speeds, until the film's images appear light as egg whites that bubble and bulge and dissolve.

Like the making of beads and musical scores, my uncle's wedding films are about linkage—in this case, a steady, virtually uninterrupted stream of domesticating ceremony. They are about longing and creativity and the missing. Sprocket holes and frames are crudely yet painstakingly spliced to fabricate continuity: picture the filmmaker as master of ceremonies pulling endless strings of lights out from within his long sleeve.

Banal and repetitive as these films might seem, there is really too much going on in them. The first sixty seconds alone—a passage from Aunt Josephine's wedding—offer a montage of eerily ethnographic acts that seem to document the struggle to be seen. It appears that my grandfather has been directed to encourage his mother to face the camera. Arm in arm, they begin slowly to approach Uncle Tony's seeing eye. Grandmother Rose pushes her way from the back of their crowded driveway toward the couple until she too is included in this bewilderingly slow-moving march of elders, who seem drawn toward the camera as though by magnetism. At this point a child runs out from the crowd and places herself squarely between the camera and Great-grandmother, whose head now appears to be perched atop the child's body. The whole scene is lit by a backdrop of rows of moving orchids on women's lapels. The child and others act as though they expect to see something in the camera's lens. The child jerks her head around, answering no doubt to a reprimanding call, bends, curt-sies, and, facing the camera, puts a finger to her mouth as if to say "ssshhh." This scene is followed by the only shot of Uncle Tony in the entire wedding montage, in profile, apart, casually picking his tooth. The footage of this wedding then concludes with a shot of a child, one knee bent and arms outspread, who clearly seems to be mimicking Al Jolson.[3]

Uncle Tony's wedding montage moves from random and self-impelled theatrics like these toward his orderly arrangement of parading wedding parties before his house, only to end with a camera that begins to wander when his subjects, now moving into the 1960s, begin to misbehave. The most deliberate attempt to create a kind of silent film narration, though, occurs at a point where the filmmaker trains his camera toward a corner of his front yard and house, then pans from left to right as if accidentally to happen upon or "find" a wedding party there: a photographer poised like a tai chi instructor bends to arrange the couple and his camera, a small cluster of the wedding party comes into view, and then the houses and moving cars and yards of the neighborhood as a whole. This is followed by two more pans beginning at the same point, that corner of the house, but each time taking in more of a sweep of the neighborhood and each time finding the photographer, couple, and party cluster at a different, later, slightly altered, and seemingly similar moment in time.

Here I see my uncle using the camera like a paintbrush, with each pan equal to one thin stroke of paint laid upon another until, out of these layered repetitions, a thickness, or difference, or presence emerges. It's an art that moves neither horizontally nor vertically but at the point where those axes cross over. It's not about direction or chronology—the passage of time through which loss keeps track of us—but space and its voluble dimensions. There are two other places in the film where forms become or assert themselves like this—unconstrained, what I want to call moments of lyrical condensation—where the form's appearance, so perfect and seductive and full of play, seems thoroughly accidental but whose inclusion in the frame exists, I am sure, by virtue of my uncle's having found, of his having fully sighted, an object, usually marginal to the subject at hand, that corresponded to something in his heart. These brief poetic films within the film could be called "The Red Hat" and "The Blue Ribbon."

A wedding party assembles in tiered rows on the front steps of the church it is exiting. In the bottom right corner a mother adjusts a headpiece on a child. The camera catches the wedding party center but soon begins to roam outside its periphery to the left, roaming uncertainly until a woman's hand holding a hat onto the back of her head, a ruby red hat, comes into the frame, shot from behind. Suddenly, the camera seems to be shooting from above, from higher ground. The camera is, for the first time, still while the red hat threads a needle through the crowd, and it is as though everyone, without knowing it, is in thrall to the hat, each person having imperceptibly moved aside to let the red-hatted woman (does it matter that it belongs to my aunt Frances?) through and around and out, and she is waving, waving.

In the very next frame—now my parents' wedding—the party begins its regular procession around my uncle's gracefully ascending stone-tiered garden plots and toward the front of his house, but a blue ribbon interrupts the lens. It flutters and snaps unpredictably; now it is pocked, now dimpled; once a corrugated ribbon, again a sprocketed loop of fabric like a loosed piece of film itself. It runs fast and free along an edge of sky, it laps the hard edge of Uncle Tony's house, it randomly, hilariously anoints the heads of promenaders. Suddenly out of scale with what surrounds it, it's a stray bell cord demanding an immense strength to make its clapper crack like lightning, a bell peal to sound its unpremeditated chord. And who can tell if the sound will satisfy, sweetly greet, alarm, or change who hears it?

Perhaps my uncle sought to weave such immediate, telling movements into his films—the red hat, the blue ribbon—sooner rather than later after his son's death, for these two films were made just outside a year of that trauma. It's as though he postponed his grieving as withdrawal in favor of a passionate intensity for exteriorized, sharable, and supple visualization. Of course, the real staple of the wedding films is that structure my uncle had made with his son—the house. Sometimes the wedding films seem less about any particular church-sanctioned coupling than about the materializing of the house that Uncle Tony designed and built. In this sense, my uncle's films fit squarely within the bourgeois impulses of 1950s home movies—as odes to the middle class house and its nuclear family.[4]

Better off than his working-class relatives, my uncle could be seen as meanly showing up each wedding party, recorded for posterity, backdropped by his house. Contrary to what another family member might recall—that Uncle Tony was mean—I found him to be mostly extraordinarily playful, though a number of competing impulses might have been mixed into his forms of play. If Uncle Tony turns his camera in the direction of his house again and again, he might be laughing at or weeping for what it fails to hold, no child at its nucleus. More hollow, more symbolic than this visceral loss, though, is the missing *church* that haunts these films. In an obvious way, I mean the extent to which his house upstaged the church as wedding proscenium. But there is also an untold family story lurking here like a ghost to the movies.

My great-grandfather (Uncle Tony's father-in-law) had, as my grandmother used to put it, a good deal of property "on the other side." She didn't mean by this the extraterrestrial heavens but the Campobassan region of Italy. When she was a child, her father's longtime altar boy partner (now a priest), wrote to him from Italy to tell him of unfunded plans to expand the town church. This church, that had memorialized the moment that "our Lord was taken down from the cross and put in the Blessed Mother's arms," needed, for reasons left untold, to be made into a cathedral. The church's symbolic patronage originated in a vision that had "come to a peasant on top of a mountain," my grandmother once explained to me, and she had "poetry" at home to prove it. My great-grandfather directed his childhood friend to sell all of the property he had left in Italy and to "do what you have to do to the church." Once the church was rebuilt, the clergy "went to the trouble," as my grandmother put it, to offer to pay for my great-grandfather's boat fare back to Italy, where they would make a banquet and parade in his honor. My great-grandfather declined the invitation, so they asked instead for a photo of him that they would place in the foyer of the cathedral among pictures of the church's founders. On Uncle Tony's 1950 trip to see *his* mother, he traveled as well to the cathedral of his in-laws, camera in hand. What he found instead and what he filmed were a grassy knoll and piles of rubble where once had stood the cathedral destroyed in World War II. Fifty years later, I am confronted with a double vacancy, for, while all of Uncle Tony's film reels are carefully labeled and securely stowed, the canister marked "Italy" is empty: the film of the vacant lot that was once a church that was made in place of a home in Italy, the film of his trip to see his mother, appears to be lost.

Convinced of my uncle's playfulness and missing it, I picture him inviting me to play a game. I am supposed to find the missing reel, which may mean learning to travel as easily as he did to old places, to new places. I am to make a pie in the film tin and feed it to those bright red birds called cardinals. I am to make a pinwheel of the void.

Once I had explained to my uncle that I wasn't a lemon (or for that matter a red hat or blue ribbon), he stopped squeezing me. Instead, he gave me back my metaphor with a smile each time I saw him. Rather than confuse me with one of his lost objects, he might come to recognize me as a fellow artisan, a cohort in kitsch. In the rapid passage of holes that perforate some frames of his film, I can almost make out words, and beyond them, poems.

IV. Poems

> Forensics establishes which is that they will rather than linger
> and so they establish.
> —Gertrude Stein[5]

By now it must be clear that this essay is as much about my own struggles with loss as it is about the lifelines forged between emptiness and creativity in the lives of my relatives. The drive to return to my great-uncle's home movies was certainly enabled by what I had been learning about the poetry of super-8 and 16mm film from a new colleague, friend, and mentor in and around 1992—the well-known experimental filmmaker, Marjorie Keller. Marjorie, a magnetic, serene, immensely generous, and resourceful woman, died suddenly of no discernible cause in the middle of a February night in 1994 on a trip with her three-year-old twin daughters to visit her parents in Florida. I read and record the coroner's words, reported in a Providence newspaper, with difficulty: "I have looked at the entire body, both at the autopsy, when we first did the autopsy, and at microscopic sections of different sections. I see no abnormality." She was in her early forties. My partner had talked with Marjorie, who spoke enthusiastically of her sabbatical projects and a feeling of well-being, just a few days before on the telephone. I would, I had thought, speak with her when she returned from Florida.

I tried to rationalize the cruel inexplicability of Marjorie's death, especially in light of the loss that her daughters must face, the loss of an utterly devoted, creative—to say nothing of "together"—mother: I told myself there was another world where harder work was called for, a world worse even than our own, that needed Marjorie even more than her three-year-old twins needed her. And Marjorie, as a generous, gifted visionary was called to that other world's need. None of this made any more sense than an event that placed itself before me at this time—like those scenes that Uncle Tony only seemed to happen upon—that soon became the basis of a symbolizing process that might make its way to poetry.

On a foggy and dark morning in early March of 1994, the rain outside sounds like a bath filling with water. I drive to school hoping for comfort but feeling unbearably heavy, until I am buoyed up by the scene of silver buckets attached to maple trees. The trees, the buckets, the winter harvester who placed them there all seem to augur a season of sweetness to come. I am tempted to go home for lunch, the way I did in elementary school, and when I arrive, there is a package from my mother that includes among its enclosures a postcard of a painting by Horace Pippin, *Maple Sugar Season* (1941), picturing the very scene I had witnessed in the morning: the trees, the buckets, the leaf-shaped footprints of the sap gatherer in snow. Pippin's footprints read like the palm of the sap gatherer, a portrait of him established by overlapping traces, deliberate steps, meandering stops and starts. It's not that I thought my mourning was taking me into a mystic circle of the synchronous but that I read the coincidence as a gift. I was struck by the idea of parallel witness—myself, my mother, Pippin—and from that day began to record such doublings in a notebook, with the thought that at the end of a very long time, one year, two years, my collection might lead to a poem.

A number of the doublings were linguistic, for example, hearing twice in a day the same phrase, "Caesar crossing the Rubicon"; the place-name "Bountiful, Utah"; the odd adjective "Lovecraftian." Others started as dreams that met up with experiences the next day: I dream that I must perform a flamenco dance. The dress and shoes are prepared. I can't remember if I know how to dance flamenco—of course I do?—if worse comes to worst, I'll improvise. The next day, I click on the car radio, and flamenco is playing. I can see the black shoes, the red dress, the upright posture, the red-brown floor. Some doublings were very literal, like finding a twin bloom on a magenta-colored daisy plant. Others were more metaphoric or associative, as in the example of cognate afterimages. When I close my eyes, I see the foliage in my garden: green stems, green leaves; when I close my eyes, I see the concert pianist's green dress. Or watching the splendid velocity, slow, of my eight-year-old nephew's bowling ball as it approaches and then ever so tentatively fells the pins. His T-shirt askew on his shoulder. The ball reminiscent of a silver-marbled bluefish hanging from a mobile in the doctor's office. Some doubles were surreal, as in the way an idle hair tie is always accompanied by a penny lying around the house, while others were very social, having emerged as the unexpected meeting point in conversation.

I also began to notice what other poets had to say about the number two. In Lyn Hejinian's *My Life*, "Reason looks for two, then arranges it from there." Brenda Hillman, in her deeply stirring, wise, and beautiful book on the sudden loss of a female friend and mentor, had written: "and I wanted to hear just one voice / but I heard two, / wanted to be just one thing, but I was several" (*Death Tractates*). Robert Hass, quoting Leonard Bernstein, had said: "Two is the rhythm of the body; three is the rhythm of the mind" (125), and in his own words, "Two is an exchange; three is a circle of energy" (130). The clinician Robert Jay Lifton, on trauma again, had spoken of psychological "doubling in the service of survival" (Caruth 137). What I thought I was searching for in my gatherings of two was a meeting place and a hunger—the breaking of a fast. An ambidextrous art. And yet I hoped to resist the idea of two equaling a kind of natural balance or easy, longed-for harmony: vision being equivalent to the practice of making two eyes work as though they were one, the importance of acknowledging that one leg was longer than the other. Partly, I was trying to love chance meetings or the stark contrasts that happen within an hour of one's life. It wasn't a likeness I was in search of, but the shadow cast by letters, language's light. I realized my emphasis on two was overdetermined: a search for a poetics based on the technique of tremolo, a grief for a pair of girl twins, a longing for the double movement of the rosary, a distinction between reassuring repetitions and the repetitions beyond our control: that the day on which the news was heard will return to meet itself into eternity. Wanting to learn to treat each day as something other than an anniversary.

My poem is not ready yet. It seems to need multiple voices and a form of orchestration. It seems to want to be a collage, but there's a question of whether I need to know more about traditions of collage or if I can use my family's forms of juxtaposition to make it so, those hidden resources I spoke of from the outset. For now, I have this writing and the way in conversation it has led others to share with me their rosary beads, or prayer beads, or worry beads, and with every set a story of secret pleasure or secret pain. And I keep pulling more rosaries out of memory's sleeve. Perched at the end of the dinner table that my father regularly overturned once sat a plastic rosary container with the kitschy rhyme: "The family that prays together, stays together." For a spell in our hot, short kitchen, my mother had us try to say the Rosary together after meals. It was a desperate time; and as I recall, the rosary gig didn't last too long, for it failed to calm my father, and it paralyzed us.

A separate, recent event helps me to see it from a different angle. I'm on a crowded lake beach outside the city of Providence in northern Rhode Island. It doesn't have the charms of seclusion held by the southern beaches, and here there's no surf to drown the noise of one's neighbors. I'm finding the number of people, the volume of squeals overwhelming, claustrophobic. It's clear I won't be able to read here or to rest. Suddenly, whistles are blaring and muscled men and women are pounding furiously, running in one direction on the tiny beach. They've ordered everyone out of the water and have announced a missing child, nine-year-old Jamie, her ponytail, her flowered swimsuit. Hand to hand, they've linked themselves to form a human chain as they walk the length of the lake, suspecting the missing girl has drowned. Behind my sunglasses I am crying. I can't seem to stop my tears. Midway down the length of the roped-in swimming area, the searchers are halted by a voice from the loudspeaker announcing a "positive I.D." Jamie has been found frolicking by a hidden corner of the concession stand. My tears, I sadly realize, are partly tears of surprise and relief that other people will look for you if you are lost. They will make of themselves a rosary. Rather than say the Rosary, my family should have gone for walks hand in hand. We should have walked and walked.

Notes

. . . .

1. The traumas that Lifton is working from are, of course, more cataclysmic than the loss of a child to "natural causes"—such brutal humanly determined devastations as Hiroshima and the Holocaust. The psychoanalytic insights he provides are, I believe, applicable (without being exactly "universal") to a range of traumatic experience.

2. I have in mind Andrew Parker and Eve Sedgwick's insights on the wedding ceremony as performative: "It is the constitution of a community of witness that makes the marriage; the silence of witness (we don't speak now, we forever hold our peace) that permits it; the bare, negative, potent but undiscretionary speech act of our physical presence—maybe even *especially* the presence of those people whom the institution of marriage defines itself by excluding—that ratifies and recruits the legitimacy of its privilege" (11).

3. This image is striking to me as a trace of what Michael Rogin discusses in *Black Face, White Noise* as the obligatory passage of certain ethnics through blackface toward assimilation in United States culture.

4. Zimmermann notes that "in the 1950s the position, function and definition of amateur film shifted from aesthetics and technology into a social configuration exclusively administrating bourgeois, nuclear family ideologies" (111).

5. I encountered the quotation in Alicia Ostriker's introduction to Giannina Braschi's *Empire of Dreams*: "To claim or demand a structure is a form of argument, which is what Braschi scrupulously avoids. As Gertrude Stein puts it, 'Forensics establishes which is that they will rather than linger and so they establish.' The reader of Braschi may prefer to linger longer and establish less" (xv).

References

Austin, J. L. *How to Do Things with Words.* Cambridge, Mass.: Harvard University Press, 1994.

Calinescu, Matei. *Faces of Modernity: Avant-garde, Decadence, Kitsch.* Bloomington: Indiana University Press, 1977.

Caruth, Cathy. "An Interview with Robert Jay Lifton." *Trauma: Explorations in Memory.* Ed. Cathy Caruth. Baltimore: Johns Hopkins University Press, 1995.

Hass, Robert. *Twentieth Century Pleasures: Prose on Poetry.* New York: Ecco Press, 1984.

Hejinian, Lyn. *My Life.* Los Angeles: Sun and Moon Press, 1987.

Hillman, Brenda. *Death Tractates.* Hanover, N.H.: Wesleyan University Press/University Press of New England, 1992.

Mekas, Jonas. *Movie Journal: The Rise of the New American Cinema, 1959–1971.* New York: Macmillan, 1972.

"On Kitsch: A Symposium." *Salmagundi* Winter/Spring 1990: 197–312.

Ostriker, Alicia. Introduction. *Empire of Dreams.* By Giannina Braschi. New Haven: Yale University Press, 1994.

Parker, Andrew, and Eve Kosofsky Sedgwick, eds. *Performativity and Performance.* New York: Routledge, 1995.

Rogin, Michael. *Black Face, White Noise: Jewish Immigrants in the Hollywood Melting Pot.* Berkeley: University of California Press, 1996.

Zimmermann, Patricia R. *Reel Families: A Social History of Amateur Film.* Bloomington: Indiana University Press, 1995.

John Agresto

What Grandma Knew

Every now and then, my very Italian grandmother would embarrass me greatly. Once I had my colleague from graduate school and his fiancée over for dinner. Looking at the woman my grandmother began the quiz: "You Italian?" (The young woman was nearly six foot, blonde, with green eyes, but Grandma was never much of a noticer.) "No." "You Irish?" "No." "You Jewish?" "No." "You Portuguese?" "No . . . I guess I'm part German, part Scandinavian, maybe some Russian, mostly just a mix of things." Downcast eyes, turned head. My grandmother then said softly: "How terrible not to be somebody."

To my grandmother it didn't matter all that much what you were, so long as you were somebody. Sure, Italians were better—no cultural relativist she. But really any answer was fine, so long as there was an answer. It mean you were a whole person, and she was happy for you.

This blend of seeing and not seeing this hope that everyone could be somebody—to be rooted, to have traditions, to live off the capital of ancestors—and still not have that ethnicity matter for the public, for citizenship, for friendship, struck me as an important American truth. America was for everyone regardless of origins, yet a place where origins were respected, even admired. One's heritage was both personally central and interpersonally irrelevant.

I remember, going back even more years, a public service jingle that would regularly come on TV between the Farmer Gray cartoons. I think I remember it exactly:

> An -off, a -ski, a -witz or -cou when added to a name
> Just teaches you the family or town from which he came.
> A name like Jefferson in some land o'er the sea

Would not be Thomas Jefferson but Thomas Jefferski,
Or Jefferoff or Jefferwitz or maybe Jeffercou,
So do not let a -ski or -witz or -cou seem strange to you.
I feel the same toward every name no matter how it ends
For people with the strangest names can be the best of friends.

Now, this says a number of true things. First, that I watched far too much TV when I was young. Second, that we have to find ways of being both respectful of and oblivious to ethnicity. It matters greatly, and it fundamentally doesn't matter at all.

Why we should respect ethnicity—or race or heritage—is fairly clear. We can talk about the enrichment ethnicity brings to both our personal and national lives. Beyond the silly and superficial habit we have of reducing ethnicity to food, heritage adds interest, charm, and above all, diversity of outlook, talents, and ways of life to country and depth and relation to our private lives. Like religion, ethnicity helps form our character and shape our horizons.

But the analogy to religion is even more apt because, like religion, ethnicity both collects and divides us. It separates us from others as it connects us to our own. And ethnicity combined with nationalism promises to be *the* centrifugal international force of the next decade.

We are not without those tendencies in America. For all their personal benefits, the antagonisms that grow out of race and heritage are still far stronger than the antagonisms of sector or class and often stronger than forces that unite us.

This is, of course, a major public policy issue. We tried for years to solve the problems by promoting the idea of the "melting pot." All would become American without the cutting distinctions of the Old World. To a real degree, it worked. Ethnic names were anglicized. Jews married Christians; Italians married Irish; French married Germans or Russians or English. We became, in the awful, virtually all-encompassing category used here in New Mexico, "Anglos"—even if you were originally Greek, Chinese, or Bulgarian. I even know Sicilians back east who are referred to as WASPs.

But the melting pot idea, well intentioned as it was, did not, could not, fully dissolve the real solidity of ethnicity. Third generations become more ethnic than their parents. Race and roots have now attained heightened significance. "Diversity" has become the rage.

This newfound attachment to "diversity" and "multiculturalism" has both educational and public policy consequences, some of them quite deleterious. Race and ethnicity have recently so captured the minds of leaders of higher education that one would think that dwelling on diversity is the core of a liberal education. It isn't. Indeed, more often than not, the call for multiculturalism and diversity has less to do with an honest examination of differing intellectual traditions than it does with using race and ethnicity as the latest handy weapon with which to beat up Western civilization. But political movements do not masquerade well in academic guise.

In the political realm proper, race and ethnicity have also become heightened, moving us from respect to empowerment, from blindness to preference. As with the rest of the world, where racial and national divisions have become the center of political life, we run the risk of so dwelling on race and nationality that we forget the idea that we can respect origins yet act regardless of origins. In dwelling on race and ethnicity, we risk releasing the ugliest aspects of ethnic and racial divisions. As with privileging certain religions, racial and ethnic preference is both wrong in principle and deadly in practice.

Still, to listen to the pundits, one would think the view that ethnicity is both personally important as well as socially irrelevant is impossible. Maybe it is, though I doubt it. All I know is that it was a principle my grandmother understood.

Marianna De Marco Torgovnick

. . . .

On Being White, Female, and Born in Bensonhurst

The Mafia protects the neighborhood, our fathers say, with that peculiar satisfied pride with which law-abiding Italian Americans refer to the Mafia: the Mafia protects "the neighborhood" from "the coloreds." In the fifties and sixties, I heard that information repeated, in whispers, in neighborhood parks and in the yard at school in Bensonhurst. The same information probably passes today in the parks (the word now "blacks," not "coloreds") but perhaps no longer in the school yards. From buses each morning, from neighborhoods outside Bensonhurst, spill children of all colors and backgrounds—American black, West Indian black, Hispanic, and Asian. But the blacks are the ones especially marked for notice. Bensonhurst is no longer entirely protected from "the coloreds." But in a deeper sense, at least for Italian Americans, Bensonhurst never changes.

Italian American life continues pretty much as I remember it. Families with young children live side by side with older couples whose children are long gone to the suburbs. Many of those families live "down the block" from the previous generation or, sometimes still, live together with parents or grandparents. When a young family leaves, as sometimes happens, for Long Island or New Jersey or (very common now) Staten Island, another arrives, without any special effort being required, from Italy or from a poorer neighborhood in New York. They fill the neat but anonymous houses along the mostly tree-lined streets: two-, three-, or four-family houses for the most part (this is a working-class area, and people need rents to pay mortgages), with a few single-family or small apartment houses tossed in at random. Tomato plants, fig trees, and plaster madonnas often decorate small but well-tended yards that face out onto the street; the grassy front lawn, like the grassy backyard, are relatively un-common.

Crisscrossing the neighborhood and marking out ethnic zones—Ital-ian, Irish, and Jewish, for the most part, though there are some Asian Americans and some people (usually Protestants) called simply Ameri-cans—are the great shopping streets: Eighty-sixth Street, Kings Highway, Bay Parkway, Twentieth Avenue, Eighteenth Avenue, each with its own distinctive character. On Eighty-sixth Street, crowds bustle along side-walks lined with ample vegetable and fruit stands. Women wheeling shop-ping carts or baby strollers check the fruit carefully, piece by piece, and bargain with the dealer, cajoling for a better price or letting him know that the vegetables, this time, aren't up to snuff. A few blocks down, the fruit stands are gone and the streets are lined by clothing and record shops, mobbed by teenagers. Occasionally, the elevated train ("the El") rumbles overhead, a few stops out of Coney Island on its way to "the city," a trip of around one hour.

On summer nights, neighbors congregate on "stoops" that during the day serve as play yards for children. Air-conditioning exists everywhere in Bensonhurst, but people still sit outside in the summer—to supervise children, to gossip, to stare at strangers. "Buona sera," I say, or "Buona notte," as I am ritually presented to Sal and Lily and Louie: the neighbors, sitting on the stoop. "Grazie," I say when they praise my children or my appearance. It's the only time I use Italian, which I learned at high school, although my parents (both first-generation Italian Americans, my father Sicilian, mother Calabrian) speak it at home, to each other, but never to me or my brother. My accent is the Tuscan accent taught at school, not the southern Italian accents of my parents and the neighbors.

It's important to greet and please the neighbors; any break in this deco-rum would serious offend and aggrieve my parents. For the neighbors are second only to family in Bensonhurst and serve as stern arbiters of con-duct. Does Lucy keep a clean house? Did Anna wear black long enough after her mother's death? Was the food good at Tony's wedding? The neighbors know and pass judgment. Any news of family scandal (my brother's divorces, for example) provokes from my mother the agonized words: "But what will I tell *people?*" I sometimes collaborate in devising a plausible script.

A large sign on the church I attended as a child sums up for me the ethos of neighborhoods like Bensonhurst. The sign urges contributions to the church building fund with the message, in huge letters: "EACH YEAR THIS CHURCH SAVES THIS NEIGHBORHOOD ONE MILLION DOLLARS IN TAXES."

Passing the church on the way from largely Jewish and middle-class Sheepshead Bay (where my husband grew up) to Bensonhurst, year after year, my husband and I look for the sign and laugh at the crass level of its pitch, its utter lack of attention to things spiritual. But we also understand *exactly* the values it represents.

In the summer of 1989, my parents were visiting me at my house in Durham, North Carolina, from the apartment in Bensonhurst where they had lived since 1942, ever since the day they had wed: three small rooms, rent-controlled, floor clean enough to eat off, every corner and crevice known and organized. My parents' longevity in a single apartment is unusual even for Bensonhurst but not that unusual; many people live for decades in the same place or move within a ten-block radius. When I lived in this apartment, there were four rooms; one has since been ceded to a demanding "landlord," one of the various "landlords" who have haunted my parents' life and must always be appeased lest the ultimate threat—removal from the rent-controlled apartment—be brought into play. That summer, during the time of their visit, on August 23 (my younger daughter's birthday), a shocking, disturbing news report issued from "the neighborhood": it had become another Howard Beach.

Three black men, walking casually through the streets at night, were attacked by a much larger group of whites. One was shot dead, mistaken, as it turned out, for another black youth who was dating a white, although part-Hispanic, girl in the neighborhood. It all made sense: the crudely protective men, expecting to see a black arriving at the girls' house and overreacting; the rebellious girl dating the outsider boy; the black dead as a sacrifice to the feelings of "the neighborhood."

I might have felt outrage, I might have felt guilt or shame, I might have despised the people among whom I grew up; in a way I felt all four emotions when I heard the news. I expect that there were many people in Bensonhurst itself who felt the same rush of emotions. But mostly I felt that, given the setup, this was the only way things could have happened. I detested the racial killing, but I also understood it. Those streets, which should be public property, belong to "the neighborhood." All the people sitting on the stoops on August 23 knew that as well as they knew their own names. The black men walking through probably knew it too—though their casual walk sought to deny the fact that, for the neighbors, even the simple act of blacks walking through "the neighborhood" would be seen as invasion.

Italian Americans in Bensonhurst are notable for their cohesiveness and provinciality; the slightest pressure turns those qualities into prejudice and racism. Their cohesiveness is based on the stable economic and ethical level that links generation to generation, keeping Italian Americans in Bensonhurst and the Italian American community alive, as the Jewish American community of my youth is no longer alive. (Its young people routinely moved to the suburbs or beyond and were never replaced, so Jews in Bensonhurst today are almost all very old people.) Their provinciality results from the Italian Americans' devotion to jealous distinctions and discriminations. Jews are suspect, but (the old Italian women admit) "they make good husbands." The Irish are okay, fellow Catholics, but not really "like us"; they make bad husbands because they drink and gamble. Even Italians come in varieties by region (Sicilian, Calabrian, Neapolitan, very rarely any region further north) and by history in this country (the newly arrived and ridiculed "gaffoon" versus the first or second generation).

Bensonhurst is a neighborhood dedicated to believing that its values are the only values; it tends toward certain forms of inertia. When my parents visit me in Durham, they routinely take chairs from the kitchen and sit out on the lawn in front of the house, not on the chairs on the back deck; then they complain that the streets are too quiet. When they walk around my neighborhood and look at the mailboxes, they report (these De Marcos descended from Cozzitortos, who have friends named Travaglianti and Pelliccioni) that my neighbors have strange names. Prices at my local supermarket are compared, in unbelievable detail, with prices on Eighty-sixth Street. Any rearrangement of my kitchen since their last visit is registered and criticized. Difference is not only unwelcome, it is unacceptable. One of the most characteristic things my mother ever said was in response to my plans for renovating my house in Durham. When she heard my plans, she looked around, crossed her arms, and said, "If it was me, I wouldn't change nothing." My father once asked me to level with him about a Jewish boyfriend, who lived in a different portion of the neighborhood, reacting to his Jewishness but even more to the fact that he often wore Bermuda shorts: "Tell me something, Marianna. Is he a Communist?" Such are the standards of normalcy and political thinking in Bensonhurst.

I often think that one important difference between Italian Americans in neighborhoods like Bensonhurst and Italian Americans elsewhere is that the others moved on—to upstate New York, to Pennsylvania, to the

Midwest. Though they often settled in communities of fellow Italians, they moved on. Bensonhurst Italian Americans seem to have felt that one large move, over the ocean, was enough. Future moves could only be local: from the Lower East Side, say, to Brooklyn, or from one part of Brooklyn to another. Bensonhurst was for many of these people the *summa* of expectations. If their America were to be drawn as a *New Yorker* cover, Manhattan would be tiny in proportion to Bensonhurst itself and to its satellites, Staten Island, New Jersey, and Long Island.

"Oh, no," my father says when he hears the news about the shooting. Though he still refers to blacks as "coloreds," he's not really a racist and is upset that this innocent youth was shot in his neighborhood. He has no trouble acknowledging the wrongness of the death. But then, like all the news accounts, he turns to the fact, repeated over and over, that the blacks had been on their way to look at a used car when they encountered the hostile mob of whites. The explanation is right before him but, "Yeah," he says, still shaking his head, "yeah, but what were they *doing* there. They didn't belong." The "they," it goes without saying, refers to the blacks.

(As I write this essay, I am teaching Robert Frost: "What had that flower to do with being white, / The wayside blue and innocent heal-all? / What brought the kindred spider to that height, / Then steered the white moth thither in the night? / What but design of darkness to appall?—/ If design govern in a thing so small." Thus Frost in "Design" on a senseless killing and the ambiguity of causation and color symbolism. My father: "They didn't belong.")

Over the next few days, the TV news is even more disturbing. Rows of screaming Italians, lining the streets, many of them looking like my relatives. The young men wear undershirts, and crosses dangle from their necks as they hurl curses. I focus especially on one woman who resembles, almost completely, my mother: stocky but not fat, mid-seventies but well preserved, full face showing only minimal wrinkles, ample steel-gray hair neatly if rigidly coifed in a modified beehive hairdo left over from the sixties. She shakes her fist at the camera, protesting the arrest of the Italian American youths in the neighborhood and the incursion of more blacks into Bensonhurst, protesting the shooting. I look a little nervously at my mother (the parent I resemble), but she has not even noticed the woman and stares impassively at the television.

.   .   .

What has Bensonhurst to do with what I teach today and write? Why did I need to write about this killing in Bensonhurst but not in the manner of a news account or a statistical sociological analysis? Within days of hearing the news, I began to plan this essay, to tell the world what I knew, though I stopped midway, worried that my parents or their neighbors would hear about it. I sometimes think that I looked around from my baby carriage and decided that someday, the sooner the better, I would get out of Bensonhurst. Now, much to my surprise, Bensonhurst—the antipodes of the intellectual life I sought, the least interesting of places—had become a respectable intellectual topic. People would be willing to hear about Bensonhurst—and all by the dubious virtue of a racial killing in the streets.

The story as I would have to tell it would be to some extent a class narrative: about the difference between working class and upper middle class, dependence and a profession, Bensonhurst and a posh suburb. But I need to make it clear that I do not imagine myself as writing from a position of enormous self-satisfaction or even enormous distance. You can take the girl out of Bensonhurst (that much is clear), but you may not be able to take Bensonhurst out of the girl. Upward mobility is not the essence of the story, though it is an important marker and symbol.

In Durham today, I live in a modern house, surrounded by an acre of trees. When I sit on my back deck on summer evenings, no houses are visible through the trees. I have a guaranteed income, teaching English at an excellent university, removed by my years of education from the fundamental economic and social conditions of Bensonhurst. The one time my mother ever expressed pleasure at my work was when I got tenure—what my father called, with no irony intended, "ten years." "What does that mean?" my mother said when she heard the news. Then she reached back into her experiences as a garment worker, subject to seasonal "layoffs": "Does it mean they can't fire you just for nothing and can't lay you off?" When I said that was exactly what it means, she said, "Very good. Congratulations. *That's wonderful.*" I was free from the bosses and from the network of petty anxieties that had formed, in large part, her very existence. Of course, I wasn't really free of petty anxieties: would my salary increase keep pace with my colleagues', how would my office compare, would this essay be accepted for publication, am I happy? The line between these worries and my mother's is the line between the working class and the upper middle class.

But getting out of Bensonhurst never meant to me a big house, or nice clothes, or a large income. And it never meant feeling good about looking down on what I left behind or hiding my background. Getting out of Bensonhurst meant freedom—to experiment, to grow, to change. It also meant knowledge in some grand, abstract way. All the material possessions I have acquired, I acquired simply along the way—and for the first twelve years after I left Bensonhurst, I chose to acquire almost nothing at all. Now, as I write about "the neighborhood," I recognize that although I've come far in physical and material distance, the emotional distance is harder to gauge. Bensonhurst has everything to do with who I am and even with what I write. "We can never cease to be ourselves" (Conrad, *The Secret Agent*). Occasionally I get reminded of my roots, of their simultaneously choking and nutritive power.

Scene One: It's after a lecture at Duke, given by a visiting professor of German from a major university. The lecture was long and I'm tired but— bad luck—I had agreed to be one of the people having dinner with the lecturer afterward. I settle into the table at the restaurant with my companions: this man, the head of the Comparative Literature program (also a professor of German), and a couple I like who teach French. The conversation is sluggish, as it often is when a stranger, in this case the visiting professor, has to be assimilated into a group. So I ask the visitor a question to personalize things: "How did you get interested in what you do? What made you become a professor of German?" The man gets going and begins talking about how it was really unlikely that he, a nice Jewish boy from Bensonhurst, would have chosen, in the mid-fifties, to study German. Unlikely indeed.

I remember seeing *Judgment at Nuremberg* in a local movie theater and having a woman in the row in back of me get hysterical when some clips of a concentration camp were shown; "My God," she screamed in a European accent, "look at what they did. Murderers, MURDERERS!"—and she had to be supported out by her family. I couldn't see, in the dark, whether her arm bore the neatly tattooed numbers that the arms of some of my classmates' parents did—and that always affected me with a thrill of horror. This man is about ten years older than I am; he had lived more directly through those feelings, lived every day at home with those feelings. The first chance he got he raced to study German. I myself have twice chosen not to visit Germany—but I would understand an impulse to identify with the Other as a way of getting out of the neighborhood.

At the dinner, the memory about the movie pops into my mind, but I pick up instead on Bensonhurst—I'm also from there, but Italian American. Like a flash, he asks something I haven been asked in years: Where did I go to school and (a more common question) what was my family name? I went to Lafayette High School, I say, and my name was De Marco. Everything changes: his facial expression, his posture, his accent, his voice. "Soo Dee Maw-ko," he sez, "dun anything wrong at school today—got enny pink slips? Wanna meet me later at the park or maybe bye the Baye?" When I laugh, recognizing the stereotype that Italians get pink slips for misconduct at school and the notorious chemistry between Italian women and Jewish men, he says, back in his elegant voice: "My God, for a minute I felt like I was turning into a werewolf."

It's odd that although I can remember almost nothing else about this man—his face, his body type, even his name—I remember this lapse into his "real self" with enormous vividness. I am especially struck by how easily he was able to slip into the old, generic Brooklyn accent, though I also have no memory of trying *not* to speak it, except for teaching myself, carefully, to say "oil" rather than "earl."

But the surprises aren't over. The female French professor, whom I have known for at least five years, reveals for the first time that she is also from "the neighborhood," though she lived on the other side of Kings Highway, went to a different, more elite high school, and is Irish American. Three of six professors, sitting at an "eclectic" vegetarian restaurant in Durham, all from Bensonhurst—a neighborhood where (I swear) you couldn't get the *New York Times* at any of the local stores.

Scene Two: In this scene, I still live in Bensonhurst. I'm waiting for my parents to return from a conference at my school, where they've been summoned to discuss my transition from elementary to junior high school. I am already a full year younger than any of my classmates, having been "skipped" a grade, a not uncommon occurrence for "gifted" youngsters. Now the school is worried about putting me in an accelerated track through junior high, since that would make me two years younger. A compromise is reached: I will be put in a special program for "gifted" children but one that takes three, not two years. It sounds okay.

Three years later, another wait. My parents have gone to school to make another decision. Lafayette High School has three tracks: academic, for potentially college-bound kids; secretarial, mostly for Italian American girls or girls with low aptitude scores; and vocational, mostly for boys with the same attributes, ethnic or intellectual. (The high school is segregated de facto so none of the tracks is as yet racially coded, though they are coded by ethnic group and gender.) Although my scores are superb, the guidance counselor has recommended the secretarial track; when I protested, the conference with my parents was arranged. My mother's preference is clear: the secretarial track—college is for boys; I will need to make a "good living" until I marry and have children. My father also prefers the secretarial track, but he wavers, half proud of my aberrantly high scores, half worried. I press the attack, saying that if I were Jewish I would have been placed, without question, in the academic track. I tell him I have sneaked a peek at my files and know that my IQ is genius level. I am allowed to insist on the change into the academic track.

What I had done, and I was ashamed of it even then, was to play upon my father's competitive feelings with Jews: his daughter could and should be as good as theirs. In the bank where he was a messenger and the insurance company where he worked in the mail room, my father worked with Jews, who were almost always his immediate supervisors. Several times, my father was offered the supervisory job but turned it down, after long conversations with my mother about the dangers of making a change, the difficulty of giving orders to friends. After her work sewing dresses in a local garment shop, after cooking dinner and washing the floor each night, my mother often did "piecework" making bows for a certain amount of money per bow; sometimes I would help her for fun, but it *wasn't* fun and I was free to stop while she continued for long, tedious hours to increase the family income. Once a week, her part-time boss, Dave, would come by to pick up the boxes of bows. Short, round, with his shirttails sloppily tucked into his pants and a cigar almost always dangling from his lips, Dave was a stereotypical Jew but also, my parents always said, a nice guy, a decent man. The first landlord I remember was Mrs. Rosenberg. My father was a sitting duck.

Years later, similar choices come up and I show the same assertiveness I showed with my father, the same ability to deal for survival but tinged with Bensonhurst caution. Where will I go to college? Not to Brooklyn College, the flagship of the city system—I know that but don't press the invitations I have received to apply to prestigious schools outside of New York City. The choice comes down to two: Barnard, which gives me a full scholarship, minus five hundred dollars a year that all scholarship students are expected to contribute from summer earnings, or New York University, which offers me a thousand dollars above tuition. I waver. My parents stand firm: they are already losing money by letting me go to college; I owe it to the family to contribute the extra thousand plus summer earnings. Besides, my mother adds, harping on a favorite theme, there are no boys at Barnard; at N.Y.U. I'm more likely to meet someone to marry. I go to N.Y.U. and marry in my senior year, but someone I didn't meet at college. I am secretly relieved, I think now (though at the time I thought I was just placating my parents' conventionality), to be out of the marriage sweepstakes.

The first boy who ever asked me for a date was Robert Zuckerman, in eighth grade: tall and skinny to my average height and preteen chubbiness. I turned him down, thinking we would make a ridiculous couple. Day after day, I cast my eyes at stylish Juliano, the class cutup; day after day, I captivated Robert Zuckerman. Occasionally, one of my brother's Italian American friends would ask me out, and I would go, often to R.O.T.C. dances; my specialty was making political remarks so shocking that the guys rarely asked again. After a while, I recognized destiny: the Jewish man was a passport out of Bensonhurst. When I married, I of course did marry a Jewish man, who gave me my freedom, and, very important, helped remove me from the expectations of Bensonhurst. Though raised in a largely Jewish section of Brooklyn, he had gone to college in Ohio and knew how important it was (as he put it) "to get past the Brooklyn Bridge"; we met on neutral ground, in Central Park, at a performance of Shakespeare. The Jewish-Italian marriage is a common enough catastrophe in Bensonhurst for my parents to have accepted, even welcomed my marriage—though my parents continued to treat my husband as an outsider for the first twenty years ("Now Mary Ann. Here's what's going on with you' brother. But don't tell you' husband").

Along the way, I make other choices, more fully marked by Bensonhurst cautiousness. I am attracted to journalism or the arts as careers, but the prospects for income seem iffy. I choose instead to imagine myself as a teacher. Only the availability of NDEA Fellowships when I graduate, with their generous terms, propels me from high school teaching (a thought I never much relished) to college teaching (which seems like a brave new world). Within college teaching, I choose offbeat specializations: the novel, interdisciplinary approaches (not something clear and clubby, like Milton or the eighteenth century). Eventually I write the book I like best, about "primitive" Others as they figure within Western obsessions: my identification with "the Other," my sense of being "Other," surfaces at last. I avoid all mentoring structures for a long time but accept aid when it comes to me on the basis of what I perceive to be merit. I'm still, deep down, Italian American Bensonhurst, though by this time I'm a lot of other things as well.

. . .

Scene Three: In the summer of 1988, a little more than a year before the shooting in Bensonhurst, my father woke up trembling and in what appeared to be a fit. Hospitalization revealed that he had a pocket of blood on his brain, a frequent consequence of falls for older people. About a year earlier, I had stayed home, heeding my father's suggestion that I remain with my children, when my aunt, my father's much-loved sister, died; only now does my mother tell me how much my father resented my missing the funeral. Now, confronted with what is described as "brain surgery" but turns out to be less dramatic than it sounds, I fly to New York immediately.

My brother drives three hours back and forth from New Jersey every day to drive my mother and me to the hospital, which is about fifteen minutes from my parents' apartment: he is being a fine Italian American son. Often, for the first time in years, we have long conversations alone. He is two years older than I am, a chemical engineer who has also left "the neighborhood" but has remained closer to its values, with a suburban, Republican inflection. He talks a lot about New York, saying that (except for neighborhoods like Bensonhurst) it's a "Third World city now." It's the summer of the Tawana Brawley incident, when Brawley accused white men of abducting her and smearing racial slurs on her body with her own excrement. My brother is filled with dislike for Al Sharpton and Brawley's other vocal supporters in the black community—not because they are black but because they are "troublemakers, stirring things up." The city is drenched in racial hatred that makes itself felt in the halls of the hospital: Italians and Jews in the beds and as doctors; blacks as nurses and orderlies.

This is the first time since I left New York in 1975 that I have visited Brooklyn without once getting into Manhattan. It's the first time I have spent several days alone with my mother, living in her apartment in Bensonhurst. My every move is scrutinized and commented on. I feel like I am going to go crazy.

Finally, it's clear that my father is going to be fine and I can go home. My mother insists on accompanying me to the travel agent to get my ticket home, even though I really want to be alone. The agency (a Mafia front?) has no one who knows how to ticket me for the exotic destination of North Carolina and no computer for doing so. The one person who can perform this feat by hand is out. I have to kill time for an hour and suggest to my mother that she go home, to be there for my brother when he arrives from Jersey. We stop in a Pork Store, where I buy a stash of cheeses, sausages, and other delicacies unavailable in Durham. My mother walks home with the shopping bags, and I'm on my own.

More than anything I want a kind of sorbetto or "ice" I remember from growing up, called a "cremolata": almond-vanilla flavored, with large chunks of nuts. I pop into the local bakery (at an unlikely 11 A.M.) and ask for a cremolata, usually eaten after dinner. The woman—a younger version of my mother—refuses: they haven't made a fresh ice yet and what's left from the day before is too icy, no good. I explain that I'm about to get on a plane for North Carolina and want that ice, no good or not. But she has her standards and holds her ground, even though North Carolina has about the same status in her mind as Timbuktu and she knows I will be banished, perhaps forever, from the land of cremolata.

Then, while I'm taking a walk, enjoying my solitude, I have another idea. Near my parents' house, there's a club for men from a particular town or region in Italy: six or seven tables, some on the sidewalk beneath a garish red, green, and white sign; no women allowed or welcome unless they're with the men; and no women at all during the day when the real business of the club—a game of cards for old men who would be much quainter in Italy than they are in Bensonhurst—is in progress. Still, I know that inside the club would be coffee and a cremolata ice. I'm thirty-eight, well dressed, very respectable looking; I know what I want. I also know I'm not supposed to enter that club. I enter anyway, asking the teenage boy behind the counter firmly, in my most professorial tones, for a cremolata ice. Dazzled, he complies immediately. The old men at the card table have been staring at this scene, unable to place me, exactly, though my facial type is familiar. Finally, a few old men's hisses pierce the air. "Strega," I hear as I leave, "mala strega," "witch," or "brazen whore." I have been in Bensonhurst less than a week, but I have managed to reproduce, on my final day there for this visit, the conditions of my youth. Knowing the rules, I have broken them. I shake hands with my discreetly rebellious past, still an outsider walking through the neighborhood, marked and insulted—though unlikely to be shot.

PART TWO

. . . .

Italian American Literature

Dana Gioia

. . . .

What Is Italian American Poetry?

If Italian American poetry can be said to exist as a meaningful part of American literature, it is only as a transitional category. Some kinds of ethnic or cultural consciousness seem more or less permanent. A contemporary Catholic poet, for example, is intrinsically no less Catholic than one from the nineteenth century. Nor will an African American writer today experience the dual allegiances of black identity less deeply than did his or her predecessors. But each new generation of Italian Americans finds its cultural links with the old country more tenuous. As the Little Italies disappear and families disperse to the suburbs, the descendants of Italian immigration gradually merge their once sharply differentiated ethnic identity in mainstream America. Values change subtly but significantly. Intermarriage becomes the rule rather than the exception. If a third generation Italian American speaks Italian, he or she usually learned it not in the kitchen but in college.

Some recent critics have analyzed the position of Italian American poets in sociological terms borrowed from black literary historians. They portray Italian American writers as individuals whose ethnic consciousness alienates them from the mainstream culture. Although this approach affords some insights, it is often misleading. The Italian American writer's identity is rooted in history, not race. It originated in one central event—the massive immigration of poor Italians to the United States between 1870 and 1930. The cultural shock waves radiating from this historical upheaval (which was America's largest European immigration in the past century) formed the Italian American literary consciousness. The concept of an Italian American poet is, therefore, most useful to describe first- and second-generation writers raised in the immigrant subculture. It has been these writers who have used the immigrant experience as their imaginative point of departure.

Although Italian American poetry began in 1805 with the arrival of Mozart's librettist, the Venetian writer Lorenzo da Ponte, it took another century and a half for enough significant authors to appear to claim the attention of the English-speaking public. The social and cultural barriers that early aspiring writers faced were enormous. Not surprisingly, few poets managed to overcome them. Most immigrants came from the destitute classes of southern Italy. Poorly educated, often illiterate, few knew Toscano, the standard literary dialect of written Italian (based on the Florentine language of Petrarch and Boccaccio). The immigrant's literary heritage was usually confined to the lively traditions of a local dialect. The poetry of the early arrivals—and there is a great deal of engaging work—was written mostly in southern dialects. This heritage remains almost entirely unexplored, except by a few dedicated scholars working outside the academic mainstream.

The first generation of Italian American writers to work in English made their most important contributions neither in poetry nor fiction but in radical politics. Carlo Tresca and Arturo Giovannitti, for example, were both published poets, but today they are remembered for their social activism. Their political journalism, which passionately addressed the timeless concerns of equality and justice, remains more vital than their verse. Selden Rodman boldly reprinted Bartolomeo Vanzetti's last speech to the court as verse in his 1938 *New Anthology of Modern Verse,* and Vanzetti's proud words spoken in slightly awkward English sustain the pressure of transcription. Few poems by his Italian American contemporaries still read so well.

The best early Italian American poetry deals with the excitement and disillusionment of life in this "new-found land." The immigrant Emanuel Carnevali (1897–1942) became the first Italian writer to make a significant, if short-lived, impact on modern American poetry. Supporting himself in Greenwich Village by shoveling snow and washing dishes, Carnevali enjoyed a special celebrity among populist Modernist poets like William Carlos Williams and Carl Sandburg. He published only one book, *Tales of a Hurried Man* (1925), but it established him in avant-garde circles. Harriet Monroe, the founding editor of *Poetry,* eventually brought him out to Chicago to work on her magazine, but he was soon stricken with encephalitis. Impoverished, disillusioned, and disabled, he returned to his homeland, where he wrote, "O Italy, O great boot, / don't kick me out again!" Poets like Carnevali, however, survive today mainly as historical figures—examples of the developing ethnic consciousness of Italian American writers. They have at best modest claims to the attention of general readers of poetry.

The first Italian American poet to make a permanent contribution to our literature was John Ciardi (1916–1986). An indefatigable critic, anthologist, translator, educator, journalist, and public spokesman, Ciardi became one of midcentury American poetry's dominant tastemakers—an unprecedented position for an Italian American. He also became modestly wealthy from poetry, another rare accomplishment, about which Ciardi, who had been raised without a father and in terrible poverty, exhibited the unabashed pride typical of his first-generation contemporaries. Ciardi remains the model Italian American poet and man of letters. He has had many followers, though none quite so versatile. Ciardi not only captured the distinctive perspective and themes of Italian American experience; he portrayed them in memorable language. Here is the opening of "Firsts," a poem that simultaneously plays with echoes from the English and Italian literary traditions:

> At forty, home from traveled intention,
> I could no longer speak my mother's dialect.
>
> I had been in Italy rinsing my vowels.
> She had been in Medford, Massachusetts
>
> thickening her tongue on English crusts.
> She had become a patois. What tongue was I?
>
> I understood what I heard her say.
> Could say it over and remember—ah, yes—
>
> a taste like cooked wine-lees mushed with snow,
> our winter *dolce* once. And how many years
>
> not thought of, not forgotten? A taste
> that slipped my tongue. Would I still like it, I doubt?

Today there are so many interesting poets of Italian descent writing that it is difficult to draw any narrow generalizations about their wide-ranging work. And yet amid all the diversity there remain some common points of resemblance. I do not pretend great scholarship in the field, but I have been reading my poetic *compaesani* now for several decades (most recently in a professional capacity as poetry editor of *Italian Americana*), and I have seriously pondered the problematic issues of expressing our ethnic and cultural identity in literature. Many things need to be said, even if only in provisional terms, so let me venture a few preliminary observations.

In Italian culture one often notices two conflicting impulses—one to preserve the richness of the past, the other to reject it in search of the new. The same dialectic between tradition and revolution exists in Italian American poetry. Surveying writers of roughly the same generation, one finds both enlightened traditionalists (like Jerome Mazzaro or Lewis Turco) and feisty iconoclasts (like Gregory Corso or Diane di Prima). Sometimes one sees both impulses in a single writer, like Felix Stefanile or Paul Violi. What one rarely sees is aesthetic complacency. Italians take their art seriously. The traditionalists tend to be as passionate and argumentative as the revolutionaries. Ciardi's engaged and combative approach to poetry no longer appears to have been a purely personal trait.

Despite the stylistic diversity, one does notice certain underlying themes that unite the work of first- and second-generation writers. I would cite four central experiences that haunt, either overtly or subtly, the Italian American poetic imagination. The first is poverty. The poets and their families have usually known genuine privation and penury both here and in Europe. This bitter memory informs their views of America and themselves. Their original status as economic and social outsiders in America also colors their political views. It often makes them suspicious or critical of established power. Anarchy appeals to the southern Italian worldview. Revolution and resistance also exercise a mythic charm. Early Italian American poets were usually political radicals, though rarely loyal and obedient members of any party. More recently, several Italian American women—most notably Sandra Mortola Gilbert—are significant figures in the feminist movement.

Second, Italian American poets reflect the Roman Catholic culture in which they were raised. The mythology and iconography of Latin Catholicism often form the symbolic framework of their poetry. Even if the poets overtly reject the religion, its worldview still permeates their imaginations. One does not often find openly religious poetry (the work of Peggy Rizza Ellsberg being a noteworthy exception), but Catholic symbols and archetypes are to be found everywhere in their verse. Likewise, Catholic rituals and sacraments (funerals, first communions, confessions, and mass) constitute a frequent setting for Italian American poems. Jerome Mazzaro's "The Caves of Love" describes morning mass in an immigrant church. Toni Conley's "Ash Wednesday" begins with the Lenten ritual of its title.

Samuel Maio's "At the Funeral Mass" exemplifies a subject so common among Italian American poets as to be nearly universal—a family funeral at which the younger-generation speaker observes the older generation from a new (and inevitably slightly alienated) perspective. Innumerable poems present scenes in the confessional. David Citino has made a career of presenting every incident of a Catholic childhood.

Third, Italian American poets have a heightened consciousness of their European Latin roots. Even those raised in poverty are oddly cosmopolitan. Their family background liberates them from the often narrowly nationalistic outlook of mainstream America. While many American poets reject European influences as harmful distractions from the search for a native voice, most Italian American poets view Europe—sometimes in its Modernistic aspects, sometimes in its older traditions—as a potential source of strength. Felix Stefanile, Linda Ann Loschiavo, Mary Fortunato Galt, Jay Parini, and Gerald Costanzo all demonstrate this unself-conscious sophistication in different ways. One also sees a European consciousness in the many distinguished translators among Italian American writers, including Joseph Tusiani, Michael Palma, Jonathan Galassi, W. S. Di Piero, Rina Ferrarelli, Paul Vangelisti, and Stephen Sartarelli, to mention only a few.

Finally, there tends to be a strong element of realism in Italian American poetry. It reflects a concern with portraying a world of common experience rather than the creation of a private verbal universe. Often this realistic urge expresses itself in the harsh description of urban life. One sometimes sees the sharp edge of naturalism in the poetry of W. S. Di Piero, Lucia Maria Perillo, and Felix Stefanile as strongly as in the cinema of Martin Scorsese or Michael Cimino. Kim Addonizio's book-length narrative sequence, *Jimmy and Rita,* for instance, unsparingly describes the downward careers of two drug addicts. Sometimes the realist impulse depicts the subtler psychological realities of a common cultural or religious consciousness, as in Jerome Mazzaro. Though their artistic solutions vary, for Italian American writers, poetry remains a public art.

The full range and quality of Italian American poetry, however, remains inadequately understood. No serious critic has yet surveyed the field with the necessary combination of knowledge, sympathy, and discrimination. Only the bare beginnings of literary history have yet been undertaken. Fernando Alfonsi's 1994 anthology, *Poeti Italo-Americani e Italo-Canadesi,* is invaluable despite its many shortcomings simply because it attempts to map out the territory. Significantly, Alfonsi found his publisher not in America but in Italy. American presses still generally view Italian Americans as a small and unattractive market. Only recently have journals like *Italian Americana* and *Voices in Italiana Americana* created the regular forums for literary essays, reviews, and commentary that are the necessary precondition for serious critical consideration and consensus.

The undeveloped nature of critical thinking and scholarship in the field is evident from the terms in which Italian American poetry is commonly discussed. Most critics still borrow fashionable theoretical methodologies (mostly off-the-rack multiculturalism or feminism) and use the concepts so mechanically that they miss the unique qualities of both the Italian American experience and the poetry it produces. Meanwhile, nonacademic commentators still indulge in indiscriminate ethnic boosterism. Neither approach does justice to Italian Americans as serious literary artists. The theoretical approach characteristically treats the poet not as an individual author but as so much sociological data. Boosterism reduces the writer—good, bad, or indifferent—to an uplifting example. Isn't it marvelous, the booster coos, that an Italian can write a poem? However well-intentioned, such criticism is condescending. Promotion is no substitute for serious criticism. If Italian American poetry amounts to anything worthwhile in artistic terms, it deserves hard and informed evaluation.

At its frequent worst, literary boosterism takes the form of a long list of authors with Italian surnames followed by a vague exhortation to take them seriously as writers. The longer the list, the compiler implies, the more persuasive the case for the literary importance of Italian American poetry. In art, however, quantity means infinitely less than quality. One Dante counts for more than a hundred mediocrities. A long, indiscriminate list of names convinces no skeptical outsider; nor will crude assertion change the cultural fact that there is still no *widely recognized* and shared body of Italian American poetry. Its public reception remains marginal, even among Italian American readers. Moreover, public recognition will not come to general categories of writers; critical esteem and sustained attention is earned one writer at a time.

Such lists also reveal a deeper irony. They almost inevitably demonstrate that even the well-wishing collector of the names has not actually read all the poetry being so heartily recommended. Published lists commonly include non-Italians with Italianate names and exclude real Italian Americans with nonethnic surnames. Patricia Storace, for example, usually appears on such lists. Yet anyone who has read the *first* poem in Storace's *only* book of verse learns that she has virtually no Italian blood and no Italian American background whatsoever. (On the other hand, Mary Jo Salter and Jack Foley, whose names never appear, are half Italian). Such lists ignore the two relevant issues for approaching the whole endeavor: first, is the poetry genuinely distinguished; and second, does the poetry speak in some meaningful way about the Italian American experience? Unless the critic can sincerely say yes to both questions, the author's name does not belong on a list.

A little research demonstrates the inadequacy of using a mere surname as a meaningful guide to culture and ethnicity. Take the interesting example of Lawrence Ferlinghetti, who universally appears on lists of Italian American poets. Ferlinghetti was born Lawrence Ferling in Yonkers, New York, in 1919. His father, Charles Ferling, was reportedly an assimilated Italian immigrant who died before his son was born, though his ethnicity is almost certainly a poetic fiction. His mother, Clemence Mendes-Monsanto, a French Sephardic Jew, was institutionalized soon after his birth. The young Lawrence Ferling was raised initially in France by his maternal aunt. His first language was French.

Returning to New York in 1924, the poet was—after seven months in an orphanage—informally adopted by an older, wealthy WASP couple in Bronxville, New York. He was educated in exclusive private schools and eventually studied at the University of North Carolina at Chapel Hill and at Columbia before returning to France in 1947. He never met any member of his putative Italian family. Lawrence Ferling did, however, Italianize his name in 1955 for the publication of his first book—to symbolize his rebirth as a poet. (It takes a dull critic to miss the deliberate pun in Ferling's witty, carefully contrived, but non-Italianate new surname.) While the dubiously authentic "Ferlinghetti" has become the most famous Italian surname in American poetry, its owner has no meaningful connection with the Italian American immigrant experience. His cultural background is French, Sephardic, and—exquisite irony—patrician American. Ferlinghetti resembles the Armenian American soprano Lucine Armaganion who changed her name to Lucine Amara to pursue her operatic career. Perhaps one might create a new category for such an artist—the voluntary Italian.

Some readers may feel uncomfortable with my insistence on making distinctions. They want to create a warm, extended literary family in which every poet is welcomed unconditionally. I will not condemn such ethnic solidarity, but neither will I call it literary criticism or informed scholarship. If we do not define Italian American poetry with some strictness and consistency, we dilute the usefulness of the category. It becomes an emotional counter rather than a legitimate critical concept. There is no value in applying ethnic categories to an assimilated writer with an Italian surname nor a non-Italian with an Italianate name. Life experience, not a surname, is what determines ethnicity in literature. Otherwise, we might as well talk about R. S. Gwynn and Rodney Jones as Welsh American poets, or Emily Grosholz and Judith Hemschemeyer as German American poets. If the only place a text displays ethnicity is its byline, then it isn't an ethnic text.

If Italian Americans hope to win a broader audience for their writers, they must begin by taking their own literary heritage seriously. They must read, discuss, and evaluate their own authors. They must create and support the necessary cultural institutions to foster informed discussion— journals, publishers, readings, lectures, college courses. They must also risk making judgments about literary quality. Broad and bland endorsement will not foster a healthy literary culture, and lip service is no substitute for intellectual engagement. One sees the beginnings of serious critical activity in journals like *Italian Americana* and *Via* and in publishers like Guernica Editions and Italica Press. So much work remains to be done, however, that it is easy to be pessimistic about the outcome. The brightest young Italian American writers and critics gravitate to mainstream academic and intellectual culture. That is where reputations are made and the greatest rewards are found. The new generation of Italian American intellectuals knows as well as their immigrant grandparents did that assimilation is the easiest road to success.

"A book is never a masterpiece," observed Edmond de Goncourt. "It becomes one." A classic emerges not merely from the pages of a book but from the sustained attention and esteem awarded by generations of readers. The same slow dialectic of validation also applies to literary traditions. No new tradition suddenly appears fully formed from a few books; it grows slowly out of the ongoing conversation a culture has about these books. In this sense, Italian American literature does not yet exist. Italian American poetry, fiction, and drama are concepts still being slowly and tentatively summoned into being—too slowly and too tentatively. Unless a new generation of readers finds cogent reasons to connect with this literary heritage it will remain a half-realized historical category of interest mainly to sociologists and antiquarians. The creation of a full and meaningful literary tradition for Italian American letters will require more intellectual energy than we have historically seen in our community. The necessary changes in attitude must happen soon—while the living connections with the immigrant experience still exist—or never. Our community has all the talent, intelligence, and influence to make the changes. What we lack is the resolve.

Fred L. Gardaphé

. . . .

Breaking and Entering

An Italian American's Literary Odyssey

> What you carry in your head you don't have to carry on
> your back.
> —Advice from an old worker

If there is one thing I've learned about advocating ethnic American literature, it's that you can't avoid getting personal about the literature that
comes from your ancestral culture. And so this essay is a personal account
of my encounter with the literature produced by American writers of Italian descent. Through this development I have come to see my life's reading and writing as entries on a historical rap sheet of the cultural crimes of
breaking into and entering mainstream America.

I grew up in a Little Italy in which not even the contagiously sick were
left alone. To be alone is to be sick. The self-isolation that reading requires was rarely possible and considered a dangerous invitation to blindness and insanity. This was evidenced by my being the first American
born of the family to need glasses before the age of ten. I would not understand their attitude toward reading for many years. In fact, it wasn't
until I came across Jerre Mangione's *An Ethnic at Large* that I realized I
wasn't the only one whose reading was treated this way. In Mangione's autobiographical writing he tells of how being Sicilian and American created
a double life inside of which he fashioned a third "fantasy life . . . well
nourished by the piles of books I brought home from the public library,
most of which I read clandestinely in the bathroom or under the bed since
my mother believed that too much reading could drive a person insane."

There was no space in the home set aside for isolated study. We had one of the larger homes of those in our extended family, so our house was the place where the women would gather in the basement kitchen after sending their husbands off to work and their kids to school. They'd share coffee, clothes washing, and ironing; they'd collectively make daily bread and prepare afternoon pastas and evening pizzas and *foccacie*. Those without children would spend the entire day there, so we always returned home from school to scenes that most of our classmates knew only on weekends or holidays. We were expected to come home from school, drop our books on the kitchen table, and begin our homework. It was difficult to concentrate on work with four children at the table, all subjected to countless interruptions from family and friends who passed through the house regularly.

The only books that entered my family's home were those we carried home from school. Reading anything beyond newspapers and the mail required escaping from my family. I would try reading, but the noise would be so great that I'd shout out, "Shut up, I'm trying to read," to which my mother would respond, "Who you tellin' to shut up? If you want to read, go to the library." But the library was off-limits to any kid who wanted to be tough. I'd leave the house with homework in hand, find a place to park my books, and join in on the action in the streets. When the action didn't consist of organized play, it was made up of disorganized troublemaking. Once, while I was being chased by the police for disturbing local merchants so my partners could shoplift, I ran into the public library. I found myself in the juvenile section and grabbed any book to hide my face. Safe from the streets, I spent the rest of the afternoon reading, believing that nobody would ever find me there. So whenever I was being chased, I'd head straight for the library. The library became my asylum, a place where I could go crazy and be myself without my family finding out.

It wasn't long my before my reading habit outgrew the dimensions of the library. I had developed a chronic reading problem that identified me as the "'merican," or rebel. My reading betrayed my willingness to enter mainstream American culture, and while my family tolerated this, they did little to make that move an easy one. Sometimes at night I would take a flashlight to bed and read; but as I shared a bed with my two brothers, this often ended up in a fight, as well as a reprimand from my father, telling me I was not only keeping my brothers from sleeping but that I was also teaching my brothers bad habits. In spite of all these obstacles I managed to become quite the bookworm. I read to escape both my home and the streets and in the process entered places in my mind I had never before seen.

While my father encouraged my studies, he wanted me to know what real work was like. So whenever he'd see me reading something that was obviously not homework, he'd put me to work in the family business—a pawnshop as well as the building we owned. Only after I'd cleaned floors, put away stock, and run errands would I be given some time for myself. There wasn't much to read in the store; the constant flow of customers would not allow for anything longer than a news article at one stretch, but I always managed to get through a newspaper and the *Green Sheet*, a daily horse racing newsletter. I'd return home and reenter the imaginary worlds others created through words, never thinking there could be a bridge between the two. For a long time it never occurred to me that literature was something that could or even should speak to me of my experience, especially not of my ethnicity. The worlds I entered through reading were never confused with the world in which I lived. Reading was a vacation. The books I read were written by others about experiences that were not mine; they took me places I had never been. This naive notion of reading was shattered the day my father was murdered.

When I read the news accounts, it seemed for the first time that my life had become a subject for writing. Since we share the same name, to see his name in print was to see my own. It was especially haunting to see that name on his tombstone. I knew that a part of me had been buried with him. From that day on, I began to read in a new way. For many reasons, I began to feel that my life was no longer in control; I began to think that the only way I could regain control of it was to be the one who wrote the stories. So shocked by reality was I that I began to search for a way out, and that way, I thought, would come through reading. Because my father was murdered in the pawnshop, my family wanted me to have nothing to do with the business, but my grandfather needed me more than ever. I returned to the store, now in my father's place in spite of the fact that I was just a kid.

Since books were nonnegotiable items in my community, the giving of them was considered not only impractical but taboo. Sometime shortly after my father's death, my uncle Pasquale gave me a copy of Luigi Barzini's *The Italians*; he just handed it to me, without even a word, assuming through his glance that I would know what to do with it. Back then I thought I knew too much about being Italian. But all I really knew was that being Italian meant being different from the ones I wanted to be like. The last thing in the world that I wanted at that age was to read about a group with which I no longer wished to be associated. I put the book on a shelf connected to my bed, the only shelf outside our kitchen;

there it would be unread for seven years. From then on I read nothing beyond my school assignments. One day—a day of no special occasion—one of my aunts again broke this book-as-gift taboo by giving my mother a copy of Mario Puzo's *The Godfather*; she told my mother that, if her nephew was so intent on reading, he might as well read a book about Italians (neither of them had read it of course). The title of the book was quite appropriate; because of my father's early death, I, at the age of ten, had been made godfather to one of my cousins.

The novel lay unread until I found out that there was an excellent sex scene on page 26. That's where I started reading. I sped through the book, hoping to find more scenes like the one in which Sonny screws the maid of honor at his sister's wedding. Along the way I encountered men like Amerigo Bonasera the undertaker, Luca Brasi the street thug, and Johnny Fontaine, who were like the regulars I knew in the pawnshop. Some would come in with guns, jewelry, and golf clubs to pawn. Men like these formed alliances in order to get things done. Because of its stock of familiar characters, *The Godfather* was the first novel with which I could completely identify. The only problem I had was that this thing called Mafia was something of which I had never heard. I was familiar with the word *mafioso*, which the people in my neighborhood used to refer to poor troublemakers who dressed as though they were rich. But that these guys could have belonged to a master crime organization called The Mafia was something I had never fathomed. They couldn't even organize a good game of baseball. In spite of this, the world that Puzo created taught me how to read the world I was living in, not only the world of the streets but the world within my family; for in spite of the emphasis on crime, Puzo's use of Italian sensibilities made me realize that literature could be made out of my own experiences.

The novel came out the year after my grandfather was killed in a holdup at the pawnshop. With him gone, the business was sold, and I was free to find my own way through the world. One of the ways I searched was crime. All throughout my high school years, I was accused of being in the Mafia. So during my senior year, I decided to investigate the subject through the semester-long thesis paper that my Irish Catholic prep school required. One way or another I had been connected to the Mafia since I left my Italian neighborhood to attend the high school, so I decided it was time to find out what this thing called Mafia was. This was the first writing project to excite me. I searched the Barzini book, and between him and Puzo, I thought I had it all figured out. When I completed the paper, I was certain of an excellent grade. The grading committee decided that the paper, although well written, depended too much on Italian sources, and because I was also Italian, my writing never achieved the necessary objectivity that was essential to all serious scholarship. I read the C grade as punishment for my cultural transgression and decided to stay away from anything but English and American literature in my future formal studies.

As soon as I graduated from high school, I leapt into the youth culture that had been held at bay by the strict rules of my prep school. But it wasn't enough for me to get some jeans, let my hair grow, and smoke some dope. I might become a hippie but not without finding a historical context by which to explain the culture I was entering. My historical reading pointed to poetry. I started tracing the hippies back in time and came upon the Beatniks, whom I followed back to the American Romantics, like Thoreau and Whitman. That's when I found the poetry of Lawrence Ferlinghetti. That he was Italian American never entered my mind back then. All I knew was that suddenly here was a man whose poetry sang without rhyme and told truths in clear and simple language. I bought up every book of his that I could find. Inspired by Whitman's "Song of the Open Road," I took a year off between my sophomore and junior years in college and hitchhiked out to California with the idea of finding Ferlinghetti. I imagined City Lights Books to be a mecca that was waiting for punk pilgrims like myself.

When I arrived, I browsed the shelves until I got up the nerve to ask the clerk if Ferlinghetti was in. He pointed me to the basement. I approached his office cautiously, rehearsing what I would say. The door was opened just enough to allow me to see the poet's profile; his head was bent slightly, as though he were pondering a half-written poem still in his typewriter. I stood there awhile, staring at him, and decided that this was ridiculous. What could I possibly say to him? How stupid he'd think I was to hitchhike all the way from Chicago. What could I have wanted from him? I ran back up the stairs, bought a book entitled *Six San Francisco Poets*, by David Kherdian, and told myself I'd come back. I never did. Kherdian's book led me to other Beat writers, like Diane di Prima and Gregory Corso, who were, like Ferlinghetti, coincidentally Italian American; and as I continued hitchhiking around the country, I'd pick up their books and read them on roadsides, in hostels, and in fleabag hotels. That was 1973. I kept a journal of my trip and returned home with the decision to be a writer.

When I returned to college, I began studying literature and film with the idea of getting a teaching job so that I could make reading and writing

my career. After a few years of teaching high school and writing bad poetry, I decided I needed to get away. So I took off to hitchhike through Europe, thinking perhaps I'd stop in Italy.

Now, my grandparents had never told me why they left Italy. They
never talked of their childhood. I guess they thought it was enough to be
in America and that all that had come before no longer made any difference in their new home. After my mother's father died, no one seemed to
care much about getting together for Sunday dinners. With him were
buried many of the Italian traditions our family had followed in his presence. Without his influence, Italians became strangers in a collage of
media images: spicy meatball eaters, Godfathers, and opera singers. In
the late seventies I decided to get as far away from the family as possible.
I planned a trip to Europe to visit friends in Denmark and Sweden. As I
gathered addresses, I thought it might be interesting to visit Italy for a few
days if I had the time. Grandma had maintained only Christmas card contact with the "other family" in Castellana Grotte. She had the address of
Grandpa's brother, and I wrote him. By the time I left, I had not received
a response and wondered if I should bother to stop in Castellana. My trip
began in northern Europe, and it seemed that the closer I came to Italy,
the more emotional I became. On the train from Venice to Bari, I began to
feel confused. I asked myself many times: "What if my family doesn't
recognize me? They have no pictures! What if they can't understand me?
I've only studied Italian for three months, and Venice proved that I can
understand it but not speak it well!" But even as I worried, the excitement
grew.

As the first of the American family to return to Castellana Grotte, I was
welcomed with tears, kisses, and strong embraces. I felt like a traveler
who had come home after a long voyage. After only a few days I knew I
belonged in Castellana. I was able to live as Grandpa did. I even worked
ten hours picking beans in the same field that he had worked in when he
was young. When I couldn't straighten out my back after picking the fava,
I understood why he had left Italy. I was able to speak to his brother and
sister, and for the first time I knew what his life in Italy had been like. I
understood that he, like so many other southern Italians, had left home to
find work in America. He would send money back to Castellana Grotte
and had promised continually that one day he would return. That one day
never came, as soon he had a family of his own to support. Learning all
this helped me to regain a part of me that was lost when he died. I was
whole and now more than ever proud of my Italian heritage.

My pride no longer stemmed from arrogance and ignorance. It was a pride of wisdom and of love for the life that he had lived. I visited the house where Grandpa was born. I spent a long time inside the stone cottage, touching what he had once touched, seeing what at one time I knew he had seen. I was so lost in emotion that I cried without trying to hide my tears. I felt that this place had some kind of power over me. When I left his home, I felt for the first time that I had a history, a history that I had never studied in school, a history that would have been lost if I had not traveled to Castellana Grotte.

When I returned, I knew I needed to write about the experience. I had come home a born-again Italian, who took to drinking espresso instead of coffee, taking naps in the afternoon, and hanging out in places where I could continue to speak Italian. I might have been obnoxious, but I was directed. I began writing screenplays and short stories but felt I needed the direction that might come from a teacher. I left my teaching position in an uptown Chicago street school, took out major school loans, and started a master's program at the University of Chicago. Under the supervision of Richard Stern, I began a novel. To support myself, I assisted in an Italian professor's first-year Italian class. Along with my English and American literature courses, I took seminars in Italian literature. At this time I renewed my search for and read books by Italian Americans. This was done outside my formal classes, of course, and I never considered them in the same light as the literature I studied in my graduate courses.

Each novel led me to another. I began with Mario Puzo's earlier work. In his novel *The Fortunate Pilgrim* (1964), I found my widowed mother, who raised four children by herself, to be very much like the protagonist, Lucia Santa, who "makes the family organism stand strong against the blows of time: the growth of children, the death of parents, and all changes of worldly circumstance. She lives through five years in an instant, and behind her trail the great shadowy memories that are life's real substance and the spirit's strength." I was so taken by the novel that I started writing letters to Puzo, none of which was ever acknowledged. I took to sending him birthday cards every year, but like the fanatic letters they too were never acknowledged.

In Pietro di Donato's masterpiece, *Christ in Concrete*, I heard my hod-carrier grandfather through Geremio's dreaming aloud while he worked on a construction site: "Laugh, laugh all of you . . . but I tell you that all my kids must be boys so that they someday will be big American builders. And then I'll help them to put the gold away in the basements. . . . But am I not a man, to feed my own with these hands? Ah, but day will end and no boss in the world can then rob me the joy of my home!"

Through John Fante's novels and short stories, I came to see not only my grandparents but the way their children might have seen them, as through his story "The Odyssey of a Wop"—"I pick up little bits of information about my grandfather. My grandmother tells me of him. She tells me that when he lived he was a good fellow whose goodness evoked not admiration but pity. He was known as a good little Wop." And later on, because of Fante, I understood why my mother used to say, "I'm a dago, you're a wop; I eat spaghetti, you eat slop." "From the beginning," writes Fante, "I hear my mother use the words Wop and Dago with such vigor as to denote violent distaste. She spits them out. They leap from her lips. To her, they contain the essence of poverty, squalor, filth."

I ate up every Fante work I could find. He became my Hemingway. Just as Puzo became my Norman Mailer; di Donato, my James Farrell. All of a sudden, American literature was not something descendant from the Pilgrims. I could make sense of the drama inside the Catholic Church and understand the sturdy pagan underpinnings of my family's fears of the "Evil Eye" and defiance of literate authorities. These writers transformed my grandparents' broken English from signs of stupidity and sources of embarrassment into beautiful music that I began re-creating in my stories. And when I did, I heard them as though for the first time; their resurrections kept me sane.

The more I read of these Italian American writers, the harder it became to focus on my master's thesis on Walt Whitman. One day, I took a wrong turn in the library stacks and stumbled on the "E 184" shelf. Between books on Irish Americans and Japanese Americans were a few books on Italian Americans. That's where I found Rose Green's study of the Italian American novel. The discovery was frightening. I picked up the book and could not believe there was such a thing as an Italian American novel, let alone so many of them. I thought, here I was, a B.A. in English from the University of Wisconsin–Madison, with a nearly completed master's degree in literature from the University of Chicago, and I had never in my life heard of this? I sat down in the aisle and read the book. I checked it out and renewed it for two years—never once getting a call from the library that someone else wanted it. Using Green's bibliography, I searched for and read every book I could find that was authored by someone with an Italian surname. It seemed that everywhere I turned I found another Italian American writer. I began scouring used bookstores and leaving lists with the owners. It wasn't long before they started calling me whenever a book by an author with an Italian surname came into their hands. One day, a tiny bookstore in Chicago's Uptown called and left a message that a book entitled *Under Tina* had just come in. Sounded like porno fiction, but I checked it out anyway. Turned out it was *Umbèrtina*, a fine first novel by Helen Barolini and the first I had read by an Italian American woman. Barolini's writing gave words to my grandmothers' silences: "She had won, but who could she tell the story to? . . . She had seven living children and twenty-seven grandchildren, but to none of them could she really speak." Through Barolini's epic novel, I learned of my culture from a woman's point of view, a perspective I had never known, either because I had never bothered to listen or because of the silence I had never realized was imposed on Italian American women.

Fante, Puzo, and Barolini all taught me how to re-see the world I lived in and how to listen to and speak about that world. They filled the gaps created by my family's refusal or inability to discuss the past. I took whatever I needed from these accounts to make sense of my life. I became obsessed with gathering everything: cookbooks, self-published novels, poems, good and bad. I began to develop a growing sense of Italian American culture that reached beyond my family and broke the stereotypes I was consuming through the American media. Through Jerre Mangione's *Mount Allegro*, I began to understand the struggle involved in forging an identity out of two competing ways of living and thinking. "We gradually acquired the notion that we were Italian at home and American (whatever that was) elsewhere. Instinctively, we all sensed the necessity of adapting ourselves to two different worlds." Here were words that explained what I had felt all my life but could never understand. Italian American literature was giving me my self. The writers took material from their families, their neighborhoods, and turned it into informative and entertaining tales of how to deal with *difference*. Often I realized that they might be revealing things about their families that I could never say in public, let alone write. But they, especially the women, were teaching me that a writer could break the cultural code of *omertà*, or silence, and still live.

While I began to see the relationships between these writers and those others who I had once believed were the real American writers—the Hawthornes, the Poes, and the Whitmans—I wondered if there was a connection between the Italian American writers and Italian literature. While there were some writers, like Ignazio Silone, who gave me insight into the conditions under which Italians immigrated to America, and Dante and Machiavelli, who revealed the roots of public behavioral codes such as *bella figura* (the maintenance of a public mask so as not to reveal any weaknesses to outsiders), I found very little direct connection between the two literatures. Where I found the connections was through my study of the oral traditions evidenced through folktales, such as those collected by Italo Calvino, and also proverbs. I realized that so much of the literature created by the early Italian American writers was the oral culture in writing. This led me to realize that Italian American literature, the child of Italian and American cultures, had been abandoned by both its parents, making it an orphan of sorts or at least giving it the sense of being an illegitimate offspring that would have to fend for itself in the world's cultural arena.

To substantiate this theory, I knew I would have to learn more about the writers I had read. Through reading their nonfiction and biographical sketches in reference books, I learned that di Donato never planned to become a writer and that Fante and Mangione both wanted nothing else. For some, like Fante and Mangione, writing was a way of becoming American. For others, like di Donato, writing became a way of dealing with the incredible experiences of immigrants as they became Americans. For all of them, there was no formal recognition in their own communities. Writing was not something necessary to the immigrant culture. In fact, as I learned through studying Italian culture, writing was a way for those in power to separate themselves and keep a distance from the poor. Reading and writing meant little to the peasant farmers and day laborers who made up a great number of those who emigrated from Italy. The Catholic Church, never having fostered literacy, thus leaving interpretation of the Bible in the hands of the clergy, used reading and writing to control its congregations.

This historical reality held fast even in contemporary American life. This became obvious to me when I began circulating through the Italian American cultural community and talking to people about these writers. While the vast majority were highly literate, very few if any, knew anything about Italian American literature. Most of the books were out of print. Writers were dying with little or no public record of their existence. If they were fortunate enough to have their books in libraries, they'd live again only if a student found them. I decided that what these writers needed was an advocate and that I would become that advocate. Why not? I had always wanted to be a lawyer, but not having the means to make it into and through law school, I could turn those yearnings into literary advocacy.

To gain a sense of how to approach Italian American writers critically, I turned to reading criticism of other ethnic literatures and discovered Houston Baker and Henry Louis Gates. In "Criticism in the Jungle," Gates provided exactly what I was looking for when he said: "W. E. B.

DuBois argued that evidence of critical activity is a sign of a tradition's sophistication, since criticism implies an awareness of the process of art itself and is a second-order reflection upon those primary texts that define a tradition and its canon. . . . All great writers demand great critics" (8). These ideas soon led me to the scene of the next cultural crime: graduate school.

After completing my master's degree with a thesis on Walt Whitman, I decided to turn my attention to Italian American writers. I found a professor who agreed to be my accomplice; after polling the other faculty, he suggested that I bail out of academia and do the work on my own. Breaking in, he suggested, would be impossible. The only alternative would be to strike a compromise by working on Henry James, who had, after all, used Italian settings and characters in his fiction. I had never been able to get through a Henry James novel in my life. But just to see if I could handle it, I picked up his *American Scene* and, after reading a few hundred pages, realized that this famous American writer was appalled by the sight of the Italian immigrant workers he had seen. No, James would not be worth my time, so I followed my professor's first suggestion and escaped.

Armed with my new understanding of a hyphenated identity, I was determined to change the mistaken notions of those professors. I believed that if I could prove there was Italian American literature and that it did not depend on a distinctive Italian American audience, then my own writing would have a tradition and I a place in it. Once I had a sense of the literature, I was ready to meet those who had created it. But you couldn't just go up and tap an Italian American writer on the shoulder, especially those who had become famous. So I decided that I needed a front. I convinced the *Fra Noi*, a Chicago monthly newspaper, that they needed a book review column, and since they wouldn't have to pay me, I was given the opportunity to do what I wished. I began by relentlessly pursuing writers I had identified as Italian American, even those writers who did not see themselves as "ethnic."

One of the first I interviewed was a local Chicago writer, Tina DeRosa, whose novel *Paper Fish* (1980) was one of the greatest works I had ever read and the first ever of the Italian American experience in Chicago written by an Italian American. Her impressionistic style reminded me of the brilliant passages of Henry Roth's *Call It Sleep*, but there was a major difference. DeRosa's writing was poetry that told stories, that created scenes I had seen. Reading her novel made me see the tiny details of my past—the strings of dried peppers hanging on my grandmother's back porch—and the large issues, such as the end of immigrant culture and the beginning of suburban assimilation of the children and grandchildren of immigrants. Through writers like DeRosa, I learned that Italian American culture was multidimensional and could never be simply categorized. I began reviewing writers, interviewing them, holding public forums, and doing all I could to promote their work. Some people, mostly scholars but sometimes even the writers themselves, suggested that I was fabricating this notion of the Italian American writer in order to jump into the new fad of ethnic studies that was hitting the universities. The result of all this was that I established a strong intraethnic identity, which was subsequently stabilized by studying the Italian language and traveling to Italy whenever possible. The result was that a year after leaving academia I felt I was ready to start sending my writing out.

It wasn't until I began to submit writing to mainstream publications that I realized that disseminating my work would demand political action. My first attempt at a novel was greeted with mixed reactions by a number of editors. One suggested that I follow in Puzo's footsteps with the Mafia material; another suggested that I change the characters' ethnicity because (1) Italian Americans do not read and so could not be counted on to buy the book, and (2) Italian American characters would alienate those who did buy books, unless of course I was willing to tell more about the many murders that occurred in my family's past. I put aside my fiction and spent most of the next ten years reading, writing criticism, and giving talks about Italian American literature. It was during this period that I finally did meet Ferlinghetti, when he came to Chicago to do a reading. I was able to use the *Fra Noi* to arrange an hourlong interview. Once I got the interview I wanted, I told him about my earlier pilgrimage. He assured me that I should have tapped him on the shoulder back then. But I knew that I needed these years of reading and critically reviewing his work in order to have the confidence to meet him on more or less equal footing.

I followed the careers of Tony Ardizone and Jay Parini, neither of whom saw himself as an Italian American writer when I first talked to him. But when I reached the older writers, such as Joseph Papaleo, Rocco Fumento, and Ben Morreale, I heard something different. Morreale felt that he had never been recognized as an Italian American writer because the Italian American community had no way of seeing the need for its writers, at least not the same way the Jewish or African American communities did. He spoke of the anger he felt when the Mafia imagery overshadowed all the efforts of American artists of Italian descent. This anger perhaps could be traced to the negative attitudes that kept the Italian American writers from wanting to identify themselves with their ethnicity.

Breaking away from the stereotypes might have been easier had these artists been supported by their own *paesani*; but for writers like Mario Puzo, gaining fame and fortune through fiction had been a way of making it, of getting beyond the constraints placed on the immigrant generation. It was a personal and individual struggle that, once rewarded, required no paybacks. And because success came in spite of, not because of, community support, there would be no sense of duty to return support to the community.

This would explain the position of a Gilbert Sorrentino or a Don DeLillo, both of whom I had never considered Italian American writers because they rarely touched on subjects peculiar to the Italian American experience. Later, when I actually found a Ph.D. program at the University of Illinois at Chicago that would allow me to do a thesis on Italian American writers, I had all but dismissed Sorrentino and DeLillo when Christian Messenger, my dissertation advisor, suggested that I include them in my study. I took a year off from my writing to read DeLillo, Sorrentino, and critics Frank Lentricchia and Sandra Gilbert. Once, while I was visiting Joe Papaleo, then director of the writing program at Sarah Lawrence, I told him of DeLillo, and he pointed out the window of his office saying, "That's his house. Sometimes I see him, in the summertime, working with tomatoes in his garden." I looked out and remembered the time I had hitchhiked to San Francisco to meet Ferlinghetti; I had learned my lesson: read the writers before you meet them. Recently, only after reading and writing about him, I invited DeLilio to be included in an anthology project. While I expected his rejection, his response was interesting. In essence, he believes that the writer is a solitary being, one who should shun public affiliations and shouldn't need to be connected to other writers except on the basis of good writing.

Very few American writers of Italian descent have ever achieved what DeLillo has, so I began thinking that perhaps he was right. In fact, the ones I found to be the most frustrated were those who felt ignored by the Italian Americans they were trying reach. The ones who felt successful were the ones who ignored their ethnic communities, the very ones who had most likely written things that had antagonized that community. But if DeLillo was right, then my whole sense of there being such a thing as Italian American literature would be destroyed. How could an American writer of Italian descent *not* write an Italian American story? The only way I could reconcile this was to understand that while ethnic identity was not a subject for his art, it could very well be a source, an underground spring of sorts, for his approach to art. I turned back to his writings and began finding themes such as identity quests and ethnic discomfort that were similar to those I had found in the writers who used their Italian American experience as the subject matter for their art. With this new understanding, I realized I had my work cut out for me.

I felt that there remained a great void in American history and that someone had to do something about acknowledging the contribution of Italian American writers. My work in the *Fra Noi* gained the attention of editors and publishers. I was able to contribute articles to magazines, journals, and books, which led to the opportunity to edit books such as *Italian-American Ways*. While I traveled promoting that book, I came to the realization that Italian Americans do buy books. They just don't go to bookstores for their purchases. They prefer to meet the author before they see his work. This led me to realize that, in general, Italian Americans don't purchase books; they acquire people. In this way they get to take the author home, because without this conviviality, the reading of their work would have less meaning.

The Italian-American Theater Company produced *Vinegar and Oil*, my one-act play based on the interactions of my two grandfathers. I had first written it as a short story and had read it at an American Italian Historical Association conference. At that conference, I met Giose Rimanelli, the celebrated Italian novelist who escaped to America when Italian politics became too much for him. Rimanelli told me that the story was not a story but a play. He was right. The play received good reviews in major papers; this drew out a large Italian American audience. I was encouraged. People like Rimanelli were giving me opportunities to talk about all this reading and writing I had been doing.

But with those opportunities came responsibilities. Rimanelli tossed me an unpublished novel, one he had written back in the 1970s when he was first learning English. I read it and hated it, but to be nice I told him he should try to publish it. He laughed and told me that I would publish it. It wasn't until I read that manuscript three more times that I realized that it was a breakthrough in Italian American literature, the missing link between modern and postmodern Italian American writing. My dissertation advisor liked the inclusion of the novel in my discussion but wondered about the validity of writing about an unpublished manuscript, especially one that was not housed in an accessible archive. He suggested I take it out if it wasn't being published. I suggested to Antonio D'Alfonso, publisher of Guernica Editions, that he publish this book. He did, with hardly a second thought, and *Benedetta in Guysterland* won a 1993 American Book Award.

So much has happened because of my pursuit of the Italian American writer. In 1988, I hooked up with Anthony Tamburri and Paolo Giordano. We gave papers on Italian American literature at a conference where we were accused, by professors of Italian, of creating a ghetto for American writers who just happened to be of Italian descent. The three of us decided to find a way to publish our essays. This search grew into the anthology project, which was rejected a number of times before it was published by Purdue University Press as *From the Margin: Writings in Italian Americana* (1991). During the production and promotion of that anthology we met so many Italian American writers that we decided we would need a journal to keep the conversation alive and current. So even before the anthology appeared, we created a *Voices in Italian Americana*. Our requests for seed money were ignored or dismissed by every major Italian American group with a history of donating money. However, when we put our request before the Fondazione Giovanni Agnelli, an Italian version of the Ford Foundation, we were granted the money to start the journal. *VIA*, now in its eighth year, has become a major forum for literary interaction.

As much of my life has been validated by these writers, my life's work has been validated by the acknowledgment of such major foundations. And while there are only a couple of courses in Italian American literature at the graduate level throughout the world, there are a number of critical dissertations in the making that will one day be books in libraries upon which future students will stumble. More and more the Italian Americans are becoming aware of the value of their writers. Books will be bought, stories will be made into films, and endowed chairs will increase the presence of role models in higher education. I have no doubt that the American writers of Italian descent will have their place in American history.

Anthony J. Tamburri

. . . .

Rethinking the Italian/American Writer

Tony Ardizzone's Expressive Stories of
The Evening News

> Most men do not think things in the way they encounter them,
> nor do they recognize what they experience, but believe their
> own opinions.
> —Heraclitus

(Re)definitions and Categories

Italian/American[1] art forms have been defined as those constructed
mainly by second-generation writers about the experiences of the first and
second generations. Frank Lentricchia once defined Italian/American literature as "a report and meditation on first-generation experience, usually
from the perspective of a second-generation representative" (125). Robert
Casillo defined Italian/American cinema as "works by Italian American
directors who treat Italian American subjects" (374). Such definitions essentially halt, willy-nilly, the progress and limit the impact of those writers
who come from later generations and thus may result in a monolithic notion of what is or is not Italian/American literature. In a similar manner,
Dana Gioia describes "Italian-American poetry . . . only as a transitional
category" for which the "concept of Italian-American poet is therefore
most useful to describe first- and second-generation writers raised in the
immigrant subculture" (3).

New publications, literary and critical, have created a need for new definitions and new critical readings, not only of contemporary works but
also those of the past. Furthermore, these new publications have originated chiefly from within an intellectual community of Italian Americans.[2]

What I propose is that we reconsider Italian/American literature as a series of ongoing written enterprises that establish a repertoire of signs, at
times sui generis, and therefore create verbal variations that represent different versions—dependent on one's generation, gender, socioeconomic
condition—of what can be perceived as the Italian/American signified.[3]
That is, the Italian/American experience may be manifested in any art
form in a number of ways and at varying degrees, for which one may readily speak of the variegated artistic representations of the Italian/American
ethos in the same fashion in which Daniel Aaron spoke of the "hyphenate
writer."[4]

Aaron sets up three stages through which an ethnic writer might pass
from "'hyphenation' to 'dehyphenation'" (214).[5] The first-stage writer is the
"pioneer spokesman for the . . . unspoken-for" ethnic or racial group, who
writes about his/her co-others with the goal of debunking negative stereotypes. Less willing to please, the second-stage writer abandons the use of
preconceived ideas in an attempt to demystify negative stereotypes.
Whereas the first-stage writer might have adopted some preconceived notions popular with the dominant culture, this writer presents characters
who have already sunk "roots into the native soil." This writer readily indicates the disparity and, in same cases, may even engage in militant criticism of the perceived restrictions set forth by the dominant group. The
third-stage writer, in turn, travels from the margin to the mainstream
"viewing it no less critically, perhaps, but more knowingly." Having appro-
priated the dominant group's culture and the tools necessary to succeed
in that culture—the greater skill of manipulating, for instance, a language
acceptable to the dominant group—more strongly than his/her predecessors, this writer feels entitled to the intellectual and cultural heritage of
the dominant group. As such, the third-stage writer can also, from a personal viewpoint, "speak out uninhibitedly as an American."

An excellent analogue to Aaron's three stages of the "hyphenate writer"
can be found in Fred L. Gardaphé's threefold Vichian division of the history of Italian/American literature. Gardaphé proposes a culturally "specific methodology" for reexamining Italian/American literary productions.
In his essay, he reminds us of Vito's "three ages and their corresponding
cultural products: the Age of Gods in which primitive society records expression in 'poetry' [*vero narratio*,] the Age of Heroes, in which society
records expression in myth, and the Age of Man, in which through self-
reflection, expression is recorded in philosophic prose." These three ages,
Gardaphé continues, have their parallels in modern and "contemporary
[socio]cultural constructions of realism, modernism, and postmodernism"

("Visibility," 24). And ultimately, the evolution of the various literatures of U.S. ethnic and racial groups can be charted as they "move from the po-etic, through the mythic and into the philosophic" (ibid., 25).

For first-stage writers, then, the *vero narratio* constitutes the base of what they write. They no more write about what they *think* than what they *experience,* their surroundings. Their art, in a sense, records more their experiential feelings than their analytical thoughts. Such writers are not concerned with an adherence to or the creation of some form of ob-jective, rhetorical literary paradigm. Second-stage writers, the "militant protesters," belong to the generation that re/discovers and/or reinvents its ethnicity. While they may present characters who have already "sunk roots in the native soil," they readily underscore the characters' unique-ness vis-à-vis the expectations of the dominant culture. As Gardaphé re-minds us, before such writers can "merge with the present," they must re-create—and here I would add, in a sui generis manner—their past: they must engage in a "materialization and an articulation of the past" ("Visibil-ity," 27). The use of ethnicity at this second stage shifts from the expres-sive to the descriptive. As a rhetoricoideological tool, ethnicity becomes much more functional and quasi-descriptive; the ethnic signs constitute the individual pieces to the ethnic paradigm second-stage writers so con-sciously and willingly seek to construct. In turn, third-stage writers (i.e., Gardaphé's philosophic writer) may seem at first glance to rid themselves of their ethnicity.[6] These writers, as Aaron reminds us, will often view the dominant culture "less critically" than the previous writers but indeed "more knowingly." Similarly, as Gardaphé continues, such writers find themselves in a decisively self-reflexive stage and can readily transcend the experiential expressivity of the first two stages by either engaging in a parodic tour de force through their art or by relegating any vestige of their ethnicity to the background of their artistic inventions. In both cases, the writers have come to terms with their personal (read, ethnic) history, without totally and/or explicitly renouncing or abandoning cultural her-itage. These writers transcend "mere parochial allegiance" and pass com-pletely out of the *expressive* and *descriptive* stages into a third and final (?) reflexive stage, in which everything becomes fair game. All this is due to the "postmodern prerogative" of all artists, whether the parodic, the local-izers, or others simply in search of rules for what will have been done.

Both Aaron and Gardaphé look at these writers from the perspective of time; their analyses are generationally based and rightfully so. However, we would not err to look at these three stages from a cognitive Peircean perspective of firstness, secondness, and thirdness, as rehearsed in his *Principles of Philosophy*. All three stages represent different modes of being dependent on different levels of consciousness. They progress from a state of nonrationality ("feeling")[7] to practicality ("experience")[8] to pure rationality ("thought"),[9] or "potentiality," "actuality," and "futuribility."

If firstness is the isolated, sui generis mode of possibly being that Peirce tells us it is, we may see an analogue in the first-stage writer's *vero narratio*. For Gardaphé tells us that primitive society records expression in poetry, in unmitigated realism, that which the writer experiences only.[10] In this sense, the writer's sensorial experiences, his/her "feelings" constitute the "very stuff of [his/her] literary material" (Aaron 214)—namely, those recordings of what s/he simply experiences, without the benefit of any "analysis, comparison or any [other] process whatsoever . . . by which one stretch of consciousness is distinguished from another."

As second-stage writers shift from the expressive to the descriptive, they engage in some form of analysis and comparison, two processes fundamental to Peirce's secondness. These writers thus become aware of the dominant culture—"how a second object is"—and do not repeat the conciliatory acts of first-stage writers—they undergo a "forcible modification of . . . thinking [which is] the influence of the world of fact or *experience*."

Third-stage writers transcend the first two stages either through parody or diminution of the significance of their expressivity because they have seen "both sides of the shield" and can therefore "contemplate them from the outside only." For that "element of cognition [thirdness] which is neither feeling [firstness] nor the polar sense [secondness], is the consciousness of a process, and this in the form of the sense of learning, of acquiring, mental growth is eminently characteristic of cognition" (Peirce, 1:381). This third mode of being is the consciousness of a process, the "consciousness of synthesis" (ibid.), which is precisely what third-stage, postmodern writers do. They can transcend the intellectual experiences of the first two stages because of all that has preceded them, both temporally (Aaron, Gardaphé) and cognitively (Peirce).

What we therefore witness is a progression from a stage of realism to that of incredulous postmodernism, with passage through a secondary stage of mythic modernism in which this monolithic, modernist writer believes to have found all the solutions to what s/he has perceived as the previous generation's *problems*. Thus, we may now speak in terms of a twofold evolution that bears three distinct writers to whom we may now attach more precise labels. The *expressive* writer embodies the poetic realist who writes more from "feelings." Through the process of analysis, on the other hand, the second is a *comparative* writer who sets up a distinct polarity between his/her cultural heritage and the dominant culture in an attempt to construct a sui generis ethnic paradigm. The third writer, through "mental growth," as Peirce states, embraces a consciousness of process (i.e., self-reflexivity) and consequently engages in a process of synthesis and "bind[s] . . . life together" (1: 381)—this I consider the *synthetic* writer. Figure 1 charts my use of the above-mentioned terminology.

It is important to emphasize that these three general categories do not represent a hierarchy. Similar to Peirce's three stages, these categories represent *different* modes of being dependent on *different* levels of consciousness. Just as literary texts in general, as Ahmad tells us, "are produced in highly differentiated, usually over-determined contexts of competing ideological and cultural clusters" (23), so too do each of the three categories constitute specific cognitive and ideological clusters that ultimately provide energy and form to the texts of those writers of the three different stages. Second, these stages do not necessarily possess any form of monolithic valence. It is possible, I would suggest, that a writer's opera, if not opus, may indeed reflect more than one, if not all three, of these stages. In this respect, we should remind ourselves that ethnicity is not a fixed essence passed down from one generation to the next. Rather, "ethnicity is something reinvented and reinterpreted in each generation by each individual," which, in the end, is a way of "finding a voice or style that does not violate one's *several components of identity*" (Fischer 195; my emphasis), these components constituting the specificities of each individual.

This said, then, we should also keep in mind that we may now think in terms of a twofold evolutionary process, both temporal and cognitive, that may and/or may not be mutually inclusive. We may have, sociologically speaking, second- or third-generation writers who find a voice or style in their recent rediscovery and reinvention of their ethnicity. Though members of the second or third generation, they may actually produce what we may now expect from the expressive or comparative writer—namely, the first- or second-generation writer. Conversely, we may actually find a member of the immigrant generation—undoubtedly, a "first-stage" writer from a temporal point of view—whose work exudes everything but that which we would expect from the work of a first- or even a second-generation writer (that is, Aaron's "first-" or "second-stage" writer). For my first hypothesis, I have in mind a writer like Tony Ardizzone, a third-generation Italian American whose work fits much better the category of the expressive writer.

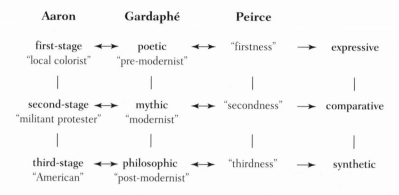

FIGURE I.

Tony Ardizzone's *Evening News*

Tony Ardizzone's *The Evening News* is a collection of eleven short stories that won the 1986 Flannery O'Connor Award for Short Fiction.[11] It offers its reader a portrait, for the most part, of the neighborhood where Ardizzone spent his childhood; he presents his reader with both working- and middle-class citizens of all ages, mostly of Italian descent. Except for a few stories about college, Ardizzone's characters are the so-called hyphenated Americans who occupy a world seemingly different from what one might expect; they are very much ensconced in a world of memory and recollection that keeps them ineluctably tied to their past, either in search of some way of understanding their present situation or, in certain cases, in an attempt to escape from their present situation.

In articulating a sense of empathy for his characters, Ardizzone becomes a sort of pioneer spokesperson—similar to Aaron's "first-stage" writer—for the unspoken-for marginalized Italian American. He offers portraits of his co-ethnics with the goal of dislodging negative stereotypes ensconced in the dominant culture's mind-set. In so doing, he also creates characters possessing at times some of the very same stereotypes that some sensitive types (e.g., thin-skinned Italian Americans) would rather see debunked.[12] In this manner, he surely succeeds in humanizing the stereotyped figure. At the same time, he does not necessarily engage directly in militant criticism of any preconceptions, restrictions, and/or oppression of ethnicity set forth by the dominant group. As a result, demystification of negative stereotypes is, at best, left for the reader to infer, for which the general reader's strategy for and/or interpretation of "dissipating prejudice" is called to the fore, and the semiotic responsibility of any sort of finalized act of signification is shifted from that of being entirely the author's to a more complicit act between author and reader. What I thus propose here is a reading of two of Ardizzone's stories as an example of his *expressivity*, as it pertains to what I have outlined earlier of my reconsideration and redefinition of the Italian/American writer.

Rewriting Ethnicity

In Ardizzone's opening tale, "My Mother's Stories," the narrator clearly speaks in his own voice, offering us a moving tribute to his ill mother of German descent married to his Italian/American father. The story opens with a brief description of how his mother was born frail and sickly. In fact, we read that "they were going to throw her away when she was a baby. The doctors said she was too tiny, too frail, that she wouldn't live" (1). What becomes significant at the outset is that this is also the opening of the entire collection, for which the frailty of the narrator's ethnic mother is also, I would suggest, a signal of the frailty of the immigrant and his/her progeny. Such frailty of one's existential condition, I would suggest here, will reappear at the end of the collection in the figure of Nonna.

All of this is couched in a much more intimate rapport between the narrator and his reader, when, in a Calvinian sense, he adopts the "You" in "You can well imagine the rest," which now transforms the reader, semiotically, into a type of listener and, emotionally, into a type of confidant. Thus, from the viewpoint of both representation and content, a shift in modality also occurs. Such a shift in levels between narrator and reader—or for that matter, any transformation in one's narrative technique—is part and parcel of the author/narrator's sense of self-awareness that informs much of this story, signaled here at the beginning: ". . . my mother and her stories. For now the sounds and pictures are my sounds and pictures. Her memory, my memory" (1). Such self-awareness first of all puts the narrator on the same level as his mother, and in a certain sense, his story telling replicates that of his mother, which he now recounts. Thus, we become witness to a type of circularity between who tells and what is being told, as the narrator engages in an act of identification with whom he describes. The act of narration is underscored by the fact that the narrator alludes to his narrating as well as to his mother, the storyteller as protagonist, and her previous story telling to him and his family. Such a layered narrative situation might be mapped out by a curious set of graphs. First, in modifying slightly Seymour Chatman's 1978 schemata (151),

FIGURE 2.

we may chart the overall narrative communication act as shown in fig. 2.

We see that Ardizzone sets up a multilayered narrative text that has embedded in his narrative communication act a second one—his mother's—including him as character. Second, in charting further the relationship between our narrator (N) and his narrated protagonist, his mother (M), we see the circularity of identification between who narrates (N) and what/whom (M) is being narrated:

$$N \to M = M/N \text{ (mother} <=> \text{narrator)} <= N$$

The narrator (N) discusses (→) his mother who soon becomes (<=>) for us also the mother/narrator (M/N) with whom our narrator eventually identifies (<=), as we saw above: "For now the sounds and pictures are *my* sounds and pictures. Her memory, my memory."

A secondary level of identification becomes equally significant here in relationship to the theme of ethnicity. Whereas above, the narrator becomes a storyteller like his mother, the protagonist of his story, here the narrator also becomes a (metaphoric) first-generation hyphenate like his mother. The storyteller's story thus replicates the life of his character. We therefore see the polysemy of the above-cited act of identification insofar as the storyteller (i.e., Narrator) as both raconteur and ethnic becomes his character the storyteller (i.e., his mother). In so doing, he signals to us that, like her, he is a first-generation storyteller. Thus, in spite of his actual ethnic status of third generation, here Ardizzone's stories appear as examples of narratives a first-generation writer might readily construct.

Along with the author's self-consciousness, we see that ethnicity is not limited to Italian Americans only; the character's mother is in fact German. Furthermore, the difference in immigrant groups is underscored by color: the Germans are light; the Italians are dark ("dark Sicilians"), as is her girlfriend and the sister of her future husband, who, in turn, is "finely muscled, dark, deeply tanned" (2). Thus, we have the usual light-versus-dark binary opposition among ethnic groups. Indeed, lest we forget, Italians were considered people of color by some sociologists in the early years of the twentieth century.[13] The initial description of the character, in fact, is presented from the young woman's perspective, the narrator's frightened young mother:

> Perhaps our Mary, being young, is somewhat frightened. The boy behind the dark fence is older than she, is in high school, is *finely muscled, dark, deeply tanned*. *Around his neck hang golden things glistening on a thin chain. He wears a sleeveless shirt—his undershirt*. Mary doesn't know whether to stay with her young friend or to continue walking. She stays, but she looks away from the boy's dark eyes and gazes instead at *the worn belt* around his *thin waist*. (2; emphasis added)

We see above that the father as a young man is an Adonis-like individual, a handsome replica of a Greek statue, who nevertheless readily recalls an image representative of the stereotype of the working-class Italian American. Tony, in a multireferential irony we should not lose, wears a sleeveless shirt, the "classic guinea T-shirt," as often called years ago, and sports, again according to a classic Italian/American semiotic, a golden chain laden with easily recognizable amulets—so recognizable that it is not necessary to enumerate them. The Italian/American sign system is further employed in the physical description of the narrator's young father. Both his muscularity and olive complexion are presented as integral parts of one another; for he is "finely muscled, dark, [and] deeply tanned," as we read. In addition, his working-class status is signaled at the end of this brief description, together with his physical attributes, as Mary, too shy from her proper raising, does not look him in the eyes but instead "gazes . . . at the worn belt around his thin waist." A most reminiscent interpretant of the Italian American of a certain social class of the early and mid-twentieth century, this portrait prefigures the good-looking athletic type (i.e., muscular) who often ended up in professional or semiprofessional sports if not, on other occasions, in the movies.[14]

Different from some father figures in the writings of other Italian Americans,[15] Tony is a sensitive husband and good father. Toward the end, in fact, his sensitivity comes to the fore. In discussing his wife's terminal illness with his son, we witness his serious demeanor; he was, as we are told, "not a man given to unnecessary talk" (12). Tony's ability to communicate his feelings of imminent loss and seeming desperation belie any notion of the stereotypically macho, emotionally hard-nosed (i.e., paralyzed) Italian/American male. For the father now confides in his son, seeking obvious comfort and reassurance, as is evident from the following conversation:

I don't know what I'd do without her, he says. I say nothing, for I can think of nothing to say. We've been together for over thirty years, he says. He pauses. For nearly thirty-four years. Thirty-four years this October. And, you know, you wouldn't think it, but I love her so much more now. He hesitates, and I look at him. He shakes his head and smiles. (12)

While it is true that the son cannot identify with his father's thirty-four years with his mother, an identification process between father and narrating son (as we saw between mother and son) is also at work. We see, first of all, that the dialogue recounted in an indirect format does not immediately distinguish between the "I" of the father and the "I" of the son: "*I* don't know what *I'd* do without her, he says. *I* say nothing, for *I* can think of nothing to say." But if this initial amalgamation of the two "I"s seems to be belied by the narrator's admitted inability to empathize and/or comprehend his father's feelings—"I cannot imagine it"—such inability is further countered by the transformation of the two singular, first-person pronouns ("I") into the first-person, plural adjectives ("our") and pronouns ("we"). Such transformation, I would add, takes place on two occasions. Immediately after the first two ambiguous "I"s we have a "we": "*I* don't know what *I'd* do without her, he says. *I* say nothing, for *I* can think of nothing to say. *We've* been . . ." The second occurrence can be found in the final, complete sentence of the paragraph, as the son responds to his father's question, "You know what I mean? he says":

> *I* say yes and *we* walk for a while in silence, and *I* think of what it must be like to live with someone for thirty-four years, but *I* cannot imagine it, and then *I* hear my father begin to talk about that afternoon's ball game—he describes at length and in comic detail a misjudged fly ball lost in apathy or ineptitude or simply in the sun—and for the rest of *our* walk home *we* discuss what's right and wrong with *our* favorite baseball team, *our* thorn-in-the-side Chicago Cubs. (emphasis added)

What starts out as an inability to understand his father's sentiments vis-à-vis his wife transforms itself into a total amalgamation of the two men as they now discuss something they both know intimately: "*our* thorn-in-the-side Chicago Cubs."[16]

The Old vis-à-vis the New

In other stories we find the interweaving of the old-world values of Italy with the New World of the United States; we also witness the cultural clash of the ethnic world with the greater world of the nonethnic. "Nonna"—the story about an old immigrant woman in a state of confusion and disconnection, seemingly senile and no longer able to cope with the changes taking place around her—best exemplifies this dichotomous world of the old versus the new. In addition, it poignantly closes Ardizzone's collection. We see how these changes affect the elderly in general as they find themselves in a state of confusion and/or conflict with change. In Nonna's specific case, her confusion and resultant indecision manifest themselves at the very beginning in her movements, as the first full paragraph signals:

> Follow her now as she *slowly* walks down Loomis toward Taylor, her heavy *black* purse dangling at her side. Though it is the middle of summer she wears her *black* overcoat. The air conditioning is too cold inside the stores, *she thinks.* (144; emphasis added)

The adverb *slowly* and the seemingly contrary-to-fact "she thinks" prefigure what is to be her constant conflict throughout this story with the actual, changing reality around her and her own version of what reality should still be. The conflict is further prefigured by Nonna's wearing an overcoat in the midst of summer because of the stores' air conditioning. Finally, her elderly, female, widowed Italian-ness is also prefigured here not only by her name but by the color of her purse and coat—black—a color that has, by this point in the collection, acquired a semiotic value of Italian-ness in general in Ardizzone's aesthetic sign system.

The story's second paragraph continues the thematics of the first in emphasizing Nonna's disconnection from and perceptual conflict with the reality around her and in prefiguring the perennial conflict between old-world and new-world values, as well as the sometimes not so respectful reception of the former by the latter:

> She hesitates, the taste of *aglio* on her tongue. Perhaps she is outside this afternoon to shop. She cannot decide. The children of the neighborhood call out to her as she passes them. *Na-na!* The sound used to call in goats from feeding. Or, sometimes, to tease. Or is it *Nonna,* grandmother, that they call? It makes no difference, the woman thinks. (144; emphasis textual)

We see that both her actions and her impression of the boys' speech underscore her confusion and disconnection. As we saw in the previous paragraph, her hesitation and initial unawareness of being inside or outside indicate Nonna's vacillation vis-à-vis the world around her. This oscillation continues when Nonna cannot decide whether the children are calling her in a respectful or disrespectful manner—"*Na-na*! The sound used to call in goats from feeding. Or, sometimes, to tease. Or is it *Nonna*, grandmother, that they call?"

Also semiotically intriguing is the verb *decide*, as if it were Nonna's choice whether reality should be one way or the other. I make this point because it not only seems to put Nonna in a position of personal enfranchisement, however limited it may be, but on a grander scale it underscores the general semiotic notion of reality as a quasi-individual entity. Inside or outside, respectful or disrespectful, Nonna as a sign source offers up to the reader multireferential signs, for which s/he has the interpretive privilege of reconstructing a reality more similar to his/her own ideological sign system.[17]

Such semiotic freedom also allows for the interpretive reconstruction of the Italian aspect of the story. First, the Italian "aglio" anticipates its linguistic counterpart "Na-na" which, in turn, anticipates its homonymous "Nonna." Second, while "aglio" is inserted in an American sentence with one reference only, garlic, the second Italian word, "Na-na," conjures up a multiplicity of meanings that all prove significant to some degree in this story. In its own right, as we read, "Na-na" can refer both to the calling of sheep or it can be a teasing sound. On the other hand, "Na-na," as stated, can also be a homonym for the Italian noun "Nonna." All of this underscores the Italian aspect of the story and brings to the fore cultural dualism and its various consequences—here prefigured by the positive and negative, as the children call to her or tease her. Finally, Nonna's initial oscillation is punctuated at the end of the paragraph with its closing sentence: "It makes no difference, the woman thinks."

Nonna's experience in her bicultural world of Chicago is one of dealing with difference that is, first of all, immigrant. She also assumes that these young men are both Italian and Catholic since they wear "cornicelli" around their necks, which thus moves her to wonder about the non-Italian names on the storefronts and to reminisce about her dead husband and their own Italian origins. In the first case, she assumes that these people, like many Italian immigrants, have shortened their names; she also wonders if they are still in touch with their culture of origin: "what part of the boot [Mr. Swanks's] family came from, and does he still speak the old language" (149). Like the first part of this sentence that alludes to Italy, the adjective *old* here also appears on a number of other occasions in this story with the distinct feature of underscoring the dichotomy of Nonna's bicultural experience—the difference between the "old" and "new" worlds.

In the case of Nonna reminiscing about her and Vincenzo's Italian origins, Ardizzone informs his text with a number of significant, multireferential signs:

> She pictures Padova on the worn, tired boot. Vincenzo called Italy that. Nonna remembers that Padova sits far up in the north, west of Venezia. She looks down at her black shoes. Italia. She was from the south, from Napoli, and Vincenzo, her husband, may he rest, came from the town of Altofonte, near Palermo, in Sicilia. The good strong second son of *contadini*. (149; emphasis textual)

Italy is the "worn, tired boot" that could not accommodate Nonna's and Vincenzo's basic needs for them to stay and live in their own country. The dichotomy of the two worlds—Italy/USA—in which Nonna has lived for so long is now replicated in the north/south dichotomy to which she alludes here in her thoughts. Padova and Venezia stand as the northern counterpart to the southern cities of Napoli and Altofonte. Nonna's dilemma is now amplified through this north/south dichotomy that is punctuated by the phrase, "She *looks down* at her *black* shoes," where the geography of north/south is signaled by Nonna's bowing of her head, and the Italy that could not offer them the sustenance they needed to remain is signaled by the color "black" of her shoes. Third, we see that Vincenzo was one of many farmers who, in U.S. metropolitan areas, were often considered unskilled workers or laborers. Finally, we should not ignore another example of Ardizzone's subtle choice and use of language, here signaled by the contrasting use of *Italy* for the country from which they came for economic reasons, and *Italia* for the area of the country about which she now reminisces and she obviously misses.

The second and third general aspects of Nonna's Catholicism and her gender dilemma are often intertwined. With regard to her Catholicism, we saw early on that while Nonna now finds herself in a differently evolved neighborhood, where she no longer recognizes the faces of the sons or grandsons of those she once knew, she is, as we saw above, relieved to see that they are still Catholics: "Well, at least they are still Catholics, she thinks, and her lips move as she says *They are still Catholics,* and her hand begins to form the sign of the cross" (148; emphasis textual).

As Nonna's state of mental disconnection continues to manifest itself during her walk down Taylor Street, in her state of confusion, which now also consists of mental shifts back to her youth in the States, she notices a young girl in the bookstore window:

She looks inside the bookstore window and sees a long-haired girl behind the counter. Her head is bent. She is reading. Nonna smiles. It is what a young girl should do when she is in a bookstore. *When she is in church she should pray for a good husband, someone young, with a job, who will not hit her. Then when she is older, she should pray to the Madonna for some children. To have one. To have enough.* (150–51; emphasis added)

Nonna immediately consents to the young woman's behavior of reading a book, for, after all, that is what one should do in a bookstore. In like fashion, Nonna's simple logic manifests itself as she suddenly shifts from the bookstore scene to a church, where we find our first intertwining of the gender and religious themes. As Nonna thinks of church, we see that the young woman should in fact pray for "a good husband, someone young, with a job, who will not hit her." She should, we see, immediately relegate herself to the role of wife, as old-world values would require. In addition, (1) the man should have a good job, (2) pure and basic economic amelioration is the end goal, and (3) he should not hit her.[18] The old-world influence continues: In order to find fulfillment, according to Nonna's semiotic, this young woman must become both wife and mother.

Nonna's disconnection is further manifested by her confusion as to where her sons are, what happened to them, when she associates the young girl in the bookstore with her imaginary Mrs. Swanks who cannot have children. At this point in the narration, two things occur. First, she momentarily realizes that Mrs. Swanks's husband's infertility is actually the problem Vincenzo had: the reason she and Vincenzo never had children. Nonna's reaction proves equally significant for the discussion at hand:

Poor Mrs. Swanks, Nonna thinks. Her Antonio must not be good for her. *It is often the fault of the man.* The doctors in New Jersey had told her that. Not once, but many times. That was so long ago. *But do you think I listened? Nonna says to herself. For one moment? For all those years? My ears were deaf! Nonna is gesturing angrily with her hands.* She strikes the store's glass window. *It was part of Heaven's test, she is saying, to see if I would stop believing. . . .* Inside the bookstore the manager closes his book and comes to the window. Nonna watches her close her book and stand, then raise her head. *She wears a mustache. It is a boy.* (152; emphasis added)

Nonna, we discover at this point, took on the responsibility of not having had children even though it was her husband who was infertile. In addition, we see that she has associated her and Vincenzo's misfortune with a test of her faith, as part of the Catholic experience to endure misfortune. At this point in the story we also realize that Nonna is, in fact, engaged in creating her own little world; as, we see here, she has reconstructed the reality around her into one that suits her own emotional needs. Mrs. Swanks, we now realize, is a re-creation of Nonna's own misfortune of long ago, and the only way for Nonna to confront her situation so many years later is to create a fictional character who reflects her own experience. This re-creation, as Ardizzone informs his text, is underscored by the impersonal narrative interspersed with Nonna's thoughts, in the case of Mrs. Swanks, and her perceptions, in the case of the bookstore manager—"Inside the bookstore the manager closes *his* book and comes to the window"—whom she sees as the young woman but who is really a male: "Nonna watches *her* close *her* book and stand, then raise *her* head. *She* wears a mustache. It is a *boy*."

Nonna's gender dilemma comes to the fore when she overhears her downstairs neighbor, young Lucia, and her boyfriend. At this point we see the intermingling of religion and gender and, more specifically, the sexual, as Nonna now thinks back to the first time she and Vincenzo made love:

> The night was hot, and that brought back to her the thin face of Vincenzo, and she was suddenly young . . . in New Jersey, in her parents' house, with young Vincenzo in the stuffed chair opposite her and . . . the soft sound of her mother's tranquil snoring. Nonna shakes her head. She knows what she must feel about that night. She was trusting, and Vincenzo was so handsome—his black curls lay so delicately across his forehead, and his smile was so wet and so white, bright—and she allowed the young boy to sit next to her on the sofa, and she did not protest when he took her hand, and then, when he kissed her, she even opened her mouth and let his wet tongue touch hers. Oh, she was so frightened. Her mouth had been so dry. On the street now she is trembling. She is too terrified to remember the rest. But the memory spills across her mind with the sound of the girls' easy laughter, and she moves back on the pink sofa and does not put up her hands as Vincenzo strokes her cheek and then touches her, gently, on the front of her green dress. And then she turns to the boy and quickly kisses him. The light from the oil lamp flickers. The snoring stops. She looks at Vincenzo, and then she blushes with the shame of her mortal sin, and now if Vincenzo does not say they will marry she knows she will have to kill herself, and that in God's eyes she has already died.
>
> Nonna is still, silent, standing in her guilt on the street, afraid even now to cross herself for fear she will be struck down. She feels the stifling weight of her sin. Vincenzo then moved back to the stuffed chair, coughing.

Neither spoke. She began to cry. The next morning Vincenzo spoke to her
father. (156)

Nonna was socialized to feel the way she does, for she "knows what she
must feel about that night," even though she felt comfortable with Vincenzo and was complicit in bringing their first experience to fruition: "She
was trusting, . . . and she allowed the young boy to sit next to her . . . she
did not protest when he took her hand, . . . she even opened her mouth
and let his wet tongue touch hers." In addition, we see that Nonna's desire to make love with Vincenzo is counterpoised to her current fear of the
consequences as she now thinks back to what they had done. Ardizzone,
we see, adroitly sets up another dichotomy that represents the difference
between Nonna's personal wishes as a young woman and the restrictions
placed on her by her Catholicism and the society in which she lived then
and still does: "Oh, she was so frightened. Her mouth had been so dry. On
the street now she is trembling. She is too terrified to remember the rest."
Nonna's fear of the moment was that she was not ready to receive Vincenzo's kiss, for "her mouth had been so dry."[19] Now, to the contrary, her
fear is a different one, as, old now, she stands "trembling. . . . too terrified
to remember the rest"; for she, we can safely assume, lived with an overwhelming sense of guilt all of her life.

The difference between then and now is underscored in the second half
of Ardizzone's narrative of the event. Nonna is a willing participant: "she
moves back on the pink sofa and . . . turns . . . and . . . kisses him." Yet she
cannot live with, what others consider "her mortal sin," where the adjective
mortal indeed proves multireferential. For she now sees in her act with
Vincenzo the consequences of both the death of her soul—"in God's eyes
she has already died"—and her own potential physical death if Vincenzo
does not now agree to marry her—"if Vincenzo does not say they will marry
she knows she will have to kill herself." Nonna, we see again, suffers from
the pressures visited on her from both her religious association and her social position. As a young *Catholic woman,* she should remain a virgin until
her wedding; otherwise, she risks the consequences of her "sin" in the
death of her soul and a general ostracism from society, because if "everyone . . . will know, [she'll] have to move to another neighborhood" (157).

From one act early in her life, an act of sentiment and affection in
which she was a co-participant, Nonna still suffers the consequences. In
fact, we see that she has blamed herself that she and Vincenzo never had
children, in spite of the fact that he was physically incapable; she never-

theless feels compelled to bear the brunt of the guilt, as the following paragraph underscores:

> Vincenzo understood why she could bear no children; it was because of their sin. Perhaps now that everyone knows, she thinks, she would not have to move anymore. Maybe since the whole world knows, I can finally rest where I am now and be finished with my punishment. And then I'll die, Nonna says. And then, if I have been punished enough, I will be once again with Vincenzo. (157)

The last and surely one of the most effective stories, "Nonna" eulogizes the passing of the old world and at the same time welcomes in a new world of new values and new immigrants. The Italian neighborhood has been transformed into a mixed ethnic locale where a Mexican population has superseded the Italian. And in a sense, the change in the neighborhood accompanies the change that may still take place in Nonna's value system, as this story, and the collection, now comes to a close:

> What she needs is next to the counter. In plastic bags. Nonna is so happy that tears come to her eyes. So this is why she was outside, she thinks, why she is now inside this *strange* store. She had wanted to try the freckled *Mexican flat breads.* Hadn't someone before been telling her about them? Nonna holds the package in her hands and thinks. . . . Someone who explained that her punishment would be over, that soon she would be with her Vincenzo. That these were the breads that were *too simple to have been baked with yeast, that these did not rise, round and golden, like other breads, like women fortunate enough to feel their bellies swell, their breasts grow heavy with the promise of milk, but instead these stayed in one shape, simple, flat.*
> The dark man behind the counter nods and smiles.
> Perhaps, Nonna thinks as her fingers unclasp her purse and search for the coins her eyes no longer clearly see, *perhaps bread is just as good this way.* (160–61; emphasis added)

The "strange store" in which she now finds herself is strange to Nonna not because it is Mexican, or for that matter of any other specific ethnic group, but because it is *not* Italian. Things have changed around Nonna, and she has not been able, cognitively, to process it all, chiefly because she has been consumed most of her life by her overwhelming sense of guilt from her one love act with Vincenzo. In fact, we see that Nonna now connects this "simple" bread to her own personal situation of being a woman who did not bear children.

In addition, as we saw elsewhere, here, too, Ardizzone informs his text with multireferential signs for his reader to decode. As a counterpoint to Nonna's life-long dilemma of sin and guilt, Ardizzone uses the simple motif of food to make his final, closing point. Something so basic and so simple as bread becomes a type of prism though which Nonna can finally begin to consider a different way of thinking. In so doing, Ardizzone inserts the ambiguous sign of consent on the part of the Mexican store owner—ambiguous since we as readers are not sure as to what he concurs with his nod and smile.[20] For the immediate antecedent is Nonna's comparison of the bread to childbearing women. Or, looking forward, we may also assume that the storeowner welcomes what we are about to see, Nonna's new propensity to change; Nonna, we can assume, is—albeit at a late age—now open to change. But it is a change that is not just the transformation of the Italian neighborhood into a Mexican one or the substitution of unleavened bread for yeast bread. Instead, it is a more fundamental change in her way of thinking about her own personal gender position in society, as well as that of other women.

General Considerations

Ardizzone challenges his reader to delve deep below the surface in order to grapple with the sense of some sort of existential unease, if not a seeming despair and hopelessness, often present in his stories. Equally significant is his self-awareness as storyteller and crafty builder of tales. As he tends to lie outside his stories as omniscient narrator, he also inserts himself in stories usually masked as one of the storytellers. In fact, as the narrator of "My Mother's Stories" tells us, writers engage in what I would label narrative *irresponsibility,* to echo the long-forgotten Wayne Booth in our theoretical/critical world of narrow-minded poststructuralism:[21] "I stand here, not used to speaking about things that are so close to me. I am used to veiling things in my stories, to making things wear masks, to telling my stories through masks" (12). The "here" of where our narrator stands is an ambiguous one. This paragraph, which appears at the end of Ardizzone's opening story, is set apart from the main text by spaces inserted before and after the preceding and subsequent paragraphs. Thus, we must, as involved readers, look for whatever possible bits of evidence lying beneath the surface—"veil[ed in] masks," as Ardizzone's narrator would tell us—might lead us down one or the other interpretive path. For we should not forget what Ardizzone's narrator tells us at the end of his first story: "but [my mother] never said what it was that she saw from the front windows. A good storyteller, she leaves what she has all too clearly seen to our imaginations" (13). We may surely borrow our initial narrator's words and, in considering Ardizzone's story telling, state that, like his narrator's mother, Ardizzone the "good storyteller, . . . leaves what [he] has all too clearly [crafted] to our imaginations."

Indeed, as his characters seem to inhabit a certain time period or possess characteristics of a period long gone, in his own way Ardizzone inhabits, in a thematic sense, an ethnic warp. To cite one of his reviewers, he "can't seem to cut himself free [from working-class, ethnic, city life]. And that's good, because his book not only entertains, it fills a void."[22] He does not engage in the militant criticism we would expect of a comparative writer; nor does he go beyond the ethnic in an attempt to synthesize his stories and characters with irony and/or ethnic dispassion. He succeeds, like those who (re)turn to their ethnicity and (re)invent it through their craft while filling in the above-mentioned void. It is, in fact, this filling of such a void—an ethnic void, I would suggest—that, in one sense, makes Ardizzone the expressive writer that he is. The characters he presents are still very much tied to individuals with the vicissitudes of those whom Aaron outlined in his essay. Ardizzone, that is, writes from the heart of the North Side of Chicago, a socioeconomic milieu where ethnicity is still very much alive and well, and class issues are up front and personal.

Notes

· ·

1. For more on the slash in place of the hyphen, see Tamburri (*To Hyphenate*, esp. 20–27, 33–42).

2. For a compilation of a recent Italian/American critical self-inventory, see Giordano and Tamburri's introduction.

3. For a recent rehearsal of a "postmodern," critical analysis of Italian/American literature, see Gardaphé (*Italian Signs*, "Visibility").

4. Ten years after Aaron's original version, Rose Basile Green spoke to an analogous phenomenon within the history of Italian/American narrative; then she discussed four stages: "the need for assimilation," "revulsion," "counterrevulsion," and "rooting."

5. To avoid repetitive textual citations, I point out that Aaron's description of all these stages is found on p. 214.

6. For a cogent example of ethnic signs relegated to the margin—what at first

glance may seem an absence—see Gardaphé's discussion of DeLillo ("Visibility," 30–31), where he also rehearses his notions of the "visible" and "invisible" Italian/American writers.

7. "By a feeling, I mean an instance of that kind of consciousness which involves no analysis, comparison or any process whatsoever, nor consists in whole or in part of any act by which one stretch of consciousness is distinguished from another" (1: 306).

8. Secondness, as "the mode of being of one thing which consists in how a second object is" (1: 24), provokes a "forcible modification of our ways of thinking [which is] the influence of the world of fact or *experience*" (1: 321; emphasis textual).

9. "The third category of elements of phenomena consists of what we call laws when we contemplate them from the outside only, but which when we see both sides of the shield we call thoughts" (1: 420).

10. I make this distinction in order not to contradict myself vis-à-vis Peirce's use of the term *real* when he discusses secondness. There, he states: "[T]he real is that which insists upon forcing its way to recognition as *something* other than the mind's creation" (1: 325).

11. The Flannery O'Connor Award of the University of Georgia Press has unearthed some fine Italian/American writers. Along with Ardizzone, other winners include Salvatore La Puma (1987) and Rita Ciresi (1991).

12. As thin-skinned Italian Americans, I have in mind those persons who see absolutely no thematic value to the works of those like Mario Puzo, Nick Pileggi, Frances Ford Coppola, Nancy Savoca, or Martin Scorsese, for example, because such works, in their opinion, glorify a negative stereotype. This is, to be sure, a curiously superficial reaction by those who then turn around and call for the biographical rendition, written or visual, of the life of someone like Amedeo Giannini. They also call for the preservation of Chicago's Italo Balbo monument, donated by Mussolini, or extol the "virtues," as they say, of Mussolini's corporate state, or, last but surely not least, invite Italy's leading neo-Fascist, Gianfranco Fini, not to mention Mussolini's own ideologically sympathetic granddaughter, to their annual gala event.

13. For an example of those who, directly or indirectly, classified Italian Americans in this manner see Rosen and Whyte. Such notions notwithstanding, I would point out that while this may seem to be a negative commentary of sociologists early on, today the notion of Italians and Italian Americans as people of color is a more positive consideration. See Birnbaum and Romano for more on a redefinition of Italians as people of color.

14. One need only think back to some of the classic names associated with Italian Americans and Hollywood, such as Rudolph Valentino, Frank Sinatra, Dean Martin.

15. One of the less sensitive figures of the Italian and/or Italian/American father figure is found in Rachel Guido de Vries's *Tender Warriors*. Other figures can be found in the fiction of Helen Barolini's *Umbertina*, in Mario Puzo's *The Godfather*, or in the poetry of Gianna Patriarca's *Italian Women and Other Tragedies*.

16. At this point, it is also important to note that one of Ardizzone's early novels is thematically couched in the metaphor of baseball: *In the Heart of the Order*.

17. For a sense of arbitrariness to which I allude here, I have in mind, specifically, Peirce's definition of sign, which states: "A sign or *representamen*, is something which stands to somebody for something in some respect or capacity. It addresses somebody, that is creates in the mind of that person an equivalent sign, or perhaps a more devel-

oped sign. That sign which it creates I call the *interpretant* of the first sign. The sign stands for something, its *object*. It stands for that object, not in all respects, but in reference to a sort of idea, which I have sometimes called the *ground* of the representamen" (2: 228). Another definition that Peirce offered during the same period refers to a sign as "anything which determines something else (*interpretant*) to refer to an object to which itself refers (its *object*) in the same way, the interpretant becoming in turn a sign, and so *ad infinitum*" (2: 303).

18. This reference to the violent male is not infrequent in Italian/American literature, and here it figures as a basic tenet of marriage. I remind the reader of the titles I mentioned in note 15.

19. We should not ignore Ardizzone's probable use of metonymy here, as the description of the kiss can readily afford an interpretation of "kiss" as a sign of the act of lovemaking. The preparation to kiss, especially, is reminiscent of the very moment before vaginal penetration. This said, I would also call attention to the pink sofa as reminiscent, at least for this reader, of Aretha Franklin's "Pink Cadillac." The rest I leave to my reader's imagination.

20. Another ambiguity is in the description of him as "the dark man behind the counter." His ethnicity, though not Italian, is signaled here by the same sign Ardizzone used in other stories to signal previous characters' Italian ethnicity. Such a use should not come as a surprise since both groups, Mexicans and Italians, share, among other things, a Mediterranean origin.

21. I am aware of the irony involved in my paraphrasing of Booth. But it is true that we, in our poststructuralist theoretical mind-frame, must not forget where the foundations of some of our new ideas lie. Our debt is too big to ignore.

22. Jim Spencer. Another reviewer suggests that Ardizzone become "a free agent from his past" (Courtney). It is his attachment to his past that indeed has made Ardizzone the Italian/American writer he is. Humor, as Courtney would have it, is not necessarily a requirement; it is a choice of style, technique, and rhetoric.

Works Cited

. . . .

Aaron, Daniel. "The Hyphenate Writer and American Letters." *Smith Alumnae Quarterly* (July 1964): 213–17.

Ahmad, Aijaz. "Jameson's Rhetoric of Otherness and the 'National Allegory.'" *Social Text* 17 (1987): 23.

Ardizzone, Tony. *The Evening News*. Athens: University of Georgia Press, 1986.

———. *In the Heart of the Order*. New York: Holt, 1986.

Barolini, Helen. *Umbertina*. New York: Seaview, 1979.

Birnbaum, Lucia Chavola. "The History of Sicilians." *Italians and Italian Americans and the Media*. Ed. Mary Jo Bona and Anthony Julian Tamburri. Staten Island, N.Y.: AIHA, 1996. 206–15.

Booth, Wayne. *The Rhetoric of Fiction*. Chicago: University Chicago Press, 1960.

Calvino, Italo. *If on a Winter's Night a Traveler.* New York: Harcourt Brace Jovonovich, 1979.

Campisi, Paul. "Ethnic Family Patterns: The Italian Family in the United States." *American Journal of Sociology* 53.6 (May 1948).

Casillo, Robert. "Moments in Italian-American Cinema: From *Little Caesar* to Coppola and Scorsese." *From the Margins: Writings in Italian Americana.* Ed. Anthony Julian Tamburri, Paolo A. Giordano, and Fred L. Gardaphé. West Lafayette, Ind.: Purdue University Press, 1991. 374.

Chatman, Seymour. *Story and Discourse.* Ithaca, N.Y.: Cornell University Press, 1978. 151.

Courtney, Mary Elizabeth. "Making Games of Allegories" *Columbus Dispatch* [Ohio] 19 October 1986. 26.

———. Rev. of *The Evening News,* by Tony Ardizzone. *Booklist* 15 September 1986.

Fischer, Michael M. J. "Ethnicity and the Post-Modern Arts of Memory." *Writing Culture. The Poetics and Politics of Ethnography.* Ed. James Clifford and George E. Marcus. Berkeley: University of California Press, 1986. 195.

Gardaphé, Fred L. *Italian Signs, American Streets: The Evolution of Italian American Narrative.* Durham, N.C.: Duke University Press, 1996.

———. "Visibility or Invisibility: The Postmodern Prerogative in the Italian/American Narrative." *Almanacco* 2.1 (1992): 24–33.

Gioia, Dana. "What Is Italian-American Poetry?" *Poetry Pilot* (December 1991): 3–10.

Giordano, Paolo A., and Anthony Julian Tamburri, eds. *Beyond the Margin: Readings in Italian Americana.* Madison, N.J.: Fairleigh Dickinson University Press, 1995.

Green, Rose Basile. *The Italian-American Novel: A Document of the Interaction of Two Cultures.* Madison, N.J.: Fairleigh Dickinson University Press, 1974.

Guido deVries, Rachel. *Tender Warriors.* New York: Firebrand, 1986.

Lentricchia, Frank. Rev. of *Delano in America & Other Early Poems,* by John J. Soldo. *Italian Americana* 1.1 (1974): 124–25.

Lopreato, Joseph. *Italian Americans.* New York: Random House, 1979.

Patriarca, Gianna. *Italian Women and Other Tragedies.* Toronto: Guernica, 1994.

Peirce, Charles Sanders. *Principles of Philosophy: Collected Papers.* Ed. Charles Hartshorne and Paul Weiss. 2 vols. Cambridge, Mass.: Harvard University Press, 1960.

Puzo, Mario. *The Godfather.* New York: Putnam, 1969.

Romano, Rose. "Coming Out Olive in the Lesbian Community." *Social Pluralism and Literary History: The Literature of the Italian Emigration.* Ed. Francesco Loriggio. Toronto: Guernica, 1996. 161–75.

Rosen, Bernard. "Race, Ethnicity and the Achievement Syndrome." *American Sociological Review* 24 (October 1959): 47–60.

Spencer, Jim. "N. Sider's Tales of Urban Life." *Chicago Tribune* 13 January 1987: sec. 5: 3.

Tamburri, Anthony Julian. *To Hyphenate or Not to Hyphenate? The Italian/American Writer: An Other American.* Montreal: Guernica, 1991.

Tamburri, Anthony Julian, Paolo A. Giordano, and Fred L. Gardaphé, eds. Introduction. *From the Margin: Writings in Italian Americana.* West Lafayette, Ind.: Purdue University Press, 1991.

Whyte, William. *Street Corner Society.* 2nd ed. Chicago: University of Chicago Press, 1960.

Edvige Giunta

. . . .

"A Song from the Ghetto"

Paper Fish represents a landmark in Italian/American literature, though few critics have ever heard of the book.[1] It was first published in 1980 by a now-defunct publishing house. Only one thousand copies were printed and it went out of print within months of its publication. Yet *Paper Fish* was saluted by its first readers as a masterpiece. A prepublished portion of the manuscript received the Illinois Arts Council Literary Award, and the novel was nominated for the Carl Sandburg Award. Jerre Mangione read the manuscript and praised De Rosa's extraordinary literary debut.[2] Fred Gardaphé, who reviewed the book for the *American Italian Historical Association Newsletter,* recalls thinking of *Paper Fish* as "one of the greatest works" he "had ever read" ("Breaking and Entering" 12).[3] In 1985, Helen Barolini reprinted an excerpt from the novel in *The Dream Book: An Anthology of Writings by Italian American Women,* while Mary Jo Bona analyzed its interweaving of issues of gender, ethnicity, and illness in an article published in *MELUS* in 1987.

Despite these unyielding efforts, *Paper Fish* and its author remained in the shadows for fifteen years. Apart from a handful of academics who occasionally taught the book in Italian/American culture courses by giving their students photocopies, *Paper Fish* was excluded from literary history. This reprint of De Rosa's book, then, represents a discovery as well as a recovery. As with other works that were published long after their composition, such as H.D.'s *HERmione* (1981), or that received late recognition, such as Zora Neale Hurston's *Their Eyes Were Watching God* (1937), *Paper Fish* urges readers and scholars to interrogate the long silence surrounding the book and its author.[4] Ironically, silence enveloped De Rosa's novel in the midst of debates about the canon, minority literatures, ethnicity, and gender—that is, in a climate that ought to have welcomed *Paper Fish*. It becomes imperative, then, to consider the politics of publication and distribution as they influence the construction of literary history and the emergence of a writer and a tradition—in this case, an Italian/American female literary tradition.

Tina De Rosa was born in Chicago, where she still lives. Her maternal grandparents were Lithuanian, but as a child De Rosa identified primarily with her paternal grandmother, Della, whom she describes as the most influential person in her life.[5] Born in Boscoreale, near Naples, probably in 1888, Della came to the United States when she was about seventeen years old. She died in 1963, when the author was nineteen years old, leaving a void that De Rosa would try to fill through her writing. De Rosa's work thus became a "home" in which she could take refuge, a site of soothing memories, where even tragedy and ugliness could be incorporated into her life and made the source of magical storytelling.

Until she was seventeen, De Rosa lived with her family in the Taylor Street area on the West Side of Chicago. One of the few people in her neighborhood to go to college, she attended Mundelein College of Loyola, a Catholic university in Chicago. After working at various jobs and gaining some writing experience, she earned a master's degree in English from the University of Illinois, where she studied under Michael Anania, who read early drafts of *Paper Fish* and encouraged her to cut and revise the manuscript. In 1977, Jim Ramholz of the Wine Press became interested in publishing the book.[6] In 1978, while trying to finish *Paper Fish*, holding two jobs, and struggling through economic hardship, De Rosa received a writer's residency from the Ragdale Foundation that enabled her to complete the book. *Paper Fish* was thus written in stages: begun around 1975, it was completed in 1979, though the author put it away for over a year in between.[7]

Cross-cultural marriages such as that of De Rosa's parents, though not frequent among first- and second-generation immigrants, did occur in the ethnically diverse Chicago of De Rosa's childhood, where different ethnic groups coexisted in the same neighborhood. This was the case on the West Side, which, although regarded as primarily Italian by "outsiders," was home to many ethnicities, including Irish, German, Mexican, Greek, Jewish, Polish, and Czech.[8] While growing up, and as she started writing, De Rosa defined her ethnicity as primarily Italian/American.[9] De Rosa's silence about her Lithuanian ancestry depends not only on the fact that her paternal grandmother kept alive her *italianità* in the family, but also on the seeming reluctance of her maternal relatives to discuss their origins and the reasons for the family's emigration. Her mother's family lore, which fascinated the young De Rosa, remained vague, almost mysterious. By contrast, she was exposed in her daily life to the Italian language and customs, both in her household and in the Little Italy where she grew up. *Paper Fish* dramatizes the author's relationship to her dual heritage. Grandma Doria, whose mind knows "only Italian" (43), is the wise and benevolent matriarch to whom everyone, including her "foreign" daughter-in-law Sarah, turns for guidance and comfort. She is also the one who tells Carmolina of a distant, mythical Italy, "the land that got lost across the sea, the land that was hidden on the other side of the world" (15). Unlike Grandma Doria, Carmolina's maternal grandmother remains a distant, unresponsive, "stiff" (46) figure. While privileging Italian culture, *Paper Fish* gives voice to the disorienting experience of cultural dislocation, which Sarah suffers repeatedly. Once married, Sarah must leave behind "the small white houses of the south side of the city," with their "picket fences between the yards" (49), and move into the little cold-water flat on Taylor Street, where "the guttural and minced Lithuanian in the throats of her family, her neighbors, was stilled" (49) while the "sweet" and "musical" Italian spoken by her husband's family "fell" "meaningless" on her ears (50). The pregnant Sarah wonders "which language the baby would speak" (50) as she listens to the Italian that remains incomprehensible to her. Although not central to the story, the author's Lithuanian background emerges in fragments such as these, shedding light on the experience of cross-cultural identity, which De Rosa also examines when she focuses on the predicament of third-generation Italian Americans like herself.

In "My Father's Lesson," an autobiographical essay published in 1986, De Rosa reflects on the expectations that her family, especially her father, had about her future, and describes her philosophy of work—a philosophy that is in harmony with her aesthetic vision:

> For a long while, I expected to find satisfaction, fulfillment, in my employment. I was the new generation, the one my father tended as carefully as my grandmother had tended her garden. My work, it was promised to me, would be, unlike my father's, fulfilling. So off I went to college, where I studied sociology, and then to graduate school, where I lost myself in literature and poetry. For a long time, I believed my father's promise, and wondered why I kept changing jobs. I suppose that I was seeking perfect employment, the kind my father always said I would have. But I was also discovering that I am a writer, and that, for me, an indestructible distinction exists between my employment and my work. Always, I would be wanting to run home. (15)

Through the distinction she draws between "employment" and "work," De Rosa both rejects the paternal promise of success and pays tribute to the father who unwittingly taught her "how to be a writer" (15). Like her father, who "spent his whole life doing the sad and hidden work of society, then came home and hid his face in the little world" of his family,[10] De Rosa finds refuge in her books, her "silent children" ("My Father's Lesson" 15).

A comparison can be drawn between De Rosa's aesthetics of work, rooted in her father's experience, and Pietro di Donato's representations of the laborer's relationship to a demonized "Job," a powerful force that "loomed up, damp, shivery gray," waiting to swallow the workers with its "giant members" (*Christ in Concrete*, 8). In his novel *Christ in Concrete* (1939), di Donato simultaneously illustrates the dehumanization of the workers—"The men were transformed into single, silent beasts" (9)—and infuses labor with the humanity of the workers themselves. Like other Italian/American and working-class authors, di Donato "elevates the common worker to the status of a deity . . . as a way of dignifying the plight of the worker." In "An Italian-American Woman Speaks Out" (1980), De Rosa expresses similar concerns, and questions capitalist ethics by asking:

> What happens to a person who is raised in this environment full of color, loud music, loud voices, and genuine crying at funerals and then finds herself in a world where the highest emotional charge comes from the falling of the Dow Jones average, or yet another rise in the price of gold? (38)

To fight alienation, De Rosa forges for herself an uncontaminated space, a home where her work becomes possible, where she can put to good use her father's lesson. In a self-conscious manner, De Rosa acknowledges the worker's need to sell her labor; yet she manages to create a space that is, as much as possible, immune from the ill effects of capitalist exploitation. In a quasi-utopian fashion, De Rosa envisions her home as separate from the alienating world of the modern laborer.

"My Father's Lesson" and "An Italian-American Woman Speaks Out" are two of the essays that De Rosa published during the 1980s. These essays constitute a disjointed, fragmentary autobiography, one that could be called, to borrow Gardaphé's description of Barolini's work an "autobiography as piecework." They document the writer's journey toward authorial self-fashioning. It is a journey that requires negotiation between Italy and America, between the myth of the tightly knit family and the myth of the individual.[11] The emphasis on a self-contained and self-sufficient individual, predominant in mainstream Anglo-American culture, is at odds with the central place of the family in the precapitalist, predominantly agrarian culture of late-nineteenth-century southern Italy. It was this Italian cultural heritage, caught in a time capsule, that the immigrants passed on to new generations of Italian Americans. These new generations were thus torn between the culture of descent, epitomized by the family, and the culture of consent, with its self-sufficient, even ruthless individualism.[12] From this perspective, *Paper Fish* develops De Rosa's autobiographical narrative in a fictional text that, while documenting the disappearance of the world of the author's childhood, testifies to the struggle between conflicting cultural values sustained by Italian/American women.[13]

For women writers, who entered a world that stood in contrast to the domestic sanctum of Italian womanhood, the struggle was indeed arduous.[14] In "Becoming a Literary Person Out of Context," Barolini writes that her aspiration to become a writer was "outlandish" in her Italian/American milieu. For her, an inextricable link exists between writing and class:

> [Frances Winwar's] story is not typical because she was born in Italy of educated parents who understood and abetted her career, as is true for women writers in Italy in general. . . . One can cite names of Renaissance court women who wrote, but again this was a function of class and privilege. And since it was primarily the uneducated masses who migrated to America, they did not carry with them, to transmit to their progeny, a tradition of literacy, much less the concept of being writers of literature. (266)

Yet these "uneducated masses" carried with them oral traditions that, through storytelling and song, would be passed on to the new generations. A deeply internalized self-hatred—characteristic of the works of many Italian/American writers but also of working-class writers—has at times stood in the way of the development of a literary tradition, even after literacy became available to the children of immigrants.[15] "I no longer belong to the Italian-American working class," De Rosa wrote in 1980. "My parents were successful in moving me out of it. After I moved far enough, I wanted to leave, and went as far as I could. But sometimes I try to go home, and that is where the heartache lies. You find out that you really can't go home again, no matter how much you might want to" ("Italian-American Woman" 39). *Paper Fish* represents De Rosa's attempt to "go home again" and soothe "the heartache." An analogy can be drawn between the separation experienced by the immigrant, and the separation from the family that moving into the middle class entails for the working-class person. Like many other working-class writers, De Rosa views the family as a homeland that can be revisited only through writing.[16]

. . .

Written after the deaths of De Rosa's grandmother and father, *Paper Fish*
represents an attempt to make the absent present: "I wanted them to be
eternal," she writes, remembering her family. "I wanted the brief, daily
lives they lived never to end." Struggling with her sorrow, De Rosa kept
trying to tell her family's story; overwhelmed by the intensity of her own
remembering and the awareness of her loss, she would temporarily abandon the writing and take it up again later, each time beginning a new section of the work. As she wrote, her family members "would die over and
over again," to be reborn in her fiction.[17] The result is a prismatic text,
whose pieces cohere into a fragmentary narrative reminiscent of the fiction of high modernism. The complex structure aptly portrays—just as it
emerges out of it—the emotional turmoil that triggered the author's creative process. De Rosa's modernist strategy becomes the means by which
she captures her memories and translates them into poetry. Her experimental, highly lyrical prose is reminiscent of H.D.'s high modernist fiction
(although literary antecedence must be excluded because H.D.'s fiction
was published posthumously, in the last fifteen years, and has received
critical recognition only more recently.)[18]

De Rosa writes poetry that tells stories and creates scenes familiar to the
Italian Americans from Chicago. The impressionistic style of *Paper Fish*
evokes a surreal atmosphere: the writer paints her characters with light, almost unfinished strokes, more concerned with evoking a feeling than completing a portrait. The story of Carmolina BellaCasa, a third-generation Ital-
ian/American child, unfolds as a series of overlapping layers in which past,
present, and future interweave in a complex temporal dimension that, dis-
regarding linearity, creates a mythical time. Yet in this mythical time the author inscribes the lives of Carmolina and her family with the scrupulous
precision of a realist writer. The eight parts into which the book is divided,
including a prelude and an epilogue, fit together like the pieces of a puzzle
that keeps undoing itself.[19] The opening words of the first section, "This is
my mother," which appear set apart from the rest of the text under the title
"Prelude" (1), stand almost as a subtitle, suggesting that the writing that follows is itself the "mother," the locus of creativity that brings the past,
through memory, back to life, incorporating it in a continuum in which past,
present, and future are inseparable. The clash of tenses soothes the sorrow
that accompanies loss, and the unobtrusive authorial voice takes everything
in, returning all the memories to the reader as a feast of voices, blending
them into one harmonious song. The prelude thus opens with the vision of
the unborn, unconceived Carmolina observing her mother and father:

My mother's skin brushes strawberries, her skin will brush my father's, that night their skin will make me, but I know none of this. I am less than the strawberries, I am less than the carving my father is making with his hands, less than the brown intent of his eyes over wood, less. (2)

Yet this "less" than life represents an all-knowing voice that seeps through the walls of houses, through the consciousness of each character, seeing and knowing everything through the creative power of its imaginative story-telling.

While Tina De Rosa lacks literary foremothers, her character, Carmolina, finds sustenance in the voice of her grandmother. A vehicle of cultural transmission and a source of emotional nourishment, Grandma Doria provides Carmolina with the material out of which the author forges the book's poetry. As Bona puts it, Carmolina "uses her grandmother's memories of the homeland as the subjective topography for her own fertile imagination." The domestic detail takes on a mystical aura as the storyteller's touch uncovers the spiritual in the most mundane objects and details. Thus, Carmolina's reversed writing on a bakery bag suggests her "access to literary creativity in the midst of everyday reality" ("Broken Images" 98).[20] Indeed, it is this "everyday reality" that provides the poetic subject matter of the book. In her essay, "Career Choices Come from Listening to the Heart," De Rosa writes:

> In our cold water flat, my father, who was a policeman, constantly played classical music, and operas. My grandmother, an immigrant from Bosca Royale [*sic*] near Naples, sang all the time. She sang while she cooked, while she cleaned, while she made the beds. I listened to their music. I could see that the lives they were living were simple, ordinary lives, lives that no one would ever notice, but that there was a beauty there that must be understood in the eyes of God. Even as a child, I knew this. Even as a child, I listened to them, watched them, and knew that they were extraordinarily beautiful, and temporary. (9)

De Rosa's pantheistic vision endows everything it comes across with life. The rugs that hung out of the houses resembled "great tongues" that "dry in the sun," that "panted out of the clutter of the tight rooms into the sunshine above the head of the horse who watched the children" (*Paper Fish* 34). In the description of the first encounter between Carmolina's parents, Sarah and Marco, which takes place in Sarah's parents' restaurant where she works as a waitress, a spiritual aura equally envelopes Sarah *and* the pots in the kitchen: as "the sunlight through the windows banged the pots hard and metallic, the silver light bounced off them and into her eyes" (4). The kitchen glows with the light of Sarah and Marco's newly born love, and the reader is transported into a universe in which the ecstasy of love is a miracle that happens inside the small restaurant, which "filled with light," to the delight of the children looking upon the scene and also to the delight of God (5).

The unorthodox religiosity of the book has its origin in Grandmother Doria, who is variously associated with God in the novel. The spiritual aura that pervades the narrative draws upon Doria's southern Italian roots and the distinct brand of Catholicism practiced in southern Italy. Blending folklore and Christian beliefs, Doria manufactures tales to explain the world to Carmolina, to teach her about sorrow and joy, life and death:

> There is a mountain in Italy filled with candles. . . . Each person has his own candle. When he is born the candle is lit; when the candle goes out, he dies. You can see this mountain, Carmolina, only in your dreams, but God will not let you see your own candle, even in a dream. If there is a mistake, and you see your own candle, you will die. This is how people die in their sleep. (24)

Doria's God is not infallible. The story of the mountain of candles, like all of Doria's fables, draws upon a mythology rooted in the storytelling of peasants who, while timorous of God and intimidated into subjection by a Church complicitous with the landlords, were undaunted in their transformation of Christian dogmas. In her travel memoir *No Pictures in My Grave: A Spiritual Journey in Sicily* (1992), Susan Caperna Lloyd documents the blending of Christian and pre-Christian elements in the Easter procession, a ritual central to Catholicism. Searching for the matriarchal roots of the procession in Trapani, Sicily—which she believes can be traced to the cult of Demeter and Persephone—the author paints a portrait of a popular and subversive Catholicism that, while seemingly bowing down to the Church, maintains its own integrity and a distinctly antiauthoritarian quality. It is this peculiar kind of Catholicism that one recognizes in the pages of De Rosa's book. In his discussion of part VI of the novel, Gardaphé points out that Grandma Doria "is carried on a chair up to Carmolina's room in a scene that recreates the traditional procession of the Madonna" to see her granddaughter dressed as a bride:

> In Italian tradition, the daughter (and quite often the son) does not leave home until she is married. Marriage is the ritual through which a young woman establishes her independence from her family. However, it also means shifting from an identification with family to an identification with

a male who then becomes her new patriarch. De Rosa's presentation of this scene signifies a defiance of the Italian tradition. Carmolina achieves her adult identity, not by attaching herself to a man, but by taking it from her grandmother who acknowledges it through the blessing she gives her granddaughter.

In preparation for the visit Grandma Doria dons her blue dress. . . . Blue is the color traditionally associated with the Madonna, and it is fitting that the blue-eyed matriarch of the BellaCasa family wears it as she is carried up to see her granddaughter.

This humanizing of religion—a recognition of the divine in the human—which, after all, is intrinsic to the origins of Christian theology, is creatively incorporated into the domestic rituals of the BellaCasa family.[21] The appreciation for the small objects of creation that prevails in Grandma Doria's fables and throughout the narrative draws upon a Catholicism linked to the people and to the earth, reminiscent of Franciscan mysticism and its rejection of the authoritarian practices of the Church. The poetry of the book lies in its capacity to uncover, through language, the sacred in the mundane; this capacity is a gift that Carmolina receives from her grandmother. While "breaking the red peppers" for the sausages that will make Carmolina laugh as she eats them, Doria is simultaneously "making the world" for her granddaughter (15). Her "shabby old fingers" perform miracles (15). It is significant that the working title of *Paper Fish* was "Saintmakers": to De Rosa, the faces of her family members and "the tiny, ordinary lives they had led," are indeed "holy, and of great value."[22]

Asked by Gardaphé about the title of her book, De Rosa said that she had chosen it because "the people in the book were as beautiful and as fragile as a Japanese kite." But the fish carries other associations as well.[23] A few pages into the book, the fish emerges through the nauseating "smell of dead fish burning"—an odor unbearable to Sarah, who is pregnant with Carmolina, and screens herself with her hand from the smell while "the smoke rested outside the window like a serpent; it stared out of its white eyes" (10). Throughout the book, death and birth intertwine in the fish imagery, replete with analogous associations in Christian symbolism, in which the fish stands for Jesus. Water imagery is endowed with similarly contradictory associations. In the opening pages, the first encounter between Marco and Sarah is described as a falling "into the sea":

He fell beneath the surface of the sea. He floated into the blue water, his head showing like a rose that has a face, like a silent animal filled with anguish, filled with joy, and his heart, his life, was liquid, fluid like a fine fish, and he fell far beneath the sea. He was a marionette without strings, the sea was his string, his ribbon, holding him gently. His life dallied below him, below the water, his life was magnificent and his smile was small, above the liquid line of the sea. He was a doll, floating, with a marvelous secret just under the water.

The fluidity of the language in this passage exemplifies De Rosa's style: her prose is dense, sensual, musical, and evocative of surrealistic images and sounds. The ambivalence of the fish (both beautiful and revolting, delicate and offensive) and the water (nurturing and threatening, liberating and suffocating) establish from the very beginning a clash of imageries and themes which is sustained throughout the novel, consistent with its function as both celebratory song and dirge.

Accordingly, Carmolina's beautiful sister Doriana is afflicted by a mysterious illness: she is a "swan, a black swan that flew into the incorrect night, followed the wrong moon," leaving her family "with glass eyes" (2). "Broken" early in her life, Doriana is the child so beautiful that she "frightened" her own mother (2). She represents the unknown, the mystery that the author never tries to solve but only contemplates in awe, resigned to the fact that "It is all leaves, leaves falling out of a tree, with no hands to catch them" (2). Doriana's origin remains a mystery even to Grandmother Doria, although she is the one who weaves the tale that makes the unfathomable accessible, describing Doriana as "lost in the forest":

In the forest the birds are. Ah, such beautiful birds. White birds. Blue and pink. Doriana she go into the forest to look at the birds. The birds they sing in the trees, they sing, they turn into leaves. Doriana she have a key to the forest. It a secret. Only Doriana know where she keep the key. One day Doriana go into the forest. She forget the key. She get lost in the forest. She get scared. Her face it turn hot like a little peach and she scream and try to get out of the forest. . . . She try to come home. From the forest. She no find her way.

De Rosa's exquisite language turns "broken" English into poetry. *Paper Fish* thus confers literary dignity upon the speech of those first-generation immigrants who struggled to express themselves in a language that often felt hostile and unconquerable. Writers such as Diana Cavallo and Maria Mazziotti Gillan have articulated the linguistic tribulations of immigrants. The speaker of Gillan's "Public School No. 18/Paterson, New Jersey," contrasts her "words smooth" in her "mouth" "at home," where she "chatter[s]" and is "proud," to her silence in school, where she "grope[s] for the right English/word," fearing "the Italian word / will sprout from . . . [her] mouth like a rose." The protagonist of Cavallo's A Bridge of Leaves describes his grandmother "stammering the brittle sounds of a new tongue that flushed waves of Mediterranean homesickness through her with each rough syllable" (14). Legitimizing orality—and Paper Fish is indeed a "speakerly" text, with its own distinct accents[24]—the novel stands as a tribute to the unrecorded beauty and poetry of the voices of women immigrants, exemplified by Grandmother Doria.[25]

Like Grandma Doria, Doriana is instrumental in what Fred Gardaphé calls Carmolina's "lyrical self-awakening" (Italian Signs 131). Doriana's consciousness represents a hidden self to which the narrative longs to gain access, though her direct perspective emerges only briefly. Throughout the novel, Doriana and Carmolina mirror each other. From the very first encounter between the baby Carmolina and the "small person" Doriana, they recognize a mysterious sameness as they look into "each other's eyes" (Paper Fish 11).[26] Frightened after overhearing her family discuss the possibility of institutionalizing Doriana, Carmolina runs away and is swallowed by the streets of Chicago. Thus, Carmolina replicates her sister's dislocation: she also cannot find her way home.[27] De Rosa plunges the reader into the mental and emotional universe of the young girl and, in doing so, endows the grim urban landscape with fantastic traits and a poetic aura.[28] "Streetlamps are blue eyes, beating. . . . The sky is black fabric. The devil will roll it away. . . . A dog barks. It is no one's dog. It is the devil's dog. It will swallow you and you will live in the devil's belly" (92). Carmolina wanders for three days through this frightening world which "someone turned . . . upside down," having "nowhere to go" (92). Her journey and subsequent illness brings all the conflicts of the novel into focus. If Doriana cannot heal, Carmolina will recover from her illness to develop an identity outside the symbiotic relationship with her sister. Unlike Doriana, Carmolina finds the "key" to exploring the forest. After three days, in a symbolic resurrection, she comes back "home"—both to the home of the past and to a new home that she will construct for herself. She ominously tells her father, "When I grow up . . . I'm going to go away forever" (107). Analyzing the final scene, in which Carmolina, as a young woman, faces her own mirror image, Bona argues;

> The fact that Carmolina's own face is reflected in the mirror (without the shadow of Doriana or the reflection of her grandmother, who had stood next to her) reinforces Carmolina's acceptance of death and her role as a

young, ethnic, American women who will keep the fire inside of her, however difficult and demanding that may be for her.

While both Doriana and Carmolina represent sacrificial, Christ-like figures, Grandma Doria's symbolic system empowers Carmolina to save herself.

Doriana's instability reflects the dislocation of the Italian family in America: "She seemed always to be moving towards another place, different from this." Linking the displacement of immigration and mental illness, Bona argues that, like other Italian/American women writers, De Rosa "uses the topic of illness both as a realistic comment on the prevalence of sickness in underprivileged communities and as a metaphor for the immigrant experience of living in a world that does not readily welcome outsiders." Indeed, Grandma Doria employs the dichotomy of home and forest to explain to Carmolina both Doriana's beauty and her illness:

> "Where is the forest, Grandma?"
> "Behind her eyes," Grandma whispered. She turned to Carmolina."
> "Doriana, she have a beautiful face, no?"
> "Yes, Grandma."
> "Her face, why you think it so beautiful?"
> Something squeezed tight inside Carmolina. It was made of glass; it could break.
> "I don't know, Grandma. Why?"
> "Her face, she so beautiful," Grandma swiped at the tears, she was angry at them, "because Doriana fight so hard to come home. She look out her eyes every day and try to come home. When you fight to come home, you beautiful." (100)

Grandma Doria holds "the city" responsible for the illness that consumes Doriana. The city is "like a spider sucking the blood of the wonderful child," and "the child bled out her brains, her smiles, her own words into the empty grey light of the city and there was nothing to feed her." "[L]ike a giant" (40), the city destroys the little family; its buildings are described as "bones crushing against little Doriana." Through the use of body imagery, De Rosa represents the urban monster as driven by a deliberate and ineluctable force, greedily devouring the fragile Doriana, reducing the family to "little pieces." If the city crushes the immigrants like a giant, De Rosa defies its destructive power and puts back together the little pieces through the redemptive force of her vision and her language.

. . .

Paper Fish depicts a world few readers have encountered before in fiction or in the stereotypical film versions of Italian/American lives. Chicago's Little Italy constitutes the setting in which Carmolina witnesses the disintegration of her ethnicity. In De Rosa's *bildungsroman,* Carmolina's growth is juxtaposed to the vanishing of the culture that nourishes her.[30] Berrywood Street disappears "as though it were a picture someone had snapped away":

> The city said the Italian ghetto should go, and before the people could drop their forks next to their plates and say, pardon me?, the streets were cleared.
>
> The houses of the families with their tongues of rugs sticking out were smashed down, the houses filled with soup pots and quick anger, filled with forks and knives and recipes written in the heads of the women, were struck in their sides with the ball of the wrecking crane and the knives and bedclothes and plaster spilled out.[31]

The demolition of the Italian ghetto resembles a carnage, and *Paper Fish* becomes the means by which the author attempts to rescue the memory of what is inexorably gone. The choral narrative in this passage, as elsewhere in the book, takes on the characteristics that Janet Zandy identifies as typical of working-class literature:

> [A]lthough it relies heavily on autobiography as a genre, its subject is rarely isolated or romanticized individualism. Rather, its *raison d' être* is to recall the fragile filaments and necessary bonds of human relationships, as well as to critique those economic and societal forces that blunt or block human development.

While De Rosa painstakingly recovers a history that otherwise would be lost, the nostalgia that pervades *Paper Fish* never becomes a pathetic longing for the stereotypical tokens of a stultified, one-dimensional Italian/American culture.[32] The imaginative and deeply personal story of Carmolina remains rooted in the collective history of Italian immigrants in Chicago, though, as Zandy writes, "Liberating this kind of [working-class] memory involves the reconstruction of a set of relationships, not the exactitude of specific events." De Rosa's book stands as an elegiac reminiscence drenched with the sounds, colors, and smells of the quotidian life of an Italian/American family living in a cold-water flat on the West Side of Chicago in the late 1940s and 1950s.

While the first Italians had arrived in Chicago a century earlier, in the 1850s, from northern Italy, the largest migration of southern Italians occurred between 1880 and 1914. The Italian population in Chicago, which never reached the numerical proportions of New York's Italian community, settled in several ethnically diverse Little Italys rather than in one large all-Italian neighborhood. If in the first half of this century Italians were not fully accepted or integrated members of the community, with the rise of Mussolini to power and the outbreak of World War II, the situation only worsened for Italians in the United States—regardless of their political beliefs. *Paper Fish*, set in the aftermath of the war, illustrates the sometimes subtle prejudice suffered by Italian Americans. Introducing Marco at the very opening of "The Memory," the narrative describes Carmolina's father as "a young man tall and thin, still not comfortable in his policeman's uniform. . . . He was, in the eyes of the department, still a rookie, Italian and stupid. He was treated politely, but with little respect." Rather than indicating trouble-free assimilation into the mainstream, Marco's position in the low ranks of the police department may represent the attempt of local authorities to send ethnic policemen back into their own neighborhoods to deal with the "locals." But it is when Carmolina is ostracized for being a "dago kid" that one recognizes De Rosa's awareness of cultural tensions and feels the full impact of her condemnation of bigotry. Imprinting itself indelibly on the reader's memory, De Rosa's portrayal of the Italian/American working-class world establishes a powerful critique of prejudice. *Paper Fish* forces one to come to terms with an American culture that simultaneously celebrated Shirley Temple and Dorothy of *The Wizard of Oz* and ghettoized "dago kids" such as Carmolina, as well as other racial and ethnic minorities.

In an essay on ethnicity and class, Rudolph Vecoli rejects the classification of Italians as "white (or persons of non-color) sans ethnicity," and argues that such a classification overlooks the "significance of class in human society." Vecoli thus addresses the overly simplistic dichotomy between European and non-European cultures, a dichotomy that oftentimes ignores specific historical and social circumstances—in this case, issues of emigration and assimilation. The history of Italians in the United States is a multifaceted one: They came from different regions, speaking a "jigsaw puzzle of . . . Italian dialects," driven by dreams of success, and, for the most part, by extreme poverty. A vast number of immigrants, specifically in Chicago, were involved in labor activities, and contributed in a significant manner to the history of the American working class.[33] Mocking and rejecting facile racial, ethnic, and class labels, the poet Rose

Romano writes: "I'm not oppressed enough. I / haven't been conquered / enough. I'm not Olive / enough. I may as well be Italian." Romano's cutting verse expresses her outrage at an American culture that at best infantilizes Italians, at worst criminalizes them. In "Mutt Bitch," Romano proceeds "to take inventory" of herself:

> I'm a woman.
> I'm a contessa
> on my father's side,
> contadina on my
> mother's side.
> I've got a
> high school equivalency diploma
> and an associate's degree
> in liberal arts.
> I'm a skilled blue collar worker.
> I'm a published poet.
> I've got a Brooklyn accent
> with Italian gestures.
> I'm a dyke.
> I'm a single working mother.
> All this stuff doesn't add up to
> just
> one
> person.
>
> Fuck it. (*Vendetta* 38–39)

Through her seemingly anachronistic juxtaposition of titles indicating radically different levels of social status, Romano rejects a simple definition of social identity and class. At the same time, she claims validation for her personhood, a personhood that explodes the strict boundaries of identity implied by the notion of a singular self. In "An Italian-American Woman Speaks Out," De Rosa voices her exasperation at the sense of displacement that she experiences as the "educated" granddaughter of Italian immigrants, "an educated lady who came from the streets of a ghetto, who didn't blink twice at fistfights, or horse shit—or the word." In *Miss Giardino* (1978), Italian/American novelist Dorothy Bryant explores an analogous sense of displacement through her character Anna Giardino, another "educated lady" from the ghetto. These writers have poured into their works an awareness of the conditions of displacement and cultural marginalization that afflict Italian/American writers, particularly those of working-class origin.

If the social and cultural status of a group is linked with that group's capacity to produce a literature that will tell its stories and record its past, then the status of Italian/American literature bespeaks the tangled history of Italian Americans. Because of their problematic status as "white ethnics," Italian/American writers do not easily fit with the paradigm of "minority writers," although they have not gained acceptance into the mainstream as the members of northern European groups have.[34] Assimilation in itself—and the ethnic self-silencing that it entails—poses questions concerning the repression of a group's cultural identity.[35] Victims, along with other southern and eastern European groups, of the harshest forms of prejudice and persecution in the early stages of their immigration, Italian Americans quickly learned that "whiteness" was the key to assimilation in Anglo-America.[36] More importantly, they learned that by suppressing their ethnic identity they could "pass"—especially if they were women, who could relinquish their surnames in marriage.[37] *Paper Fish* rejects the notion of a monolithic "white ethnicity" and brings to the forefront the marginalization suffered by a particular group of "white ethnics."[38]

Popular cultural representations of Italians in Chicago have focused on the Mafia wars and on such notorious figures as Al Capone. These figures, like Mario Puzo's and Francis Ford Coppola's Don Vito Corleone, appeal to the fantastic vision of Italians that mainstream America has cultivated—and that critics have not, for the most part, scrutinized.[39] After all, the gangster is an American hero: he is defiant of the law, a warped descendant of the American colonist, with whom he shares the fearless determination to explore and expand his territory.[40] De Rosa defies stereotypical representations of Chicago Italian Americans as mobsters by portraying the very neighborhood ruled by Al Capone in a completely different light: "It was Al Capone's neighborhood," she recalls, "we were always in fear of that. . . . We were so denigrated. People were afraid to come to my neighborhood." Thus she turned to writing to show what was "beautiful" about the world she grew up in: "I wanted to tell people that they couldn't trash us like that."[41] The Italian Americans in Chicago, De Rosa demonstrates, have other stories to tell, like the lyrical and moving story of Carmolina and her family.[42]

Excluded from both the literary mainstream and the margin, Italian Americans occupy an ambivalent position, complicated by their connection with a humanistic tradition to which the majority of Italian immigrants had no access.[43] Nor could they count on an already established literary tradition to articulate their issues and conflicts, or legitimize their cultural identity.[44] Yet Italian/American literature exists and has

228 :: *Edvige Giunta*

flourished. Scholars such as Olga Peragallo, Rose Basile Green, Fred Gardaphé, Anthony Tamburri, and Mary Jo Bonna have documented the existence of this tradition. Literary journals such as *VIA: Voices in Italian Americana, Italian Americana, MELUS* and *Differentia* have created a forum for Italian/American writers and critics.[45] *La bella figura,* a journal that Rose Romano published and edited from 1988 to 1992, and malafemmina press, Romano's valorous publishing enterprise, published exclusively writings devoted to Italian/American women, while Guernica, a Canadian publishing house, consistently brings forth the works of Italian/ Canadian and Italian/American writers. But while forums do exist, barriers still prevent most Italian/American writers from achieving recognition, both in the academic world and in the publishing market at large.[46] An Italian/American classic such as *Christ in Concrete,* after a brief moment of notoriety, suffered from years of neglect, remaining, like di Donato's other works, out of print for years.[47] On the other hand, Mario Puzo's *The Godfather,* mistaken by mainstream America as the authoritative text on Italian Americans, became a best-seller and the basis for three enormously popular films. Other Mafia best-sellers have included Nicholas Pileggi's *Wiseguys,* followed more recently by *Casino,* which Martin Scorsese adapted, like *Wiseguys* (retitled *Goodfellas*), into yet another motion picture on the mob.[48] Yet the literature produced by such writers as Gilbert Sorrentino, John Fante, Felix Stefanile, Joseph Tusiani, and Anthony Valerio disputes such reductive and bigoted views of Italian Americans. And when an author like Giose Rimanelli turns to the Mafia as subject matter, it is from quite a different angle, and the result can be a daring literary experiment such as *Benedetta in Guysterland: A Liquid Novel.*

If Italian/American male authors have been struggling to achieve recognition, the problems of invisibility and legitimization are magnified for Italian/American women. What Barolini has called "The Historical and Social Context of Silence" lies at the core of the literary production of many Italian/American women.[49] Writers such as De Rosa have written with little knowledge of the community of writers and readers at work forging literary spaces for the representation of Italian Americans.[50] From Frances Winwar, born Francesca Vinciguerra, who anglicized her name at her publisher's request, to Rita Ciresi and Agnes Rossi, two contemporary writers who inscribe an internalized sense of cultural invisibility in narratives that both expose and suppress ethnic identity, Italian/American women have for the last fifty years waged a war against silence, a war fought through written words that rarely have reached a large audience.[51]

It is only when voices are heard, and when other voices reply, that a literary tradition can be formed.[52]

Paper Fish was published a year after *Umbertina* (1979), a female immigration narrative by Helen Barolini.[53] With the combative purpose of demonstrating the existence of an Italian/American female literary tradition, in *The Dream Book* (1985) Barolini gathered under the same umbrella authors as diverse as Sister Bandanna Segale, Frances Winwar, Antonia Pola, Mary Gordon, Dorothy Bryant, Sandra Mortola Gilbert, Leslie Scalapino, Louise DeSalvo, Anna Monardo, Daniela Gioseffi, Diane di Prima, and Tina De Rosa. In an interview, Barolini lamented the general exclusion of Italian/American women authors and described *The Dream Book* as her "literary manifesto," through which she wanted to ensure that "some acknowledgment be given to Italian American women writers, that their names be part of the literary record, that redress be made for having neglected and overlooked a whole segment of writers."[54]

Before Barolini, other authors had written about Italian America between between the 1940s and the 1960s in narratives filtered through the lens of their gender: Mari Tomasi in *Deep Grow the Roots* (1940) and *Like Lesser Gods* (1949), Julia Savarese in *The Weak and the Strong* (1952), Antonia Pola in *Who Can Buy the Stars?* (1957), Diana Cavallo in *A Bridge of Leaves* (1961), Octavia Waldo in *A Cup of the Sun* (1961), and Marion Benasutti in *No Steady Job for Papa* (1966).[55] All of these works, with the exception of *Like Lesser Gods,* are currently out of print. The fact that many of these authors told in their books of the struggle for survival of Italian/American workers—be it in the city, as in *The Week and the Strong,* or in the granite mines of Vermont, as in Tomasi's fiction—suggests the extent to which the combination of working-class consciousness and ethnicity in literature has not seemed palatable to mainstream publishing. The fact that many of these authors never published a second novel signals the fragility of a tradition that lacked a community to sustain and nurture its growth.[56] To this day, the most established and prolific Italian/American woman writer (in terms of publications) is Helen Barolini, who, while well known by scholars of Italian/American culture and some scholars of ethnic literature, remains virtually unknown in most academic circles.[57] Authors such as Dorothy Bryant, Rose Romano, Mary Russo Demetrick, and Maria Famà have resorted to self-publishing, which helps to keep one's books in print; but even this becomes an increasingly difficult task in the corporate publishing world.[58]

While *Umbertina* has by no means reached the popularity or critical recognition of such feminist novels as Sandra Cisneros's *The House on*

Mango Street (1984), Alice Walker's *The Color Purple* (1982), Bharati Mukherjee's *Jasmine* (1989), or Amy Tan's *The Joy Luck Club* (1991), Barolini's work has received at least some critical recognition.[59] *Paper Fish,* on the other hand, was swallowed by a void even darker than that from which it emerged.[60] This lyrical novel can indeed be described, in the author's own words, as "a song from the ghetto":[61] for her, literary isolation replaced urban marginalization. De Rosa's "individual talent" surfaced without a tradition to support and facilitate its emergence. The author's claim that her novel has more in common with a book like Anne Frank's *The Diary of a Young Girl* (1952) than with an Italian/American tradition sheds light on the writer's fear of the consequences of racial hatred and clarifies the multiple links that *Paper Fish* establishes with autobiography, *bildungsroman,* and the literatures of various ethnic and racial minorities. It also signals the distance between the author and other Italian/American writers created by the lack of any recognized tradition. If one thinks of the importance of Zora Neale Hurston for Alice Walker and other African/American women writers, one can begin to appreciate the courage necessary to write in isolation. Walker claims that she realized her "need" for Zora Neale Hurston even before she knew Hurston's work "existed." Indeed, Hurston's relatively recent canonization has consolidated the sense of a tradition for African/American women authors.

Writing about the marginalization she experienced as an Asian/American woman, Amy Ling remarks that she found solace in reading such texts as Helen Barolini's *The Dream Book,* Alice Walker's *In Search of Our Mothers' Gardens,* Audre Lorde's prose and poetry, and Virginia Woolf's *A Room of One's Own.* Arguing that "Italian American women have suffered similar oppression from the men of their own culture, a similar sense of alienation from the dominant Anglo-American tradition, and the same affinity with black women writers that Chinese American women feel," Ling writes that she "fear[s] that the Italian American woman's perspective may have been overlooked, again." Ling's observation seems accurate when we think that *The Dream Book* is currently out of print and the *Umbertina* is available only in the few surviving copies of a small print edition, making Barolini's efforts, if not vain, then largely unrecognized by the mainstream press, academe, and the general reading audience. With its commitment to publishing and reprinting women's, and especially working-class, literature, the Feminist Press has opened an important door for *Paper Fish* and for Italian/American women's literature in general.[62]

In a compelling essay on ethnic discrimination, Rose Romano denounces the silencing of Italian/American voices and asserts that "censorship doesn't always have to be censorship in order to be effective." *Paper Fish* puts an end to fifteen years of "effective" censorship and claims a place in literary history for Italian/American women. Yet such a victory does not come easy. Explaining that "the immigrant genre presents readers with the repeated coalescence of wonder and shame in relation to one's place in a given culture," Frances Bartkowski argues:

> What speaks to the victory of wonder over shame is the ethno-autobio-graphical text itself as a document of having claimed a place, culturally speaking. Yet the narratives of this coming-into-place are replete with the brutal lessons of shame, even as they recount the exultation of instants of shamelessness.

The history of *Paper Fish* is the history of a journey toward cultural recognition. Recognizing the shame that lies at the core of her writing, De Rosa triumphantly affirms the power of "wonder" to transcend shame. "Though I grew up in what the world would call a ghetto," she writes, "I was surrounded constantly by beauty." Finally claiming a place in the history of American literature, *Paper Fish* overcomes the isolation of both urban and literary ghettoes, and transforms "the disempowered experience of an unshared tongue" into a poetic feast of words that enables the tradition personified by Grandma Doria to sing.

Notes

. . . .

1. On the use of the slash (solidus) rather than the hyphen in the adjective form of Italian/American and other similar terms see Tamburri, *To Hyphenate or Not to Hyphenate*. Tamburri argues that the slash avoids privileging one of the two cultures and signals a relationshp in which Italian and American engage in a dialectical exchange.

2. Mangione's statement, which appeared on the back cover of the book, reads: "*Paper Fish* is an outstanding literary event, a first novel that breaks through the barriers of conventional fiction to achieve a dazzling union of narrative and poetry. . . . Hers is a delightfully fresh voice, filled with ancient wisdom which is new and probing, miraculously translating the most ineffable nuances of human existence in a language that is consistently beautiful and vital."

3. Gardaphé, who was the first critic to write about *Paper Fish*, thus sums up the particular significance that this book held for him: "Through writers like De Rosa, I learned that Italian-American culture was multi-dimensional and could never be simply categorized" ("Breaking and Entering" 12).

4. A roman à clef, *HERmione* was written in 1927 but was published posthumously, not only because of its overt autobiographical elements but because of the centrality of lesbian love in the novel. See Friedman and Du Plessis. The late recognition of *Their Eyes Were Watching God* has received much critical attention. See Mary Helen Washington's foreword (vii–xiv) and Henry Louis Gates Jr.'s afterword to the book (185–95), and Alice Walker's "Zora Neale Hurston: A Cautionary Tale and a Partisan View" and "Looking for Zora" (*In Search* 83–116).

5. In "An Italian-American Woman Speaks Out," De Rosa writes that the "ghost of one's grandmother" is "as real as the food on one's plate" (38).

6. Ramholz received a grant from the National Endowment for the Arts to publish *Paper Fish*.

7. The biographical information is based primarily on Gardaphé's interview with the author and on my conversations with her.

8. This multiethnicity is reflected in *Paper Fish;* a Mexican-American family lives on the floor below the BellaCasa family (*Paper Fish* 10).

9. De Rosa's self-identification as an Italian American is testified to by her essay "An Italian-American Woman Speaks Out" (1980) and by her other published works: *Paper Fish*, a biography of Bishop Scalabrini (1987), and a handful of essays she wrote in the 1980s.

10. "BellaCasa," the last name of the family in *Paper Fish,* means "beautiful home."

11. The struggle between the family and the individual in Italian/American culture has been examined in various disciplines. See Boyd et al.; De Rosa, "An Italian-American Woman Speaks Out"; Barolini's introduction to *The Dream Book;* and Bona's dissertation, "Claiming a Tradition."

12. See Werner Sollors's classic distinction in *Beyond Ethnicity.* Although this distinction has undergone much criticism, it nevertheless maintains a broad epistemological validity.

13. Grandmother Doria's storytelling enables Carmolina to "make her inevitable journey away from the family and into her self," Gardaphé argues. "To help her reach this goal, Grandma Doria teaches Carmolina to turn memory into strength." In "Feminism, Family and Community," Jeanne Bethke Elshtain sheds light on the creative and radical potential within the family which, she contends, stands in opposition to "the 'needs' of capitalism" and the "market images of human being" created by capitalism (260). The collection of essays edited by Penny A. Weiss and Marilyn Friedman in which Elshtain's essay appears, *Feminism and Community,* provides a multiplicity of perspectives on the function of various kinds of communities in shaping women's self-definition. The question of whether or not ethnicity, race, and nation define one's identity is one De Rosa indirectly takes up in *Paper Fish,* a book that emphasizes the instrumental role of ethnic heritage in forging the author's artistic talent. In her poem "Ethnic Woman," Rose Romano rejects the view of "ethnicity" as something she "drag[s] out / of the closet to celebrate quaint holidays," and eloquently explains the connection between self and ethnicity: "I could write my life / story with different shapes in / various sizes in limitless patterns of / pasta laid out to dry on a thick, white / tablecloth on my bed." She asks her imaginary interlocutor, "Must I teach you / to read?" Yet this is not an ethnicity that "define[s]" you, rather "you define it."

14. For studies of the historical and social conditions of Italian/American women

see Boyd et al. and Gabaccia. In the opening poems of *Italian Women and Other Tragedies*, entitled "Italian Women," "My Birth," and "Daughters," Gianna Patriarca, an Italian/Canadian writer, powerfully inscribes the experience of womanhood in the patriarchal Italian family.

15. Torgovnick, "On Being White, Female and Born in Bensonhurst." Many Italian/American writers, male and female, have lamented the lack of support within the family for fledgling writers. See Ciresi, "Paradise below the Stairs." The literate children and descendants of Italian/American immigrants, thrown into a world in which their culture does not receive recognition, have often camouflaged their ethnic and class identities. Writers like Rose Romano, Maria Mazziotti Gillan, and Tina De Rosa reclaim, through their writings, those very identities. In "Reclaiming Our Working Class Identities: Teaching Working Class Studies in a Blue-Collar Community," Linda Strom writes of the painful gap that her "education" had created between her and her family, though her family had encouraged her in her pursuits.

16. On working-class literature see "Working-Class Studies," an issue of *Women's Studies Quarterly* edited by Janet Zandy, and *Calling Home and Liberating Memory*, also edited by Zandy.

17. Information on the composition of *Paper Fish* was given to me by De Rosa during telephone conversations that took place in 1995.

18. Interestingly enough, H.D.'s experimental fiction is represented primarily by a number of romans à clef, a category that can be used to describe *Paper Fish*. *HERmione*, written in 1927, was published in 1981, a year after the publication of *Paper Fish*, while other novels by H.D. were published later: *Bid Me to Live* in 1983, *The Gift* in 1984, and *Asphodel* in 1992. *The Gift* is especially akin to the child's perspective of *Paper Fish*, with its focus on the memories of Hilda Doolittle's childhood in her hometown of Bethlehem, Pennsylvania.

19. On the structure of *Paper Fish* see Bona, "Broken Images" and Gardaphé, "The Later Mythic Mode" in *Italian Signs*. For a discussion of time in *Paper Fish* see Bensoussan.

20. Other authors endow the quotidian and monotonous domestic activities with a creative function. In the poetry of Sandra M. Gilbert, domestic chores become poetical subject matter, as in "Doing Laundry." Helen, one of the two female protagonists of Louise DeSalvo's novel *Casting Off*, thinks of how "one could read the progress of her life in the spills of mysterious substances that now nearly obliterated her favorite recipes. . . . this dripping and this dribbling had been Helen's way of making history, and she had been reluctant to give it up in favor of the pristine page with no splotches and no spills. . . . Sometimes she wondered why she always remembered events in terms of the things that she had eaten" (28–30).

21. For a feminist analysis of Catholicism, and specifically the Marian cult, see Hamington. See also Torjesen. Martin Scorsese's *The Last Temptation of Christ* (based on the novel by Alikos Kazantzakis), a film that attempted to capture the paradox of the divine in the human (or vice versa), caused one of the most explosive controversies in film history due to the virulent responses of many Christian groups.

22. "Doriana's face was the ivory-white face of the Virgin Mary, praise God. Grandma Doria watched the sleeping face of the child on the pillow. The eyelids closed perfectly, like the lines in a saint's statue; the eyelids seemed carved by the hands of a saint-maker" (*Paper Fish* 63).

23. The sleeping Doriana, "Stuffed in under all the sheets and blankets," is compared to a "dead fish." The skin of Sarah's hand is described as "puckered and scaly like a fish flat and dead on a beach where the ocean tossed it away."

24. According to Henry Louis Gates Jr.'s definition, the "speakerly text" is "a text whose rhetorical strategy is designed to represent an oral literary tradition . . . the narrative strategy signals attention to its own importance, an importance which would seem to be the privileging of oral speech and its inherent linguistic features" (181). See also Gardaphé, "From Oral Tradition to Written Word: Toward an Ethnographically Based Criticism" in Tamburri, Giordano, and Gardaphé, eds.

25. On ethnic women's voices see Krause, ed.

26. On the relationships between sisters see Foster, ed.

27. *Alice's Adventures in Wonderland* and *The Wizard of Oz* come to mind as possible—though distant—literary antecedents, especially because of their combination of enchantment and darkness.

28. The stream of consciousness of De Rosa's prose and the crucial function of topography in the novel recalls the experiments and the representation of urban setting by modernist authors such as James Joyce, Virginia Woolf, and Jean Rhys. Sandra Cisneros's critically acclaimed novel *The House on Mango Street* (1984) places Esperanza Cordero, a girl growing up in the Latino section of Chicago, at the center of the narrative. A comparative study of *Paper Fish* and *The House on Mango Street,* including a reception study, might shed light both on ethnic self-representation and on the cultural construction of ethnicities in American culture.

29. "It is truly no secret that life for ethnic groups in America has been equated to a Dantean hell; that alongside the usual hardships of poverty and hunger come serious and debilitating mental illnesses that arise in America and cannot be cured there; that the family, however much loved and passionately honored by men, is often unrelentingly painful for women" (Bona, *Voices* 13).

30. For a dicussion of *Paper Fish* as a *bildungsroman* see Bona, "Broken Images" and Gardaphé, "The Later Mythic Mode" in *Italian Signs*.

31. See Candeloro 244. Ironically, the neighborhood was destroyed to make room for the University of Illinois, whre De Rosa would receive her M.A. in English and where she would begin to outline *Paper Fish*. To this day the few surviving residents blame the university for the destruction of the community and the uprooting of its members.

32. In 1987 the Academy Award for best film was given to such a misguided and misleading portrayal of Italian/American culture as *Moonstruck*. Despite their artistic value, Coppola's *The Godfather* and Scorsese's *Goodfellas*—possibly the most popular Italian/American films of the last twenty-five years—propose images of Italian Americans that perpetuate stereotypical views. See Sautman.

33. For an account of Italian/American working-class history see Vecoli.

34. Candeloro notes that the Italian Americans in Chicago, for example, have achieved better economic status, but they have not yet reached a much sought after "respect" (247–48).

35. See Rose Romano's controversial essay on her relationship to the lesbian community, "Where Is Nella Sorellanza?" and her poem "This Is Real.

36. The trial of the Italian anarchists Nicola Sacco and Bartolomeo Vanzetti and the lynching of Italian Americans in New Orleans in 1891 represent two chapters in

the history of Italian Americans in the United States. In "Dago Street," Rose Romano remembers, as if she had witnessed it, the 1891 lynching. Bona points out that the interweaving of past and present "allows Romano to reinforce the insidious persistence of ethnic prejudice in America" ("Learning to Speak Doubly" 165). Also see Nazzaro.

37. In a review essay of Romano's *The Wop Factor* (1994), Bona argues that "the poet who talks back . . . compels the reader to recognize the potential cultural genocide inherent in . . . passing." She quotes Romano: "Most Italians escape by hiding / don't teach the children Italian, / use Italian to tell the old stories, / and never complain. / Now most Italians pass / and don't know it" (*Wop Factor* 22). Scholars such as Sandra M. Gilbert and Marianna De Marco Torgovnick have only recently begun using their Italian family names. Gilbert wrote to Helen Barolini: "I am really Sandra Mortola Gilbert . . . and my mother's name was Caruso, so I always feel oddly falsified with this Waspish-sounding American name, which I adopted as a 20-year-old bride who had never considered the implications of her actions!" (*Dream Book* 22). Gilbert's Italian/American voice emerges, significantly, in her poetry, which she seems to consider as unrecognized, somewhat clandestine writing: "As for my poetry . . . I don't feel myself to be a tremendously established poet. In fact, I'm always interested when people even know that I write poetry." See Gilbert's book of poems, *The Summer Kitchen* (1984) and also "Piacere Conoscerla: On Being an Italian American," in Tamburri, Giordano, and Gardaphé, eds. In *Crossing Ocean Parkway: Readings by an Italian American Daughter* (1994), Torgovnick considers her marriage to a Jewish man, which enabled her to "cross," as epitomizing the self-silencing of the *"paesani"* who "often sport last names that aren't Italian" (viii). For a discussion of white ethnicity see di Leonardo.

38. For a discussion of white ethnicity and race see Ignatiev.

39. In her poem "Mafioso," Sandra Mortola Gilbert questions mainstream views of Italian Americans: "Frank Costello eating spaghetti in a cell at San Quentin, / Lucky Luciano mixing up a mess of bullets and / calling for parmesan cheese, / Al Capone baking a sawed-off shotgun into a / huge lasagna— / are you my uncles, my / only uncles?" (Barolini, *Dream Book* 348).

40. "Turning to crime," argues Humbert Nelli, "was not a denial of the American way of life, but rather comprised an effort by common laborers who lacked skills to find 'success'" (quoted in Candeloro 241).

41. Telephone conversation with the author, 26 September 1995. Referring to Humbert Nelli's research, Candeloro points out that during the Capone era, "the members of the corrupt syndicates were *American*-born practitioners of the *American*-ethic of success" (241).

42. *Paper Fish* is the first novel about Italians in Chicago, although several sociological studies about Italians in Chicago exist. See Nelli, *Italians in Chicago* and *Role of the "Colonial" Press.* Candeloro's essay, "Chicago Italians: A Survey of the Ethnic Factor, 1850–1990," provides much information about the history and changing status of the Italians in Chicago.

43. See Lucia Chiavola Birnbaum in Tamburri, Giordano, and Gardaphé, eds., 282–93.

44. In 1994 the *New York Times Book Review* published an article by Gay Talese entitled "Where Are the Italian American Novelists?" See the responses of some Italian/American scholars and writers in *Italian Americana* to Talese's article (Gioia et al.).

45. Most scholarship on Italian/American literature has been published in these journals as well as in the proceedings of Conferences of the American Italian Historical Association. Gardaphé's book, *Italian Signs, American Streets,* is the first comprehensive study of Italian/American literature to be published in twenty years. See also the special issue of *VIA: Voices in Italian Americana,* devoted to women writers, which I guest-edited.

46. On the questions of recognition and identity in a multicultural society see Gutman, ed.

47. See Gardaphé's introduction to the 1993 reprint of *Christ in Concrete,* x–xviii.

48. Other Italian/American male writers who have achieved success, such as Don De Lillo, have for the most part avoided Italian/American subjects. On De Lillo as an Italian/American writer see Gardaphé, "Visibility or Invisibility."

49. For a discussion of the connections between gender and authorial emergence see Barolini's introduction to *The Dream Book.*

50. See Barolini, "Becoming a Literary Person." See also Bona's introduction to her dissertation, "Claiming a Tradition," and Giunta, "Blending 'Literary' Discourses."

51. See Louise DeSalvo's essay, "A Portrait of the *Puttana* as a Middle-Aged Woolf Scholar." On Frances Winwar see Barolini's introduction to *The Dream Book,* 6. For a discussion of the question of ethnic self-representation in Rossi, see Giunta, "Narratives of Loss" and "Reinventing the Authorial/Ethnic Space." On Ciresi see Fausty, "Masquerading Narratives" and his review of *Mother Rocket.* In De Salvo's *Casting Off,* a novel published only in England and currently out of print, the characters are Italian/Irish/American working-class women, but their Italian/American identity emerges obliquely, expressing a position common among individuals of Italian and Irish ancestry. Because of the more socially accepted status of the Irish, in intermarriages the Italian element was often subsumed, even concealed. Such a conflicting position emerges powerfully in *Casting Off* and in the writings of Italian/Irish/American writers such as Agnes Rossi. (See my essay "Reinventing the Authorial/Ethnic Space.") Louise DeSalvo encodes the Italianness of her characters in their Irishness, though their Italian identity also emerges powerfully in other ways. Her novel thus explores questions of ethnic identity—and identification—on many different levels. For an analysis of ethnic invisibility, see Gardaphé, "Visibility and Invisibility" and "(In)visibility: Cultural Representation." See also Romano's autobiographical essay "Where Is Nella Sorellanza?"

52. In an unpublished interview, referring to her response to reading Carole Maso's *Ghost Dance* (1986), De Rosa commented, "After calling for so long, I finally hear an echo" (Fausty and Giunta).

53. In 1978, Dorothy Calvetti Bryant published *Miss Giardino,* a novel that explores issues of gender, age, ethnicity, and class.

54. The question of an aesthetic value that would determine inclusion in, or exclusion from, the canon is inseparable from the social and cultural contexts in which these works were produced. Virginia Woolf's question comes to mind: "What conditions are necessary for the creation of works of art?"

55. In her dissertation, Mary Jo Bona traces the history of an Italian/American literary tradition from the 1940s through 1980. Mary Frances Pipino, a graduate student at the University of Cincinnati, is completing a dissertation on Italian/American women that also examines the development of an Italian/American female literary tradition.

56. Virtually all traces of some of these writers are seemingly lost, as in the case of Antonia Pola, author of *Who Can Buy the Stars?* (1957), a book that gives "an account of an Italian immigrant woman which is forceful, unsentimentalized, and sharply different from the portraits of submissive women which seemed to be the standard for her time." The book's exploration of issues of gender, class, age, and sexuality makes it a particularly intriguing text.

57. For a discussion of Barolini's career see Gardaphé's "Autobiography as Piecework" and my essay "Blending 'Literary' Discourses." For a study of the field, see my article "Crossing Critical Borders."

58. Hale Mary Press was "founded to commemorate all women who lost their ethnic, given names at Ellis Island and who were renamed 'Mary' in legal, immigration papers" (back cover of Demetrick and Famà, *Italian Notebook*).

59. For a discussion of *Umbertina* see Gardaphé, "The Later Mythic Mode," in *Italian Signs, American Streets*; Giunta, "Blending Literary Discourses"; and Tamburri, "Helen Barolini's Umbertina" and "Umbertina: The Italian/American Woman's Experience" in Tamburri, Giordano, and Gardaphé, eds.

60. Mary Jo Bona argues that, "separated from their literary foremothers in Italy, Italian women in America have perceived themselves to be writing in a void, without support from early models or from contemporary writers similarly concerned to legitimate the connection between ethnicity and literary creation" ("Broken Images" 90). The relationship between Italian/American women and their Italian "foremothers" is a complex one. Who are such foremothers? Can Italian/American women writers claim a connection with other writers by virtue of their national origins? This is a topic that has not yet been explored in criticism.

61. During a telephone conversation with the author that took place in August 1995, she described *Paper Fish* as a "song from the ghetto," akin to Anne Frank's *Diary*.

62. In 1997 the Feminist Press will reprint three works by another Italian/American woman, Dorothy Bryant: *Miss Giardino, The Confessions of Madame Psyche,* and *Ella Price's Journal.*

PART THREE

. . . .

Identity Politics

Michael Barone

. . . .

Italian Americans and American Politics

It has been just over a century since Italians started migrating to America in large numbers. For most of that period, Italian Americans have been no more than a minor force in American politics. The first Italian American elected governor and senator, John Pastore of Rhode Island, won those offices in 1946 and 1950, half a century after the great migration began in the 1890s. The first Italian American cabinet member, Secretary of Health, Education and Welfare Anthony Celebrezze, was appointed in 1962. Italian Americans had been mayors of major cities but not very often. And the best-known Italian American mayor, Fiorello LaGuardia of New York, elected in 1933, 1937, and 1941, was not at all a typical product of the Italian American community; he grew up in Arizona, was an Episcopalian, was elected to Congress as a Republican and Socialist, and drew a greater percentage of support from Jewish, white Protestant, and African American voters than from Italian Americans.

Yet today, Italian Americans are so successful in politics it is difficult to count their numbers. They come from unlikely constituencies—Senators Pete Domenici from New Mexico and Mike Enzi from Wyoming and Congressman Romano Mazzoli from Kentucky, for example. They include men with un-Italian names, like Senator Patrick Leahy of Vermont. Seldom has their Italian heritage been much of an issue one way or the other. There are exceptions: Governor Mario Cuomo thrilled the nation by speaking of his immigrant father in his keynote speech to the Democratic National Convention in 1984; and the Democratic vice presidential nominee that year, Congresswoman Geraldine Ferraro, was attacked for her husband's alleged contacts with organized crime. But for the most part, Italian Americans are making their way ahead in politics more or less like anyone else and in greater and greater numbers.

How did this happen? What made it so difficult for Italian Americans to move ahead in politics for so long, and what has made it so easy, relatively, for them to succeed in the past quarter-century? For the answers to these questions we need to look at the political habits of Americans of Italian descent, going back to the first large wave of Italian immigrants in the 1890s.

The First Generations

The vast bulk of the Italian immigrants in the period 1890–1924 were from southern Italy, mostly from the territory that was, until Garibaldi's successes of 1860, the Regno of the Two Sicilies. The basic outlook of people in this part of Italy has been described by Edward Banfield as "amoral familism" and by Robert Putnam as "a culture of distrust." Loyalty extends to the family and to a limited extent the village—and no farther. There is no trust in the good intensions of strangers and certainly none in the state or its agents. Nor is it thought that the state has legitimate claims on the ordinary person. Even toward the church there is little loyalty; especially among the men there is strong anticlericalism.

These first waves of Italian immigrants tended to settle in what have been described as "urban villages." People from a particular village would cluster on one block or street and would remain there for generations. Staying in school, moving up in socioeconomic class, making large amounts of money—all were discouraged, on the theory that they would break up the family, the one connection that people could rely on. Many Italians intended to and did return home as they earned enough money— the first immigrant group to follow this pattern, which has since become common among Greeks and Latin Americans. Italian American incomes remained relatively low; well into the 1940s they were still below the national average, though Italian Americans were concentrated in East Coast and Great Lakes metropolitan areas with income levels far above the national average. Italian Americans' participation in the Catholic Church was limited; all the positions seemed to be taken by Irish Americans, and the anticlericalism of the early immigrants often continued. Their children were educated typically in public schools and very often did not graduate from high school.

Italian American participation in politics was limited. They did vote, and some ran for public and party office but not very many. They encountered in the Democratic Party what they encountered in the Roman

Catholic Church: coteries of Irish Americans adept at hierarchy and organizational politics and uninterested in working with others. As a result, Italian Americans in some communities became Republicans; examples include Philadelphia and New Haven, Conneticut. But overall the first two generations of Italian Americans showed relatively little ethnic solidarity. Their loyalty was still to their family or perhaps to their urban village. "Italy" was an abstraction, a recent political phenomenon. Their native language was not the Italian of Dante but a local dialect, in most cases far more different from Tuscan Italian than Mexican or Argentine Spanish is from Castilian.

Politics for these Italian American immigrants was not a means of advancing abstract principle or even for displaying ethnic identity; it was a means of getting something concrete for your family or community. In the 1920s, 1930s, and 1940s such voters accepted baskets of coal and city jobs from machine politicians, Republicans as well as Democratics, and gave them votes in return. Nationally, they showed no overwhelming allegiance to either party, such as Irish Americans then gave to the Democrats and African Americans do today. And as Nathan Glazer and Daniel Patrick Moynihan wrote in *Beyond the Melting Pot,* "there never developed among the Italian proletarian group a generalized ideology in support of liberalism and progressivism." Italian American voting patterns were the results of a very large number of local decisions and accommodations.

The Third Generation

After World War II, Italian Americans started dispersing from their "urban villages." These "Little Italy's" remained cohesive and were more resistant to racial change than were any other ethnic communities, as a traveler to Boston's North End, surrounded by office buildings and tourist destinations, or Cleveland's Little Italy, near the museum quarter and surrounded by largely African American communities, can see even today. But the population density within these neighborhoods declined as wage earners made more money and started moving to the suburbs in the 1950s. Concentrated in high-wage, high-salary metropolitan areas, especially in the Northeast, Italian Americans' incomes rose to the national average by the 1950s, at a time when that average was rising rapidly; this was vast economic progress. But "as Italians emerged from the grip of neighborhood and family which had maintained the peculiar cast of south Italian culture, they did not enter into an unmodulated and abstract

Americanism," Glazer and Moynihan wrote in 1963, "The Italian migrant to the suburbs found in the new, ethnically mixed Roman Catholic church of the suburbs an important expression of his new status as a middle-class American."

Politically, Italian Americans thus became part of what has arguably been one of the two major pivotal segments of the American electorate in the years after 1960, the northern urban/suburban ethnics (the other being white southerners). In 1960, Italian Americans voted heavily for the first Catholic president, John F. Kennedy. But a first Catholic president can be elected only once. The 1960 election settled once and for all that Catholics would be accepted as fully American, at just about the same time that Vatican II and the responses to it made American Catholics far less distinctive than they had been even in the late 1950s. Catholics no longer prayed in Latin, refused to eat meat on Friday, eschewed contraception, and had distinctively large families.

Italian Americans, with less of a history of ties to the Democratic party than Irish or Polish Americans had, became a key swing voting bloc. In the 1960s and 1970s they tended to be liberal on national economic issues; they wanted the New Deal maintained and even extended. But they were conservative on cultural issues, strongly opposed to the urban riots of the 1960s, the fast-expanding welfare budgets of the 1970s, and the racial quotas of the 1970s and 1980s; they had, in Glazer and Moynihan's phrase, "the ideological outlook of small homeowners," which increasingly they were. By the late 1960s they had swung away from the Democrats and helped to elect Conservative party candidate James Buckley to the Senate in 1970. They were the core group opposing Mayor John Lindsay (New York) in 1969, supporting Mayor Frank Rizzo (Philadelphia) in 1971 and 1975, and comprising Richard Nixon's big majority in 1972. Italian Americans swung toward Jimmy Carter in 1976, mainly because of the issue of federal aid to New York City. But they supported Ronald Reagan in 1980 and 1984 and voted against Mario Cuomo for governor of New York in 1982.

One reason Italian Americans were not more successful in politics during the first two generations was their reputation for being involved in organized crime. "The vulnerability of Italian American political figures to charges of links with criminals will remain great as long as substantial wealth in the Italian American community is derived from illegitimate enterprises," Glazer and Moynihan wrote in 1963. But in the years that followed, as more and more Italian Americans accumulated wealth and achieved professional success without any contact with organized crime, the plausibility of such charges vastly diminished. In addition, two Italian Americans played a key role in unraveling the Watergate scandal and rendering accountable those who broke the law and violated their trust—Judge John Sirica and House Judiciary Committee chairman Peter Rodino. Their performance, under enormous pressure and against the wishes of a president of the United States just reelected by an overwhelming margin, showed complete integrity and adherence to principle. Sirica, an active Republican before he became a judge, and Rodino, a Democrat who served in Congress for thirty-eight years, proved to all Americans that Italian Americans could be trusted with the highest responsibilities. Their example destroyed the stereotype that had trailed behind Italian Americans for so long.

The Fourth Generation

By 1990 Italian Americans were mainly suburban, not urban, voters. In the New York area they were still clustered around old Italian neighborhoods—Bensonhurst, Canarsie, Howard Beach, the East Bronx. But many more lived on Long Island, on suburban in all but name Staten Island, in Westchester County, or out on various freeways in northern New Jersey. Similar patterns were apparent in other metropolitan areas. And the character of their politics had changed. They still wanted lower taxes, but they also wanted government to subsidize or favor their community institutions: expensive suburban school systems, well-established labor unions. Although they remained conservative on many cultural issues, they became more laissez-faire or even liberal on others, notably abortion; Italian Americans were part of the strongly pro-choice majority in the East Coast states.

The prototypical Italian American politician is New York's Senator Alfonse D'Amato, with deep roots in the town of Island Park and a long, tumultuous relationship with the Nassau County Republican machine. He has shown dogged persistence in aiding his own communities and a willingness to oppose liberal Democrats when they are unpopular but also a proclivity to go with the winner. D'Amato affects a familiar, even vulgar style, but he has also shown high intellect, an ability to master difficult substantive issues, and a willingness to work hard. In many respects he seems typical of the average Italian American voter—a person with strong community roots and impressive economic achievement, a survivor in a difficult marketplace with little interest in political theory or procedural reform. Italian Americans swung toward Bill Clinton in the elections of 1992 and 1996, but they also voted to oust Mario Cuomo for George Pataki (a Hungarian American and D'Amato's hand-picked choice) in 1994. That same year they also voted heavily for Republican governors in Massachusetts, Connecticut, Pennsylvania, Ohio, Michigan, and Illinois, as they had for Christine Todd Whitman over James Florio in New Jersey in 1993. In 1996 they again picked winners: Clinton for president and Republicans for Congress.

In a country in which one of the two most popular foods is the pizza it should not be too surprising to find that Italian Americans have become typical American voters and successful politicians in all manner of constituencies. Italian Americans have overcome some of the handicaps their southern Italian heritage imposed in a commercial, industrial, historically Protestant democracy. At the same time, they have not entirely lost touch with that heritage and have employed to advantage the strengths it has conferred. If Italian Americans for the most part do not seem entirely comfortable with either of the two cultural blocs that provide the greatest enthusiasm and support for the two major parties—the religious right for the Republicans and the feminist left for the Democrats—perhaps they are well positioned to act as a moderating force on both. If so, the Italian Americans who were so unimportant in American politics one hundred or even fifty years ago have become one of the decisive forces in American politics today.

Linda Hutcheon

. . . .

Cryptoethnicity

The obvious question that will be going through some readers' minds is what someone with the name of Hutcheon is doing writing about ethnicity. Yet I would remind you that Hutcheon is a resolutely Scottish name, and you do not have to visit the Highlands to recognize that the Scots—with their kilts and their haggis—most certainly possess as recognizable a set of ethnic customs as anyone. In addition, if you know the conflicted history of the British Isles you will realize that many Scots still think of themselves today as culturally minoritized and politically marginalized. Sir Walter Scott wrote his *Minstrelsy of the Scottish Border* in 1883 in order to contribute to the history of his native country, "the particular features of whose manners and character are daily melting and dissolving into those of her sister and ally" (51–52). Nevertheless, the secret ethnic life of the Scots is *not* the subject of this exploration of "cryptoethnicity."

My starting point, however, is the fact that I was not born a Hutcheon; I was born a Bortalotti. The fact of a hidden or, more accurately, a silenced marker of Italian heritage is one I share with a generation of women "of a certain age," married at a time when social custom meant taking their husbands' surnames. For example, there is Cathy N. Davidson, professor of English at Duke University and editor of *American Literature*. But the N. in her name stands for Notari—or as she prefers, Notari-Fineman-Kotoski. Here in one small, not quite hidden letter is the sign of a crypto-*multi*-ethnicity, the sign of growing up Italian, Russian, German Jew, and Polish Catholic in working-class Chicago.[1] And then there is Marianna Torgovnick, or so I thought her to be named. But then, in 1994, she published a book entitled *Crossing Ocean Parkway: Readings by an Italian American Daughter*. When telling of her crossing from Italian to Jewish Brooklyn when she married, she chose to write as Marianna *De Marco*

Torgovnick. The feminist scholar we know and respect as Sandra Gilbert, the president of the MLA and the collaborator with Susan Gubar in those ground-breaking studies of women's writing, graduated from high school as Sandy Mortaro. In other words, beneath the Gilbert, the Torgovnick, the Davidson is an encrypted Mortaro, De Marco, Notari. Of course, there are male scholars in the literary field with similar Italian backgrounds: Frank Lentricchia, Dominick LaCapra, John Paul Russo, Joseph Pivato. But for the men, there is no cryptonym, no social cryptography.

What I also share with these women is the fact that we are cryptoethnic *professors of English*. In other words, we, like most of you, teach and study in academic departments structured along the lines of dominant linguistic traditions with intimate connections to the nineteenth-century politics of nation-building (see Perloff 249). But what does it mean to become an *English* professor when you grow up in an Italian household where "the English" were seen to possess a distinct and different ethnic identity, where roast beef and Yorkshire pudding were considered foreign but osso buco and polenta were the norm. "The English" were as different, as strange to us as no doubt we were to them; they too were "ethnic," other, alien—at least from our point of view. This is ethnicity as positionality.

But Sandra, Marianna, and Cathy are all Italian American; I am Italian Canadian. Does this difference in nationality entail different experiences of either ethnicity or its encrypting? After the attention given in the U.S. media in the fall of 1995 to the Québec referendum on separation, Americans may now have an even greater sense of the differences in politics, culture, and national self-image between Canada and the United States as well as between English and French Canada. With no melting pot ideology and no equivalent of even a pluralist "American" national identity to rally around, Canadians—be they of British, Italian, Somali, Chinese, or Pakistani origin—have only the paradoxically multiple model of multiculturalism in which to configure their sense of self-in-nation. This is probably one of the reasons Canadians suffer from their infamous and perpetual identity crisis.

It was during the so-called culture wars that I first realized that the word "multicultural" had very different political associations in Canada and in the United States. Then, in books such as Peter Brimelow's *Alien Nation: Common Sense about America's Immigration Disaster* or Richard Bernstein's *Dictatorship of Virtue*, I read political denunciations of multiculturalism as a social policy destined to "disunite" America (Schlesinger). Most often I found multiculturalism defined as the dominant ideology on college campuses, contaminated (as they were said to be) by political correctness.

However, Dinesh D' Sousa was not the only one to worry about what he called the "ethnic cheerleading" (31) implied in some curricular changes: Henry Louis Gates Jr., too, expressed concern about potential "ethnic chauvinism" ("'Ethnic'" 288) within the multicultural academy. Some raised questions about the possibility that multiculturalism's politics of difference might simply be another way of reconfiguring white racial supremacy (Wiegman); others voiced fears that the recent interest in ethnic studies would elide the historical realities of race through the use of a European immigrant paradigm as the master narrative of difference (San Juan 132).[2] Despite urgent defenses of minority studies and despite sincere attempts to render more complex the more dangerously simplistic views of the new changes in university curricula,[3] the associations of the word *multiculturalism* in the United States often included issues of gender, sexual choice, and occasionally class.[4]

It was precisely these associations that were so confusing to me as a Canadian, for multiculturalism in Canada is not so much a question of the canon[5] or campus politics but one of national self-definition—and it is so *by law*. In Canada the majority culture's self-understanding is in part forcibly defined by its designation as multiple, rather than single. The history of the term *multicultural* goes back to the part of the 1970 report of the Royal Commission[6] on Bilingualism and Biculturalism that was entitled *The Cultural Contribution of the Other Ethnic Groups*, where "ethnic" signified all who were not native North American. Out of this came Prime Minister Pierre Elliot Trudeau's 1971 multicultural policy statement and, in 1988, Bill C-93, the Act for the Preservation and Enhancement of Multiculturalism in Canada. The Canadian Charter of Rights and Freedoms also includes within it a commitment to the protection of the multicultural heritage of the nation. Such legal provisions are perhaps typical of Canadian political society, which Charles Taylor has characterized as "more committed to collective provision, over against American society that gives greater weight to individual initiative" (*Reconciling* 159). In Québec, as in what is really a very polyglot and misnamed "English" Canada, as Taylor suggests, there exists a "plurality of ways of belonging"—what he calls "deep diversity" (183).

It is no accident, however, that it was Pierre Elliot Trudeau, the fierce federalist opponent of Québec separation, who formulated the policy statement about multiculturalism in the early seventies. Changing Canada's self-image from bicultural to multicultural was not simply a matter of recognizing a demographic reality (see Itwaru); it had a political purpose and, in some people's eyes, a political result.[7] On the night of the

1995 separation referendum, Québec premier Jacques Parizeau lamented that the (French) Québécois chance for independence had been ruined by what he controversially referred to as "money and the ethnic vote."[8] It is no coincidence that multicultural policies were put in place at the same time that Québec was developing its own discourses of decolonization— derived from theorists of French colonialism such as Albert Meumi and Frantz Fanon. Today, in same critics' eyes, these policies still function as implicit barriers to the recognition of both Québécois demands for inde- pendence and also the land claims and demands for self-government of First Nations Peoples.

A proudly (and self-proclaimed) assimilated Canadian like Neil Bis- soondath has voiced other objections to multiculturalism as government policy. In his book *Selling Illusions: The Cult of Multiculturalism in Canada*, Bissoondath argues that he does not feel part of the Trinidadian community in Canada, that he moved away from the West Indies to start a new life, to expand horizons and to go beyond the confines of his cultural heritage. Reviewers of the book were quick to note that not everyone had arrived in Canada with such choices and such hopes; many had not sought the displacement of enforced migration. Readers were also quick to his- toricize, to point out that the ease of acculturation felt by Bissoondath had been made possible by the very policies he was attacking: the situation be- fore 1971 in Canada was anything but hospitable to immigrants, especially non-white immigrants.[9] Part of what Bisscondath is responding negatively to is the very idea of government intervention in something he feels to be as personal as ethnicity and culture. He is also reacting against the reduc- tion of ethnicity and racial difference to institutionalized, grant-supported folklore or, worse, to ethnic food festivals, folk dancing, and parades.[10]

Yet another worry is that, with multiculturalism as national policy, eth- nicity could become a compulsory and limiting identity label. The fear is that "familial genealogies, or biologism," could become the only defining terms of subjectivity (Kamboureli 27). But one reply to this concern is that, with the inevitable changes that come with displacement, any sense of ethnicity is bound to be configured differently in a new and different place. Human life, as "communitarian"[11] (and Canadian) Charles Taylor has argued, is "dialogic"; it is formed in relation to other people and other customs ("The Politics" 32).[12] In Michael Fischer's terms, "ethnicity is something reinvented and reinterpreted with each generation by each in- dividual. . . . Ethnicity is not something that is simply passed on from gen- eration to generation, taught and learned; it is something dynamic, often unsuccessfully repressed or avoided" (195)—even by cryptoethnics.

As the opponents of Canadian multiculturalism policies helpfully remind us, ethnicity should not be something reified, frozen in time; it
should never only be the site of nostalgia. Indeed, instead of insisting on
difference and specificity, Stuart Hall has urged that we should be looking
toward models of mobility and syncretism.[13] Cultures interpenetrate;
"transculturation" occurs.[14] Despite the ethnic conflicts raging in various
parts of the globe today, the meaning of ethnicity in the late-twentieth-
century diasporic world should logically no longer entail concepts of purity and authenticity; as Joseph Pivato and others have noted, for many
people it is more in the meeting of cultures that ethnicity today is lived.[15]

I want to resist the urge to find any more precise-sounding (or at least
more convenient) metaphor for this meeting of cultures that constitutes
ethnicity for me. As a model or metaphor, cultural "hybridity"—in either
its utopian or dystopian varieties—seems to depend implicitly on an idea
of purity, of authenticities brought together (see Young). It also seems
paradoxically to be dependent on keeping the very borders it seeks to dissolve. So too do metaphors of "'in-between' spaces" (Bhabha, *Location* 1)
or even "collage" (Munson 289). I am a second-generation Italian Canadian and cryptoethnic, living in multiracial, multiethnic Toronto. I do not
really feel caught between what has been described as the "experience of
loss and of being othered in a web of old and new cultural registers"
(Kamboureli 22); for me ethnicity has much more to do with the process
of what Fischer calls "inter-reference between two or more cultural traditions" (201). Marianna De Marco Torgovnick's image of crossings—between ethnic groups and social classes, between being an insider and an
outsider, among the roles of "wife, mother, daughter, mourner, professional woman, critic, and writer" (x)—strikes me as a fruitful one for
many different situations (as her own list indeed suggests), but it is not
precisely descriptive of my personal sense of what ethnicity means.

In a provocative and even prophetic essay written a decade ago, called
"A Critique of Pure Pluralism," Werner Sollors urged that the categoriza-
tion of both writers and critics as members of ethnic groups be understood as "very partial, temporal, and insufficient characterization at best"
(256). In arguing instead for a dynamic "transethnic" focus based on the
complexities of "polyethnic interaction" (257), he wrote of the dangers of
choosing—timidly—to speak with the "authority of ethnic insiders rather
than that of readers of texts" (256). When Sollors wrote that "literature
could become recognizable as a productive force that may Americanize
and ethnicize readers" (275, italics in original), he implied that you are
what you read.

Perhaps, however, you are also *how* you read (as well as how you are read). This is what Henry Louis Gates implied when he argued that "under the sign of multiculturalism [here used in its American sense], literary readings are often guided by the desire to elicit, first and foremost, indices of ethnic particularity, especially those that can be construed as oppositional, transgressive, subversive" ("Beyond the Culture Wars" 8).[16] The impact of ethnicity—like race and gender—on the act of interpretation is a much debated topic (see Mukherjee). But like the cultural construction of "nationness" (as Homi Bhabha has argued), the cultural construction of ethnicity may also be a "form of social and textual affiliation" (Bhabha, "DissemiNation" 292)—for readers as for writers, for both are formed (as readers and writers) by being placed in an order of words; both emerge as a function of different and perhaps conflicting encodings.[17]

However, some crypto-Italians—like myself, like Cathy Davidson, Sandra Gilbert, Marianna Torgovnick—end up as professional readers and writers, the kind called professors of English. The question is, do "English" professors have to do "English" readings? I received my education in English literary studies in Canada and therefore largely within the normalizing, ethnocentric context of Leavisite humanism: the immigration of British professors of English to the colonies had guaranteed that Leavis's "great tradition" would be my tradition. In other words, I learned to do what Frances Mulhern calls "English reading." The realization of this particular and particularly insidious form of cryptoethnicity may well be what drove me into Italian studies and finally comparative literature; it may even have dictated the choice of theory as my scholarly research area.[18] One part of my academic "life-script"—the narrative I use to shape and tell my life story as a reader and writer—would have to include my realization that, in the academy too, the English (as they were known in my family) constituted a specific ethnic group and not the voice of the universal. Rather than eradicate foreignness in the name of universal naturalization, we should "persuade everyone of their own foreignness vis-à-vis everyone else" (Kadir 247). At the same time, we could work toward models of interculturalism that facilitate the meeting of these ethnicities.

In the end (and at the end), I cannot in fact resist offering an image of what ethnicity and cryptoethnicity might mean to me. I borrow it from *In the Skin of a Lion*, a novel by Sri Lankan Canadian writer Michael Ondaatje. It is a novel about the history of Toronto, the city in which I live and work; the image, however, is one used to describe an Italian Canadian man, evocatively and ironically named David Caravaggio. In prison for theft (he thinks of himself as a "professional displacer" [191]), Caravaggio learns that his name is a carrier of ethnicity, a mobile attractor of scorn and abuse, for he is called "wop" and "dago." One of his tasks while in prison is to paint the roof of the penitentiary blue. (Caravaggio thus lives up to his namesake's profession even if in a debased sense.) As he goes about his job, he realizes that he is losing all sense of the boundaries between blue sky and blue roof. With this realization comes a sense of liberation and empowerment for the imprisoned man—but not only for the visual illusion of freedom it offers. In an act of cunning self-cryptography, he has his fellow inmates paint him blue, thereby erasing all visible boundaries between himself, the roof, and the sky. Caravaggio then escapes.

Cryptoethnicity, for me, is a fact of life; so too is ethnicity. From these there is no escape. But in the very fact of the encrypting there is a potential challenge to purist, imprisoning boundaries that (most of the time, at least) I find liberating. I think of blue Caravaggio on the blue roof, and he becomes for me the image not only of cryptoethnicity but of ethnicity itself—ethnicity as positionality.

Notes

. . . .

1. In 36 *Views of Mount Fuji: On Finding Myself in Japan*, writing about a Christmas dinner when she was seven, Davidson states: "Three generations and we were still foreigners masquerading as participants in the American dream. The Chianti for the children is a dead giveaway that this is not a WASP gathering in the suburbs" (260).

2. Cornell West argues that European immigrants arrived in North America perceiving themselves as "Irish" or "Sicilian" and had to learn that they were "White" "principally by adopting an American discourse of positively-valued Whiteness and negatively-charged Blackness" (29). In Canada this process is not as straightforward because of a smaller black population with a very different history. One of the worries among scholars of ethnicity in Canada is that European ethnic minorities groups will all get homogenized into the category of "white." This view was forcefully expressed by Enoch Padolsky in a paper entitled "Ethnicity and/or Race: Canadian Minority Writing at the Crossroads," presented at the Windy Pines conference, August 1995.

3. See, for instance, the essays in Goldberg, and Arthur and Shapiro. See also Worth; Appleby, Hunt, and Jacob; Gillan and Gillan.

4. On multiculturalism as the product of "an economic strategy developed by the multinational corporations," see Massey 20. See also Jameson on the "neo-ethnic" and the "neoregional" as flights from "the realities of late capitalism, a compensatory ideology, in a situation in which regions (like ethnic groups) have been fundamentally

254 :: Linda Hutcheon

wiped out—reduced, standardized, commodified, atomized, or rationalized" (148).

5. On the difference in the canon debates in Canada, see Lecker.

6. Canadians have long used royal commissions to study cultural issues. In 1928 one was set up in response to worries about the Americanization of Canadian commercial airwaves. This fear of foreign and corporate control of culture industries has driven the creation of Canadian national culture as a public and publicly funded endeavor. There is a distrust of the U.S. notion of the marketplace as the guarantee of cultural democracy. See Berland 515.

7. For more on this issue, see the special issue of the *Journal of Canadian Studies* 17.1 (1982), titled "Multiculturalism: Retrospect and Prospect."

8. The vote was 50.56 percent against separation, with almost 93% of eligible voters casting ballots. Of the 49.44 percent who voted for separation, Parizeau claimed that they represented 60 percent of francophones in the province, and therefore the so-called *pure laine* Québécois had indeed voted for independence.

9. On continuing racism as an inhibitor to integration and the particular Caribbean cultural patterns that "feed and reinforce" racism, see Henry. On racist discourse in Canada, before and after 1971, see Bauer.

10. "Our approach to multiculturalism encourages the devaluation of that which it claims to wish to protect and promote. Culture becomes an object for display rather than the heart and soul of the individuals formed by it. Culture, manipulated into social and political usefulness, becomes folklore" (Bissoondath 88).

11. This is the term Habermas (111) uses to describe Taylor.

12. Historically and geographically, the settling of Canada (so different from that of the United States) also illustrates this theory well. There was no drive westward from an Atlantic beginning but rather, in Cole Harris's terms, a disjointed and discontinuous archipelago, settled island by island by different European groups at different times with different technologies and economies, not to mention languages and customs. The result was "dense networks of kin and local traditions that amalgamated elements of the different regional backgrounds of founding populations into distinctive folk cultures" (Harris 465). Compare, on the language issues, Canadian Marc Shell's historical account of the American predilection to take "the fiction of original American monoglottism for the reality of American polyglottism" (104).

13. Hall's remarks from "Minimal Selves," *ICA Documents* 6 (London: ICA, 1987) are cited in Ang 29. In a similar vein, Herbert Lindenberger, writing about growing up in the 1930s and 1940s, notes that for him "the thing that mattered for most of us was what linked you to other people, not what made you different or ethnically distinct— and this is precisely the reverse of what it is today" (49).

14. See Cristl Verduyn's use of this term to mean a "creative process of cultural transition" in "Transculturation/Transformation: Ecriture migrante féminine au Québec" (paper presented at the ACQS biennial conference, Montreal, 20 November 1992).

15. See Pivato (*Echo* 57, *Contrasts* 30) on this image of ethnicity in writing as a meeting of cultures, in his Canadian (language-based) model—the meeting of anglophone or francophone with some other ethnic group.

16. He continues, making a point Sollors too stresses: "In a critique of liberal individualism, we debunk the supposed 'stability' of the individual as a category, and yet we sometimes reconstitute and recuperate the same essential stability in the form of

an ethos that allegedly exhibits all the regularities and uniformities we could not lo-cate in the individual subject" ("Beyond the Culture Wars" 8).

17. See Blodgett on ethnic writing as a matter of "code, discourse and the con-struction of a specific subject" (2).

18. Torgovnick feels this more strongly and in a different sense than I do: "Much of my recent work has been about 'us/them' relations in American culture" (x).

Works Cited

. . . .

Ang, Ien. "Hegemony-in-Trouble: Nostalgia and the Ideology of the Impossible in Eu-ropean Cinema." *Screening Europe: Image and Identity in Contemporary European Cinema*. Ed. Dundan Petrie. London: British Film Institute, 1992. 21–31.

Appleby, Joyce, Lynn Hunt, and Margaret Jacob. *Telling the Truth about History*. New York: Norton, 1994.

Arthur, John, and Amy Shapiro, eds. *Campus Wars: Multiculturalism and the Politics of Difference*. Boulder, Colo.: Westview, 1995.

Barthes, Roland. *Roland Barthes by Roland Barthes*. Trans. Richard Howard. New York: Hill and Wang, 1988.

Bauer, Julien. "Racism in Canada: A Symposium." *Viewpoints*. Suppl. to *Canadian Jewish News* 16.5 (1988): 1–2.

Berland, Jody. "Marginal Notes on Cultural Studies in Canada." *University of Toronto Quarterly* 64 (1995): 514–25.

Bernstein, Richard. *Dictatorship of Virtue*. New York: Knopf, 1994.

Bhabha, Homi K. "DissemiNation: Time, Narrative, and the Margins of the Modern Nation." Bhabha, *Nation and Narration* 291–322.

———. *The Location of Culture*. London and New York: 1994.

———, ed. *Nation and Narration*. London and New York: Routledge, 1990.

Bissoondath, Neil. *Selling Illusions: The Cult of Multiculturalism in Canada*. Toronto: Penguin, 1994.

Blodgett, E. D. "Towards an Ethnic Style." *Canadian Review of Comparative Literature* 22.4 (1995): 1–16.

Brimelow, Peter. *Alien Nation: Common Sense about America's Immigration Disaster*. New York: Random House, 1995.

The Cultural Contribution of the Other Ethnic Groups. Book 4 of *Report of the Royal Commission on Bilingualism and Biculturalism*. Ottawa: The Queen's Printer, 1967–70.

Davidson, Cathy N. *36 Views of Mount Fuji: On Finding Myself in Japan*. New York: Penguin/Dutton, 1993.

D' Sousa, Dinesh, and Robert MacNeil. "The Big Chill? Interview with Dinesh D'-Sousa." *Debating P.C.: The Controversy over Political Correctness on College Cam-puses*. Ed. Paul Berman, New York: Dell, 1992.

Fischer, Michael M. J. "Ethnicity and the Post-Modern Arts of Memory." *Writing Culture: The Poetics and Politics of Ethnography.* Ed. James Clifford and George E. Marcus. Berkeley: University of California Press, 1986.

Gates, Henry Louis, Jr. "Beyond the Culture Wars: Identities in Dialogue." *Profession* 93 (1993): 6–11.

———. "'Ethnic and Minority' Studies." *Introduction to Scholarship in Modern Languages and Literatures.* Ed. Joseph Gibaldi. New York: MLA, 1992. 288–302.

Gillan, Maria Maziotti, and Jennifer Gillan, eds. *Unsettling America: An Anthology of Contemporary Multicultural Poetry.* New York: Viking, 1995.

Goldberg, David Theo, ed. *Multiculturalism: A Critical Reader.* Oxford and Cambridge, Mass.: Basil Blackwell, 1994.

Gutman, Amy, ed. *Multiculturalism: Examining the Politics of Recognition.* Princeton, N.J.: Princeton University Press, 1994.

Habermas, Jürgen. "Struggles for Recognition in the Democratic Constitutional State." Trans. Shierry Weber Nicholsen. Gutman 107–48.

Harris, R. Cole. "Regionalism and the Canadian Archipelago." *Heartland and Hinterland: A Geography of Canada.* Ed. L. D. McCann. Scarborough: Prentice-Hall Canada, 1982. 459–84.

Henry, Frances. *The Caribbean Diaspora in Toronto: Learning to Live with Racism.* Toronto: University of Toronto Press, 1995.

Itwaru, Arnold. *The Invention of Canada: Literary Text and the Immigrant Imaginary.* Toronto: TSAR Publications, 1990.

Jameson, Fredric. *The Seeds of Time.* New York: Columbia University Press, 1994.

Kadir, Djelal. "Comparative Literature Hinterland." *World Literature Today* 66.2 (1995): 245–48.

Kamboureli, Smaro. "Canadian Ethnic Anthologies: Representations of Ethnicity." *Ariel* 25.4 (1994): 11–52.

Lecker, Robert. "A Country without a Canon? Canadian Literature and the Esthetics of Idealism." *Mosaic* 26.3 (1993): 1–19.

Lindenberger, Herbert. "Between Texts: From Assimilationist Novel to Resistance Narrative." *Jewish Social Studies* 1.2 (Winter 1995): 48–68.

Massey, Irving. *Identity and Community: Reflections on English, Yiddish, and French Literature in Canada.* Detroit: Wayne State University Press, 1994.

Monson, Ingrid. "Doubleness and Jazz Improvisation: Irony, Parody, and Ethnomusicology." *Critical Inquiry* 20 (Winter 1994): 283–313.

Mukherjee, Arun P. *Oppositional Aesthetics: Readings from a Hyphenated Space.* Toronto: TSAR Publications, 1994.

Mulhern, Francis. "English Reading." Bhabha, *Nation and Narration* 250–64.

Ondaatje, Michael. *In the Skin of a Lion.* Toronto: McClelland and Stewart, 1987.

Perloff, Marjorie. "'Living in the Same Place': The Old Mononationalism and the New Comparative Literature." *World Literature Today* 69.2 (1995): 249–55.

Pivato, Joseph, ed. *Contrasts: Comparative Essays on Italian-Canadian Writing.* Montreal: Guernica, 1985.

———. *Echo: Essays on Other Literatures.* Toronto and New York: Guernica, 1994.

San Juan, S., Jr. *Racial Formations/Critical Transformations: Articulations of Power in Ethnic and Racial Studies in the United States.* Atlantic Highlands, N.J.: Humanities Press, 1992.

Schlesinger, Arthur M., Jr. *The Disuniting of America: Reflections on a Multicultural Society.*

Scott, Sir Walter. *Minstrelsy of the Scottish Border: Consisting of Historical and Romantic Ballads.* London, 1883.

Shell, Marc. "Babel in America; or, The Politics of Language Diversity in the United States." *Critical Inquiry* 20 (1993): 103–27.

Sollors, Werner. "A Critique of Pure Pluralism." *Reconstructing American Literary History.* Ed. Sacvan Bercovitch. Cambridge, Mass.: Harvard University Press, 1986. 250–79.

Taylor, Charles. "The Politics of Recognition." Gutman 25–73.

———. *Reconciling the Solitudes: Essays on Canadian Federalism and Nationalism.* Montreal and Kingston: McGill-Queen's University Press, 1993.

Torgovnick, Marianna De Marco. *Crossing Ocean Parkway: Readings by an Italian American Daughter.* Chicago: University of Chicago Press, 1994.

West, Cornell. "The New Cultural Politics of Difference." *Out There: Marginalization and Contemporary Culture.* Ed. Russell Ferguson, M. Gever, Trinh T. Minh-ha, and Cornell West. New York: New Museum of Contemporary Art; Cambridge, Mass.: Massachusetts Institute of Technology Press, 1990. 19–36.

Wiegman, Robyn. *American Anatomies: Theorizing Race and Gender.* Durham, N.C.: Duke University Press, 1995.

Worth, Fabienne. "Postmodern Pedagogy in the Multicultural Classroom: For Inappropriate Teachers and Imperfect Spectators." *Cultural Critique* 25 (Fall 1993): 3–32.

A. Kenneth Ciongoli

. . . .

The Way of the WASP

In recent years, people across the ideological spectrum have been troubled, as well they should, by a growing number of horrors, including child
murders and teenage pregnancies. They have told us that America is expe-
riencing a crisis of values, and we must take this assessment seriously. It is
also undeniable that the America conceived by our Founding Fathers was
perceived by the rest of the world as a fountainhead of enlightenment, a
place where reasonable people confront their problems rationally. If we are
to correct this national malaise, it is crucial for us to understand exactly
what values we have lost and their origin so that they might be restored.

The founders of this country were largely northern Europeans and, by
religion, Protestant. But it would be a great mistake to assume that they
wanted America to emulate eighteenth-century-English, medieval Anglo-
Norman, or even pre-Norman Anglo-Saxon values. The original immigrant waves, whether English or Dutch, were seeking a better world, and
they saw America as the new Roman republic. The ancient wisdom of
Rome was indeed their guiding light as much as anything they had left behind in northern Europe.

What went wrong here? How have we lost sight of the Roman origins
of this republic?

Like cosmopolitan Rome in its decline, we are currently beset by fac-
tionalism and cultural relativism. We seem unable to agree that anything
resembling transcendental truth exists. Unless we resolve these problems,
we may well suffer Rome's fate.

Here is a proposal. We should identify an American subgroup whose
culture still works for them, analyze its value system, and decide if it is
compatible with the original American vision. It should not surprise many
that the Italian American core value system closely parallels the Roman

258

vision of our founders in America. In 1991, Richard Brookhiser suggested, in *The Way of the WASP*, that for America to recover from its philosophical crisis, it must return to the provenance of our WASP Founding Fathers. In this spirit of identification of the cultural repository for American salvation, I will attempt to define what I call the way of the "WAXP."

The provocative nature of my title serves two purposes. The first is to connect with Brookhiser's thesis, and the second is to identify the Roman roots seminal to the creation of American ideals. I want to suggest a repossession of our Roman past that might just be therapeutic in these times.

My "in your eye" self-deprecatory slur is not meant to reap ethnic hate mail but merely to grasp the attention of those who ordinarily would ignore a more estimable title about something Italian. As Brookhiser has informed us, contemporary Americans have exchanged the high-minded traditions of our Founding Fathers for gratification, blunt ambition, and selfishness. I cannot argue with this. We should, in fact, celebrate the ideals of Washington, Franklin, Jefferson, Madison, and Mazzei. They were almost all WASPs, but they aspired to create a world different from the one they had left behind in Europe.

Let us take the case of Jefferson. Willard Sterne Randall, his biographer, tells us that Jefferson longed to relieve English culture of the Norman yoke. Jefferson despised the Norman vices that infected Anglo-Saxon virtue after the eleventh-century conquest of England. He accused the Normans of fostering in the English spirit an addiction to monarchy, feudalism, and rough justice by crown-appointed judges rather than by juries of one's peers. He disdained what he perceived as inherent Norman savagery, land theft, and predatory manners. These are not the preferred ways of the WASP. Instead, Jefferson and his contemporaries grafted the virtues of Roman Britain (which had lasted for five centuries) onto Anglo-Saxon stock. The American utopia was not to be defined by the liberties of the ancestral Germanic woods of the Anglo-Saxon so much as by the early Roman republic.

This historical brief is not intended to foster Norman bashing, although that would be novel, but to demonstrate that an important segment of our heritage has affinities beyond those usually attributed to the Anglo-Saxon world. Whatever group or groups are responsible for the transformation of American culture from liberal (in the traditional sense of British eighteenth- and nineteenth-century liberalism) to libertine, it is incontrovertible that it happened. The social experimentation of the past half century has, in my view, been disastrous. I suggest looking back to

Cicero and to the Roman republic for models for the restitution of a lost sense of virtue.

There are close parallels between what our Founding Fathers proposed for this nation and the lives of Italian Americans—the heirs of ancient Rome on American soil. A few cautionary notes, however, are in order. I do not accept the media stereotypes of Italian Americans: the Fonz, the poolhall boys of the *Bronx Tale*, John Gotti, the street toughs of *Do the Right Thing*, or even Mamma Teresa's Tomato Sauce. I'm not talking about houses full of plastic slipcovers or French provincial furniture— the suburban stereotype encountered, as ever, in the media. I refer to the average Italian American family—hardworking, independent-minded people whose political votes are sought but whose cultural opinions are seldom considered.

When I consider the core values of Italian American life, the idea of the family is paramount. The family is sacrosanct, in Italian as well as Italian American culture. The well-being of our children—I speak personally, of course, having been raised in an Italian American family in south Philadelphia—is our first priority. Honor thy father and thy mother is almost an Italian American mantra. A recent study showed that more than 90 percent of Italian Americans over the age of sixty-five live with a blood relative, an astounding fact in late-twentieth-century American culture. Routine sympathy, congeniality, fairness, self-control, loyalty, and duty, as propounded by Cicero, are seen by most Italian Americans as essential to civilization itself. But the family is primary, with daily habits that include eating together at the dinner table (a habit that, not incidentally, has been shown to raise SAT scores in high school students).

Let me give an example of Roman values at work. Some neighbors told my cousin's wife, Cathy: "In the next life make us you and Tony." These neighbors envy the confident ease with which Cathy and Tony guided their three teenage daughters through the social miasma of teen America without the help of a Baedeker. Tony is an executive for a national retail chain, and like many educated Italian Americans he decries the damage the child psychology gurus have wrought on the psyches of American children and their parents. Cathy comes from a very similar family background and education. Both know from their childhood experiences that they were more important to their parents than their parents were to themselves. Even so, they did not get a lot of what they wanted but did get a fair amount of discipline they did not want. The atmosphere generated by their parents contributed a great deal to their success as parents.

It's the kind of thing you can't really teach, but you learn it by osmosis in an Italian American home.

A second example. A cultured Italian American friend confided to me that he recently read Cicero's beautiful description of the soul of a wise man; in that description he found his parents. They had never read Cicero, of course, but the virtues of moderation and constancy were part of their lives. He was reminded of them when reading about Cicero's call to civic virtue, too. They felt duty-bound to work for others.

Not incidentally, I have heard similar tributes to parents and grandparents over the past eighteen years as a member of the National Italian American Foundation; again and again, the foundation's honorees each year—drawn from the business sector, education, politics, religion, and the world of entertainment—have praised their families, which provided an atmosphere of honor and virtue, where the work ethic was prized, where a sense of community values was passed on, as well as the Ciceronian ideal of self-restraint, a trait woefully missing in the world these days.

As I write, I hearken to a distant Roman superstition that murmurs, "The public disclosure of the state of our family may destroy us." But for the restitution I am talking about to occur, we must take such a risk.

Italian Americans have much to contribute to this country. For complex reasons we have had little or no voice in the major media outlets. The Italian American tradition—or even the Italian tradition—is rarely studied in our universities, which supposedly pride themselves on studying a broad range of cultural backgrounds. It may well be time for a fresh look at Roman humanism, its legacy in the world of Italian culture, and of course, its transmission to America in the lives of Italian Americans.

Matilda Cuomo

. . . .

Italian Americans Address America's Problems

Families and Children in the Twenty-First Century

Of all God's creatures, a child is most vulnerable to the world. From the moment of birth and for many years after, a child is absolutely dependent upon its family—its parents and in a larger sense, the community—for the essentials of life: love and safety, shelter and nourishment. This is something that Italian Americans have long understood: It is essential to our self-definition.

As we bear witness to the slow erosion of basic services to the neediest of our citizens, we all know that there is one group that suffers more than any other. They are all our children. We see in their eyes their great need and profound powerlessness—tiny boats on a wide sea, at the mercy of the forces that surround them.

Because government is defaulting, the rest of us must seize every chance we can find to focus the nation on these smallest but most important members of the human family, to appreciate their strength, understand their vulnerabilities, celebrate the joy they give us, and assess what we must give them in return.

Our message—as Italian Americans and, of course, U.S. citizens—should be a clear one. This is the richest and most powerful nation in the world, and for some people, our strong free enterprise system is working beautifully: We have more millionaires and billionaires than ever before. But at the same time, the fact is that of all the Western industrialized nations, the U.S. record on childhood poverty ranks among the worst. The gap between our poorest and richest children is the widest.

And of course the problem is not simply poverty: There are hundreds of stories about children with AIDS, children abused and neglected at home or caught in the crossfire of the streets, children robbed of the hope or direction even to stay in school, and children so lost they are having children themselves because they know no other avenue to dignity.

For too many children, it can be devastating—and even deadly. Among those fifteen to twenty-four years old, suicide has tripled in the past three decades across all socioeconomic levels, and for the first time we're seeing significant increase in suicides among ten to fourteen-year-olds. When Marian Wright-Edelman of the Children's Defense Fund declares that "no child is physically, economically, and morally safe in [1990s] America," she speaks an ugly and sad truth.

It is not only the poor children who are suffering, although their agony is usually more vivid. The Child Care Action Committee tells us that in more than two-thirds of all two-parent families, both parents work. In effect, we are now raising a generation of middle-class children who are in many ways raising themselves. Sixty-five percent of all children come home after school to an empty house.

The world we live in has changed dramatically in the past half century, but the needs of young children have not changed since the beginning of time. No woman—and increasingly, encouragingly, no man—can afford to assume that "career" is the real point of living and that "family" will take care of itself.

We will never have a responsibility greater than raising a child. If and when we choose to have a family, we need to take that seriously. Representative Charles Rangel of New York made this observation: "When a child is willing to shoot and be shot, to go to jail and not be afraid to catch AIDS, to do drugs, I think all of society ought to be afraid as to why it is, that the child has so little hope and so little confidence."

We know that the fundamental health and developmental well-being of children is an interlocking system and requires that we do many things simultaneously. It involves everything from a strong family unit to good schools, proper shelter, and stable communities, from nutritious food to good medical care. It depends on steady jobs for their parents, as well as tax codes that make it easier for families to stay together and afford a good education for their children. And in the end, the child must have the tenderness of a loving home and a reason to hope for the future. But the reality is that a large number of our children today have neither a community, a neighborhood, nor a supportive family structure in which to grow.

What is the response from our current political leaders? Mostly, it is one of two things: they either deny the gravity of the situation by ignoring it, or they blame government for having created it, which is very much like blaming the bandage for the wound! We must correct the misinformation. We must fight the rising tide of defeatist thinking that says, because we haven't found perfect answers to poverty and family breakdown, we just quit trying.

Over decades of changing social policies, the American experience has taught all of us a few fundamental lessons about how we can help families and children flourish. First, when we deal with families, there is nothing more important than *prevention*. We must concentrate intensely on helping families cope with little problems before they turn into catastrophes.

Government today, in Washington and across the country, is slashing away at education and the community-based services that we know are the best tools of prevention. Short-term, we save money; but long-term, we stand to lose another generation of our children. We should not have to apologize for spending dollars to promote prevention and strengthening families.

If we want to help a child who is hungry or ill or illiterate, it will take more than just bread or an antibiotic or a lesson in the alphabet. We have to be willing to comprehend these problems as symptoms of a larger social and economic disorder and understand that their causes are so deeply intertwined that we cannot effectively treat them one symptom at a time.

In the current climate, it may not be popular to say this, but it is nonetheless true that we must continue to find ways to strengthen birth families, the extended family, and the community and to make them all part of the solution. It is essential that we do everything we can—all at once—to help the whole family and to address the total well-being of the child.

We must find ways to help all those children who are poor because their parents are uneducated and are uneducated because their parents are poor. We must find ways to help the children who are sickly because they are neglected and are neglected because they are sick. We must find ways to help parents know better how to help their children and ways to help the children who grow up in violent surroundings and become indifferent to the value of a human life—because the world has never valued their lives. Surely, this is not the best universe we could offer our children.

We must all understand—and make sure our leaders recognize—not only the worthiness of every individual family but our *interconnectedness* as well. We all need one another.

And so we come to the second lesson of the American (and Italian

American) experience: that just as the problems of our children are inter-connected, our efforts to help them must be interconnected, too—requir-ing cooperation and networking between the agencies of government; be-tween government, business, media, and voluntary community groups; and within and between the government and families themselves.

As governor of New York State, my husband based his administration on the idea of "family"—on the principle that we become stronger and better when we share benefits and burdens, addressing our vulnerabilities with the collective strength of all our people. The idea of family motivated his principal policy and program judgments. It's an idea that makes sense, not just to Democrats but to Republicans and Independents, to farmers and physicists and factory workers. It makes sense to policymakers—and it certainly makes sense to parents.

The idea of family and interconnectedness guided New York's decision in 1988 to establish the Decade of the Child, a long-term, comprehensive commitment to help children and families. This initiative linked together all of the human service agencies in state government in a cooperative ef-fort to serve the complex needs of children. Never before had the state devoted so many of its resources to family and children's issues.

As we have come to recognize the value of prevention and the depth of our interconnectedness, we have also learned another lesson: that one key to our success, especially in a time of economic strain and instability, is to get help from the business community, to form *partnerships* between the public and private sectors. More and more companies are coming to un-derstand that it is in their own best interest to help their employees build strong families and strong communities, because today's children will be tomorrow's citizens and tomorrow's work force. Our job is to show those businesses how they can help.

For example, one successful initiative in our administration was known as Partners for Prevention of Child Abuse and Neglect. Businesses worked with state government to sponsor training and counseling pro-grams to help employees who are working parents balance the competing demands of work and family. Every employer should offer flexible work schedules and parental leave policies. When working parents can give their children the love and time they need, we all benefit. Only parents can give the love, but employers can help furnish the time.

A fourth principle for shaping our approach to the problems of chil-dren and families insists that we must focus more on *outcomes*. Process is important, but results are all-important. We have to be honest with our-selves. Are the strategies we're using really changing children's lives for the better? Are they the best we can do? Could we serve more children, more effectively, if we gave up some old assumptions?

Take foster care as an example. We have only to look at the crisis in foster care to know that something is amiss. We spend $1,975 per child per year on AFDC but $10,945 per child living with a foster care family and a whopping minimum of $40,000 per child in a residential foster care facility.

You all know how it works: traditionally, we have paid a daily fee for services rendered to foster children. The longer the child stays in foster care, the more money the provider receives. No wonder the foster care population continues to rise dramatically. The incentives are absolutely backward.

We must move to a performance-based financing system so that we pay for positive outcomes—like the reunification of a child with his or her birth family or finding a permanent, loving home for the child as soon as possible. This was the goal of the "Families for Kids ASAP" spearheaded by New York State. Through our efforts, New York City received a grant of nearly $5 million from the Kellogg Foundation to implement the "Families for Kids" initiative.

We shouldn't be afraid to tie reimbursement to performance. Instead, we should embrace it as the best way to help children and families recover and move on. If we fail to put the spotlight on results, we fail to serve the children.

Prevention; interconnected, cooperative solutions; public/private partnerships; and focusing on outcomes: these are all enduring principles that should guide our thinking permanently for the sake of our children's well being.

There is one final lesson that is crucially important at this moment in our history, when America seems poised to walk out on sixty years of the most humane and intelligent progress any government ever achieved. The current political rhetoric has persuaded much of the public that nothing works, that we have no idea how to help the children and might as well spend the money elsewhere. But the truth is, all across the country little miracles are performed every day. Not-for-profit organizations, governmental agencies, and businesses are gently lifting children from the dark chasm of poverty, neglect, and violence on the bright, steady wings of programs that work.

A wonderful success story—and a great partnership—was the New York State Mentoring Program (NYSMP), which we began in 1987 to prevent children from dropping out of school. It was a unique school-based, statewide, early-intervention program, kindergarten through eighth grade, that relied entirely on volunteer mentors whom we trained and organized. Before the program was eliminated by the current state administration, we had more than 250 mentoring programs throughout New York State with almost 4,000 children mentored on a one-to-one basis.

The children's grades went up, and school absenteeism went down. In a five-year study our records indicated that not one mentee dropped out of school, slipped into drug use, or became pregnant. I know from my own experience as a mentor to Ely that she was helped directly. Indirectly, we also helped her siblings, and her mother, Paula, gained better parenting skills and self confidence.

In 1995, I established MENTORING USA (MUSA) to replace the NYSMP model. Today, MENTORING USA continues to support the former NYSMP program. New initiatives are heavily concentrated in New York City, where we are implementing mentoring programs in New York City Housing Authority sites and in targeted public schools in need of special support. MUSA, with programs now underway in eight states, is expanding across the country as well.

MUSA is also now part of the continuum of care services offered by H.E.L.P. (Housing Enterprise for the Less Privileged), the nation's largest provider of transitional housing and comprehensive independent living programs for homeless families. There are MUSA programs at two Genesis sites, H.E.L.P.'s permanent housing sites located in Brooklyn and Manhattan.

We need leaders who will encourage effective partnerships. The answer to bad programs is not for government to run away from its responsibilities, to dump the entire burden on states and localities. Private charities cannot compensate for the losses. Do we believe in the "thousand points of light"? Of course! Our charities are the most generous in the world. But they cannot offer enough heat to comfort all the shivering children, nor enough light to show the way home for all the people who have lost their way.

We need leaders who have the courage to make fundamental reforms to the system with intelligence, who will cut waste with a surgeon's scalpel, not a meat ax. We need leaders who have the courage to stand up for principles, even against popular sentiment, whenever it's necessary. We need strong leaders who will not sacrifice the health or safety of our most vulnerable citizens to satisfy the fickle gods of politics, leaders who will not fuel their political careers by igniting our prejudices and insecurities.

The United States is being rocked today by a disturbing wave of conflict and fragmentation. But surely, if we can be united on anything, it should be the welfare of our children. In the fight for our children's rights and well-being, we have to pray for the strength never to give in to fatigue or frustration, and to be always on guard against the most dangerous enemy—the indifference of the powerful—and against our own indifference, every one of us. It is the power of the people together that will change our policies for children and families. If we fail to help them, we will all pay for the consequences.

Mother Teresa has said that "the most terrible poverty is the feeling of being unwanted." We have to understand that the world we are offering our children—a world too full of confusion and injustice, bitterness and pain—does not look like a world that wants them very much.

We must find the resources to help our poor, forgotten children and all the middle-class children who will need to compete in a tough new world: make sure that they can go see a doctor when they need one, that their schools are safe and stimulating places to learn, that they're mastering the skills to succeed in the world of work, and that they have all the adult help and counsel and love they need to grow. Not as a handout, not just as the response to compassion, not to purge our moral guilt but as an investment in the human resources without which we cannot make it in the fierce global competition of the new millennium.

All the children are our precious natural resources. Where else but in America could you find such extraordinary diversity of children, representing the languages and culture of the whole world? We must not let apathy and selfishness steal the beauty and the future of this magnificent place.

Together, with confidence, we can make this the beginning of a new era of hope and justice for all our children—and therefore for the future of our nation. We can take whatever we have learned in our own families into the world at large, where we can make a difference.

Richard Gambino

· ·

The Crisis of Italian American Identity

> A whole nation walked out of the middle ages, slept on the
> ocean, and awakened in New York in the twentieth century. . . .
> My parents needed their energies for making sense of a world
> their own parents scarcely began to understand, so that the
> genealogy of their predicament was a luxury they had neither
> the leisure nor the means to think of pursuing. In my generation,
> time and money were provided, but it turned out that the
> genealogy was not for sale.
> —Robert Viscusi, *Astoria*[1]

Much of the Italian American experience is trapped in inauthentic myths.
The distortion of Italian realities is so extreme that we are grateful if a
work stereotypes us benignly, for example, as merely an "operatic" (emotionally overexpressive and therefore ridiculous) but likable people, as in
the film *Moonstruck*. Overcoming this state of affairs requires both analysis of what's wrong and a fresh look at that Italian American experience
that is authentic.

A few years ago a film producer unwittingly revealed himself as at sea
in the imbroglio. A young Italian American who had grown up in New
York, he was at the time in charge of making films for one of the three
major broadcast television networks. Later he went on to the same position at a second of the three networks. "All this Italian ethnic stuff," he
confided to me, "is just jerking off." Another man, an Italian American editor of a newspaper in Chicago, told me that Italian Americans "just want
to be told how great they are."

The scenario has three parts. First, Italian Americans are largely in a surrealistic limbo regarding their identity. This is so partly because a people's identity needs to be expressed in the arts and reflected in the social sciences to be adequately realized. Second, wildly successful inauthentic myths of Italian Americans have come to serve as a substitute among Italian Americans for an authentic, developed identity. Thus, Italian Americans are left in a quandary about their ethnic experience.

Luigi Pirandello, in plays like *Six Characters in Search of an Author* and *Henry IV*, was fascinated with the idea that a person does not have an identity except as defined entirely by the events that happen to him. There is no "me," no "you," and no "him" or "her" apart from what happens to us in the world. Pirandello made the case that Descartes's "I think, therefore I am" is a delusion. So is every other effort to establish an individual's real and continuing identity as he goes through life's happenings. There are only the happenings. Pirandello's point of view reminds one of an old joke. A desperate man shouts at the sky, "God, do you exist?" And a voice comes thundering back, "Who's asking?"

Italian Americans disturbingly come closer and closer to living Pirandello's condition. They resemble characters in search of an author. But many authors and others give them a character that is a caricature at best. Italian American identity is in danger of being dissolved in a sea of inauthentic myths. Italian Americans shout "We are!" but an army of those who define them answers, "Look who's talking! Criminals, buffoons, racists, and *cafoni.*"

For some time now, there has been running in New York a theatrical piece called *Tony n' Tina's Wedding*. This is "participatory theater." The audience (at $60 a ticket) gets to share in a mock Italian American wedding held, scandalously, in an actual church—St. John's at 81 Christopher Street. Then the cast and audience go to a mock reception at a "catering hall." The actors play an Italian American family and friends as chaotic clowns, vulgarians, hysterics, and religiously superstitious, sex-driven, and vengeance-prone obsessives. In short, Italian Americans are presented in a range of grotesquely negative stereotypes. The audience joins in the fun by trying to outdo the cast in caricaturing Italian Americans at the church, in the hall, and in the streets en route from one to the other. It seems that *Time* magazine's critic, John Patrick Shanley, was right when he wrote of Italian Americans (November 7, 1988, issue) with reference to movies, the stage, and television, "They are the last ethnic group America can comfortably mock." And investigative reporter Jack Newfield was correct when he wrote in the February 4, 1992, issue of the New York *Post,* "Prejudice against Italian Americans is the most tolerated intolerance."

Italian Americans live as if in a dream of a certain type. Applying Pirandello's view, we recall a Shakespearean phrase. Italian Americans "are such stuff as dreams are made on." Italian Americans hold myths about themselves, but the rest of America insists on other, very different myths about them. The two sets of myths stand in a perverse chiaroscuro relationship wherein the darkness of the inauthentic views saturates and kills the light. The word *myth* is used here not to mean mere fiction but in the critically important sense explained by Joseph Campbell:

> . . . the individual has had an experience of his own—of order, horror, beauty, or even mere exhilaration . . . and if his realization has been of a certain depth and import, his communication will have the value and force of living myth—for those, that is to say, who receive and respond to it of themselves, with recognition, uncoerced.
>
> Mythological symbols touch and exhilarate centers of life beyond the reach of vocabularies of reason and coercion.
>
> . . . The first function of mythology is to reconcile waking consciousness to the *mysterium et fascinans* [great and fascinating mystery] of this universe *as it is*: the second being the interpretive total image of the same, as known to contemporary consciousness. Shakespeare's definition of the function of his art, "to hold, as "twere, the mirror up to nature," is thus equally a definition of mythology. It is the revelation to waking consciousness of the powers of its own sustaining source.
>
> A third function, however, is the enforcement of a moral order: the shaping of the individual to the requirements of his geographical and historically conditioned social group. . . . The fourth and most vital, most critical function of a mythology, then, is to foster the centering and unfolding of the individual in integrity, in accord with (*d*) himself, (*c*) his culture, (*b*) the universe, and (*a*) that awesome ultimate mystery which is both beyond and within himself and all things.[2]

Real Italian American identity is in danger of extinction, in at least the first three of the four ways in which Campbell explains how identity functions: (1) authentically to express Italian American realities, (2) to reflect Italian American realities, and, (3) to shape the individual, all in noncoercive ways solely by the force of the identity's power to compel individuals to respond positively to it. Therefore, the last, or religious, function of identity is also greatly hobbled; because to the extent that an individual's identity shows little integrity in the first three ways, it provides a shaky foundation for integrity on the spiritual level. Italian American identity is being annihilated at its soul by lies, many of which "strut their stuff" as art, journalism, and scholarship.

"Art," said Pablo Picasso, "is a lie that enables us to see the truth." But as Picasso indicates, art does not tell literal truths. In fact, liberalism and art are mutually exclusive. Much has been made in recent years about "found art," as in an exhibit at the Whitney Museum in the mid-1980s. The show consisted entirely of some seven hundred used-car tires strewn randomly about in a large, bare room. But if experience of such found art has proved anything, it is that if something is a literal representation, it isn't art. If something is art, it is not a literal representation.

For lack of a better word, art is *interpretive*, highly interpretive. Other disciplines are also interpretive (e.g., history and sociology). But unlike them, art is not bound at all by rules of literal truth. The relationship between art and the social sciences is extremely complicated. But three errors are to be avoided. First, to subordinate art to the social sciences leads to dull, didactic art, epitomized, for example, by the worst "socialist realism" art of the Communist world. Second, to be literal-minded is to be a Philistine, a person who cannot appreciate genuine art. And third, to take art as if it were history is ridiculously to take fiction, Picasso's "lie," as literal truth. Yet this last mode has been the case regarding Italian Americans. For example, the Mafia myth found in so many films and TV shows about Italian Americans is taken as history. It is also important to understand that to the extent that any historical experience has to be ceaselessly defended regarding its accuracy, that is, "getting the story straight," all expressions of the experience suffer. Thus, much of Italian American expression seems boring because it is telling us some literal truth. It isn't showing us truth of the kind art enables us to see as a deeper reality. That type of truth, artistic truth, is mythic in nature.

Again, "myth" is used here in the sense of *an account that illuminates an important general truth about the essential nature of a people or their condition*. Myth is, to use Plato's sense, "a likely story" through which we can intuit the essence of something. For example, the ancient Greek myth of Oedipus has been a rich lode of truth about human nature and the human condition, from Sophocles to Freud to Woody Allen (although not all their insights are of equal depth).

A people's myths are interpretations of its experiences. To repeat, myths are meant to tell vital truths intuited as the heart of the experiences. In the most famous of Michelangelo's *Pietà*s, the body of Jesus is proportional to that of a twelve-year-old boy in relation to the figure of

Mary. Mary appears to be a thirty-year-old woman cradling the body of her thirty-three-year-old son. Michelangelo's "incorrect" interpretation here is in the service of telling greater truths. Michaelangelo was after essential truth about Jesus, Mary, and suffering, and he sacrificed literal truth to capture it.

Still, myths and the "literal" social sciences aid and abet each other. "History never embraces more than a small part of reality," observed La Rochefoucault. We attempt to gain greater parts of reality by creating myths, largely through art. Myths then return the compliment. *Myths aid and abet history, sociology, and the other social sciences by indicating to social scientists where and how to look at reality.* For example. Look at Italian American history as a story of *la famiglia,* work, Italian Catholicism, and other Italian values. Or look at Italian American history as a story of crime as an upward-mobility ladder for an ethnic group. Where you look and what you will find will be biased accordingly.

Contrary to popular linguistic usage, a myth is not just a fiction or a lie. A complicated myth is a tangle of truths, distortions, insights, facts, fictions, legends, fears, and ideals. For example, take the historic American myths of success, equality, and progress. Or take some myths currently shaping our lives: those of self-fulfillment, female liberation, male chauvinism, or yuppie good living.

Myth originates from the Greek *mythos,* which means "statement." Myths are statements we all live by and use to understand and explain ourselves, to explain others, to explain the human condition, and to explain the universe. Rich myths give us thorough and fair meanings that augment the literal knowledge of the social sciences. Poor myths yield only misunderstandings. Only the philosophically naive believe there is only a single, one-to-one correspondence between reality and truth. A wonderful triple spring of understanding flows from the mingling of the social sciences, art, and myth. But it is anything but simple.

As already indicated, however, to the extent that a people have myths about themselves forced upon them, they will often be preoccupied with the inauthentic myths' distortions, which purport to explain vital truths about the people and their experience. This is especially so if the inauthentic myths are negative and are accepted over the people's own attempts to explain themselves. In this we find the key to what are more authentic myths and what are less authentic myths. Myths that ring true are those that evolve in time through lived experience that is reflected upon. It is essential that myth have its feet in experience. Less authentic myths are at best less informed by experience. They lead to perceptions that are less true, less illuminating; and this is so regardless of how artful the art and how talented the artist. (So the standard advice given to artists is not to lose touch with their experience.)

To the extent that a people find inauthentic, negative myths about them given more credence and importance than their own attempts to explain themselves, the group's own self-understanding and expressions about themselves often suffer from three problems. One is that much of the group's understanding of itself bows to the preponderant myths held by the dominant larger society. Self-expressions reflect the outsiders' myths of the group. The group's deference to the less authentic myths occurs either because the members of a group have truly accepted the less authentic myths or because they are playing to the inauthentic myths because these myths are better received by the larger American population. Self-understandings and self-expressions produced in this mode by the group's members reinforce the less authentic myths, inspiring more belief in them and inspiring the production of more art in the same vein.

The cycle can go on endlessly, as seems to be the case, for example, of Mafia dramas since the fantastic commercial success of The Godfather movies. The fact that the less authentic art is produced by artists of the group itself is especially convincing. As is thought of Mario Puzo, Francis Coppola, or Martin Scorsese, "He's one of them, so you see, that view of them must be true." Or even "He's one of us; therefore it's true." Of course, as is the case with The Godfather, the adding of some authentic family characteristics and other Italian American cachets—done brilliantly, especially in the films—to the dominant myths that Italian American culture is in its essence criminal and that Italian American upward mobility in America was achieved through crime (which is quite different from the simple and undeniable proposition that there are Italian American gangsters) gives the myths great credibility and great "legitimacy."

The Godfather myth has had a great impact on art about Italian Americans coming after it, as well as on how Italian Americans are understood, by guiding people in how to look at Italian Americans. For example, one film producer responded sincerely to the idea of an Italian American Roots. "It's been done," he said, "The Godfather." "Oh," he added, his eyes glazing over, as it was explained to him that criminality and the Italian American experience are not synonymous. The popular conviction is that "everybody knows" that the Mafia is all there is to know about Italian Americans, all one needs to know about them, all that is worth knowing about them, or all that is interesting about them. Claims to the contrary are just expressions of ethnic oversensitivity, if not ethnic paranoia. Such claims are to be humored but not taken too seriously.

Again, one "knows" all of this to a large extent because of the incredible popularity of films like *The Godfather*. One knows it is true also, of course, from reading the newspapers, which are heavily informed in how they deal with crime stories and features by the dominant artistic myths of society. Code phrases are used to reinforce the myth that Italian American gangsters are not just gangsters and that racketeering by Italian Americans is not mere racketeering. For example, what is a "crime family"? Its members are not related by blood or by marriage. Why not just call the gangs "gangs" or "rings" or any of the other terms used for gangs of non-Italian thugs active in the same types of crime? Similarly, the A&E cable TV channel in 1995 broadcast a biography of Al Capone, which ended with Jack Perkins on camera saying that "the crime family founded by Al Capone is still thriving in Chicago." This fantastic statement is very different from the proposition that there are still Italian American racketeers in Chicago. So we all appear to be captive on a carousel of prevailing myths for one more go around after another.

Another result of the predominance of inauthentic myths is to force Italian Americans into a preoccupation with setting the Italian American record straight. It is an onus ceaselessly pressed on Italian Americans by the daily fare of Mafia dramas and other distortions in print, on film, in the broadcast media, and in schools. Therefore, there are great pressures on Italian Americans to be defensive. When they, in fact, become defensive, they are then dismissed.

Still a third response by Italian Americans is both genuinely historical and scholarly rather than inauthentic or defensive. But this too often is dismissed as not conforming to "the truth." This means, of course, it doesn't jibe with the inauthentic myths used by the larger society to explain the Italian American experience, myths "everyone knows are true." These authentic expressions are frequently denigrated, when not rejected altogether, as "ethnic," meaning, of course, that they have meaning only in terms of the peculiarities of the group and not in terms of others' lives. For example, Pietro Di Donato's 1937 novel, *Christ in Concrete*, is excellent in terms of presenting valid Italian American myths of family, sacrifice, love, and work and excellent also in technical accomplishment. The author pulls off a rare feat in presenting the syntax and idioms—and therefore the thought processes—of one language and culture, Italian, in another language, English. Yet despite the acclaim it received as a "worker's novel" when it was published, it is ignored today as a work of "ethnic art."

Another example is found in a recent favorable introduction to a re-publication of Jerre Mangione's 1942 book, *Mount Allegro*. Herbert J. Gans labels it "a classic of ethnic American literature." This is like calling the novels of Henry James ethnic literature because they are about WASPs.

In the world of painting, Ralph Fasanella is celebrated as an American primitive painter in the class of Grandma Moses. But he is further labeled a folk artist and pigeonholed. The label "folk artist" would limit his value to the literal themes of his paintings—in a word, to nostalgia: the past struggles of the American labor movement, the politics of the Old Left, the densely populated ethnic life of American cities of a generation or more ago, and Italian American immigrants, their families, work, and religion. Yet Fasanella's works are of much more value. Fasanella said it in a prospectus for a 1979 showing of his works in New York. "It's always a triple play in art, you know what I mean. DiMaggio didn't see the ball, he'd sense something behind him and then he'd start to run. Well, that's how it is in art; it's not a single or double play, it's sixteen things at once."

The point is, the works of James, Mangione, Di Donato, and Fasanella transcend the ethnicity each portrays to reach universal human meaning. But for many critics and others, it is less than possible to see this if a work departs from the accepted myths held about Italian Americans in the larger society. Quite simply, Fasanella, Di Donato, Mangione, and many others explain Italian Americans in ways that have nothing to do with crime, buffoonery, anti-intellectualism, mindless reactionaryism, or racism. (With revealing language, film critic David Denby, in the June 26, 1989, issue of *New York* magazine called an Italian American character in the movie *Do the Right Thing* "an Italian tribal racist.") By conventional stipulation, any work that does not conform to the prevailing negative myths of Italian Americans must be ethnocentered, folksy, parochial, defensive, or ethnopropagandistic.

I suggest that this maddening state of affairs reflects an essential truth about Italian Americans—the Italian American surrealistic state of being. It remains a potent conceptual model for understanding. A motto of the ancient Stoics was *Amor fati,* "love of fate." The current fate of Italian Americans is surrealistic. They need not love it, but if they are going to understand themselves, they'd better at least come to terms with it, for surrealism is the most marked quality of their experience today.

Before the 1970s, portrayals of Italian Americans dealt overwhelmingly in two sets of myths. One, of course, is the Mafia. Sadly, it has become part of American popular consciousness, running from the film *Little Cae-*

sar in 1930 to the 1980s *Prizzi's Honor, Married to the Mob, Cookie,* the 1990s *The Client, Get Shorty,* and *Casino,* and the English Opera Company's performing Verdi's *Rigoletto* in New York in modern dress as a Mafia story set in New York. The Mafia mania shows no sign of abating and will no doubt continue to be the dominant myth about Italian Americans in the foreseeable future.

The second set of myths standard before the 1970s concerned the now familiar themes of the trials of Italian immigrants in a new land, the conflicts between them and their American-bred children, and the accommodations between Italian immigrants and their children and of both to *l'America.* Not coincidentally, this second set of Italian American myths took off at about the same time as the advent of talking pictures. Just before *Little Caesar* was made, its star, Edward G. Robinson, played the leading role in the film, *A Lady to Love,* about the life of an Italian American grape grower in California seeking a bride through the mails. In the movie, and in the 1950s Broadway musical based on it, *The Most Happy Fella,* Tony Patucci is portrayed sympathetically as a would-be romantic hopelessly outclassed in the mores of American culture. Thus, another perennial pattern was already evident in the film. Italian Americans, when not shown as Chico Marx buffoons or *cafoni* having no culture at all, are depicted in the nativist American bias of being, despite their good hearts, ill-equipped in the United States because they have an inferior Italian culture. They are gruff, irrational, crude, benighted, medieval, operatic, oversexed, overly physical, impulsive, violent, and hidebound. In short, they have many of the negative qualities attributed to children, adolescents, and fools.

Italian Americans often suffer defeat in the pre-1970s works. When they triumph, most often they do so largely because they outgrow their Italian American values. In short, the works reinforce the standard version of the melting pot ideology. To be American, one cannot be Italian. Even in the film *Marty* (1955), one of the most sympathetic toward Italian Americans of these works, the title character has to courageously break the lonely, anxious lock on him by his immigrant Italian mother in a strange land. In the 1950s film of Tennessee Williams's *Rose Tattoo,* an Italian immigrant, Serafina, struggles almost unto death to allow her sexuality to emerge and seek fulfillment. The obstacle to this is her antisensualist Italian culture, a standard, if absurd, oxymoron of the American nativist tradition in its twentieth-century liberal version. Whatever Italian Americans may be, they are not James Joyce's Dubliners. The provocateurs who lead to Serafina's liberation are her earthy, oversexed Italian immigrant lover and her "Americanized" daughter, also fixtures of American nativism.

Still, films and other works in the assimilation-travails vein, such as the film version of Arthur Miller's *A View from the Bridge* (1962), portrayed Italian Americans as multidimensional human beings. The immigrant and second-generation culture-conflict themes did much better in some Italian American literature of the period, notably Di Donato's *Christ in Concrete,* Mangione's *Mount Allegro,* and Mario Puzo's *Fortunate Pilgrim.* (Not so fortunately, the recent TV film of Puzo's moving novel reverted to classic Hollywood inane stereotypical treatment.)

In the past twenty years or so there have been added to the Mafia and culture-conflict myths the surrealistic condition of contemporary Italian Americans. It is seen in films like *Lovers and Other Strangers* (1970), *Mean Streets* (1974), *Rocky I* (1976), *Saturday Night Fever* (1977), and *Moonstruck* (1987) and in literature, as in some of Albert Innaurato's plays and Helen Barolini's novel *Umbertina.* Of course, many of these works also rely on the older myths. For example, all of the films dip deeply into the honey-and-lye bath of Italian Americans as good-hearted *cafoni* or buffoons. (Even Nintendo got on the wagon with its Super Marios video game.) And the Mafia is often thrown in gratuitously. Rocky Balboa earns his living at the film's beginning as a loan shark's goon. And the young denizens of Little Italy's *Mean Streets,* are, in the perception of viewers, mafiosi-in-training.

Innaurato's long-running Broadway drama, *Gemini,* is set, as is *Rocky,* in the Italian neighborhood of South Philadelphia in the year 1973. It centers on a crisis of sexual identity in a twenty-one-year-old Italian American man, Francis, who is torn between his heterosexual and homosexual urges. It also treats other themes (e.g., the difficulties of communication between fathers and sons, the search for love, and the loss of love) in a context permeated by today's Italian American surrealistic state of being, both overtly and more subtly. Judith, Francis's classmate at Harvard (Radcliffe), "an exceedingly, perhaps even intimidatingly, beautiful Wasp" majoring in Italian, early in the play tries out her linguistic skills in a futile effort to make cultural contact with Francis's family. Francis's father, Fran, replies, "Hanh?" Lucille, Fran's Italian American lover, explains, "You see, dear, that's Harvard Italian. We don't speak that."

Later, at his twenty-first birthday party, an emotionally tortured Francis turns on both Italian American and WASP culture—and for good measure, on a non-Italian neighbor named Bunny,—by ethnically stereotyping and insulting the people who love him. What he says is a bitter example of the rage born of despair that the Italian American surrealistic state of being can produce:

> I would first like to thank my father, now that I am officially an adult, for teaching me how to dance and sing and cough and fart and scratch . . . then I would like to thank my next-door neighbor Bunny for demonstrating once and for all that motherhood ought to be abolished, along with drunks and whores; Lucille, for teaching me how to ruin the happiest of occasions with one glance and the cheapest insect spray; . . . and then Judith, our brilliant, bubbly, and let's not forget, mature Italian major from Radcliffe will recite to us in her Main Line Italian all the nonsense syllables of her upbringing and her recent reading.[3]

Innaurato's *The Transfiguration of Benno Blimpie* is a play also set in the milieu of an Italian American family. In fact, it is steeped in working-class Italian American life. Unlike the successful *Gemini*, it ran only for some two months. It is easy to see why: it is an excruciatingly painful play to watch. We see a grotesquely fat man, Benno, literally eating himself to death because those close to him have abused him and failed to love him all of his life. Guided by the mature Benno, we watch his life as a child. The young Benno is routinely abused and neglected by his family. His mother refers to the fat boy as "this *disgraziato* freak." In one episode, Benno is being sadistically assaulted by some other boys, but his grandfather is too preoccupied with sexually molesting a thirteen-year-old Irish girl (who dominates the man and eventually stabs him to death) to respond to the pained cries of his grandson, a boy he despises.

In another scene, Benno panics at the sight of the old man's sexual play with the teasing girl. The young boy cries hysterically, if improbably, "I want, I want, I want Brunelleschi, Botticelli, Rafaello, Michelangelo" and names a string of other Renaissance individuals, *all of them synonymous with Italian beauty and truth*. The play ends with a psychotic Benno about to chop off his own flesh with a meat cleaver so that he can eat it. His last speech can be read as another psychological response, albeit in extremis, to the Italian American surrealistic condition. It is "eating yourself up" in the frustration of being unappreciated (not to say unloved) as one is, until one is "liberated" by numbness. Benno says of himself after being once again brutalized by neighborhood sadists:

> He lay there; and in that instant, time stopped. And feeling, it stopped too, and seemed to merge with time, and with space. My sense of identity seeped out of me into the cracks in the concrete. And for a few seconds, I

was out of myself, totally free of myself. Totally. Free. Free. And this I call: The Transfiguration of Benno Blimpie.[4]

Not surprisingly, the critics all but ignored the Italian American character of Innaurato's two plays. The plays present the wrong ethnic myths, ones the critics don't comprehend. Where are the mafiosi, the Rockys?

Helen Barolini's *Umbertina* (1979) is a novel of four generations of Italian American women, focusing heavily on Umbertina, who migrates to America from Calabria in the great wave of Italian immigration; her granddaughter Marguerite, and Marguerite's daughter Tina, born in 1950 and named after her great-grandmother. Tina is a graduate ("the only one in her class with an Italian name") of Bryn Mawr College. In Italy she tells a WASP friend from New England, a graduate of Bennington College, "Missy, you know what I love about you? You have no existential predicament in your nature. . . . I've never understood where I belong." Whether in the United States or Italy, Tina explains, Missy unthinkingly and securely knows she is simply an American.

Tina, whose "school Italian" is perfect and who has been raised partly in Venice, the home of her father, bumps up against her ethnic background in Italy in meeting Italian American tourists who typically speak bad Italian. Meeting them evokes in her the Italian American surrealistic existence she ran from in leaving the United States:

> They were ruining her morning, Tina thought sourly. . . . She thought of herself in the States angrily explaining that she was not Italian American. My father is Italian and my mother is a third generation [Italian] American who never heard Italian until she got to Italy to study; I am part Italian and part American, not Italian-American. It was a splitting of hairs that convinced no one, not even Tina. But she felt obliged each time to put up her defense against being merged in the ethnic mess she saw and despised in the States. She thought of a bumper sticker that disgusted her: "Mafia Staff Car, Keepa You Hands Off."[5]

As Tina's story unfolds, back in the United States she is told she is like her namesake great-grandmother, who, unlike Tina's mother, "was a strong person and stuck to her guns." Unlike her Italian American relatives, Tina is determined to study the culture of Italy and maintain a living relation to it. This is the novel's solution to the question of how to live with the Italian American surrealistic condition, "the ethnic mess she saw and despised back in the States." Tina asks herself, "What was wrong with the immigrants' children that it left them so distrustful of their *italianità?*"

Toward the end of the novel, Tina looks back on her costly evasions of her own identity and is reminded of Dante's view, as she sees it, that hell is what a person does to himself when he goes against the grain of his own character.

If cultivating *italianità* via a living relationship with today's Italy is Tina's answer to resolving the Italian American surrealistic condition, the films of the past twenty years seem to take it as axiomatic that resolutions, if they are to come at all, are to be found in looking toward American rather than Italian culture. Although redolent of the Italian American buffoon stereotype, *Lovers and Other Strangers* is a sad comedy about married life, a theme used to carry the anomie of third-generation Italian Americans. They are alienated from their parents' dogged second-generation values. From the perspective of the film, this is just as well. A second-generation couple, played by overweight Richard Castellano and a booming Bea Arthur, have nothing to offer their two grown sons except empty rituals of food and overeating. They are at a loss to understand one son's failed marriage to an Irish American woman and the upcoming marriage of the second, also to a non-Italian woman.

The bewildered father repeatedly asks his son, "So, Richie, what's the story?" Grudgingly satisfied with his second-generation compromise of maintaining an outward shell of a traditional Italian marriage, the father lamely characterizes himself and his wife as "content." But he betrays his deeper feelings by blurting out to his son at one point, "Happy? Who said you had to be happy? You think you're better than me?" The film's message is that third-generation Italian Americans have a worse than useless legacy. Their way out of the surrealistic conflict of the deadening myths of what they are supposed to be as "Italian" and their actual emptiness is not to look back to their bankrupt heritage. Instead, it is rootlessly but bravely to muddle through the guideless chaos of values that is current American culture.

The same message about young Italian Americans (and *to* them)—forget your supposed ethnic inheritance and just bravely struggle through as rootless individuals—is also the theme played with variations in *Rocky I.* In fact, "Rocky" is given no family whatsoever, and his Italian American girlfriend's family is limited to an embittered middle-aged working drudge of a brother. Still another variation on the theme is presented in the film *Saturday Night Fever.* In this movie, not only is Tony Manero's working-class family just a sink of painful failure, including the failed religious life of his Catholic priest brother, but Tony also becomes disillusioned with the false "cultural style" he and his Italian American peers have produced.

It is built on the narrow neighborhood glory of disco dancing ability, sex bereft of any value, even that of sensuality, and a generalized stupid freneticism of pointless lives. The thin hope offered to young Italian Americans to get out of this ethnic hell is to forsake it altogether. It is the example given to Tony at the end of the film by a female dancer who has embarked on the lonely, guideless quest out of the surrealistic ethnic muck by moving to Manhattan, with all its dehumanizing urban woes. (It seems that in our time even the melting pot Eden has been defined downward.)

Mean Streets carries the same message of no valuable cultural inheritance for young Italian Americans. In the end, the criminal, sordid, ignorant, crazed, racist, and violent existence of young adults in New York's Little Italy in the 1970s overcomes even the modest hope of hapless Charlie and his girlfriend, ostracized because she is epileptic, to escape it all by getting an apartment "uptown." Charlie is slaughtered in a drawn-out orgy of gunfire, graphically presented with endless pain and blood. *Mean Streets* makes a glancing attempt to portray Italian American religious sensibilities. But it is very limited—one of the characters holds his hand near a flame and mutters "You can't fuck around with God." The surrealistic state of Italian Americans is further evidenced by the fact that so few artists have tried to tap the mythically deep-textured Italian religious piety "incarnated" in everyday life. A few paintings by Ralph Fasanella and Gian Carlo Menotti's opera *The Saint of Bleecker Street* come to mind as works by those artists who do try.

Moonstruck contains one of Hollywood's few affirmative messages to young Italian Americans that their cultural inheritance may have living value for them. In this case, la *famiglia* is presented as the saving legacy. But the film takes the easy way out of the surrealistic relationship between Italian American culture and larger America's different, very insistent view of it. Larger America is all but ignored in the film. It is as if Italian Americans today could live a ghettoized life akin to that of their ancestors eighty or even fifty years ago. They cannot.

When we turn to an authentic, scholarly view of Italian Americans and compare it to what some intellectuals see, we encounter much of the same surreal view of the group as we see in popular culture. Let us begin with some facts. According to the 1990 census,[6] there are 14.8 million Italian Americans. Their household income ($44,865), family mean income ($51,442), and per capita income ($17,834) are significantly higher than the national averages—respectively, $38,453; $43,803; and $14,420. The percentage of Italian Americans, ages eighteen to twenty-four, with a bachelor's degree or higher is 11.2 percent versus 7.5 percent as the national average. This is a dramatic change from only three to four decades ago, when Italian Americans still had one of the lowest records of educational achievement, nationwide, of all groups.

In other words, Italian Americans since the 1960s have caught up with *and surpassed* the national average for formal schooling, as well as for income. Italian Americans are relatively recently arrived in the economic middle class and are increasingly successful in it. In addition to formal education (and probably even more important before the 1970s), one outstanding statistic accounts for the dramatic economic upward mobility among Italian Americans in the past thirty-five years. That is that the rate of business ownership among Italian Americans is 70 *percent higher* than among the general population in the United States.

Among the paramount values of traditional Italian American culture is that of cultivating responsible adults. This would seem a humdrum statement were it not for the fact that we live in a time when a major characteristic among many adults is narcissism, in a mass culture that encourages and affirms a particular type of self-centered self-absorption above all other values. The mode of narcissism is marked by the ego run amok in adolescent fantasies of "self-fulfillment" without commitments. I am *not* primarily referring to parents of "latchkey children." Even when narcissistic parents are present, *their children are alone*. I am thinking more of parental *authority*, the kind of authority that must rest on parents being responsible adults, which in turn rests on the parents knowing who they are and being comfortable with who they are. Narcissistic parents fit one description of narcissistic personalities given by the American Psychiatric Association: "They expect to be catered to . . . this sense of entitlement combined with a lack of sensitivity to the wants and needs of others may result in the conscious or unwitting exploitation [or neglect] of others."[7]

The consequences to children in a society composed of such adults was cogently stated by Edward Shorter in a review by him of an excellent 1994 book on the subject, *Ties That Stress: The New Family Imbalance*, by David Elkind:

> The "new family imbalance" referred to in his title is the systematic privileging of pleasure for adults at the cost of the developmental needs of children. Elkind argues that a sea change has struck American family life, destroying a social system once friendly to children and replacing it with one congenial to adults but pernicious for the young.
>
> . . . The big losers, says Elkind, have been children, who are now shorn

of the security and protection essential for healthy growth and left to fend for themselves in a hostile world. Although the rights-oriented jargon under which this diminishing of childhood has occurred is characterized by terms such as "competency" and "empowerment," the bottom line is that people who are far too young to deal with autonomy are now cast adrift in it.[8]

Think about a TV program that was very popular when today's young parents were children and teenagers—*Magnum, P. I.* The program presented a handsome hunk of a grown man living a teenage boy's fantasies. Magnum lived in another man's home, that of a very rich man, a luxurious seaside mansion in Hawaii. Magnum drove the rich man's expensive sports car as his own. Best of all, the rich man was never there. Magnum had no real job but indulged himself instead in a child's version of a private investigator's career. His comings and goings in the pursuit of fun brought an endless succession of sexy women into his arms. They made no demands on him but lived to satisfy and please him. In his "career" he regularly tore up the landscape of Hawaii with no moral or legal consequences to himself. Magnum, it goes without saying, had no children to burden him in his chosen life-style.

Decades ago, Noël Coward sang a song, a line of which was "What will happen to the children when there are no more grown-ups?" The answer surrounds us in the plague of teenage pregnancies, violence, and alcohol and drug use that started in the 1960s when certain adults exploited young people's disgust with the Vietnam War to assume a mantle of authority, which they used to tell kids to "tune in, turn on, and drop out." Even today as these aging disciples of the self-styled wisdom—"Don't trust anybody over thirty"—pass from the scene, the Abby Hoffmans and Gerry Garcias are still eulogized in the press as cultural heroes.

On October 12, 1995, newspapers reported a study showing that actual risks *to their lives*, brought on by so many teenagers' behavior, are now brought upon themselves by *subteens*. The Carnegie Council on Adolescent Development, a committee of the Carnegie Corporation, issued a report of a ten-year study of children from ages ten to fourteen. As reported by Elizabeth Shogren of the *Los Angeles Times*, "profound societal changes have left young Americans with less adult supervision while subjecting them to growing pressure to experiment with drugs, engage in sex, and turn to violence to resolve conflicts."[9]

Also at the core of traditional Italian American values is a yearning for justice, a desire and intense respect for it brought from the memory of centuries of ordinary people routinely and brutally denied justice in southern Italy. Centuries of experience had bred in the bones of the often illiterate immigrants landing at Ellis Island a profound moral understanding, which was expressed early in Mediterranean history when Aristotle repudiated Plato's collectivist notions of justice. Justice, said Aristotle, is only had if it is had by each and every individual as such. We'd do well to ponder this as we read our newspapers. Claim after claim is made that group justice has been set above individual justice.

The Catholicism of the immigrants encompassed a morality of incarnated piety. Put in its simplest terms, it stressed that one's Christian morality is not measured by one's churchliness, nor by understanding abstract theologies but by one's de facto lived values, no more, no less—especially in one's relations with other people. The morality also involved an ethic of *personalist* civic responsibility, not one of being responsible merely through belonging to grand causes. A current slogan of the ecological movement comes to mind: "Act locally; think globally." The same Italian ethic produced the Italians' peculiar definition of *crisitiani*—the immigrants used the word as a synonym for "human beings," not in the sense of reducing humanity to Christians alone but elevating the very concept of humanity to one of lived Christian morality.

Of course, the values of adult responsibility and authority, of noncollectivist justice, and of incarnated morality cannot be kept vital or rejuvenated simply by harking back to the past. Any identity based on nostalgia alone in useless. Values can be kept alive and developed to meet changing circumstances *only* if we know about their roots and evolution—and care about what we know. Italian American experiences will continue to contribute to America only to the extent that Italian Americans and other Americans have an educated knowledge of the history, literature, and present social realities of Italian Americans. What Thomas Jefferson said of freedom is also true of living identity: it is incompatible with ignorance.

Yet, many intellectuals present a very different picture of Italian Americans. It should be astonishing that, in the 1990s, southern Italian culture and Italian American culture are still frequently cited by intellectual writers as examples—and egregious ones at that—of "amoral familism." The phrase and the theory were introduced by Edward C. Banfield in his 1958 book, *The Moral Basis of a Backward Society.* Banfield, who did not speak Italian, studied a town in southern Italy for nine months. Incredibly, he not only missed the most conspicuous and powerful institution of southern Italy, the extended family (not to mention the social networks of related extended families created by marriages and the custom of *comparraggio,* only poorly translatable by the English term "godparenthood"), he in fact denied it existed. In his words, his preposterous conclusion was that he saw in southern Italy "the absence of the institution of the extended family."[10]

In the June 1993 issue of *Commentary*, a man widely accepted as an expert on American morality, James Q. Wilson, cited the family system of southern Italy as an example of systems that are socially and politically dysfunctional because they are socially amoral. America, Wilson wrote, has no need of such social systems. In the August 1993 issue of *Commentary*, an exchange of letters was published: Peter Brimelow, one of the leading advocates of stopping the current immigration to the United States and a virulent critic of today's immigrants, and Francis Fukuyama, who defended today's immigrants, both *accepted* the theory of "amoral familism," applied it to the Italian immigrants of decades ago and to Mexican immigrants of today, and also alleged, in Fukuyama's words, that these groups have "a knack for organized crime."

A 1992 book about today's immigrants, *Who Prospers,* by Lawrence E. Harrison,[11] also employs the theory of amoral familism, applying it to Latin American cultures. Paradoxically, it is a theory all the more easily accepted because Italian Americans are regularly scapegoated in American universities by proponents of multiculturalism—anathema to Harrison— who blame them for racism, sexism, organized crime, and other vices.

Given this intellectual climate, it should have come as no surprise when on March 15, 1995, a day after the 104th anniversary of the lynching of eleven Italian Americans in New Orleans in 1891 (the largest lynching in American history), columnist and Pulitzer Prize winner Murray Kempton wrote a piece in New York *Newsday* justifying the lynchings. Kempton wrote: "the victims in this instance were probably gangsters whose awful fate was inspired by the highest public spirit.[12] I am the author of a book about the 1891 lynchings[13] and probably the leading authority in the world on the case. But such is the unthinking acceptance of anti–Italian American bigotry that I had to argue with the "Viewpoints" editor at *Newsday* that (1) it is outrageous to justify a lynching and (2) Kempton had gotten the case all wrong from the overall story to the spellings of the principals' names, including those of the mayor and police superintendent of New Orleans. (Kempton did poorly by relying on a certain sensationalist book on crime, which no scholar takes seriously.) Finally, the editor agreed to publish a rebuttal from me.

Shortly thereafter, *Newsday* published another piece by Kempton, about Nancy Sinatra's posing for *Playboy* magazine, in which he mused about her "Italian Skin."[14] Kempton is buttressed by the still-current tradition of the American press that takes note of Italian Americans' ethnicity only when individuals are of a criminal, clownish, or scandalous type. As another example, *Time* magazine, in a burst of creativity, labeled Joey Buttafuoco, at the height of his notoriety, an "Italian stud." (Contrast this with the press's treatment of the more recent story of Congressman Mel Reynolds, who like Buttafuoco, was convicted of having sex with a sixteen-year-old girl—statutory rape, which is a felony. Little mention was made of Reynolds's ethnic background. Indeed, there would have been, justifiably, a storm of protest if the press had emphasized that he is African American.)

The point of all this is not that the distortion of Italian American culture and defamation of Italian Americans threatens Italian "pride"—such a point of view itself trivializes the matter. The point is that the defamation and trivialization of Italian Americana threatens to wash away altogether Italian American history and culture in never-ending tsunami waves of nonsense. Little wonder that a 1990 survey by a professional polling agency found that 74 percent of Americans associate Italian Americans with organized crime *and also that 78 percent of Italian Americans make the same association.*[15] In short, for these reasons, Jerome Krase's view that "Italian Americans have an unknown past and an uncertain future" is not only accurate but urgent.

Luigi Pirandello gave two views in *Umorismo* that may be useful to both Italian Americans in their surrealistic cultural and psychological condition and to artists and social scientists addressing that state. "There lives in our spirit," he wrote, "the spirit of the race or of the collectivity of which we are a part; we respond, unconsciously, to the pressure of others, to their ways of judging, their ways of feeling and functioning." And he warned, "The more one's own weakness is felt in the struggle for life the more important becomes the need for reciprocal deceit.[16]

Notes

. . . .

1. Robert Viscusi, *Astoria* (a novel about Italian Americans) (Toronto/New York: Guernica Editions, 1995), p. 22.

2. Joseph Campbell, *Creative Mythology: The Masks of God* (New York: Penguin Books, 1968), pp. 4–5, 6.

3. Albert Innaurato, *Gemini,* in *Bizarre Behavior: Six Plays by Albert Innaurato* (New York: Avon Books, 1980), p. 57.

4. Albert Innaurato, *The Transfiguration of Benno Blimpe,* in *Bizarre Behavior: Six Plays by Albert Innaurato* (New York: Avon Books, 1980), p. 98.

5. Helen Barolini, *Umbertina* (New York: Seaview Books, 1979), p. 315.

6. Census demographic statistics age taken from the following. U.S. Bureau of the Census (Washington, D.C., 1990): *Detailed Ancestry Groups for States, 1990 Census of the Population* (CP-S-1-2); *Summary Tape File 3C, 1990 Census of Population and Housing* (CD-ROM); *Ancestry of the Population of the United States, 1990* (CP3-1); *Summary Tape File 3A, 1990 Census of the Population and Housing* (CD-ROM); *Detailed Ancestry Groups for the United States, 1990.* (CPH-L-97), Suppl. to CP-S-1-2).

7. American Psychiatric Association, *Diagnostic and Statistical Manual of Mental Disorders,* 4th ed. (Washington. D.C.: Author, 1994), p. 659.

8. Edward Shorter, review of *Ties That Stress: The New Family Imbalance,* by David Elkind, *Readings: A Journal of Reviews and Commentary in Mental Health* 10(3) (September 1995): 14.

9. Shogren's story was published in New York *Newsday,* October 12, 1995.

10. Edward C. Banfield, *The Moral Basis of a Backward Society* (New York: Free Press, 1958), p. 10.

11. Lawrence E. Harrison, *Who Prospers* (New York: Harper Collins, 1992).

12. Murray Kempton, "Mafiosi Forget to Honor Their Martyrs," New York *Newsday,* March 15, 1995, sec. A.

13. Richard Gambino, *Vendetta: The Largest Lynching in American History* (New York: Doubleday, 1977).

14. Murray Kempton, "Nancy Sinatra Has Found Her Own Way," New York *Newsday,* April 13, 1995.

15. Response Analysis Corporation, *Americans of Italian Descent: A Study of Public Images, Beliefs, and Misperceptions* (Princeton, N.J.: Author, 1990), Table 12.

16. Luigi Pirandello, *Umorismo,* in *Modern Drama,* ed. Anthony Caputi (New York: W. W. Norton, 1966).

Joseph V. Scelsa

. . . .

The 80th Street Mafia

On April 21, 1986, Dr. Joel Segall, president of Baruch College, one of the twenty-one colleges of the City University of New York (CUNY), in a memorandum to the entire College community referred to the CUNY chancellor's Office as "the 80th Street Mafia." Ironically, at that time neither the CUNY chancellor nor any of his vice chancellors was Italian American. This incident resulted in an outcry of bias from the New York Italian American community. On May 12, 1986, President Segall issued a public apology for using an ethnic slur. He retired thereafter.

It was a hot, humid afternoon on September 9, 1992. I found myself standing in the corridor of the federal courthouse at Foley Square in New York City. There were no windows nor air-conditioning in the hall of the prewar building. The sweat was pouring down my head as my professional life passed before me. I was keenly aware that I had just taken a step that was irreversible, one that I knew was the right thing to do for myself and for my family. I had been brought up to believe in the American Dream, the U.S. Constitution and the belief that the federal courts would ensure its fulfillment. As a youngster, I loved my civic courses at P.S. 97 in the Bronx, where I attended school in the 1950s. In high school and college, social studies and American history were my favorite courses. In college, I majored in political science at Long Island University and later earned two master's degrees from Lehman College of the City University of New York, in social studies and counseling. Ultimately, I completed my formal education with the degree of doctor of education in sociology from Columbia University Teachers College. At Columbia, I studied civil rights but never dreamed that I would be compelled to avail myself of the protection of those laws that were drafted for "minorities."

It seemed like an eternity that afternoon as I stood outside the chambers of Judge Constance Baker Motley. I did not know at the moment that Judge Motley had been a civil rights activist with Justice Thurgood Marshall on the famous 1954 *Brown vs. Board of Education* case, which overturned the "separate but equal" doctrine, making it unconstitutional. What I did know was that I had just filed a federal civil rights suit against the chancellor and the City University of New York, asking the federal court to intervene to stop the university from discriminating against Italian Americans by dismantling its Italian American Institute and removing me as its director.

The door to the judge's chamber opened, and my attorney, Philip Foglia, came out and stated, "The judge wants to see you." As I entered the chamber, I was impressed with the stateliness of the room, with its oak wood paneling and leather chairs and couch. The judge sat at the head of her long conference table with my attorneys at one side and the CUNY vice chancellor of legal affairs and an attorney from the Office of the Attorney General of New York on the other side. I took a chair at the far end of the table facing the judge. Judge Motley asked me to explain in my "own words" why I was there. I responded that the university was trying to dismantle the John D. Calandra Italian American Institute and remove me as its director because of my activism on behalf of Italian American faculty and staff employed in the CUNY system.

The judge appeared to have a head cold and had a box of tissues next to her, which she kept reaching for while university counsel tried to assert that they had just made a "management decision and there was no retaliation or discrimination." Judge Motley listened attentively, but she was not persuaded. She had dealt with matters of discrimination all her professional life, and the scenario must have sounded all too familiar. Judge Motley wanted to learn more, so she granted a temporary restraining order (TRO) and set a hearing date for a preliminary injunction in three weeks.

Despite knowing the massive power structure I was confronting, I felt compelled to push ahead. I later realized that my strong conviction for justice is derived from my heritage and from those Italians who believed in justice for all. Was it not the Italian Cesare Beccaria who with his short thesis, "On Crimes and Punishment," in 1764 humanized the courts of Europe in their administration of the law and is credited with having ended torture and laid down the philosophy and framework for the Fifth Amendment to our Constitution, which guarantees "equal protection" under the law for all citizens? Although my battles in court were just beginning, this confrontation between the Italian American community and CUNY was a long time in coming.

During the 1960s, the City University of New York experienced a period of unprecedented expansion. Within its ranks, members of traditional minorities and ethnic groups started to become more visible. One of these groups was the Italian Americans, the first generation of descendants of Italian immigrants from the mass immigration period of 1880 to 1920 to have obtained higher education and pursue academic careers.

Initially, these Italian American faculty members met socially to discuss academic issues of mutual interest, but when an increasing number of individuals were denied tenure and/or promotions, they decided to form the Italian American CUNY Faculty Association for mutual support and assistance. Soon they focused their energies on matters of representation and the development of ethnic studies programs and later on discrimination in the workplace.

From 1971 on, they met with representatives of the chancellor's office and endeavored to enlist the support of outside agencies as well as state legislators. In October 1971, the state commissioner of human rights, Dominic Massaro, threatened a writ of mandamus against CUNY to obtain compliance from the university with a demand for a statistical analysis on Italian Americans. CUNY officials, alas, claimed they were "incapable" of compiling such information.

During the same period, the Italian American faculty, under the leadership of Dr. Richard Bossone, began gathering information for a status report on the extent of discrimination at CUNY, titled *Status of Italian Americans at the City University of New York*. It was published in November 1973 jointly by the Italian American Center for Urban Affairs, Inc., and the Association of Italian American Faculty of CUNY. In their report, they found that "despite the fact that Italian Americans constitute 25% of the population of New York City, and despite a progressively increasing number of Italian Americans graduating with a doctoral degree, the representation of Italian Americans at The City University of New York was at a low 5% level."

At this time, I was enrolled as a graduate student at CUNY's Lehman College, and while Italian American faculty members were courageously sharing stories of discrimination, I, along with other Italian American students (now making up as much as 25 percent of the student body at the various campuses of CUNY), also complained of ineffective counseling services as well as the inequitable distribution of the student activities fees. We formed a CUNY-wide association for Italian American students, chaired by Anita Cuttita, and sought the support of state officials. As a result of the combined efforts of both the faculty and students, CUNY chancellor Robert Kibbee was prompted to address our joint concerns, which he did in a letter dated March 17, 1976. This letter was sent to all CUNY college presidents and stated the following:

> Over the past ten years, The City University has moved aggressively to offer the possibility of a higher education to populations previously excluded. Beginning with College Discovery, then SEEK, and finally, through open admissions, the opportunities of the University were expanded to even larger segments of the City's youth.
>
> Among those which have entered the University in ever-growing numbers are Italian Americans, young people from all sections of the City. I would like to call your attention to this expanding component of the University's enrollment and to urge you to consider ways in which their particular need can be served better.
>
> The young Italian Americans come to us with a proud and rich cultural tradition in literature, music and the arts. They also carry with them customs and values that flow from their ancestral homeland, their religious heritage, and their American experience. It is important to them and their communities that the University represent a congenial, understanding and sympathetic environment. If this is to be so, it behooves all of us faculty, administration, and staff to recognize, understand and respect traditions, customs and beliefs of this large and important component of our academic community.

Chancellor Kibbee then outlined seven specific points for consideration:

> *Point 1.* The development of a series of programs that draw upon the cultural and the folk tradition of Italian and the Italian American community.
>
> *Point 2.* The encouragement of student and faculty organizations on the campus that are oriented toward the preservation and promotion of academic, cultural or spiritual value of importance to Italian Americans.
>
> *Point 3.* The development of academic programs and/or courses that appropriately reflect the contributions made by Italians to history, literature, science and the arts.
>
> *Point 4.* The encouragement of outreach programs to serve the special needs and aspirations of those Italian American communities within the natural orbit of the college.
>
> *Point 5.* The development of orientation programs for counselors designed to sensitize them to the cultural, social and spiritual heritage of Italian Americans. In establishing such a program, every effort should be made to draw upon the resources of the community and its leadership.

Point 6. The creation of advisory committees to the President with which you can consult as to how the college and its various components can improve their services to Italian American students and the communities from which they come.

Point 7. Periodic consultation with the Italian American faculty and student organizations on the campuses so that you can be alert to incipient problems and through which you may ascertain ways in which the college can more effectively fulfill its obligations to its students and faculty.

In justification and explanation for the above remedies, Chancellor Kibbee ended his memo by stating:

> I urge you to consider additional measures that might be taken on your own campus to quicken the colleges' response to the City's Italian American communities to heighten campus sensitivity. We are concerned here with the City's largest minority and one which, like other minorities, has over time suffered the degrading effects of bigotry, misunderstanding and neglect.

However, this letter did not address the faculty's primary concern: the inclusion of Italian Americans as an affirmative action category.

In May 1976, the second faculty report on the status of Italian Americans at CUNY was published. In this document, entitled *Italian Americans: The Neglected Minority in City University,* jointly sponsored by the Italian American Center for Urban Affairs and the Association of Italian American Faculty of CUNY, they called for affirmative action to be extended to Italian Americans: "We are asking the university and administration to redress the grievances of Italian Americans, as well as those of other minorities, without pitting one group against the other."

Prompted by this publication and the ever-increasing activities of the students, faculty, and community, on May 7, 1975, Judge Samuel DeFalco, chair of the National Italian American League to Combat Defamation called for "affirmative action" at CUNY. Chancellor Kibbee responded do this call in a memorandum dated December 9, 1975, to the CUNY Council of Presidents.

> It is my belief that the present situation requires the University to take positive action to assure that qualified persons of Italian American ancestry are identified so that they can be considered fairly along with other candidates for positions that might become available at the University. I am equally concerned that the processes of the university are such that Italian Americans receive fair consideration in the processes that lead to promotion and tenure within the University.
>
> *To this end, I am designating Italian Americans as an affirmative action cat-*

294 :: *Joseph V. Scelsa*

egory for this University, in addition to those so categorized under existing Federal statutes and regulations. I also have instructed the Affirmative Action office to include Italian Americans in the data collected for affirmative action purposes.

Now, having been designated an affirmative action category by the university, one might think that the need for Italian American community activism might not be necessary any longer. Unfortunately, this was not the case. The complaints continued until finally, under the leadership of New York State senator John D. Calandra, then head of the New York Italian American Legislative Caucus, a series of legislative hearings was conducted at the City University of New York during the months of December 1977 and January 1978 to ascertain the effect of the Kibbee memorandum.

While completing my second master's degree in guidance and counseling, I was elected vice chairperson for legislative affairs of the CUNY Student Senate, which represented the 180,000 students at the University. As such, I assisted in the analysis of the data that was collected and ultimately became part of a new report, published in January 1978: *A History of Italian American Discrimination at CUNY.* This report analyzed the status of Italian Americans and concluded that discrimination existed vis-à-vis the working conditions throughout the CUNY system. The report made specific recommendations as to the remedies required to ameliorate these adverse conditions. Among them was a recommendation to establish an institute for Italian Americans at CUNY.

Following this report, two items were added to the New York State 1979–1980 budget: one created an Italian American institute to be housed at CUNY, and the other provided funding for eighteen university counselor positions. These new counselors were to provide services to the Italian American community, and I was offered the position of the institute's first director of counseling.

I worked closely with the institute's executive director, the Rev. Nicholas Russo, and CUNY's upper-level administration as the institute's liaison officer to implement the counseling program and place the counselors on CUNY campuses. Unfortunately, on March 23, 1980, Father Nicholas Russo had a fatal heart attack, leaving the institute without an executive director at its formative stage and at a critical time in the budget season. Although the institute's director of student affairs, Anita Cuttita, valiantly attempted to maintain equilibrium after the death of Father Russo, this and the inability to find a suitable replacement for his position resulted in the institute's not being funded the following year. Fortunately,

I was maintained by the university to continue the work of coordinating the integration of the new counselors during the 1980–81 academic year, as their funding was continued.

This was a difficult year. It was obvious that the campuses did not like the idea that they had been forced to accept the counselors. The hostility ranged from the covert cold-shoulder treatment to out-and-out hostility. Through all this, the counselors and I endured. However, when the institute was refunded in 1981 and a new executive director, Louis Cenci, was finally chosen, I made a career decision to complete my doctoral dissertation at Columbia University on a full-time basis.

Some three years passed. In 1984, while on a trip to the legislature in Albany, New York, to advocate for professional standards in the counseling profession, I stopped to pay a courtesy call on my state senator, John D. Calandra. He appeared very happy to see me and indicated that the position of executive director of the Italian Institute was once again vacant, since Mr. Cenci had taken a position on the CUNY board of trustees. He inquired if I was interested in returning to working with Italian American issues and wanted to recommend me for the position. I decided to accept his offer and was ultimately hired as director of the Italian American Institute, starting August 1, 1984.

I was not so naive or arrogant to think that I was the only one who could effectively lead the institute, but rather, since I knew the machinations of the CUNY system, I felt confident that I had the knowledge and skills to participate and function within the system. So I set about the task of building the institute from the ground up, based on the objectives that had been enumerated by the legislators in 1978. Little did I realize how formidable a task it would be.

I soon realized that the situation for the Italian American community had not improved and that in many cases it was worse. The students continued to complain about the lack of Italian and Italian studies courses, as well as counseling services, faculty, and staff; they voiced repeated concerns regarding future hires, promotions, and tenure and the negative attitudes of some CUNY administrators toward them.

To send a message out to the CUNY community, I, along with my colleagues at CUNY and the New York Italian American state legislators, were able to persuade chancellor Joseph S. Murphy, on the tenth anniversary of the Kibbee directive, December 9, 1986, to reaffirm the university's stated commitment to affirmative action for Italian Americans in a memorandum issued to the CUNY Council of Presidents. In his memo he stated:

In December 1976, Chancellor Robert J. Kibbee established Italian Americans an Affirmative Action category within The City University of New York, a decision I now reaffirm. The 1976 action represented a formal extension of the federally defined protected classes for purposes of the University's affirmative action program to include an additional group as a protected class. It also served to underscore the commitment of the University to a broad ethnic diversity. The City University of New York will continue to recruit actively for Italian Americans for available faculty and staff positions.

Unfortunately, this memo fell on deaf ears. The Italian American situation was just not getting better, and we had lost our biggest supporter in the legislature when Senator John D. Calandra suddenly died on January 20, 1986. As a sign of their solidarity, the New York Conference of Italian American State Legislators met with Governor Mario Cuomo in the spring and asked that the institute budget be made a discrete item in the state's executive budget, along with changing the name of the institute to the John D. Calandra Italian American Institute in honor of the efforts of the late state senator. Governor Cuomo agreed, and it became state law.

During the 1986–87 academic year, the Calandra Institute's Faculty Fellow was Professor Richard Gambino, director of Italian American Studies at Queens College. Professor Gambino conducted a yearlong study that led to his research report, *Italian American Studies and Italian Americans at the City University of New York: Report and Recommendations*. Chapter 3 documents in detail the Italian American experience at CUNY and concludes that, despite numerous efforts on the part of students, faculty, administrators, and public officials, there had been no substantial change in the overall picture for Italian Americans with respect to faculty representation.

Following the publishing of the Gambino report, the organized Italian American community in New York asked for a meeting with CUNY chancellor Joseph Murphy. That meeting took place on April 22, 1988, in the chancellor's conference room. The next day the *New York Post* reported on the meeting:

> Stress Test. If Dr. Joseph Murphy seemed shell shocked yesterday, he had an excuse. The Chancellor started the day with a group of angry Italian Americans. Limo king, Bill Fugazy, president of the Coalition of Italo-American Association, led a delegation that included City Council Majority Leader Peter Vallone, State Senator Guy Velella and Assemblyman Eric Vitaliano. Armed with statistics showing that the number of Italian American

CUNY deans and professors had dropped from 6½% to 5% in the past 10 years. The group demanded redress.

I attended that meeting, and it was difficult.

Realizing that a political solution to the Italian American problems at CUNY might not be possible, we decided to create a legal defense fund, and so the Italian American Legal Defense and Higher Education Funds, Inc. (IALD&HEF), was born on July 22, 1988.

Following the April 22 meeting, in the summer of 1988 I met with the deputy chancellor of CUNY, Laurence Mucciolo, who had been instructed by the chancellor to work with me to locate suitable midtown space for the Calandra Institute, since the space in which we had been housed since 1984 was wanted by the Graduate School. It seemed that we were getting too prominent and asking for too much! Deputy Chancellor Mucciolo also promised to help me to get a faculty appointment at the university, "if I could find a department which would approve my credentials."

One of the ways an institute receives academic recognition is through the academic rank of its leader. This was consistent with Professor Gambino's recommendation in his report that the director of the institute be elevated to faculty and dean status. During the fall of 1988 and spring of 1989, with the help of Professor Gambino, I interviewed in two departments at Queens College, his home campus. The faculty of the Department of Youth and Community Programs at the Queens College School of Education unanimously found me acceptable and recommended my appointment as a full professor. I shared the good news with Dr. Mucciolo in June 1989 but have never heard from him again regarding this matter.

I decided to report what happened to the New York Conference of Italian American State Legislators. Concomitantly, the IAD&HEF was not wasting any time. They were exploring the possibility of filing a class action complaint of Italian American discrimination at CUNY with the U.S. Department of Labor. We filed a complaint alleging discrimination at CUNY with respect to Italian Americans in hiring, promotion, and tenure on July 27, 1990.

Additional meetings took place in 1988, 1989, and 1990, between the representatives of the CUNY chancellor and the Italian American legislators, in which CUNY agreed to find space for the institute, to appoint a Distinguished Professor in Italian American Studies, and to participate on an advisory committee on urban public higher education. The chair of the committee was Justice Dominic R. Massaro. It was to be joined a joined committee established by the Italian American legislators of New York State and the CUNY central administration. Its purpose would be to offer advice and counsel on the needs of Italian American students and faculty. What follows are the three resolutions as adopted by the Massaro Commission on June 6, 1991.

Recommendation I: Affirmative Action
    BE IT RESOLVED that the Advisory Committee on Urban Public Higher Education recommends to The City University of New York that during the Summer of 1991, the Chancellor's Office complete the development of availability data for Italian Americans in order that they will be able to proceed with a utilization analysis during the Fall 1991.

Recommendation II: Italian and Italian American Studies
    BE IT RESOLVED that the Advisory Committee on Urban Public Higher Education recommends to The City University of New York that it establish a Ph.D. program in Italian Studies and that alternative funding sources, i.e., non-tax levy monies, be explored for support, for example, the Italian government and private foundations.

Recommendation III: John D. Calandra Italian Institute
    BE IT RESOLVED that the Advisory Committee on Urban Public Higher Education recommends to The City University of New York that the status of the John D. Calandra Italian American Institute be elevated with the goal of developing an organizational structure that would permit the Institute to sponsor appropriate research activities involving University faculty and students, and that the leadership of the institute hold a title or titles commensurate with their qualifications and responsibilities and that the Institute retain its student services activities and expand these efforts to include recruitment of Italian American high school dropouts into CUNY's General Equivalency Diploma Program.

In the months that followed the issuing of the Massaro Report, the City University formulated a clandestine plan to dismantle the Calandra Institute and remove me as its head. This was done as an attempt to thwart the Italian American community's legitimate efforts to move forward. In early January 1992, I started receiving information from legislators that City University officials were meeting with them regarding the status of the Calandra Institute. I was not a participant in these discussions, and several of the legislators were concerned as to why I was not present. As a matter of fact, several legislators called me to find out what I thought of "the plan," a plan that would become known as the Volpe Plan, named after the president of the College of Staten Island, Dr. Edmond Volpe, where the institute was supposed to be relocated. The plan had been circulating since November 1991, but it was still a big secret. Since I had not seen it or been invited to comment on it, I could only say that I had no official knowledge of any plan to change the Calandra Institute.

In spring of 1992, phone calls from outside, particularly from legislators, were coming on a daily basis, inquiring about my reactions to the impending plan, to which my answer was always the same: I had no knowledge of any plan and could not comment. However, since I did not believe that it was in the best interest of the Italian American community to move the institute from its central midtown location, I made my thoughts known to that extent. Needless to say, with all these rumors there was an atmosphere in the institute of impending doom, especially since I was left out of the process. The University was in effect undermining my leadership.

By late May 1992, after more disastrous talks and meetings between the community and the chancellor's office, my assistant, Maria Fosco, asked me, "What will become of us?" I remember looking at her with a very stone-faced expression and stating: "We're going to walk into federal court." I also remember her face turning white as she silently walked out of my office.

The "blood of my blood" was patiently waiting its time, the moment when I would spring into decisive, impassioned action, when I could avenge my CUNY family and move it forward. As Richard Gambino, in his now famous thesis on the dilemma of the Italian Americans, *Blood of my Blood,* explains: We are people who are accustomed to waiting in silence till the right moment, never resigned to accept the faith of our oppressors but "doggedly rebellious against it."

By June, relations between the Italian American legislators and the City University had broken down so severely that the president of the New York Conference of Italian American Legislators, Senator Nicholas Spano, wrote directly to the CUNY board of trustees to express their anger and frustration over the policies of Chancellor Anne Reynolds and the university. I was convinced that if the chancellor was going to move us, the perfect time would be after July 1, when the legislature was not in session. Luckily for us, we were dealing with a chancellor who heads a bureaucracy that has its own timing. The summer is always somewhat quiet, but this was too quiet. We heard absolutely nothing from the chancellor's office. It was as if they had already psychologically and geographically cut us off.

The chancellor's response came on August 28, 1992, when she acted without any notice on her plan to dismantle the Calandra Institute by sending letters out on a Friday when no one would be around to turn to for help. Some members of my staff received their letters on Saturday, August 29. My assistant was the first to call me at home. I learned that we were ordered to be out of our offices by September 1. The news was devastating but a relief. The relief was that the anxiety, worry, tension, and suspense were now over. The lines were drawn, and war was declared. I now knew what I had to do: gather the troops and respond to this act of arrogant hostile discrimination.

I instantly left my house to go to the office, and on my way down, I picked up my assistant. We hardly spoke during the ride, but silently we knew what we had to do. The crisis had begun. We were in a state of war. My trunk was full of extra briefcases and empty shopping bags. She carried her usual tote bag and an extra duffel bag. Surely, CUNY would have bolted the office doors. After all, wasn't this a coup d'état? How would we get in? My assistant had the key in her hand, and as we approached the lock we both held our breaths praying that the door would open. It did. We immediately grabbed important files, pulling and dumping everything that we could carry in our bags. We knew the guard would be suspicious if he saw us walking out with so many files. My assistant took any file that was important but that we couldn't hide. We were out within a half hour. We felt like political dissidents on the run. Back at her mother's house the campaign was launched. Reynolds had blundered. Through her unethical act, she instantly galvanized the Italian American community and we were proclaimed martyrs.

On Monday the first thing I had to do was console my staff, who were in crisis; I promised them that I would do everything in my power to resolve this problem. The shock was overwhelming. Everyone was walking around in a daze. Word was spreading like wildfire. The month of October (Italian Heritage and Culture Month) was approaching, and the plans for the Columbus Quincentennial celebration were in progress. The institute had a central role and was responsible for handling many of the events and activities in addition to distributing the calendar of events for that year. However, my staff and I were now fighting for our survival. The university wanted the office empty by the next week, but I was to be out, by orders of the chancellor, by Tuesday, September 1. I would have only one day to pack. I instructed the staff to start packing.

My assistant, Maria Fosco, immediately took leave and positioned herself at the offices of the Coalition of Italo-American Associations, where Bill Fugazy and Richard Grace would coordinate the political campaign to save the institute. They were continuously on the phone and faxing memos to garner support through letter-writing campaigns, petitions, rallies, and press conferences planting stories in the newspapers—anything that would help to save us. By Thursday, September 3, the coalition had put together a rally in front of the CUNY Graduate Center. The Italian American community, including legislators, came out in full force. It was a big rally and got coverage on the 6:00 P.M. news. Once the rally was over, if CUNY did not capitulate, I knew it would be all over. On Friday, September 4, I started packing, and Ms. Fosco returned to the office. She appeared exhausted and ill from the toll of a week of intense emotional stress. In fact, Ms. Fosco had lost seven pounds, was barely able to stand or function, and as I later learned, she had not changed her clothes for several days. By Sunday, Ms. Fosco had to be hospitalized for exhaustion and dehydration.

That was the last straw. *Basta!* It was time. I had to do something. I contacted Dr. Lawrence Castiglione, president of the IALD&HEF, and my friend Philip Foglia, chief legal counsel for the IALD&HEF. Phil was a former assistant district attorney for the Bronx, then for Queens, and at that time in private practice. I told them both I wanted to go to federal court. Phil was first taken aback by my boldness but agreed to listen to me. Larry was ready to back me through the Defense Fund. It was the Labor Day weekend when we started preparing. Phil contacted his partner, Michael Marinaccio, and another attorney, Howard Birnbach, who was more familiar with civil rights laws. We worked feverishly that weekend. We would be seeking a temporary restraining order (TRO) and then asking for a preliminary injunction in federal court. It would be the only way I knew justice would be served.

On Wednesday, September 9, 1992, we walked into the U.S. courthouse at Foley Square. The CUNY attorneys were notified and totally taken by surprise. My attorneys and I had prepared this case right under their noses. It was probably the last thing they thought we would do. Fortunately, we were assigned to Judge Motley. Judge Motley signed the TRO while the CUNY attorneys were still pleading their case and then said to them, "I'll see you on September 21st." The hearing was set for that date.

One of CUNY's attorneys' opening remarks on September 21 was that CUNY could not discriminate against me because they had no way of knowing I was Italian American. That was the beginning of the end for them. The judge completely ignored them and continued the hearing process. Witness after witness, we were clobbering them. Sometimes, the

CUNY attorneys did not have the nerve to get up and say, "No questions, Your Honor." At one point we realized that CUNY officials were even lying to their own attorneys or not giving them the facts. Their lawyers were learning more from us than from their own client. Testimony lasted a full week.

Next it as CUNY's turn. As each CUNY official took the witness stand, no one took responsibility for the plan to dismantle the institute, and several indicated that they were "taking orders" from their supervisor. Orders from whom? Our vice chancellor, who carried out the orders, was ordered to testify by the judge. Her testimony turned into a disaster. She maintained that she had no knowledge of the institute or of the plan to reorganize us. Finally, Judge Motley had heard enough and stated, "I've had enough of this snow job." She then ordered Chancellor Reynolds in to testify. Reynolds's attorneys gave every excuse as to why she was unable to come to court. To which Judge Motley replied, "There is no more important work than the work of the federal court. If she's not in on Monday, September 28th, I will have the federal marshals escort her in." That remark appeared in the newspapers the next day. Chancellor W. Ann Reynolds appeared in court on Monday as ordered.

For one full day my attorney, Philip Foglia, grilled Chancellor Reynolds on the witness stand. The entire courtroom was packed with spectators from the community and the media. There was standing room only. Chancellor Reynolds stated that Italian Americans were not a protected class at CUNY, even though two previous chancellors had extended them that protection. She also said that the president of the College of Staten Island had been the orchestrator of the institute's reorganization plan and was in full agreement that the institute should be moved to his campus. She had made him her scapegoat. Unfortunately for her, the president of the College of Staten Island, Edmond Volpe, had faxed her a letter on August 28, 1992, disavowing the plan as it was constituted, especially in light of the fact that he would, in essence, be given a program with no funds to operate it. Dr. Volpe knew all too well what that would mean—the institute's certain failure and the wrath of the Italian American community. He testified that he did not agree with the plan as the chancellor had described it.

Several individuals gave testimony as to their treatment on the CUNY campuses, but it was Dr. Maria Grace LaRusso's testimony that silenced the courtroom with her tales of exclusion from faculty meetings, being given isolated facilities, and the general contempt with which she was held on her campus, Hunter College, because of her affiliation with the Calandra Institute. Ironically, Hunter College is known nationally as

CUNY's women's college for its alleged support for women, both students and faculty.

By this point (two weeks), Judge Motley had heard enough. In her stunning remark to the court, she said she had had enough of a "snow job" from CUNY. Needless to say, we were startled by her bluntness.

CUNY wanted time to bring in statistical experts from the University of Chicago. She told the university to present their CUNY expert and with all due speed. They presented Professor John Melloncoff of the CUNY Graduate Center, who apologized in the hall outside the courtroom for using the word *capo* in a recent conversation, since he realized it was seen as an ethnic slur. His testimony, although professional, was not persuasive.

On October 6, after twelve days of testimony, the hearing ended. Now it was our time to wait again for Judge Motley's decision as to whether or not she would grant a preliminary injunction.

Of course, pending her determination, the temporary restraining order was to stay in place. On November 18, 1992, at approximately twelve noon, I received a call from a reporter from New York *Newsday*. Apparently, Judge Motley had filed her opinion concerning us earlier that day, and it was picked up by the Associated Press and United Press International wires. We were being bombarded with phone calls from all the major newspapers. She had granted us the preliminary injunction. It stated:

> . . . a preliminary injunction is granted enjoining discrimination against Italian Americans with respect to faculty recruitment and promotions and enjoining the dismemberment of the Institute and the removal of Dr. Scelsa as Director of the Institute, pending the trial of this action. (92Civ. 6690 [CBM], pp. 1 & 2)

Needless to say, there was great rejoicing in the community. I could hardly absorb the news, especially in light of Judge Motley's instructive language, which I was hearing about from the reporters. The news was picked up by every major newspaper in New York and around the country. With regard to CUNY's position on the inclusion of Italian Americans in affirmative action, she said, "Defendants [CUNY] clearly assumed the duty to include Italian-American as an Affirmative group. For defendants to argue that this language has no effect is disingenuous. The mere fact that CUNY has not kept its promise to the Italian-Americans does not mean such promises do not exist."

Judge Motley saw the university as trying to curtail my activist role as director of the institute and said, "CUNY is seeking to curtail the independence of the Institute and put Dr. Scelsa on a shorter leash, one in which he lacks the ability to bite his master, CUNY." She went on to say that, as director of the institute, I could legitimately represent the interests of the Italian American community in court, "since civil rights suits seeking to vindicate the rights of a minority have historically been presented in this fashion." Furthermore, she said that as director of the institute, I was the "flagbearer for the Italian-American community" and as such demonstrated to the court that the planned move would cause irreparable harm to the entire Italian American community, not just myself.

In speaking to New York State claims of immunity from prosecution under the Eleventh Amendment, Judge Motley said, "This case is a perfect illustration of the exception to the exhaustion doctrine, as forcing plaintiff to first exhaust administrative remedies would be futile, given the time constraints. CUNY cannot tarry until the last minute in announcing its plans and then argue that for plaintiff to seek relief through the courts is premature."

With the procedural issues and the questions of whether an individual could sue the state put to rest, Judge Motley turned her attention to substantive issues. Judge Motley stated, "Plaintiffs have shown either a likelihood of success on the basis of the merits or fair ground for litigation" for both Title VI and Title VII claims. Judge Motley made the following points: that Italian Americans are covered by Title VI, national origin discrimination, and that since CUNY receives federal financial aid, the court had jurisdiction. Judge Motley concluded that CUNY was motivated by "retaliation for the Institute's role in assisting in the filing of civil rights complaints by Italian American faculty and staff members." Retaliation in this instance is discrimination, and CUNY was trying to "inhibit the Institute's effectiveness in seeking to validate the civil rights of Italian Americans."

This "current policy," Judge Motley added, "represents either an attempt to renege on the promises of the past or, by denying that such promises were made or intended to be kept, a reaffirmation of the original finding of discrimination against and underrepresentation of Italian Americans that motivated the original Kibbee memorandum and its reaffirmation with the Murphy letter."

Having established that there would be irreparable harm to the Italian American community, Judge Motley also wrote:

Defendant CUNY undertook an obligation to increase the numbers of Italian Americans employed in its workforce, an obligation it failed to dis-

charge. Plaintiff is granted the relief sought, on the ground that his presence at the Institute, as currently configured, has acted as a spur to CUNY.
This court lacks the confidence that, pending trial, CUNY will address
these problems without Dr. Scelsa at his present position. Dr. Scelsa must
remain in place, pending trial. At trial, CUNY is invited to present for the
court's satisfaction a plan to set the goals and fulfill the promises first undertaken in the 1976 Kibbee Memorandum but ignored since then.

Judge Motley then granted a preliminary injunction barring defendants
from discriminating against Italian Americans in employment and relocat-
ing the institute pending trial. Needless to say, her opinion was scathing
and devastating to CUNY.

On December 14, 1992, Judge Motley issued her order of preliminary
injunction to the City University of New York enjoining them from the
following:

> 1. Transferring the John D. Calandra Italian American Institute from its
> current location;
> 2. Removing Dr. Joseph V. Scelsa from his current position as Director
> of the John D. Calandra Italian American Institute or in any way modify-
> ing, amending, altering or diminishing his responsibilities and powers as
> Directors;
> 3. Discriminating in any way against Italian Americans with respect to
> hiring, promotions, transfers, compensation, terms, conditions or privileges
> of employment because of their national origins.

As I previously stated, everyone at the Institute was relieved, as was
everyone in the community that supported us. This important battle to
obtain equality and justice for our community in higher education had
been fought and won, but we cannot rest. One must be constantly vigi-
lant, or whatever gains have been made will be taken away. One must be
ready to come down from the mountains when the call to arms comes
again, ready to fight for and defend the ground we have taken.

When I look back at the events that took place, the resources that we
harnessed, and the tenacity of our community to obtain justice for its people, I could not be prouder to be an American of Italian descent. Unfortunately for me, my parents were not here to see this victory. After all, it
was the nurturing I received from both of them that gave me the strength
to endure and the belief that in this country the American dream can be
the American reality if you are willing to work for it. However, this should
not be seen as a victory for me or for the New York Italian American

community but for all Italian Americans in the United States. My office is now inundated with new cases of discrimination against Italian Americans, and our community is rising up in protest and winning all over the country. These victories are for all our children. I have lived this experience and shared it with my son. I hope you will share my experience with your children as well, for they, the next generation, need to know of our struggles to break the "glass ceiling" of prejudice and discrimination. If our children are to wear their identity as Americans of Italian heritage proudly, they must know of the struggles and sacrifices for their civil rights that we have made for them and know what they must be ready to do for *their* children to ensure that what we have gained will not be lost.

Rudolph J. Vecoli

· ·

Are Italian Americans Just White Folks?

Although Chicago is not my hometown, the Windy City holds a special
significance for me, personally and as a scholar. Chicago was my first big-
city experience, coming into town on liberty from the Great Lakes Naval
Training Station in 1945. But that is another story. I want to tell you about
my experience when I was researching my dissertation on Italians in Chicago during the fifties.[1] Over a period of several years, I witnessed the
death of Chicago's Little Italies. The old neighborhoods were under siege
from urban "renewal," highway construction, and changing population
patterns; but when I first arrived, they were still there. Halsted Street was
still the heart of the West Side colony, lined with *fruttistendi, grosserie,*
and *stori*.[2] Hull House was still a functioning institution, not a museum.

As my research stretched over several years, I witnessed the destruction of that neighborhood. Images remain etched in my memory: a vast
desolate area (like the bombed-out cities of wartime Europe) where
houses and stores had been bulldozed; finally, the only building standing
was the Italian Church of the Guardian Angel (La Chiesa dell'Angelo
Custode). One day, as I watched from a distance, a procession emerged
from the church and paraded through the empty streets with the statue of
the patron saint—a Felliniesque vision. On the Near North Side was Little Sicily (also called Little Hell), where Father Luigi Giambastiani had
presided over the parish of St. Philip Benizi for fifty years. Though the
church still stood, the houses of his parishioners had been leveled to
make way for public housing. Padre Luigi was a bitter man, his parishioners scattered and his church soon to be destroyed. Many Italians I
spoke with during those years were bitter. Their lives were literally reduced to heaps of rubble.

I tell you this not to indulge in nostalgia about life in the old neighborhoods but to remind us that the death of the Little Italies in the fifties (a subject that deserves a book and a film), not only in Chicago but across the country, marked the end of the first chapter of the history of the Italians in America. At the time I thought it was the end of the story. The old immigrants were dying; their children were headed for the suburbs, hell-bent on becoming 100 percent American. My own research was driven by the fear that they (including part of me) would disappear without a trace. Oblivion is the worst thing that can happen to a people.

In the fifties there was no American Italian Historical Association (AIHA); there was no field of Italian American studies. The last substantial work, Robert Foerster's *The Italian Emigration of Our Times*, had been published in 1919. The assumption dominating the public culture, including history and the social sciences, was that the European nationalities (the term *ethnicity* did not come into currency until the sixties) were rapidly disappearing from the American scene. Israel Zangwill's "melting pot," it seemed, had worked its magic.

Of course, today we know that was not the case. For varied and complex reasons, the sixties brought an explosion of repressed identities that erupted through the surface of Anglo-American hegemony and revealed the true pluralism of this society. And lo and behold, the Italian Americans had not disappeared after all; here they were tarantella-ing in public, staging protest rallies, and writing books about themselves. By and large those were not the old *paesani*, but second- and third-generation Italian Americans. As part of this phenomenon, the founding of the AIRA in 1966 signified the emergence of a mature scholarship on the Italian American experience, one that was to yield a bountiful harvest of monographs, dissertations, articles, novels, poems, films, and plays. The decades of the sixties and seventies also witnessed a revitalization of Italian American communal life. While the old *società di mutuo soccorso* became less and less pervasive, new cultural, political, and social organizations sprang up. And the voices of Italian Americans could be heard in the public dialogue about the character and future of this "new pluralism," as it was called. Italian America was alive and well, or so it seemed.

Then came the eighties and nineties, and suddenly we are told it was all a mirage, that we don't really exist, that we are in the "twilight of Italian American ethnicity." What happened? In the parlance of football, we were blindsided; we were hit high and low. In the late seventies, neonationalists began decrying what they termed the excesses of ethnic "tribalism" that threatened the ungluing, the fragmenting of America, what Arthur M. Schlesinger Jr. has described in his shrill polemic *The Disuniting of*

America. At the same time, they sneered that the "ethnic revival" was nothing more than a pipedream of would-be ethnic demagogues and called for a return to the melting pot.

If the neonationalists/assimilationists perceived European American ethnicity in general (and Italian American ethnicity in particular) as annoying distractions that did not need to be tolerated, as did ethnicity among "people of color," neo-Marxists dismissed "white ethnicity" as a smokescreen for racism. While the ethnic nationalism of people of color could be accommodated under their model of indigenous resistance to colonial oppressors, Americans of European ancestry who affirmed their ethnicities were simply reactionary fascists.

Much of the intellectual underpinnings for this attack on the "new ethnicity" has come from sociologist Herbert Gans and his followers. Gans's theory of symbolic ethnicity is based on the assumption of straight-line, inevitable assimilation; Gans argued that what had been perceived by some as an "ethnic revival" was really a form of acculturation and assimilation.[3] What was new was that the "symbolic ethnicity" of European Americans consisted of subjective identity that was not based in lived culture or social networks. Gans recognized that Italian Americans still ate spaghetti, attended religious *feste*, and might on occasion dance the tarantella, but he dismissed those as leisure-time activities, simply hobbies like collecting stamps or butterflies. In serious matters, Italian Americans were becoming indistinguishable from their suburban, middle-class European American neighbors.

In recent years, Richard Alba and Mary Waters have buttressed the theory of symbolic ethnicity with their sociological studies. They have particularly sought to resolve the contradiction that they perceive between high levels of ethnic identity and alleged low levels of actual ethnic involvement. It is Alba who condemned Italian Americans to the "twilight of ethnicity."[4] Seconding Gans, he concluded that particularly for the third and fourth generations, ethnicity had become muted, voluntary, and private. What some thought was an ethnic revival was really an expression of receding ethnicity. But Alba has further argued that a new ethnic group is emerging from the melting pot, the European Americans, in part a result of extensive intermarriage but also as a response to African American militancy. In her book *Ethnic Options*, Waters distinguished between the ethnicity of people of color, which is due to oppression and thus real and involuntary, and that of whites, which is symbolic and voluntary and she adds, "contentless."[5] Further, white ethnics oppose removing barriers for ethnics of color because they do not understand the difference between the two forms of ethnicity. Waters describes traditional European ethnic groups as sexist, racist, clannish, and narrow-minded. Obviously, I disagree vigorously with Gans et al. for reasons I hope to make clear.

First, however, a word about multiculturalism.[6] In the seventies we thought that persons who shared a common identity (a sense of peoplehood) constituted an ethnic group and that pluralism described a society in which there were a number of such ethnic groups. Now we are told that the appropriate term is multiculturalism, a word I first encountered when the Canadian government adopted a policy of inclusive multiculturalism in 1971. However, in the American version of multiculturalism, certain "preferred minorities" are to be nurtured by the benign rays (and funds) of multiculturalism while "others" are condemned to the eternal night of non-groupness. Race, Gender, and Class became the trinity worshipped by the cult of multiculturalism; however, social class is assigned a minor role, and biological differences stemming from skin pigmentation and sexual organs are regarded as the significant sources of group identity.

Drawing eclectically upon postmodern, semiotic, and feminist theories, American multiculturalism in its more extreme forms has as its agenda the radical transformation of the polity and curriculum of American universities—and other institutions as well. Given their project of deconstructing patriarchy, racism, and capitalism, which are identified with European American male domination, multiculturalists privilege (to use one of their favorite terms) the literatures, histories, and cultures of "people of color" and of the third world. Meanwhile, the ethnicities of European Americans are suspect as an ideological cover for racial and sexual exploitation.

If radical theories of postmodernism and feminism have provided the intellectual firepower behind the multicultural movement, strangely enough, the political clout has come from the federal government. While the Civil Rights Act of 1964 mandated equal opportunity "regardless of race, color, religion, sex, or *national origin*" (emphasis added), its subsequent implementation specified particular racial/ethnic populations, as well as women, as the beneficiaries of affirmative action programs. In 1977 the Equal Employment Opportunity Commission's Directive No. 15: *Race and Ethnic Standards for Federal Statistics and Administrative Reporting*, established the following categories for compliance purposes: "White, not of Hispanic Origin; Black, not of Hispanic Origin; Hispanic, regardless of race; American Indian or Alaskan Native; and Asian or Pacific Islander."

Those categories, of course, have no basis in biology or ethnology, mixing egregiously racial, cultural, and geographic criteria and lumping together populations that have wildly divergent histories and cultures—and, be it noted, totally ignoring class as a determinant of disadvantage. Yet this bureaucratic formula has legitimated the five-part division of the American people; university administrators, educators, foundation officers, and the like have embraced those categories as designating distinctive peoples. Private-sector as well as governmental programs in ethnic studies, institutes on pluralism, diversity curricula, fellowships, and multicultural workshops and conferences legally restrict their scope to those "protected classes" to the exclusion of persons of European, North African, and Middle Eastern origins, who are classified as "white."

How often have you been confronted with forms in which you are asked to indicate your "race and ethnicity" by checking a box for "White" (or the totally dehumanizing "Other") as the only alternative to American Indian or Alaskan Native, Asian or Pacific Islander, black or Hispanic? Does this upset you? It upsets me, not only because the "white" option automatically excludes me from the multicultural umbrella with all its perks but even more because of the impudence of those who would deny me my history, my culture, and my identity and relegate me to the realm of nonbeing.

The Office of Management and Budget held hearings this past summer on the revision of the race and ethnic standards for federal statistics. The hearings make fascinating reading. Forceful objections were voiced by several witnesses to the "white" category on the grounds that the term did not describe either a race or an ethnicity. A number argued for a European American category, but others demanded specific recognition of their groups as Arab Americans, Hawaiians, or German Americans. I was disappointed that no one appeared to protest the submergence of Italian Americans into the white pool.[7]

Perhaps you can understand my personal chagrin in finding myself (and my people) consigned to the shadowlands of peoplehood just as we were forty years ago! As in the fifties, the public and academic cultures deny the validity of Italian American claims to a place in the country's ethnic spectrum. Perhaps I was witnessing the last chapter of Italian American history in the fifties. But I think not. I am persuaded that this is not the twilight of Italian American ethnicity, for several reasons. First, my conception of ethnicity as a dynamic, evolving form of adaptation is the antithesis of the Gans et al. notion that it is a static quantity, a commodity, which once dissipated is gone forever. In my conception, ethnicity is protean, capable of taking a variety of forms, of being expressed in a range of behaviors, and of being revived. Does one need to speak the mother tongue, live in a particular neighborhood, worship in a specific church, or even eat spicy foods to be ethnic? I think not. What is essential now, as it always has been, is a subjective sense of peoplehood based in common memories and manifested in symbols that evoke those memories (a flag, a ritual, a song, a fig tree).[8]

Second, I believe in my own experience as a participant in and student of Italian American life more than I do in the charts and tables of sociologists.[9] That experience teaches me that, while the context and content of Italian American identity have been drastically altered over the past half century, that identity persists in significant ways for many. For how many? I am suspect of statistics and cite them sparingly. But the fact that the 1990 U.S. census reported almost fifteen million persons, identifying themselves to be of Italian ancestry (making them the fifth-largest ancestry group) cannot be dismissed offhandedly. While the census report does not tell us what that response meant, the fact that they were willing to claim Italian ancestry means something—as does the fact that only 5 percent of all respondents reported their ancestry as just "American" and less than 1 percent answered "white."

Beyond statistics, I spy abundant evidence of vitality and creativity in Italian American life, which, compared to its moribund status in the fifties, tempts me to speak of a *rinascimento*. What is this evidence? Certainly not a revitalization of the Little Italies, except as tourist attractions. But in this age of faxes and e-mail, group affiliation does not depend on physical proximity. In recent years, old organizations such as the Order of the Sons of Italy in America (OSIA) and UNICO have taken a new lease on life, and new organizations, devoted to cultural and heritage activities, have proliferated. A new generation of Italian American publications has seen the light of day: community newspapers like Chicago's excellent *Fra Noi* and scholarly journals such as *VIA* and *Italian Americana*. And of particular importance, more than ever before Italian Americans are articulating their experiences through fiction, poetry, films, theater, and exhibits. Meanwhile, in their search for roots, many journey to ancestral *paesi*, scour archives and cemeteries, and reestablish ties with long-lost cousins. If you know genealogists, you would not demean their passionate quest for ancestors by dismissing it as simply a hobby.

What distinguishes this interest in Italy today from the philofascism of the 1930s is that it is not inspired by politics. Rather, it increasingly takes the form of a reaffirmation of specific regional or local origins. Associations based on such ties are burgeoning: Figli di Calabria, Piemontesi nel Mondo, Trentini nel Mondo, Cuore Napoletano, Lucchasi nel Mondo, for example. Noting this trend, the late Robert Harney commented that this revival of *regionalismo* and *campanilismo* was the "undoing of the Risorgimento."[10] Indeed, it reflects the growing regionalism in Italy since the devolution of authority and funds to the regions in 1970. Of course, the regions and provinces promote contacts with their far-flung emigrants and descendants for reasons of tourism and commerce. But my experience suggests that genuine interest in distant *paesani* also animates these initiatives. For myself, I find my Lucchese American identity, based on specific cultural traditions personally more satisfying than the abstract idea of being Italian American. Since I abhor the idea of all melting pots, I applaud this revival of localized dialects and traditions.

By now you probably have guessed my answer to the question posed by the title of this essay. If Italian Americans are not just plain white folks, what are they? I have elsewhere presented my ideas about Italian American ethnicity, and rather than recapitulate them here, I refer you to those writings.[11] Suffice it to say that to be an Italian American today obviously means something very different from what it meant fifty or seventy-five years ago. We have learned from our AIHA conferences that that meaning varies according to geography, generation, gender, social class, and political disposition. We would be hard pressed to define what it is that we share as Italian Americans today, but of one thing I am certain: we are once again in the process of reinventing our ethnicity.

In the meantime, how do we position ourselves in this increasingly diverse and contentious American society? If we reject being lumped together as white European Americans, what are our options? Could we pass as African Americans or Latinos? I don't think our black or Chicano brothers would have us—which brings us to the subject of race and Italian Americans. In the years of massive immigration, the racial classification of Italians was in doubt. Many Anglo-Americans questioned that those swarthy sons of sunny Italy were really white. Employers and labor leaders referred to them as "black labor," while the color line was invoked to keep them out of certain neighborhoods, schools, and organizations. Nor was this peculiar to the South. I recently discovered the charter of the Washington League of Knights and Ladies of Minneapolis, established in 1902, which specifically excluded Negroes and Italians.

I need not remind you of the animus of racial nativists towards southern and eastern Europeans—and Italians in particular. The current controversy swirling about *The Bell Curve* reminds me that, in the 1920s, IQ scores were cited to prove the inferiority (and thus undesirability) of Italians.[12] Innocent of the racial code in this "free country," newly arrived immigrants often worked with and lived among African Americans. Such association was itself taken as confirmation of the Italians' ambiguous racial status. Once they became aware of the terrible price to be paid for being "black," they hastened to distance themselves from African Americans and to be accepted as white. The historic relationships of Italian Americans and African Americans are, of course, much more complex than that; they would require a big book, a book that needs to be written.[13]

Let me tell you where I stand. As an unreconstructed pluralist, I believe that true multiculturalism must be inclusive of the full range of ethnic groups that compose the society and that ethnicity is a cultural, not a biological, phenomenon. Races, as discrete populations sharing unique hereditary qualities (common gene pools), have not and do not exist; in this conclusion, I am in the company of geneticists and anthropologists. But race as a cultural construct and racism as an ideology have played a powerful and pernicious role in the history of the past two hundred years. The source of peoplehood is not blood but shared history and culture. On that basis, we Italian Americans have as much a claim to our peoplehood as any other segment of society.

Since ethnicity is not transmitted to the next generation through germ plasm, it has to be learned from parents, teachers, clergy, community leaders, the media. How good a job have we been doing of teaching our children about their Italian American heritage? Despite my earlier upbeat remarks, we have reason for concern about the future of Italian America. In part, this is because the mainstream institutions—the schools, films, press, television—either omit Italian Americans or portray them in an ugly, distorted fusion. An irony is that persons of Italian ancestry who fill important positions in such institutions, either because they are de-ethnicized or because of ethnic self-hatred, acquiesce in or even propagate such stereotypes. I applaud the work of the Commission on Social Justice of the OSIA, the National Italian American Foundation, and the Joint Civic Committee of Italian Americans in Chicago. But we need to do more, and we need more muscle to put an end to such group defamation.

Yet we must admit that the transmission of cultural heritage within families and by Italian American institutions is often done poorly, if at all. The result is that we are raising a generation of lost souls. As other groups adopt militant forms of ethnic assertion, young people without a clear and strong identity are at a disadvantage. We encounter them in our classrooms—kids with Italian names but without an inkling of the history those names carry with them. Some hunger to be Italian American but don't know how. Some adopt as their role models the mafiosi of the gangster films. Or they take on the dress, music, and behavior of other ethnics; they become Latinos or Wiggers; yet others become skinheads.[14] I am not faulting the youth; *it is we who have failed them.*

To quote Lenin: "What is to be done?" I have no panacea, but I think that we who are the self-chosen custodians of Italian American heritage have a special role and responsibility. Ethnicity is a form of memory, and many Italian Americans are suffering from amnesia. Freud observed that forgetting is "the avoidance of the pain of remembering." And there was much that was painful in the Italian American experience. I don't believe that we should connive in those silences; our job is to bring to the surface the painful memories of bigotry, repression, and conflict. In addition to writing our books and articles, we need to connect with Italian Americans where they live. Exhibits, oral history projects, films, family histories— those are the means of engaging Italian Americans in the process of re-covering often traumatic but also inspiriting memories. As we deal with our real history, I think we will engage the imaginations of our young peo-ple. Let me share with you a letter I recently received from an aspiring fourth-generation student: "I have a strong attachment to my ethnic roots and am eager to learn more about the true story of Italian Americans—not the stereotypical, thin version presented by the media and so widely be-lieved. The Italian experience . . . is complex and varied and I hope to fur-ther flesh out, in my small way, the incomplete story of my ancestors."

The AIHA, which from its inception has been dedicated to the pur-pose of disseminating understanding of the Italian American experience, has made enormous contributions to a reawakening of Italian American consciousness. What too often has been lacking has been the political and economic support of Italian American organizations and individuals whose resources could have amplified manyfold the work of the AIHA. A long-rooted tradition of anti-intellectualism among Italian Americans has restricted the essential linkage of wealth and power with intellect and creativity.

But you may ask, why bother? Why invest our time, energy, and money in revitalizing Italian American ethnicity when there are so many other ur-gent matters to attend to? Why not simply submerge ourselves in the vanilla frosting and enjoy the perks of being "white" in a racist society? Replies will vary, but I have a couple of answers for myself. First, let me say I am not into ethnic chauvinism. I am as opposed to Italocentrism as I am to Anglocentrism or Afrocentrism. Beyond the personal significance of the Italian American experience in which I am willy-nilly a participant, as a humanist I argue for the intrinsic significance of that experience. It is an epic story of a diaspora, the story of the tragedies and triumphs of millions, the story of generations struggling to reconcile the old and the new. It is neither grander nor meaner than the story of other migrant peoples, *but it is our story.* Knowledge of that story can enrich and inspire our lives; it can provide us with a center and a compass in these turbulent times.

But the Italian American experience has a larger significance, which transcends its meaning for us as individuals. Over the past century we have collectively comprised a considerable segment of the American population; there is no sphere of life in which our presence has not been manifest. To delete that experience is to omit a big slice of American history. Further, we need to ponder what meaning that experience has for understanding the character of this society and the critical issues that confront it today. Sheldon Hackney, the chairman of the National Endowment for the Humanities, has called for a "national conversation" about our sources of diversity and of unity. What makes us different? What makes us American? Italian American voices used to be heard in that conversation. Based on our historic experience, I think we have something to contribute to it. Of course, we would not speak with one voice; there have been a variety of Italian American experiences subject to a variety of interpretations.

I would argue that our experience has taught us firsthand of the evils of racism and nativism. Guido Calabresi was recently sworn in as a judge of the Second U.S. Circuit Court of Appeals (on the fifty-fifth anniversary of the arrival of his family from Italy). Speaking of American history, Judge Calabresi observed: "Our tragic moments—for which we are still paying and will long pay—are those times when our laws furthered bigotry and discrimination." We, as Italian Americans, should resonate to those words, particularly in these times when the latest arrivals in this Promised Land are the object of nativist attacks. We, the descendants of *contadini*, should not tolerate those who say, "Oh, but our immigrant ancestors were different. They suffered hardships, but because they were hardworking, self-reliant, honest, etc., they made it."[15] Anyone who has studied Italian American history knows that this is a gross oversimplification, if not falsification, as well as a slander on the new immigrants.

Our experience has taught us the fallacy of the very idea of race and the mischief of racial labels. It has taught us that both total assimilation and total separatism are will-o'-the-wisps, unachievable and undesirable if they were achievable. It has taught us that a healthy ethnicity is compatible with, indeed essential to, a healthy America. For these reasons, we Italian Americans have something important to contribute to the national dialogue.

Finally, we must say no to both the neonationalists and the multiculturalists who would deny us the right to define our own identities as Italian Americans. We must say no to the xenophobes and bigots whether we or others are their targets. Neither white nor black nor brown nor red nor yellow, we are distinguished by our unique experience in these United States. Let us claim our rightful inheritance as Italian Americans.

Notes

. . . .

1. "Chicago's Italians Prior to World War I: A Study of Their Social and Economic Adjustment" (University of Wisconsin, 1963).

2. For a superb study of the linguistic adaptation of the Italian immigrants, see Hermann W. Haller, *Una lingua perduta e ritrovata: L'italiano degli italo-americani* (Florence: La Nuova Italia, 1993).

3. Herbert Gans, "Symbolic Ethnicity: The Future of Ethnic Groups and Cultures in America," in *On the Making of Americans: Essays in Honor of David Riesman* (Philadelphia: University of Pennsylvania Press, 1977), 193–220.

4. Richard D. Alba, *Italian Americans: Into the Twilight of Ethnicity* (Englewood Cliffs, N.J.: Prentice-Hall, 1985). See also Alba, *Ethnic Identity: The Transformation of White America* (New Haven, Conn.: Yale University Press, 1990).

5. Mary C. Waters, *Ethnic Options: Choosing Identities in America* (Berkeley: University of California Press, 1990).

6. The literature relating to the controversies swirling about multiculturalism is extensive, but for a critical review of its extreme form, I recommend Richard Bernstein, *Dictatorship of Virtue: Multiculturalism and the Battle for America's Future* (New York: Alfred A. Knopf, 1994).

7. Ramona Douglass, however, did testify before the House Subcommittee on the Census on behalf of establishing a "multiracial/multiethnic category." Ms. Douglass, who is president of the Association of MultiEthnic Americans, identified herself as Sicilian American on her mother's side, while her father is of Ogalala Indian and African American ancestry.

8. For an elaboration of this view I refer you to Kathleen Neils Conzen, David A. Gerber, Ewa Morawska, George E. Pozzetta, and Rudolph J. Vecoli, "The Invention of Ethnicity: A Perspective from the U.S.A.," *Journal of American Ethnic History* (fall, 1992): 3–41.

9. For an attempt to articulate the influence of personal experience on the writing of history, see Rudolph J. Vecoli, "Italian Immigrants and Working-Class Movements in the United States: A Personal Reflection on Class and Ethnicity," *Journal of the Canadian Historical Association*, 4 (1993), 293–305.

10. "Undoing the Risorgimento: Emigrants from Italy and the Politics of Regionalism," in *If One Were to Write a History . . . : Selected Writings by Robert F. Harney*, ed.

Pierre Anctil and Bruno Ramirez (Toronto: Multicultural History Society of Ontario, 1991), 201–26. In a personal communication, Andrew Canepa confirmed my impression of the resurgence of regional and local associations, citing a lengthy list of such organizations in California.

11. "The Search for an Italian American Identity: Continuity and Change," in *Italian Americans: New Perspectives in Italian Immigration and Ethnicity*, ed. Lydio Tomasi (New York: Center for Migration Studies, 1985), 88–112; "The Coming of Age of the Italian Americans," *Ethnicity* 5 (1978): 119–47.

12. William McDougall, professor of psychology at Harvard College, presented essentially the same argument regarding the hereditary and racial basis of intelligence in *Is America Safe for Democracy?* (New York: Charles Scribner's Sons, 1921). McDougall (p. 64) reported that Italians scored 84, and colored scored 83, as compared with the score of 106 of "all Americans." He noted, however, that "the recent Italian immigrants are not probably a fair sample of the population of Italy."

13. For provocative discussions of the ambiguous racial status of Italian immigrants, see Robert Orsi, "The Religious Boundaries of an Inbetween People: Street *Feste* and the Problem of the Dark-Skinned Other in Italian Harlem, 1920–1990," *American Quarterly*, 44 (September 1992): 313–47; and David R. Roediger, *Towards the Abolition of Whiteness* (London: Verso, 1994), particularly chap. 11, "Whiteness and Ethnicity in the History of 'White Ethnics' in the United States."

14. Donald Tricarico, "Guido: Fashioning an Italian American Youth Style," *Journal of Ethnic Studies* 19 (spring 1991): 41–66, is a fascinating account of an Italian American youth culture.

15. Anna Quindlen, "Hypocrisy from a Nation of Immigrants," *Star Tribune* (Minneapolis). Quindlen's maternal grandparents were immigrants from Italy. A leading proponent of Proposition 187 in California, Sally Vaughn, who also had Italian grandparents, declared: "I resent them [current immigrants] comparing themselves to my grandparents, who came here legally, worked hard, learned to speak English and tried to be good citizens," *Star Tribune*, November 6, 1994.

CONTRIBUTORS

John Agresto is President of St. John's College in Santa Fe.

Michael Barone is a journalist and television commentator.

Regina Barreca is an essayist and scholar. She teaches at the University of Connecticut. Her books include Sweet Revenge and Perfect Husbands (and Other Fairy Tales).

Mary Cappello is Associate Professor of English at the University of Rhode Island. She writes poetry, creative nonfiction, and literary and cultural criticism. Her memoir is published by Beacon Press.

A. Kenneth Ciongoli is Professor of Neurology at the University of Vermont School of Medicine and President of the National Italian American Foundation.

Matilda Cuomo has founded a program called MENTORING USA, which works with underprivileged children. She was the First Lady of New York for many years.

Louise DeSalvo is a literary and cultural critic who recently published her memoir, Vertigo. She teaches at Hunter College.

Richard Gambino specializes in the field of Italian American studies and has published widely in this area.

Fred L. Gardaphé is the author of Italian Signs, American Streets: The Evolution of Italian American Narrative. He teaches at Columbia College and is an editor of VIA: Voices in Italian Americana.

Claire Gaudiani is President of Connecticut College. She has written numerous books of literary criticism.

Sandra M. Gilbert is a poet and literary critic who teaches at the University of California at Davis.

Dana Gioia has published several books of poetry and a volume of essays.

Edvige Giunta teaches at Jersey City State College and has published many articles on Italian American women's literature and cinema.

Linda Hutcheon is Professor of English and Comparative Literature at the University of Toronto. She has published numerous books of criticism.

Maria Laurino will soon publish *Scents,* a memoir. She lives in New York City.

Frank Lentricchia teaches in the Literature Program at Duke University and is a well-known literary critic and novelist. His most recent book, *Johnny Critelli and The Knifemen*, is two novellas published in one volume.

Alane Salierno Mason is an editor at W. W. Norton.

Jay Parini is a poet and novelist. He teaches literature at Middlebury College.

Joseph V. Scelsa is Director of the John D. Calandra Italian American Institute.

Gay Talese is the author of many well-known books, including *Unto the Sons,* an Italian American memoir.

Anthony J. Tamburri teaches Italian literature at Purdue University, where he edits *VIA: Voices in Italian Americana*.

Marianna De Marco Torgovnick teaches in the English department at Duke University. Her memoir of Italian American life is called *Crossing Ocean Parkway*.

Rudolph J. Vecoli teaches at the University of Minnesota and was a pioneer in the field of Italian American studies.

University Press of New England publishes books under its own imprint and is the publisher for Brandeis University Press, Dartmouth College, Middlebury College Press, University of New Hampshire, Tufts University, and Wesleyan University Press.

Library of Congress Cataloging-in-Publication Data
Beyond the Godfather : Italian American writers on the real Italian American experience / A. Kenneth Ciongoli and Jay Parini, editors.
    p. cm.
    ISBN 0–87451–845–8 (alk. paper)
    1. American literature—Italian American authors—History and criticism.   2. Italian Americans—Social life and customs.
3. Italian Americans—Politics and government.   4. Italian Americans—Intellectual life.   5. Italian Americans in literature.
I. Ciongoli, A. Kenneth.   II. Parini, Jay.
PS153.I8B49   1997
810.9'851—dc21   97–19535